Praise for *The Unholy Trinity*

Michael Lockwood shows that God's use of the Law—for Christians as well as for non-Christians—includes the sufferings of life that destroy our self-sufficiency, which is the root of all idolatry. His book is full of practical suggestions for pastoral care and evangelistic outreach and will be an enormously helpful resource for pastors.

—Gene Edward Veith, PhD
Professor of Literature, Emeritus
Patrick Henry College

In *The Unholy Trinity*, Michael Lockwood eschews simple causes and facile explanations of the problem of idolatry in the individual and society and takes a deeper and more systemic approach to the issue. Lockwood presents multiple examples from Luther's teaching as well as other contemporary authors. An advantage to his perspective is that being Australian as well as a pastor and scholar, he is able to observe American culture as a relative outsider, yet he has done the work and lived in the USA enough to make a fair assessment and bring to bear solutions to actual issues and problems. In so doing, he succeeds in making the issue of both idolatry and its cure in the Gospel of Jesus Christ relevant to the work of today's pastors, missionaries, laity, and theologians alike.

—Rev. Timothy P. Dost, PhD
Associate Professor of Historical Theology
Concordia Seminary, St. Louis

In two ways, Michael Lockwood has done us all a great service: he has rendered a fundamentally important theme in Luther's theology accessible, and he's shown us why it matters. In nine, deeply researched and highly readable chapters, Dr. Lockwood not only describes Luther's analysis of idolatry, but he also explains how idolatry functions. For Luther, idolatry is false faith. It's a lethal trust in the wrong thing in the wrong way. Luther didn't regard idolatry as misplaced philosophy, with merely academic consequences, but as a deadly peril because of what it actually *does*. Functionally, idolatry unseats faith in each of the persons of the Godhead, replacing it with a counterfeit trust, not just in "god" generically, but by creating a bogus equivalent of each person. The Father, the Son, and the Spirit are each and all supplanted by "me, myself and I." Michael Lockwood's writing is saturated with Luther in the best possible way. He shows not only what Luther said in the past, but why it's important to keep hearing it in the present. This volume is not just an important contribution to Luther studies, it's a seminal book for understanding the distinctive work of Christian ministry and the uniqueness of the Christian Gospel.

—Rev. Dr. Noel Due
Ministry and Mission Support Pastor
Lutheran Church of Australia, SA/NT District

How does a preacher best commend the Christian faith to people who have no need for the Gospel, let alone any desire to participate in the Divine Service? Dr. Lockwood provides us with a diagnostic tool for effective proclamation by his excellent analysis of Luther's teaching on human idolatry and the impact of its delusive claims. Luther held that the cause of idolatry lay in the mistrust of God and his Word. The human heart relies on its own idols, rather than God's Word, to secure, justify, and empower itself. It replaces the triune God with the unholy trinity of Me, Myself, and I. These idols are debunked and destroyed by the proclamation of God the Father, who loves us and provides for us; God the Son, who justifies us and gives us access to the Father in the Divine Service; and God the Holy Spirit, who enlightens and empowers us spiritually through his Word. This thoroughly biblical, culturally relevant study is a joy to read.

—Rev. Dr. John W. Kleinig
Professor Emeritus of Biblical Theology
Australian Lutheran College
Author of *Grace Upon Grace* (CPH, 2008)
and *Concordia Commentary: Leviticus* (CPH, 2004)

Luther's reading of the First Commandment interlocks with his catechetical exposition of the Apostles' Creed. Michael Lockwood has provided an attentive reading of Luther's theology while drawing out insights for a robust and engaging apologetic in our culture populated by idols fabricated by the self-justifying mind. This is a book that will be appreciated not only by Luther scholars and missiologists, but also by pastors and ordinary Christians seeking to sharpen their confession of Christ in today's world.

—John T. Pless
Assistant Professor of Pastoral Ministry & Missions
Director of Field Education
Concordia Theological Seminary, Fort Wayne, IN

Saint Augustine spoke of idolatry as worshiping anything that ought to be used, or using anything that is meant to be worshiped. John Calvin spoke of the human mind as a perpetual forge of idols, daring to imagine a god suited to its own capacity. And now we have mighty Luther, who shares the stance of Augustine and Calvin, but whose many statements on idolatry have never before been gathered together or considered in such a substantial, accessible, and pastorally fruitful manner. In carefully drawing out Luther's triune-shaped theology of idolatry and applying it to the contemporary scene, Dr. Lockwood reminds us of at least two realities. First, five hundred years after sparking the Protestant Reformation, Martin Luther is still to be studied with great profit. Second, each of us is an idolater at heart and in need of the liberating love of our Lord Jesus Christ. Given the light that is shed upon Luther's theology as a whole and the fact that readers will find themselves pointed afresh to Christ and the Gospel, I truly hope this helpful and stimulating volume will be read by many within (and well beyond) evangelical Lutheranism.

—Mark P. Ryan
Adjunct Professor of Religion and Culture, Covenant Theological Seminary
Director, Francis A. Schaeffer Institute

Today, secularism is seen as social policy, agnosticism and atheism appear to be respectable, and the ranks of the "nones" are swelling, while indifference to religious views and affiliations grows. So at first glance, idolatry is an unpromising topic for the church's life and witness. But, as Michael Lockwood shows, a deeper look at idolatry, especially through the eyes of Martin Luther, is revealing and compelling. Tying together many strands and uncovering varied connections in Luther's thought on false gods, Lockwood presents a rich trinitarian account of idolatry and uses it to uncover and overcome the idols hiding in plain sight today.

—Joel P. Okamoto, Th.D.
Waldemar and Mary Griesbach Professor of Systematic Theology
Chairman, Department of Systematic Theology
Concordia Seminary, St. Louis, MO

The Unholy Trinity

It is the trust and faith of the heart alone that make both God and an idol. . . . Anything on which your heart relies and depends, I say, that is really your God.

—Luther, Large Catechism I 2–3.

For You are my God [Psalm 143:10]. That is, I do not make for myself an idol out of my wisdom and righteousness, as my enemies do; instead, I cling to Your grace and receive from You wisdom and righteousness, which are found in You and endure forever.

—Luther, *The Seven Penitential Psalms* [1525], WA 18:527.34–37 = LW 14:202.

The highest forms of religion and holiness, and the most fervent forms of devotion of those who worship God without the Word and command of God, are idolatry. . . . every such form of religion, which worships God without His Word and command, is idolatry. The more spiritual and holy it appears to be, the more dangerous and destructive it is; for it deflects men from faith in Christ and causes them to rely on their own powers, works, and righteousness.

—Luther, *Galatians Commentary* [1535], LW 27:87–88 = WA 40.ii:110.14–25.

THE UNHOLY TRINITY

MARTIN LUTHER AGAINST THE IDOL OF ME, MYSELF, AND I

Peer Reviewed

MICHAEL A. LOCKWOOD

CONCORDIA PUBLISHING HOUSE · SAINT LOUIS

Published by Concordia Publishing House
3558 S. Jefferson Ave., St. Louis, MO 63118–3968
1-800-325-3040 • www.cph.org

Manufactured in the United States of America

Library of Congress Cataloging in Publication Data

Names: Lockwood, Michael A., author.
Title: The unholy trinity : Martin Luther against the idol of me, myself, and I / Michael A. Lockwood.
Description: St. Louis, MO : Concordia Publishing House, 2016. | Includes bibliographical references.
Identifiers: LCCN 2016023643 (print) | LCCN 2016042532 (ebook) | ISBN 9780758656971 (alk. paper) | ISBN 9780758656988
Subjects: LCSH: Luther, Martin, 1483-1546. | Idolatry. | Self--Religious aspects--Christianity. | Christian life--Lutheran authors.
Classification: LCC BR333.5.I46 L63 2016 (print) | LCC BR333.5.I46 (ebook) | DDC 284.1092--dc23
LC record available at https://lccn.loc.gov/2016023643

2 3 4 5 6 7 8 9 10 25 24 23 22 21 20 19 18 17

Contents

Acknowledgements

I would like to thank the following people, whose support, guidance, and encouragement has been invaluable in completing this research project:

- Rev. Dick Keyes, Rev. Mark Ryan, and Dr. Timothy Keller, whose work on idolatry first inspired me to see how fruitful the conceptual framework of idolatry can be for understanding contemporary society.
- Dr. Joel Okamoto, for constantly challenging me and sharpening my thinking with his "big picture" questions.
- Dr. John Kleinig, for encouraging me to focus on Luther's view of idolatry, and for suggesting sources and connections that were vital to chapter 7.
- My father, Dr. Greg Lockwood, for patiently reading my work and offering constructive feedback, for helping me to see important biblical connections, and for helping me to chase down references.
- LCMS World Mission, the LCA Scholarship Fund, Dr. Ian Hamer, Merv Mibus, Tony and Alexis Hesseen, the Lutheran congregations in Tarrington and Warrayure, Victoria, and an anonymous donor for their financial support that enabled me to do this research.
- Dr. Noel Due, for his assistance in turning my doctoral research into a publishable book.
- The people of Immanuel Lutheran Church, Kadina, South Australia, for their patience and encouragement while I completed this project.

And finally, a special thank you goes to my wife, Naomi. You are God's gift to me. Thank you for all your patience and support that has enabled me to dedicate myself to this work.

Abbreviations

LC	Large Catechism
LW	Luther, Martin. Luther's Works, American Edition. 56 Volumes. St. Louis: Concordia; Philadelphia: Fortress, 1955–86.
SA	Smalcald Articles
SC	Small Catechism
SD	Solid Declaration
WA	Luther, Martin. "Schriften." Part 1 of *Luthers Werke im WWW: Weimarer Ausgabe*. 88 Vols. Ann Arbor: ProQuest, 2000–2010. luther.chadwyck.com.
WA BR	Luther, Martin. "Briefwechsel." Part 3 of *Luthers Werke im WWW: Weimarer Ausgabe*. Part 3, 18 Vols. Ann Arbor: ProQuest, 2000–2010. luther.chadwyck.com.
WA DB	Luther, Martin. "Die Deutsche Bibel." Part 4 of *Luthers Werke im WWW: Weimarer Ausgabe*. 15 Vols. Ann Arbor: ProQuest, 2000–2010. luther.chadwyck.com.
WA TR	Luther, Martin. "Tischreden." Part 3 of *Luthers Werke im WWW: Weimarer Ausgabe*. 6 Vols. Ann Arbor: ProQuest, 2000–2010. luther.chadwyck.com.
WLS	Luther, Martin. *What Luther Says: A Practical In-Home Anthology for the Active Christian*. Compiled by Ewald M. Plass. St. Louis: Concordia, 1959.

Abstract

As Christians we know that Christ is the solution to the human plight. Yet what exactly is this plight? And why do so many people feel no need for the solution he provides? Luther's answer is that we feel no need for the true God until we are disenchanted with the false gods we have put in his place, which we think can provide all we need.

This book provides a trinitarian account of Luther's theology of idolatry, and is the first comprehensive systematic study of this area of Luther's thought. It then uses this account as a tool for understanding contemporary society and its resistance to the gospel. Luther's view—that anything we fear, love, or trust more than the true God is effectively our god—is widely applicable to the contemporary Western world, and unmasks the religious nature of many of our ostensibly secular commitments.

In particular, Luther can teach us that: (1) the self-seeking and self-reliant self is always the greatest idol and the driving force behind other idols; and (2) when we refuse to fear, love, and trust the true God we are compelled to find substitutes for him and all the work he does for us in his plan of salvation. This means finding substitutes for the Father and his work of providence, the Son and his work of redemption, and the Holy Spirit and his work of enlightening those who believe. It also means replacing God as the goal of our life and the object of our love. Applied to contemporary society, Luther's analysis reveals things like human activism, the cult of self-esteem, human rationalism, and the pursuit of personal happiness to be key idols, as we seek to provide for ourselves, to justify ourselves, to walk in the light of our own understanding, and to make the world revolve around us and our desires. Only when the futility of these projects is exposed can the gospel be heard as good news: that the true God gives us by grace all the good things we have vainly sought to provide for ourselves.

Introduction

Why Study Luther on Idolatry?

Spiritual Diagnosis

The first step in treating any disease is an accurate diagnosis. A wrong one may kill you; it certainly will not cure you. This is true not only for diseases of the body, but also for those of the soul. If we as Christians are to be servants of the great Physician, bringing his healing to a world sick with sin (Luke 5:31–32), then it is vital that we recognize the true nature of this illness.

So what diagnostic tools do we have at our disposal? Do we rely on human powers of analysis, and gravitate toward human disciplines like psychology, sociology, and philosophy to lay bare the secrets of our souls? If so, we may gain many insights, but we will not get to the bottom of our problem. As the prophet Jeremiah tells us, "The heart is deceitful above all things, and desperately sick; who can understand it?" (Jer 17:9). Or as the psalmist asks, "Who can discern his errors?" (Ps 19:2). Yet "he [God] knows the secrets of the heart" (Ps 44:21; cf. Ps 139:1–4).

This book is based on the conviction that if we are to truly understand ourselves and our spiritual malaise, then God must reveal to us the true nature of our disease. This means that we must rely on the diagnostic tool that God himself has given us—his Law, as summarized in the Ten Commandments. This Law acts as a mirror to show us our sin, and thereby our need for repentance, forgiveness, and renewal. This "theological" use of the Law makes the Ten Commandments an indispensable tool for understanding what ails us and our society.

This is especially true for the First Commandment, "I am the Lord your God. . . . You shall have no other gods" (Exod 20:2–3; Deut 5:6–7). This commandment is not only first in number but also first in importance. When we put first things first, and seek first the Lord and his kingdom, then secondary things fall into place. Not only does he provide us with everything we need, but our hearts also find their right alignment. If we fear, love, and trust the true God above everything else, then we will delight in following his will and keeping the rest of his commandments. Yet the reverse happens when we set our hearts on other things as if they are more important than he is. We then look for help in the wrong places, and the rest of God's commandments become burdensome, since we are ruled by these new allegiances instead of by love for him and his will. This means that not only do we lose sight of the most important thing in life, but the rest of life starts to unravel as well.

Like all the commandments, the First Commandment both defines what is good and reveals what is evil. Positively, it tells us what spiritual health is: to fear, love, and trust the true God above everything else. Negatively, it exposes the disease of our idolatry. That is, it reveals our propensity to turn things that are not God into false gods by investing in them the fear, love, and trust that belong only to God.[1] As painful as it may be, this exposure is the first step in our healing. In this way God drives us to Christ, who alone can restore our fellowship with the true God, and thereby make us whole.

DETHRONING CHRIST'S RIVALS

The true and living God has always opposed all pretenders to his throne. In the Old Testament, he rescued his people from slavery to the gods of Egypt (Exod 12:12; Num 33:4; Josh 24:14),[2] prohibited them from worshipping any gods besides him (Exod 20:3–6), and sent his prophets to battle the gods of the surrounding nations that threatened to seduce his people. Likewise, in the New Testament, the apostle Paul describes conversion to Christ as turning from idols to serve the living God (1 Thess 1:9; Gal 4:8–9). In the Western world today we are more likely to talk about conversion as turning from sin to faith in Christ. This, too, is a biblical way of speaking. Nevertheless, the danger with it is that we forget that idolatry lies at the heart of all sin, and therefore we always need to repent of more than just the obvious sins we see on the surface. Repentance that goes right to the heart must also include renunciation of the underlying idolatry. Therefore we cannot convert anyone without disenchanting them from their idols in some way.

---

[1] This is how Luther defines idolatry (SC I 2 = WA 30/1:354; LC I 1–25 = WA 30/1:133.1–136.3), and is the understanding of idolatry that I will be using throughout this book. When referring to cultic images, the other common meaning of the word *idol*, I will call them cultic images, unless I am stressing their role as false gods rather than their nature as images.

[2] Pharaoh was regarded by the Egyptians to be divine (Samson Najovits, *Egypt, Trunk of the Tree: A Modern Survey of an Ancient Land* [New York: Algora, 2003–4], 2:13, 71–75). He was also responsible for all state religion and for the maintenance of Ma'at, the sacred order the Egytians believed was essential for their nation's flourishing (ibid., 2:137; Jan Assmann, *The Search for God in Ancient Egypt*, trans. David Lorton [Ithaca, NY: Cornell University Press, 2001], 3–6). Therefore service of Pharaoh entailed service of the gods of Egypt, and victory over Pharaoh was victory over these gods.

Missionaries to foreign lands have long observed that the existing religious commitments of a culture have a significant impact on people's receptiveness to the Gospel. For instance, animists around the world have readily embraced the Christian faith in large numbers,[3] whereas Muslims and Buddhists have been far more resistant. In other words, Christian missionaries have found it easier to disenchant animists of their old gods than to destroy people's faith in Allah or the teachings of the Buddha. Likewise, missionaries to India have had significant success in converting low caste Hindus, but have struggled to convert those from high castes. This makes sense, as the gods of the Hindu pantheon offer more to a Brahmin than to a Dahlit.

Pastor Simon Mackenzie, the first Lutheran missionary to be sent from Australia to Thailand, recently returned to Australia after eight years of service. Although Christian missionaries have been working in Thailand for centuries they have gained only a small number of converts. However, my friend was working in a new mission field among the Lua people of northern Thailand. These people have been converting to Christianity at a rapid rate. So what is the difference? Most obviously, the ethnic Thais are Buddhists, whereas the Lua are traditionally animists.

Experiences like these should not lead us to conclude that attempts to convert Buddhists or Muslims or high caste Hindus are a waste of time. These efforts still have some success, and Christ calls us to bring the Gospel to all people. Nevertheless, they should help us to see that the existing gods of a culture matter when it comes to evangelism. Christian proclamation always assaults these gods, as Christ comes to dethrone all rivals. Therefore any competent missionary should understand the particular gods that he or she is up against and the barrier they present to the Christian faith. This is just as true in the Western world as in any foreign land.

I was born and raised in Papua New Guinea (PNG), where my parents were part of a large Lutheran effort to bring the Gospel to the people of PNG. The first Lutheran missionary to PNG was sent from Australia in 1886, and many more followed. It is now estimated that there are 1.3 million Lutherans in PNG, many of whom refer to the Lutheran Church of Australia as "mother church." Yet the LCA, of which I now serve as a pastor, boasts less than 75,000

---

[3] It is true that animists who convert to Christianity frequently combine their new faith with vestiges of their old beliefs. This leads many Christians in the West to question the genuineness of these conversions by saying things like "African Christianity is a mile wide and an inch deep." While this is a legitimate concern, we should hesitate to dismiss the faith of these people simply because we see elements of syncretism in their beliefs, or because we see many nominal converts along with the genuine ones. We have no shortage of nominal Christians in the West, and none of us is free from syncretism. Before we judge, we should remember that syncretism is easier to see in others than in ourselves. This book is an attempt to open the eyes of Western Christians to our own syncretistic beliefs.

active members and is both aging and declining in numbers. So why have our efforts to bring the Gospel to our own people borne so little fruit, when our endeavors overseas have yielded so much? It is not as if we have tried less hard to reach our own people. So why are secular Australians so resistant to the Gospel? And why is this story being repeated around the world, with churches in the Western world struggling while churches in many other parts of the world are flourishing? A significant part of the answer is the barriers that the gods of secular Western culture create for the Gospel, and our frequent failure to even identify these gods let alone address them.

THE NEGLECT OF IDOLATRY AS AN ANALYTICAL TOOL

Idolatry is a much-neglected topic in contemporary theology in the Western world. Even scholars who are interested in how the Gospel relates to the wider culture rarely talk about the idolatry of the culture or seek to analyze society through this lens.[4] Instead, they have made many attempts to analyze and engage with contemporary people using human tools derived from sociology, psychology, and philosophy. They have discussed at length whether people are modern, postmodern, post Constantinian, post Christian, or post postmodern. They have talked about target audiences such as the Baby Boomers or Generation X or Generation Y. They have debated the merits of evidentialist vs. presupposionalist apologetics, and whether we should use a foundationalist or a non-foundationalist epistemology. They have discussed different theories of communication and education, proposed strategies for managing our resources and programs more effectively, and attempted to repackage the church to grab people's attention and appeal to their felt needs. I do not want to dismiss all this talk. When such discussions are conducted wisely and kept in perspective, they can be examples of faithfully using the gifts of reason God has given us. Yet they cannot replace the analysis of the human situation God has given us in his Word. Only God can look past all outward appearances to see the human heart and its plight clearly, and only he can provide the solution. Therefore, if we truly want to understand the fallen state of our society and the people we hope to reach, we cannot ignore the analysis of their situation given in the Bible. Central to this analysis is the First Commandment.

It is easy to see why people would overlook idolatry as a useful category for understanding secular Western society. After all, in a secular society peo-

[4] When I reviewed the contents of leading missiological journals from recent decades I found hardly any mention of idolatry. One author even suggested that secularization and atheism have had the benefit of clearing away the idols from society and thereby preparing the field for the proclamation of the unknown God, as if secularism does not have idols of its own (Tomas Halik, "The Soul of Europe: An Altar to the Unknown God," *International Review of Mission* 95 [Jul–Oct. 2006]: 269).

ple's primary commitments are worldly rather than religious, at least at first glance. Few people in our society bow down to gods of wood or stone in a literal sense, and the society as a whole claims to have no public commitments to any gods. Furthermore, while religions besides Christianity are a part of the private commitments of a significant minority within our multi-cultural society, they are not the main things that draw people away from the Christian faith. Therefore it is easy to conclude that the study of idolatry is not much use in our context. Only when we reflect more deeply on the First Commandment—and see that anything we fear, love, or trust more than the true God is an idolatrous substitute for him—does its diagnostic value become plain. We have no shortage of things that we love and trust more than the true and living God, and the First Commandment unmasks the religious nature of these ostensibly secular commitments.

A second reason why idolatry has rarely been utilized as an analytical tool is the lack of a systematic framework for this analysis. If idolatry is to function as a diagnostic tool for assessing false belief, then we need to do more than simply catalogue idols. We also need to reflect on the underlying spiritual dynamic that drives people to create idols, and causes these idols to have such power. If people latch onto idols at random without any rationale for their devotion, then a theology of idolatry will be of limited diagnostic value. Yet if we can discern a deep structure to idolatry we can use it to understand and predict many hidden aspects of the heart.

In my training as a Lutheran pastor I was taught to use the Ten Commandments diagnostically, to expose my own sin and the sins of my people to prepare us for the hearing of the Gospel. I also learned from Luther's Large Catechism to treat the First Commandment as primary, and to see idolatry at the root of all sin. Yet, because I lacked a systematic framework for analyzing idolatry, I struggled in my early years of ministry to deal with contemporary idolatry in more than a superficial way. I was able to identify obvious idols like money and sex and power, but my thinking rarely went deeper than that. When I discussed this topic with colleagues, I discovered that their thinking was no deeper than mine. Therefore it is no surprise that we only put this category to limited use.

Since then I have discovered a handful of contemporary scholars who have bucked the general trend and used idolatry as the primary category for talking about the false beliefs and commitments of our culture. Some of these scholars have made significant steps toward developing a framework for analyzing this idolatry, and inspired me to see that such a framework is possible.

Yet none of them has proposed a framework that is truly comprehensive, and their work calls for further development.[5]

LUTHER'S CONTRIBUTION TO UNDERSTANDING IDOLATRY

It is here that Luther can be helpful. Scattered throughout his writings are literally thousands of references to idolatry, from comments on idolatry in the biblical text to reflections on how idolatry manifests itself in a culture where the obvious gods of paganism have been replaced by subtle idols of the heart. When Luther's thoughts are drawn together in a systematic way they provide a framework for analyzing idolatry that is both comprehensive and profound.

Moreover, Luther's theology of idolatry is solidly grounded in Scripture. In common with his general approach to theology, Luther resisted philosophical speculations regarding idolatry and instead developed his views primarily through his close reading of Scripture.[6] This lends credibility to his thought, at least for those who share Luther's respect for biblical authority. Furthermore, this devotion to Scripture means his thoughts share in the richness and clarity of biblical truth, and are able to transcend his age to speak to ours as well. Luther's genius is his ability to draw together biblical teachings and draw out their implications in ways that might seem obvious once pointed out, yet escape the attention of most of us when we read the Bible by ourselves.

Unfortunately, Luther's thoughts on idolatry are not readily accessible. This is partly because Luther never drew them together into one place or laid them out in systematic form. The closest he came to doing this was in his treatment of the First Commandment in his Large Catechism. Yet here he was acutely aware that he was producing material for family heads to teach to their households, and did not want to confuse the children with his more subtle insights.[7] If one wants to find his theology for mature adults, such as he taught to his students at the university, then one needs to look elsewhere, particularly his biblical commentaries.

---

[5] Some of the more helpful works include those by Richard Keyes, Charles Taber, David Powlison, Paul Achtemeier, Greg Beale, and Timothy Keller that are listed in the bibliography.

[6] From early on in his career Luther's stated goal was to eschew philosophical speculation and strive for a biblical theology (*Letter to Johann Braun* [1509], WA BR 1:17.42–46). This led him to delve into Scripture like few before or after him. As the Luther scholar Eugene Klug points out, Luther took an oath of fealty to Scripture when he was made a Doctor of Theology in 1512, and considered it his sacred duty for his whole life to be a Doctor of the Holy Scriptures (Eugene F. Klug, "Word and Scripture in Luther Studies Since World War II," in *Biblical Authority and Conservative Perspectives: Viewpoints from Trinity Journal*, ed. Douglas Moo [Grand Rapids, MI: Kregel Publications, 1997], 117). The more I have studied Luther and the Scriptures in parallel the more I have come to realize what an outstanding exegete Luther was, and the extent to which his theological insights emerged from prolonged wrestling with Scripture.

[7] LC I 23 = WA 30/1:135.27.

The other reason this area of his thought is not readily accessible is that it has been largely neglected by Luther scholars. While most discussions of Luther's theology mention how important the First Commandment was to him, scholars rarely go beyond the Large Catechism to give a more detailed treatment of his views on idolatry. Many Luther scholars have dealt with idolatry tangentially as part of a discussion of faith, worship, the theology of the cross, or the catechisms, yet few have made Luther's theology of idolatry their specific focus or attempted to draw it together in a systematic way.[8]

The first goal of this book is to do exactly that, to examine the copious number of places in Luther's writings where he talks about the First Commandment, or uses terms like *idolum*, *idolatria*, *Abgott*, and *Abgötterei*, and to pull his thoughts together in a systematic and accessible way. When one attempts to do this, it becomes evident that although Luther generally did not write in a systematic manner he thought in an orderly and consistent way, with key themes and insights that tied all his thoughts together. In particular, we can learn from Luther that:

1. Since idolatry lies at the heart of all sin, idolatry is everyone's problem.
2. The human self is always the most significant idol that lies at the heart of all other outward expressions of false belief and devotion.

---

[8] The most significant exception is a PhD dissertation completed at Drew University: Tae Jun Suk, *The Theology of Martin Luther between Judaism and Roman Catholicism: A Critical-Historical Evaluation of Luther's Concept of Idolatry* (Ann Arbor, MI: UMI Dissertation Services, 2001). However, Suk is more interested in an historical approach to Luther's theology on idolatry, and how it explains his polemics against Catholics and Jews, than he is in giving a systematic account of Luther's thought that can be of use to us today. Other works that discuss some aspect of Luther's theology of idolatry include: Vilmos Vajta, *Luther on Worship* [Philadelphia: Muhlenberg Press, 1954], 67–84, 125–48; Carlos M. N. Eire, *War Against the Idols: The Reformation of Worship from Erasmus to Calvin* (Cambridge: Cambridge University Press, 1986), 65–73; Charles P. Arand, "Luther on the God Behind the First Commandment," *Lutheran Quarterly* 8 (Winter 1994): 397–423; Heinrich Bornkamm, *Luther and the Old Testament*, trans. Eric W. Gritsch and Ruth C. Gritsch, ed. Victor I. Gruhn (Philadelphia: Fortress, 1969), 46–55; Michael Parsons, "Luther on Isaiah 40: the Gospel and Mission," in *Text and Task*, ed. Michael Parsons (Waynesboro, GA: Paternoster, 2005), 69–70; B. A. Gerrish, *Grace and Reason: A Study in the Theology of Luther* (Oxford: Oxford University Press, 1962), 100–113; John A. Maxfield, "Martin Luther and Idolatry," in *The Reformation as Christianization: Essays on Scott Hendrix's Christianization Thesis*, ed. Anna Marie Johnson and John A. Maxfield [Tübingen: Mohr Siebeck, 2012], 141–68; Ingemar Öberg, *Luther and World Mission: A Historical and Systematic Study*, trans. Dean Apel (St. Louis: Concordia, 2007), 37–81; Albrecht Peters, *Commentary on Luther's Catechisms: Ten Commandments*, ed. Charles P. Schaum, trans. Holger K. Sonntag (St Louis: Concordia, 2009), 103–48; Randall C. Zachman, "The Idolatrous Religion of Conscience," in *The Assurance of Faith: Conscience in the Theology of Martin Luther and John Calvin* (Minneapolis, MN: Fortress, 1993), 19–39.

3. When people refuse to fear, love, and trust the true God they are compelled to find substitutes for him and all the essential roles he plays in human life. This means finding substitutes for all three members of the Trinity and all the work they do in God's administration of his creation.

My aim in pulling these thoughts together is not primarily historical. Instead, it is to retrieve from Luther what is of value for us in understanding idolatry today. This leads to the second goal of this book, which is to engage with Western culture—as described by contemporary psychology, sociology, philosophy, and theology—to illustrate how Luther's thoughts can be reappropriated to unmask and critique contemporary idolatry. The goal is not to give an exhaustive account of our culture's idolatry, but to demonstrate the usefulness of Luther's framework for analyzing idolatry, and to stimulate further thought and discussion. To limit the scope, most of the examples will be drawn from U.S. society, although occasional references will be made to my home country of Australia, which shares similar issues.

The final goal of this book is to help to focus the church's proclamation of Law and Gospel in contemporary society. If we proclaim the Law in terms of the other commandments, without identifying how our sins against these commandments relate back to our failure to keep the First Commandment (i.e., our idolatry), we have only proclaimed the Law superficially without going to the heart of the problem. If our diagnosis of the problem through the lens of the Law is superficial, then our administration of God's remedy in the Gospel will also be superficial. Therefore an understanding of idolatry is vital to our proclamation of Law and Gospel, and our efforts to call people in our society to repentance and faith. The ultimate reason to study idolatry is not to wallow in negativity, but to bring freedom through the Gospel of Jesus Christ.

When I first became interested in the topic of idolatry my interest was sparked by a concern for evangelism. I wanted to understand the non-Christians around us as a first step to bringing the Gospel to them. Yet the more I studied the idols of those outside the church, the more I realized that I struggled with the same idols, as did the rest of the church. Therefore an understanding of idolatry is just as useful in shaping the message we give to ourselves and our own people as it is in focusing our proclamation to outsiders. If Luther can sharpen our thinking regarding the idolatry of our culture, this means he can aid us with every part of Gospel proclamation: from evangelism to preaching to catechesis to pastoral care.

OUTLINE OF THE BOOK

In part one of this book I will introduce the three key themes identified above that give shape to Luther's theology of idolatry. I will also briefly sketch out the biblical justification for understanding idolatry this way. In parts two, three, and four I will look in more detail at how Luther develops these themes in relation to each person of the Trinity, with each part focusing on a different Article of the Creed. Each chapter in these parts will focus on a different aspect of God's saving plan. It will begin with a summary of Luther's thought, proceed to an analysis of contemporary Western society in this light, and conclude with some thoughts on how this can aid us in proclaiming the Gospel.

Part One

Luther's Reappropriation of a Biblical Theme

Chapter One

Idolatry Is Everyone's Problem

Idolatry is everyone's problem, because the true God looms so large over all of life that everyone has to deal with him. If God were distant and uninvolved in human affairs, or a figment of wistful imagination like Santa Claus and the Easter Bunny, then it would be possible to live as truly secular people, and simply ignore God most of the time without this causing any difficulties. But the true God is not like this. When we turn our backs on him he still casts an enormous shadow over life. This means that even the lives of the most adamant atheists are shaped by what they seek to deny, and their attempts to compensate for that they claim does not exist.

Luther recognized that the triune God plays too big a part in human life for us to be able to abandon him without attempting to fill the resultant void with something. He writes, "The human heart must necessarily have something to love, and something to believe and trust in."[1] The one thing we cannot do is live with a spiritual vacuum. Therefore idolatry is not optional. We may not think of ourselves as religious, but if we refuse to fear, love, and trust the true God in any part of our lives we are compelled to construct some idol to take his place.

Luther considered this idolatry to be the fundamental human problem, and the root cause of all human sin. Therefore he spoke of the First Commandment as the primary commandment, and "the chief source and fountainhead that flows into all the rest."[2] By this he means that when we keep the First Commandment—by fearing, loving, and trusting the true God—we will also be happy to do all the other things he calls us to do, such as revering his name, delighting in his Word, honoring father and mother, and doing good to our neighbors. Conversely, whenever we break any of these other command-

---

[1] Martin Luther, *Martin Luther's Complete Commentary on the First Twenty-Two Psalms*, trans. Henry Cole (2 vols.; London: W. Simpkin and R. Marshall, 1826), 1:141 = WA 5:104.14–15.

[2] LC I 329 = WA 30/1:181.21–22; cf. Luther, *Commentary on the First Twenty-Two Psalms*, 2:45 = WA 5:392.26–35; LC I 321–28 = WA 30/1:180.3–181.24; LW 1:329; 9:69–70; 13:150; 31:353; 34:154.

ments it is evident that we have a deeper problem with the First Commandment at that point in our lives. This not only means we have failed to love and trust the Lord as we ought, it also means we have put something else in his place by prioritizing it ahead of him. For example, the Lord commands us to tell the truth, yet despite this "all mankind are liars" (Ps 116:11). So why do we lie? Perhaps we lie because we are afraid of what others will think of us if they know the truth. In that case, at that point in our lives human opinion is more important to us than the God of truth, and we have turned human opinion into an idol. In a similar way, one form of idolatry or another lies beneath every sin we commit. Therefore everyone with a sin problem has a deeper idolatry problem; and since we all sin, idolatry is everyone's problem.

IS THIS BIBLICAL?

Instead of merely focusing on those types of idolatry that involve belief in supernatural beings or the use of cultic images, Luther defines an idol as anything that supplants God as the focus of our trust and devotion.[3] He challenges us to see that we all live by faith, and that all faith commitments are ultimately religious in nature, regardless of how secular they may appear at first glance. Our faith must either be centered in the one true God, or else it will be centered in some idol that takes his place. Such a broad understanding of idolatry makes it broadly applicable, and is necessary if we are to use the category of idolatry to critique things like the secularism or the dis-incarnate spirituality that are prevalent in Western culture.

Yet is this legitimate from a biblical perspective? Has Luther enlarged the category of idolatry to the point where it is no longer the same phenomenon that is dealt with in the Bible? Or does the Bible itself talk about idolatry in these terms?

The main scriptural warrant for looking at idolatry this way is provided by the words of the *Shema* (Deut 6:4–9),[4] as they are recorded in Deuteronomy and reiterated by Jesus in the Gospels: "You shall love the Lord your God with all our heart and with all your soul and with all your mind and with all your strength" (Mark 12:30; cf. Deut 6:5; Matt 22:37; Luke 10:27; 1 Cor 8:5–6). This way of stating the First Commandment suggests that anything we are more devoted to than God has usurped his place. Furthermore, there is precedent in Scripture for calling anything that supplants him in this way a false

---

[3] LC I 2–28 = WA 30/1:133.1–136.26.

[4] These verses, either by themselves or recited together with Deut 11:13–21 and Num 15:37–41, are known as the *Shema*, and have been used as a creed in Jewish liturgies from biblical times up to the present day. The title *Shema* comes from the first word of Deut 6:4, and means "hear" in Hebrew.

god or idol. Habakkuk says that the Babylonians made their own might their god (Hab 1:11). When the people of Judah put their confidence in their alliance with Egypt to keep them safe instead of trusting in the Lord, Isaiah accused them of rebelling against the Lord and trusting in a false god (Isa 31:1–3). In Ephesians and Colossians, Paul calls πλεονεξία (*pleonexia*) idolatry (Eph 5:5; Col 3:5). Πλεονεξία literally means "wanting more." This usually means the desire for more wealth, but can include any kind of covetousness such as the desire for more power, fame, pleasure, and so on.[5] Therefore all these "secular" things can be idols as far as the New Testament is concerned (e.g., Luke 16:13). In Philippians, Paul talks about the enemies of Christ whose "god is their belly" since their "minds [are] set on earthly things" (Phil 3:19). Finally, although he has not made any mention of gods of wood or stone, John summarizes his First Epistle by concluding, "Little children, keep yourselves from idols." Earlier he had spoken about the love of the world (1 John 2:15), "the desires of the flesh, the desires of the eyes, and pride in what one has and does" (1 John 2:16; author's translation),[6] the attachment to our possessions that prevents us from giving to those in need (1 John 3:17), and the devil's deceptions that lead people away from Christ (1 John 2:3–6, 22–23; 3:4–10; 4:1–6; 5:19). His conclusion reveals that his theme all along was idolatry, and that he regarded all of these as idols.

Once we start to look at idolatry this way, it becomes evident that idolatry is an enormous theme in the Bible. In fact, a strong case can be made that the First Commandment and how we relate to it is the number one theme in Scripture. This is not to downgrade other themes such as Law and Gospel, but to point out that the First Commandment provides the essential background for such themes as judgment and grace. This is particularly clear in the Old Testament. The teachers of the Law in Jesus' day recognized that the command to worship God alone, as expressed in the First Commandment and the Shema, is the most important commandment in the Law (Luke 10:25–27). Jesus concurred that this is the linchpin of the Old Testament (Matt 22:24–40). Unless we see the importance of the First Commandment, most of the Old Testament remains opaque: from the way the Deuteronomic history (Joshua–2 Kings) views Israel's faithfulness or unfaithfulness to God as the decisive factor in determining the course of its history, to the way the

---

[5] Gerhard Kittel, Gerhard Friedrich, and Geoffrey W. Bromiley (ed.), *Theological Dictionary of the New Testament*, trans. Geoffrey W. Bromiley (Grand Rapids, MI: Eerdmans, 1964), 6:266–68.

[6] Βίος (*bios*) can mean either mean "manner of life" or "means of subsistence" (Walter Bauer, *A Greek-English Lexicon of the New Testament and Other Early Christian Literature*, trans. and ed. William F. Arndt, F. Wilbur Gingrich, and Frederick W. Danker [Chicago: University of Chicago Press, 1979], 141). Therefore "pride of life" can mean both pride in the way we live or pride in our possessions.

prophets interpret the exile, to God's rejection of Saul (for sins that are trivial or perhaps even commendable from a modern secular perspective), to his commendation of the adulterer and murderer David as "a man after God's own heart" (1 Kings 11:4; 14:8; Acts 13:21–22).

While the Old Testament prophets never stop railing against idolatry, at first glance there appears to be far less mention of idolatry in the New Testament. Yet here we must keep in mind two things. First, after the Babylonian exile the Jews no longer bowed down to gods of wood or stone. Therefore, if idolatry was present among the Jews of Jesus' day, it was of a more subtle kind, which might not immediately appear to be idolatry. Second, the Old Testament is always in the background for the New Testament writers. Only when one is sensitive to this do a number of key references to idolatry become apparent. For instance, Jesus quotes Isaiah 6:9–10 in all four Gospels, as does Luke in his conclusion to Acts:

> Go, and say to this people: "Keep on hearing, but do not understand; keep on seeing, but do not perceive." Make the heart of this people dull, and their ears heavy, and blind their eyes; lest they see with their eyes, and hear with their ears, and understand with their hearts, and turn and be healed. (Isa 6:9–10)[7]

A reader who is well versed in the Old Testament will note that Isaiah 6 is a fulfillment of Psalm 115 and its parallel passage in Psalm 135. Psalm 115 reads,

> Their idols are silver and gold, the work of human hands. They have mouths, but do not speak; eyes, but do not see. They have ears, but do not hear; noses, but do not smell. They have hands, but do not feel; feet, but do not walk; and they do not make a sound in their throat. Those who make them become like them; so do all who trust in them. (Ps 115:4–8)

It then becomes evident that God's judgment on Israel in Isaiah 6 was not a random judgment for sin, but a specific judgment for idolatry. God was forcing them to experience the natural consequence of their idolatry, to become as blind, deaf, and lifeless as their idols.[8] Therefore, when Jesus quotes and applies these words to the people of his day, he is suggesting that their hardness of hearing is a result of their idolatry. Likewise, when Jesus says of

---

[7] This passage is quoted in Matt 13:13–15; Mark 4:12; 8:17–18; Luke 8:10; John 12:39–40; and Acts 28:26–27. It is also alluded to in the common New Testament refrain, "He who has ears, let him hear" (Matt 13:9; Rev 2:7 i.a.). Cf. G. K. Beale, *We Become What We Worship: A Biblical Theology of Idolatry* (Downers Grove, IL: IVP Academic, 2008), 163, 198–200, 271.

[8] Beale, *We Become What We Worship*, 36–64.

the Pharisees, "in vain do they worship me, teaching as doctrines the commandments of men" (Matt 15:9), an astute reader will observe that he is comparing the worship of the Pharisees to the idolatry condemned by Isaiah and the self-chosen worship of Jeroboam, who set up the golden calves (Isa 29:13; 2 Kings 12:25–33; 2 Chron 13:8–12).

Paul continues with this theme by charging his fellow Jews with idolatry, despite the fact that they did not bow down to gods of wood or stone. This is most obvious in Romans 1–3. Here Paul begins by censuring the gentiles for their idolatry, but then says that the Jews share the same guilt. He brings this to a head in Rom 3:9–12, where he says, "Are we Jews any better off? No, not at all." For "no one seeks for God. All have turned aside." This is a stunning conclusion, that the Jews, with all their zeal for God's Law, were not seeking God. So what were they seeking? Perhaps they imagined that godliness is a means for gain (1 Tim 6:5). Perhaps they were seeking human praise (Matt 6:5, 16; 23:5). Perhaps they were so focused on justifying themselves through their own rules and traditions that they had forgotten what the true God requires (Matt 15:9). Perhaps their religion was more focused on manipulating God into giving them the things they really wanted, such as wealth or political power, than it was about seeking him (Luke 16:14; John 11:47–50). One way or another what they were really seeking was some idol, not God. In Galatians, Paul makes a similar accusation against the Judaizers.[9] He says that if Christians think they must be justified on the basis of Jewish laws and ceremonies they have turned from God and become enslaved to that which is not God (Gal 4:8–10).

From this it should be evident that when Luther treats idolatry as a central theological theme, and extends it to anything that usurps God's place in our hearts, he is faithfully echoing Scripture. If idolatry was a problem for first century Jews, who would never dream of bowing to a pagan image, then it is legitimate for Luther to conclude that idolatry was a problem for Christians in his day. Likewise, it is legitimate for us to extend this analysis to the secularism that effects people today. The book of Revelation tells us that the bulk of humankind will never repent of their idols until the last day (Rev 9:20). Therefore idolatry is a problem for all times and places.

---

[9] The Judaizers were Jewish Christians in the first century who wanted to insist that Gentiles could only become Christians if they submitted to circumcision and other parts of the Old Testament Law.

GRACE AND FAITH: THE FUNDAMENTAL INGREDIENTS OF HUMAN LIFE

Luther's contention that idolatry is the fundamental human problem flows naturally from his understanding of the God of the Bible and his relationship with humankind. The author of Hebrews presents all of Israel's history from Abel to Christ as a story of faith: that is, of a God who makes gracious and reliable promises, and of human life that is shaped by people's trust or distrust of these promises (Heb 3:1–4:16; 11:1–12:2). In the same way, Luther interprets the whole sweep of the biblical narrative as the story of God the gracious Giver, who calls us to live by faith in him as he gives us himself and all we need.

The main character in this story is God, the exceedingly rich Giver. Luther spells this out in his *Confession Concerning Christ's Supper* of 1528:

> These are the three persons and one God, who has given himself to us all wholly and completely, with all that he is and has. The Father gives himself to us, with heaven and earth and all the creatures, in order that they may serve us and benefit us. But this gift has become obscured and useless through Adam's fall. Therefore the Son himself subsequently gave himself and bestowed all his works, sufferings, wisdom, and righteousness, and reconciled us to the Father, in order that restored to life and righteousness, we might also know and have the Father and his gifts.
>
> But because this grace would benefit no one if it remained so profoundly hidden and could not come to us, the Holy Spirit comes and gives himself to us also, wholly and completely. He teaches us to understand this deed of Christ which has been manifested to us, helps us receive and preserve it, use it to our advantage and impart it to others, increase and extend it. He does this both inwardly and outwardly—inwardly by means of faith and other spiritual gifts, outwardly through the gospel, Baptism, and the sacrament of the altar, through which as through three means or methods he comes to us and inculcates the sufferings of Christ for the benefit of our salvation.[10]

Here we can see how Luther talks about all of life—from our original birth as God's creatures to our new birth as his children—as a gift of the God who is the exclusive Giver of every good thing. Furthermore, we can see how God's primary gift to us is himself.

---

[10] LW 37:366 = WA 26:505.38–506.12.

As the other characters in this story, our lives are shaped by our relationship to this gracious Giver. God's nature as the Giver of every good thing compels us to relate to him as recipients of his gifts. Since God gives from pure generosity, without any merit in us, it is right for us to thank and love him in return. Since we remain dependent on him for his ongoing provision, we must live by faith in him or else flounder. Since our faithlessness has caused us to flounder ever since the fall, only a restoration of faith can bring us healing. This all means that the call of the First Commandment to love and trust God with all that is in us is not an arbitrary imposition, but the only just and sane response to God and his gifts.[11]

Luther talks about how central faith is to all human life in his *Disputation Concerning Man* (1536). The philosophical tradition defined human beings as rational animals. Instead of accepting this definition, Luther consulted the words of St. Paul, "we hold that a person is to be justified by faith apart from works" (Rom 3:28).[12] On this basis he defined the human person as *hominem iustificari fide*, "a human being is to be justified by faith."[13] By giving this definition he is saying that our need to live by faith is not merely one aspect of our nature among others, but the most fundamental characteristic of our being. He then spells out three dimensions to this: only through God our Creator can we receive life;[14] only through God our Redeemer can we be freed from sin, death, and the devil, and receive eternal life;[15] and only through God can our lives find their glory and fulfillment as he remolds and perfects us in his image.[16] Therefore we must live by faith when it comes to every aspect of our lives: our creation, redemption, and final glorification.

If faith is really as central to human life as Luther's reading of Scripture would indicate, then whenever we refuse to live by true faith in the true God we inevitably live by false faith in false gods. This is as much the case in a secular society as in a pagan one. To illustrate this, consider the observation of Charles Taber, the past president of the American Society of Missiology and the Association of Professors of Mission. Taber notes that ancient pagan divinities were often personifications of different powers in the world that are

[11] I am indebted to Oswald Bayer for this perspective on Luther's theology (Oswald Bayer, *Martin Luther's Theology: A Contemporary Interpretation*, trans. Thomas H. Trapp [Grand Rapids, MI: Eerdmans, 2008], 95–105). Bayer summarizes Luther's theology of the Trinity as a "theology of categorical gift" (ibid., 254).

[12] As quoted by Luther in *Disputation Concerning Man* (WA 39/1:176, thesis 32). Author's own translation.

[13] WA 39/1:176, thesis 32. Author's own translation.

[14] *Disputation Concerning Man* (1536), Theses 14, 17, and 21 (LW 34:138 = WA 39/1:175–76).

[15] *Disputation Concerning Man*, Theses 22–34 (LW 34:138–39 = WA 39/1:176–77).

[16] *Disputation Concerning Man*, Theses 35–38 (LW 34:139 = WA 39/1:177).

real but not divine. People in our society rarely personify these powers in the same way, yet this does not mean we are any less fixated on harnessing them for our own advantage. People continue to worship Eros, the god of sexual pleasure; Dionysos, the god of wine and self-indulgence; Mammon, the god of wealth; Prometheus, the god of human power and achievement; and Mars, the god of race, land, and nation. In one regard these faith commitments are even more dangerous in a secular society, since they are generally not identified as idols, and people are invited to join the church without being asked to renounce them.[17] Luther urges us not to be fooled in this way.

[17] Charles R. Taber, "God vs. Idols: A Model of Conversion," *Journal of the Academy for Evangelism in Theological Education* 3 (1987–88): 23–29.

Chapter Two

Me, Myself, and I

The Chief Idol and Source of All Other Idolatries

I don't need reminding to look after myself
So maybe when you wave goodbye
You could think of something else
I don't need reminding who is number one
On my list of priorities when all is said and done
I've never grown from the terrible two's
I've just learned to hide it from all of you
Who is gonna sing my selfish song?
Well the answer is me so don't sing along
Who is gonna change this heart of stone?
Oh my God my life is a selfish song[1]

Two-year-olds have not yet learnt how to hide their sin the way adults do. Put one toy between a pair of two-year-olds, and what happens? World War III, as each one claims it as "mine." This undisguised selfishness reveals the sin that comes naturally to us all.

Human self-centeredness not only leads us to take possession of the things we desire. It also leads us to take credit and take control. As a two-year-old, my son beamed with pride when he could do something "all by myself." Even when he was not yet capable of doing something all by himself he would

---

[1] Paul Colman, "Selfish Song," *New Map of the World* (Franklin, TN: Essential Records, 2002), track 8.

insist on trying, refuse to accept help, and then take credit even if he did receive help. While much of this behavior is healthy enough as a boy learns independence from his earthly parents, it is disastrous when transferred to our dealings with God. In relation to him we can never have more than a vain pretense of independence.

Idolatry results from a spiritual life that is stuck in the terrible twos. The First Commandment tells me to love and trust the true God above all things, and to give all glory to him. Yet when I do what comes naturally (that is, when I follow the dictates of my sinful nature, rather than the leading of God's Holy Spirit), who do I really love? Myself. Who do I want to rely on? Yours truly. And who do I want to reap the accolades? Me, myself, and I.

Luther saw this kind of self-orientation at the root of human sin. His characteristic way of talking about human depravity was to say that we are curved in on ourselves.[2] When we follow the dictates of our sinful nature, we place ourselves at the center of our universe in two ways. On the one hand, we think first and foremost of ourselves and our desires, so that we seek to use all other things for our advantage, and even treat God as if he exists merely for our benefit.[3] On the other hand, we operate with an overblown sense of our importance and a misplaced confidence in our ability, as if the world depends on us.

For Luther this self-orientation spawns all idolatry. For example, in his lectures on Romans he identifies self-interest as both the greatest idolatry and the source of further idolatry. He says that since fallen human nature tries to use all things including God to achieve its own aims,[4] it

> sets itself in the place of all other things, even in the place of God, and seeks only those things which are its own and not the things of God. Therefore it is its own first and greatest idol. Second, it makes

---

[2] Luther borrowed this way of speaking from Augustine (*City of God*, 14.13, 14.28). Luther spoke about us being turned or curved in upon ourselves particularly in his 1513–15 lectures on Psalms (LW 10:241; 11:69, 262, 289, 386) and his 1515–16 lectures on Romans (LW 25:245, 291–92, 313, 345–46, 351, 426, 513). This was while his understanding of the Gospel was still developing and had not yet come to full flower. Yet it would be wrong to think that he abandoned the thought later in his career (see for instance his comment in *The Bondage of the Will* [1525], LW 33:176 = WA 18:709.14; see also Martin Luther, *Martin Luther's Complete Commentary on the First Twenty-Two Psalms*, trans. Henry Cole [2 vols.; London: W. Simpkin and R. Marshall, 1826], 1:202 = WA 5:139.12). He just found different language to express it. Luther used this understanding of human depravity throughout his career when talking about the root cause of idolatry.

[3] LW 21:309 = WA 7:556–57; LW 25:345–46 = WA 56:356–57.

[4] *Lectures on Romans* (1515–16), LW 25:291 = WA 56:304–5.

> God into an idol and the truth of God into a lie, and finally it makes idols of all created things and of all gifts of God.[5]

Later, in his lectures on Deuteronomy, Luther argues that we only learn to love God above all else when we learn to trust him above all else. He therefore writes, "You need to humble, and despair of, yourself, lest you make many gods, and that you may have one God."[6] Later still, in his Isaiah commentary, he calls trust in ourselves—including our own power, wisdom, wealth, and righteousness—"the supreme idolatry,"[7] and "the fountain and source of all idolatry."[8]

Such statements are crucial for understanding Luther's theology of idolatry as a whole. This may not be evident in the Large Catechism, where he barely mentions the idol of the self, but instead calls money "the most common idol on earth."[9] Yet as we saw in the introduction, in the Large Catechism Luther was acutely aware that he was writing for the benefit of young pupils, and therefore did not want to burden them with his more subtle insights.[10] As we have seen, in other places he had no qualms about calling the self the greatest idol. Only on this basis can we make sense of the material we will deal with in subsequent chapters, where he treats things like self-interest, self-justification, self-enlightenment and self-invented religion as the most insidious expressions of idolatry.

When Luther talks about the self as the greatest idol, he is not asserting that it is our only idol, or is always the presenting idol. Instead, it is the idol that lurks beneath other forms of idolatry. It is what causes us to "make many gods," as we recruit other idols to fulfill our desires, increase our power, and magnify our glory, all in the service of the chief god in our pantheon, ourselves.

IS THIS BIBLICAL?

So is this something Luther dreamed up for himself, or is it scriptural?

As several contemporary theologians have noted, the Bible's treatment of idolatry begins with Adam and Eve, whose desire to "be like God" led them to

---

[5] *Lectures on Romans* (1515–16), LW 25:346 = WA 56:357.2–6. While his lectures on Romans predate Luther's evangelical breakthrough, Luther continued to identify self-interest with idolatry later in his career (e.g., *Commentary on the Magnificat* (1521), LW 21:309 = WA 7:556–57).

[6] *Lectures on Deuteronomy* (1525), LW 9:68 = WA 14:609.22–23.

[7] *Lectures on Isaiah* (1527–30), LW 16:216 = WA 31/2:153.31.

[8] *Lectures on Isaiah* (1527–30), LW 17:17 = WA 31/2:273.14; cf. LW 17:107.

[9] LC I 6 = WA 30/1:133:23–25.

[10] LC I 22–23 = WA 30/1:135.17–27.

assert their autonomy in rebellious self-will. Instead of listening to the Word of the Lord, they sought what they thought was godlike freedom to determine good and evil for themselves, and set themselves up as their own lords by doing as they pleased. Since then, their offspring have preferred false gods to the true God, since these are less threatening to our presumed autonomy (Gen 3:4–6).[11]

The rest of Scripture unpacks how this original sin has set the pattern for the whole of fallen human history, which is characterized by pride, self-love, selfish ambition, self-justification, self-reliance, and reliance on false gods we think we can control, rather than trust in the Lord.

THE OLD TESTAMENT

This can be seen in the Old Testament narrative. Not long after the account of the fall in Genesis we encounter the tower of Babel, whose builders attempted to provide for their own security and make a name for themselves (Gen 11:4–7). Next, God called Abraham to surrender all the usual human sources of security and blessing—his nation, his home, and even his son and heir—and to trust solely in God's promises (Gen 12:1–3; 15:1–6; 22:1–18). A similar pattern is recounted in the lives of numerous other biblical characters. For instance, Jacob, who originally tried to obtain blessing through human conniving, finally obtained it when he came to the end of his human rope: first when he was alone and fleeing for his life (Gen 28:10–17), and then when he was again in fear for his life and God came and knocked him to the ground (Gen 32:22–32).

This pattern continues with the nation of Israel. As they entered the Promised Land, God told them it was not because of their strength or righteousness that he had chosen them as his own, but simply because he was faithful to his gracious promises (Deut 7:6–9; 9:4–29). Only confidence in him could make them great and prosperous. Therefore God tested them, humbled them, and urged them not to forget his provision by saying in their hearts, "My power and the might of my hand have gotten me this wealth" (Deut 8:17; cf. Deut 7:12–8:20). Yet instead of trusting in the Lord, in the time of Samuel the people demanded a human king in the mistaken belief that this would make them great (1 Sam 8:4–20).

---

[11] Paul J. Achtemeier, "Gods Made with Hands: The New Testament and the Problem of Idolatry," *Ex Auditu* 15 (1999): 48–50, 58; Charles R. Taber, "God vs. Idols: A Model of Conversion," *Journal of the Academy for Evangelism in Theological Education* 3 (1987–88): 26–27, 29; Richard Keyes, "The Idol Factory," in *No God but God: Breaking with the Idols of our Age*, ed. Os Guinness and John Seel (Chicago: Moody, Chicago, 1992), 31–32, 48; Richard Keyes, "The Dynamics of Idolatry."

Throughout their time of settlement in the land, God repeatedly warned the people of Israel not to put their confidence in their armies or political alliances, but in him (Judg 7:2; 2 Chron 17:7–10; Isa 30:1–31:3; Hos 14:3). They brought disaster on themselves when they failed to heed these warnings. When they humbled themselves God's wrath turned from them (1 Kings 21:27–29; 2 Kings 22:19; 2 Chron 12:6–12; 32:26; 33:12–13, 19, 23–24; 34:26–28; 36:12; cf. 2 Sam 22:8), but eventually he destroyed them because they failed to heed his warnings about their pride (Isa 28:1–4; Jer 13:8–19; Ezek 7:10, 20, 23; Hos 5:5; 7:10; Amos 6:8). Even two of their more godly kings, Uzziah and Hezekiah, brought God's wrath upon themselves because of pride (2 Chron 26:16; 32:25).

This judgment for pride also extended to the surrounding nations (Jer 48:29–31; 49:16; 50:31–32; Isa 13:11; 16:6–7; 23:9; 25:10–12; Ezek 31:10–11; Obad 3; Zeph 2:9–10). Sennacherib boasted that he was so mighty that no god could deliver its people from his hand (2 Kings 18:28–35), so the Lord destroyed his army in one night. He also rebuked and humbled Nebuchadnezzar and Pharaoh for claiming to be the creators of their realms (Ezek 29:9; Dan 4:29–32), destroyed the King of Tyre for claiming "I am a god" (Ezek 28:1–10), and put Belshazzar to death for failing to humble himself before the Lord (Dan 5:18–23). Habakkuk and Isaiah tell us that the Babylonians made their own might their god and were destroyed for their divine pretensions (Hab 11:1; Isa 14:12–15; 47:8–11), while Jeremiah pronounced God's curse on anyone who trusts in human beings instead of the Lord (Jer 17:5–6).

Similar themes are evident in the wisdom literature. In Proverbs, trusting in the Lord is contrasted with leaning on one's own understanding (Prov 3:5), and God declares that he is against the proud to bring them low (Prov 8:13; 15:25; 16:18–19; 21:4; 29:23). The Psalms tell us that pride goes together with a denial of God (Ps 10:4), and they call on the Lord to judge the proud (Ps 59:12; 31:18; 94:2; 123:4). The Psalms are also replete with calls not to fear humans or trust in them, but to trust in the Lord. "Grant us help against the foe, for vain is the salvation of man!" (Ps 108:12). "Put not your trust in princes, in a son of man, in whom there is no salvation" (Ps 146:3). "Arise, O LORD! Let not man prevail. . . . Let the nations know that they are but men!" (Ps 9:19–20. See also Ps 10:2–6; 20:7–8; 33:16–17; 49:5–20; 127:1–2; 147:10–11). Then Psalm 46 tells that despite all our struggling and fighting for preeminence, it is not we humans who will be exalted among the nations but the Lord.[12]

---

[12] "Come see the works of the Lord, the horrible things he has caused in the earth. [What are these horrible things—for humans who are trying to exalt themselves with their weapons of war?] He makes wars to cease to the ends of the earth, he breaks the bow, and shatters the spear, he burns the chariots with fire. Stop it!—and know that I am God. I will be exalted among the

It could be argued that gods of wood and stone are a greater problem in the Old Testament than human pride. Yet, as the Old Testament scholar Christopher Wright points out, pagan idolatry and pride go hand in hand. Not only is the biblical critique of such idolatry frequently coupled with a plea not to trust in human strength,[13] but most commonly the Bible describes pagan idols as "the work of human hands."[14] This is not naiveté or unfairness on the part of the biblical writers, as if they were unable to recognize that people who bow down to cult statues make a distinction between the transcendent gods and the statues that represent them. Instead, this is precisely the sting in the biblical critique. When the biblical prophets call idols "the work of human hands" they are not merely observing that cult statues are constructed by human craftsmen. Instead, they are claiming that the so-called gods represented by the statues are nonentities. They are no more than a projection of human hopes and proud aspirations, and are therefore no more powerful than the people who dream them up.[15] Hence trusting in them amounts to trusting in human strength and is a mask for human ambition.

We see this coupling of idolatry with human pride in the book of Daniel, where Belshazzar expressed his pride by praising the gods of metal, wood, and stone instead of the Lord (Dan 5:22–23). Elsewhere we are told the same about Amon and the people of Judah and Jerusalem (2 Chron 33:22–23; Jer 44:2–10). Yet this pairing of pride with the worship of false gods is most clearly seen in Isaiah, where the prophet rails against pride and idolatry in the same breath:

> Their land is filled with silver and gold, and there is no end to their treasures; their land is filled with horses, and there is no end to their chariots. Their land is filled with idols; they bow down to the work of their hands, to what their own fingers have made. So man is humbled, and each one is brought low—do not forgive them! Enter into the rock and hide in the dust from before the terror of the LORD, and from the splendor of his majesty. The haughty looks of man shall be brought low, and the lofty pride of men shall be humbled, and the LORD alone will be exalted in that day. For the LORD of hosts has a day against all that is proud and lofty, against all that

---

nations, I will be exalted in the earth!" (Ps 46:8–10. Author's translation. This interpretation of the Psalm was suggested to me by Dr. John Kleinig, professor emeritus, Australian Lutheran College.)

[13] Christopher J. H. Wright, *The Mission of God: Unlocking the Bible's Grand Narrative* (Downers Grove, IL: IVP Academic, 2006), 147–61; cf. Isa 2:6–22.

[14] Wright, *The Mission of God*, 147; e.g., 2 Kings 19:17–19; Ps 115:1–4; Hos 8:4, 6; Hab 2:18–19; Jer 10:3–5, 9, 14; Isa 40:18–20; 44:9–20.

[15] Wright, *The Mission of God*, 149–57.

> is lifted up—and it shall be brought low; against all the cedars of Lebanon, lofty and lifted up; and against all the oaks of Bashan; against all the lofty mountains, and against all the uplifted hills; against every high tower, and against every fortified wall; against all the ships of Tarshish, and against all the beautiful craft. And the haughtiness of man shall be humbled, and the lofty pride of men shall be brought low, and the LORD alone will be exalted in that day. And the idols shall utterly pass away. And people shall enter the caves of the rocks and the holes of the ground, from before the terror of the LORD, and from the splendor of his majesty, when he rises to terrify the earth. In that day mankind will cast away their idols of silver and their idols of gold, which they made for themselves to worship, to the moles and to the bats, to enter the caverns of the rocks and the clefts of the cliffs, from before the terror of the LORD, and from the splendor of his majesty, when he rises to terrify the earth. Stop regarding man in whose nostrils is breath, for of what account is he? (Isa 2:7–22)

THE NEW TESTAMENT

The New Testament narrative presents to us Christ, the humble and gentle king (Matt 21:5), who comes to lift up the humble and bring down the proud and mighty (Luke 1:51–52). Paul then tells us that Christ's humility and trust in his Father provide for us an example to emulate (Phil 2:3–8).

Jesus spends a significant portion of his earthly ministry trying to open the eyes of the Pharisees and scribes to the folly of their self-righteousness (Luke 5:19–32; 7:36–50; 15; 18:9–14; 19:1–10; John 8:1–11), by telling them that he has not come to call the righteous but sinners to repentance (Luke 5:32). His disciples vie for positions of power, but he teaches them that greatness in the kingdom of heaven is to take last place and be servants of all (Mark 9:33–37; 10:35–45; John 13:13–15). Indeed, if they want to enter the kingdom of heaven they must become humble like little children (Matt 18:1–4), since God opposes the proud but gives grace to the humble and poor in spirit (Matt 5:3, 5; 23:12; Luke 1:51–52; 14:11. Cf. James 4:6; 1 Pet 5:5–6).

By contrast, Herod Agrippa was eaten by worms for failing to give glory to God when the people of Tyre and Sidon called him a god (Acts 12:20–23). Many in Israel believed in Jesus but failed to confess him, since "they loved the glory that comes from man more than the glory that comes from God" (John 12:42–43). St. Paul on the other hand, who had taken great pride in his own righteousness according to the Law (Phil 3:4–8), was humbled and made an effective servant of the kingdom. To keep him from becoming conceited and trusting in his own strength God gave him a thorn in his flesh (2 Cor

12:7–10), and he and his coworkers had to experience great hardships "to make us rely not on ourselves but on God who raises the dead" (2 Cor 1:9). While the super-apostles in Corinth boasted of their super-spirituality, and the Galatians boasted of their works of the Law, Paul would boast only of his weakness and of Christ's power at work in him (2 Cor 11:1–12:10; Gal 6:12–14; 1 Cor 3:21).

This narrative is consistently reinforced by New Testament teaching. Christ and his apostles repeatedly warn us not to put confidence in our piety or works (e.g., Rom 9:16; Eph 2:8), nor to trust in other human things such as family (Matt 10:37), wealth (Luke 12:13–34; 1 Tim 6:17), earthly pleasures (Luke 8:14), social status or reputation (Luke 14:7–14; Heb 13:12–14), our race or nation (John 8:39ff; Acts 10:34–35), human wisdom and philosophy (1 Cor 1:18–2:16; Col 2:8, 22), or human traditions (Matt 15:1–9; Col 2:8). Rather than allowing us to exalt ourselves in this way, God has chosen the foolish, the weak, the low and the despised of this world so that no one may boast before him (1 Cor 1:27–29). St. Paul tells us that people are estranged from God not because of a lack of knowledge about him, but because of their refusal to glorify him. This causes them to suppress, through idolatrous worship, the knowledge available to them (Rom 1:18–25). Therefore we must learn to despair of our works and wisdom and all human and earthly things, and live solely by faith in God's mercy (e.g., Rom 1:16–17; Gal 2:16–3:29).

Sadly, the haughty self-seeking of humankind will continue as long as this world endures. In his instructions to Timothy, a young minister of the Gospel, St. Paul writes,

> But understand this, that in the last days there will come times of difficulty. For people will be *lovers of self, lovers of money, proud, arrogant*, abusive, disobedient to their parents, ungrateful, unholy, heartless, unappeasable, slanderous, without self-control, brutal, not loving good, treacherous, reckless, *swollen with conceit, lovers of pleasure rather than lovers of God*. (2 Tim 3:1–4; emphasis added)

Since this proud self-seeking will be a continual problem, Paul's next instruction to Timothy—and to us today—is to hold firmly to the Spirit filled Word that points us to Christ (2 Tim 3:10–17).

Summary

Clearly, the idolatry of the self, and God's response to it, is not a peripheral theme in Scripture. The evils of pride, self-reliance, and self-justification on the one hand, and our need for humble trust in God's mercy on the other, are teachings that permeate the whole Bible. Biblical teaching as a whole makes no sense without this key. For instance, anyone expecting the biblical characters to be virtuous exemplars for us to imitate will find them sadly lacking. Their stories only make sense when we read them as tales of human failure and divine mercy. Likewise, anyone who comes to Scripture expecting help in the human quest for God will hear instead, "no one seeks for God. All have turned away" (Rom 3:11–12), and "no one can come to me unless the Father who sent me draws him" (John 6:44).

The Scriptures are ultimately about fall and redemption. The fall means that left to our own devices we all choose to do what is right in our own eyes (Judg 21:25), and turn aside to our own way (Isa 53:6; 1 Pet 2:25). Redemption means that while we are still sinners (Rom 5:6–10), bent on pursuing our own self-centered will, Christ comes to seek and save the lost (Luke 19:10).

THE HUMAN SELF VERSUS THE GOD OF GRACE

So how does Luther's picture of human beings as essentially self-oriented fit with his picture of God as a generous Giver? Surely selfish people would delight in a God who gives them things for nothing? Yet this is not so. On the one hand, the Giver is a problem. We happily take the gifts, but the Giver always threatens to dislodge us from our preferred place at the center of the universe. On the other hand, the pure "giftedness" of the gifts is a problem. Giftedness also means "givenness," and as self-oriented people we have trouble accepting all the "givens" of life. If something is simply given, it means we cannot choose, control, define, or take credit for it ourselves.[16] It means we are dependent on the Giver, and this threatens our autonomy. Luther expresses it this way:

> What, then, is the grace of God? It is this, that from sheer mercy, for the sake of Christ, who is our beloved Bishop and Mediator, God forgives all our sins. He abates all His anger, leads us by faith from idolatry and error to truth. And the Holy Spirit purifies our hearts, enlightens, sanctifies, and justifies us, chooses us as children and heirs, adorns us with His gifts, redeems and protects us from the power of the devil, and finally gives us eternal life and blessedness. And yet He also supplies this transitory life with everything needful, gives and preserves it, through the service and co-operation of all creatures of heaven and earth. The whole world could not deserve even the tiniest of these gifts. . . . If this is true—and it undeniably is—then it follows that our works, wisdom, and holiness are nothing before God. For if it is God's love, then it cannot be our merit. And if it is our merit, then it is not God's love

[16] I owe this thought to Joyce Little (*The Church and the Culture War: Secular Anarchy or Sacred Order* [San Francisco: Ignatius Press, 1995], 38, 124).

> (Rom. 11:6). . . . Why do they all fight this teaching of God's grace and call it heresy? Because they do not want to see their own teaching and works despised and discarded. That God's grace gives us so much, as I said above, they are willing to accept; but that their own doings should be nothing and only pure and simple grace should count before God, why, that has to be heresy. They want to have a hand in the game and through free will do so much that they will earn God's grace and buy it from Him, together with all the aforementioned goods. Then not the love of God but our own merit achieves grace. Then we are the workmen who lay the cornerstone on which God then builds His grace and love, so that He must praise, thank, and adore us. Then we become His gods instead of the other way around.[17]

Here Luther articulates once again that God alone is the source of all good gifts in every area of life: in redemption, in sanctification, and in his provision for our earthly lives. Yet he also articulates what an offense this is for people who want to take control and take credit for themselves. When we are guided by our sinful nature, we refuse to look to God as the exclusive Giver of every good gift, and think that we can play a hand in grasping his gifts for ourselves. Therefore we put ourselves in his place, and distort our picture of him, so that he becomes a puppet who must dance to our tune.

This discomfort with God's grace does not mean that self-oriented people are necessarily irreligious. Rather, the temptation is to deal with God on our own terms. This is what Luther addressed in his well-known distinction at the *Heidelberg Disputation* between a theologian of glory and a theologian of the cross. This terminology is simply a different way of phrasing his more common distinction between true faith and idolatry,[18] which he describes using

---

[17] *Commentary on Psalm 117* (1530), LW 14:25 = WA 31/1:243a.12–244a.6.

[18] Luther frequently talks about the theology of the cross throughout his career. Yet he never contrasts this with the theology of glory except in the *Heidelberg Disputation* and his *Explanations of the Ninety-Five Theses* (LW 31:227). The expression "theology of glory" or "theologian of glory" does not appear anywhere in his writings apart from these two works from 1518 (as far as I can tell from my search of the American Edition and the *Weimarer Ausgabe*). By contrast the distinction between true, Christ-centered faith on the one hand and idolatry on the other is extremely common throughout his writings. Despite this, the distinction between the theology of the cross and the theology of glory has received enormous attention in Luther studies, while the distinction between the theology of the cross and idolatry has received very little. This is an unbalanced state of affairs. The expression "theology of glory" does draw attention to the outward show associated with idolatry in contrast to the shame and humility of the cross. Since idolatry must appeal to the sinful nature it always makes a show of things that appear glorious to sinful human beings. Yet "theology of glory" is also a more obscure expression, which is perhaps why Luther dropped it.

exactly the same themes and biblical texts.[19] A theologian of glory is nothing other than an idolater.

In his *Heidelberg Disputation*, Luther identifies two characteristics of a theologian of glory. First, he tries to grasp the invisible God through his own reason—by reflecting on the things God has made—instead of through God's Word and the crucified Christ.[20] Second, he hopes to secure righteousness and fellowship with God through his works, instead of through the cross of Christ.[21] In both these ways he seeks to grasp hold of God by himself. He misuses the best things in the worst manner, since he "takes credit for works and wisdom and does not give credit to God."[22] He cannot hope in God since he has not despaired of himself and therefore is not prepared to put all confidence in God.[23] Instead, he enjoys his own works and adores himself as an idol.[24] Nor can he know God as he is, because "true theology and recognition of God are in the crucified Christ."[25] He is like one who tries to climb into heaven to grab some glory for himself, but in the process only grasps an empty idol. A theologian of the cross on the other hand finds God in the place where he freely gives himself to us, in Christ and the cross.[26]

---

[19] Romans 1:20 is Luther's key passage for talking about the natural knowledge of God and how it leads to idolatry, as we will see in the next chapter. Jesus' words in John 14, "No one comes to the Father, but by me" and "he who has seen me has seen the Father" are used by Luther to distinguish the true knowledge of God through Christ and the Gospel from the idolatrous knowledge of God that comes from natural reason (LW 12:84; 24:23–24; cf. LW 22:148–59; 43:54–55). Exod 33:18–23 is used by Luther to argue that the true, non-idolatrous knowledge of God must be revealed to us under coverings (LW 22:157). These are the key texts and themes that Luther is dealing with in Theses 19 and 20 of the *Heidelberg Disputation*.

[20] Theses 19–22, 24, and 29–30 (LW 31:40–41 = WA 1:354–55).

[21] Theses 1–18 and 21–28 (LW 31:39–41 = WA 1:353–54).

[22] Luther's discussion of thesis 24, LW 31:55 = WA 1:363.29–30.

[23] Luther's discussion of thesis 11, LW 31:48 = WA 1:359.

[24] Luther's discussion of thesis 7, LW 31:46 = WA 1:358.

[25] Luther's discussion of thesis 20, LW 31:53 = WA 1:362.18.

[26] For Luther, the "God hidden in suffering" (LW 31:53) is not the hidden God but the revealed God. The hidden God is the one whose invisible attributes people think they can make visible by reflecting on the things he has made (Thesis 19, WA 1:354.17–18). The revealed God is the one who comes to us under the coverings of suffering and the cross (Thesis 20, WA 1:354.19–20; LW 31:40, 52–53). This is a hidden revelation, since people do not expect God to look like this, and therefore do not recognize Christ as God (Alister E. McGrath, *Luther's Theology of the Cross: Martin Luther's Theological Breakthrough* [Oxford: Basil Blackwell, 1985], 149–50). Yet in Christ the true God is on display for all who have eyes to see.

CONCLUSION

For Luther the human self, with its self-chosen efforts to grab hold of divine things, lies at the heart of all idolatry. In subsequent chapters we will see how he develops this in relation to every area of God's plan for humankind. For now it is sufficient to establish the point that idolatry involves pushing ourselves forward when God alone should be at work. It is God's job to reveal himself to us. We create an idol when we think we can form our own picture of him. It is God's job to provide for us. We latch on to many idols when we think we can care for ourselves. It is God's job to justify us. We make an idol of our righteousness when we attempt to justify ourselves. Whereas God wants to give us all things by grace, we want to define and control for ourselves our relationship with him and his gifts. The living God always comes as a gift. Idols, on the other hand, are our own accomplishment.

This attempt to put ourselves in the place of God causes an enormous problem. We are simply not up to the task. This leads to immense insecurity and causes us to latch onto many idols outside ourselves that we hope will aid us in our endeavor. Richard Keyes, director of the Massachusetts branch of L'Abri, talks about a "theology of insecurity" that lies beneath idolatry, as we seek to compensate for the God we have abandoned and seek to fill his shoes.[27] In the next chapter, we will see how Luther deals with this theme.

[27] Keyes, "The Idol Factory," 31–36; Richard Keyes, "The Dynamics of Idolatry."

Chapter Three

Trying to Fill a Triune-Shaped Hole

The Triadic Structure of Idolatry

Whenever we leave God out of our lives, this leaves a God-shaped hole in our lives, which we are compelled to fill in one way or another. More specifically, it leaves a triune-shaped hole in our lives. This forces our idolatry into a triadic shape, as we seek to find substitutes for all three members of the Trinity and the essential roles they each play in human life. To borrow some language from the early church, idolatry involves finding substitutes for all three members of the "economic" Trinity—that is, God as he relates to us and reveals himself to us within his "economy," or his plan for administering and redeeming his creation.[1] This yields for us a systematic structure for analyzing idolatry, as we consider it in relation to each member of the Trinity in turn.

This is not something Luther ever articulates in so many words. Nevertheless, it emerges from a close reading of his theology and is the best way to make sense of his thought as a whole. What we see in Luther is copious instances where he discusses idolatry in relation to either the Father, the Son, or the Holy Spirit, and the work that each of these members of the Trinity carries out in the divine plan. Thus the range of idols he discusses has a triadic structure to it, as he deals with the different idols people use to do the work of God in each Article of the Creed.

So let us now unpack in more detail why idolatry should have a triadic structure to it that mimics the triune God.

---

[1] When it is used within discussions of trinitarian theology, the word *economy* refers to God's plan for administering his creation, including his creation, redemption, and final beatification of humankind. The "economic Trinity" is the triune God as he relates to us and reveals himself to us in this plan. This is frequently contrasted with the "immanent Trinity," or God as he is in and of himself.

IDOLS ARE SUBSTITUTES FOR THE REAL TRIUNE GOD

When Luther approaches the topic of idolatry, he never treats idols as substitutes for a generic god. Instead, he recognizes that they are substitutes for the true God, who is triune. Therefore, any attempt to replace him means replacing Father, Son, and Holy Spirit.

The best way to detect a forgery is to be intimately acquainted with the original, so you can tell the difference between it and a fake. The same is true with idolatry. The best way to recognize an idol is to know the true God. Once we have identified what it is for us to have the Lord as our God, it is easy for us to identify the idols we put in his place.

This is the approach Luther takes to identifying counterfeit gods. He first asks, "What does it mean to have a god? Or, what is God?"[2] Since the true God for Luther is always the triune God, he then looks for things that people put in the place of Father, Son, and Holy Spirit. What do we trust in to provide for our physical needs in place of God the Father? What alternative means do we have of justifying ourselves instead of Christ the Redeemer? How do we seek to become wise and holy, if not through the Spirit and his Word? Questions such as these reveal our idols.

IDOLS ARE SUBSTITUTES FOR THE ECONOMIC TRINITY

More specifically, the object of true faith is the economic Trinity, or God as he has chosen to relate to us. For Luther, the doctrine of the Trinity is not simply a theoretical matter, but an immensely practical one, which is grounded in the way God reveals and gives himself to us in his plan of salvation.

Luther insists that the only way we can either know or have access to the true God is through this economy. Ever since the fall we no longer have unmediated access to God. We cannot talk with him face to face as Adam and Eve did in the garden, and as we will when we enter into glory. In our present fallen state our sin incurs God's anger, and we are unprepared to stand before him in his full majesty. So instead, God wraps himself in coverings such as his Word and the humanity of Christ so that we can receive him in grace without being terrified and crushed by the weight of his glory.[3] He accommodates himself to our weakness and condescends to deal with us in a human manner so we can understand and receive him.[4] Only as God has chosen to reveal

---

[2] LC I 1 = WA 30/1:132.34–133.1.

[3] LW 1:11–14 = WA 42:9–12; LW 5:44 = WA 43:458–59; LW 12:312–13 = WA 40/2:329–30; LW 16:54–56 = WA 31/2:38–39; cf. LW 6:148.

[4] *Lectures on Genesis* (1538–42), LW 4:143–44 = WA 43:239.

himself in this way can we know him. This means knowing him through his Son and his Spirit, and the specific words, signs, and promises he has given us in his economy.[5]

In other words, Luther insists that the true object of faith must be the revealed God and his revealed will, not the hidden God and his hidden will. Yes, there are many things about God that he has not revealed to us in Christ and his Word. Yet it does us no good to speculate about such things. Instead, we must stick with the revelation, and grasp hold of God there, rather than speculating about things God has not chosen to reveal, or trying to grasp hold of God in places he has not chosen to be found. If we try to know the hidden God in this life we will not succeed, but will only find an idol of our own creation.[6] Yet in the revealed God we can be certain we have the real God. Here we grasp hold of God as he truly is. When we enter into glory we will discover many things about God that are currently hidden from us, yet we will find the same God who has given himself to us in Christ and his Word.[7]

Idolatry is always a substitute for true faith in the true God. True faith does not involve grasping hold of God as he exists apart from us in heaven, but receiving him as he gives himself to us here on earth. Likewise, idolatry does not challenge God as he exists apart from us, but rather as he relates to us and is known by us in the economy of salvation. Luther makes the point

---

[5] *Lectures on Psalm 51* (1532), LW 12:352 = WA 40/2:386–87.

[6] "For one must debate either about the hidden God or about the revealed God. With regard to God, insofar as He has not been revealed, there is no faith, no knowledge, and no understanding. And here one must hold to the statement that what is above us is none of our concern. For thoughts of this kind, which investigate something more sublime above or outside the revelation of God, are altogether devilish. With them nothing more is achieved than that we plunge ourselves into destruction; for they present an object that is inscrutable, namely, the unrevealed God. Why not rather let God keep His decisions and mysteries in secret? . . . for this is what Christ says in John 6:65 (cf. John 14:6): 'No one comes to the Father but by Me.' Therefore when we approach the unrevealed God, then there is no faith, no Word, and no knowledge; for He is an invisible God, and you will not make Him visible" (*Lectures on Genesis* [1538–42], LW 5:44 = WA 43:458.37–459.11–14). Cf. LW 1:11–14; 4:143–44; 5:43–50; 16:54–55; 51:27–28; 28:125–26; 33:138–40; 49:63; 54:249, 385.

[7] " 'From an unrevealed God I will become a revealed God. Nevertheless, I will remain the same God. I will be made flesh, or send My Son. He shall die for your sins and shall rise again from the dead. And in this way I will fulfill your desire, in order that you may be able to know whether you are predestined or not. Behold, this is My Son; listen to Him (cf. Matt. 17:5). Look at Him as He lies in the manger and on the lap of His mother, as He hangs on the cross. Observe what He does and what He says. There you will surely take hold of Me.' For 'He who sees Me,' says Christ, 'also sees the Father Himself' (cf. John 14:9). If you listen to Him, are baptized in His name, and love His Word, then you are surely predestined and are certain of your salvation. But if you revile or despise the Word, then you are damned; for he who does not believe is condemned (Mark 16:16)" (*Lectures on Genesis* [1538–42], LW 5:44–45 = WA 43:459.24–34). Cf. LW 4:144; 5:43–50; 23:195; 28:125–26; 33:289–92; 42:147.

that not even the Antichrist can exalt himself above God in his hidden majesty. Yet he can exalt himself above the preaching and worship of God, and above God in our knowledge and dealings with him.[8] In the same way, when we elevate other things above God and turn them into idols, we cannot elevate them above God's essence as he dwells in glory. Yet we can elevate them above God's Word and his worship, and assign them a higher place in our hearts. Luther writes that "God becomes God and changes in accordance with the change in our feeling toward Him,"[9] and "the confidence and faith of the heart alone make both God and an idol."[10] By this he does not mean that God's essence changes based on our feelings toward him, but rather our relationship with him changes. When we come to faith, he is born in our hearts, and if we fall away, an idol takes his place. Thus the contest is always between our idols and the economic Trinity, or God as he relates to us and is known by us.

One significant implication of this is that if we adopt a different economy of salvation we effectively adopt a different god. Our self-directed steps will not find the true God, nor will our self-chosen piety please him. Instead, it will be directed toward a god of our own imagining. When Aaron made the golden calf at Sinai, he claimed that this was a means of worshipping the Lord, who brought Israel out of Egypt (Exod 32:4–5). When King Jeroboam set up his golden calves at Bethel and Dan he made the same claim (1 Kings 12:28). The Pharisees claimed to worship God with their human traditions, and the Judaizers with their zeal for the Jewish law. All of these claimed to be worshipping the God of Israel, yet the Bible rejects all this as idolatry (1 Kings 14:9; Matt 15:1–9; Gal 4:8–10). In a similar way, when people claim to worship the triune God, but choose to deal with him in their own way instead of through the economy he has chosen, they are not worshipping God as he really is, but only as they imagine him to be.[11] Thus idolatry results whenever we adopt a different economy of salvation.[12]

---

[8] LW 9:67–68 = WA 14:608; LW 33:139; 22:470; 3:121–22; Martin Luther, *Martin Luther's Complete Commentary on the First Twenty-Two Psalms*, trans. Henry Cole [2 vols.; London: W. Simpkin and R. Marshall, 1826], 1:530 = WA 5:331.

[9] *Lectures on Deuteronomy* (1525), LW 9:67 = WA 14:608b.26–27; cf. LW 33:116–17.

[10] LC I 2 = WA 30/1:133.4.

[11] LW 17:17; 35:269, 272.

[12] In the ancient Near East, cultic images were understood as a means of gaining access to the gods. They facilitated the divine-human relationship. In other words, they had a central place in the economy of salvation.

The Devil Can Only Ape God

A further thought from Luther that suggests a reason why idols would mimic the economic Trinity is that the devil always tries to imitate God. Luther calls the devil God's ape.[13] Likewise, he says that heretics and idolaters always ape true worship and doctrine.[14]

The way Luther develops this is to say that the devil, and those who follow his lead, imitate the outward forms of true piety while removing the substance. They remove the kernel and retain the husk.[15] The devil apes God by countering true prophesy with false signs and visions.[16] Those who follow him copy godly works, ceremonies, traditions, and doctrine, yet leave out God's Word and Spirit. They perform outward deeds with a great show of piety, yet dispense with God's commands and promises, and leave out faith in Christ.[17] Instead of placing their confidence in God as he truly comes to us, they want to outshine Christ and his Spirit.[18] So they preach their own knowledge with an appearance of wisdom, but without bringing peace to the conscience.[19]

All of this implies that the devil is not truly creative. He can only twist, distort, and misuse what God has already made, rather than making anything new. It also explains why idolatry would be a distorted reflection of true faith.

This same thought can be seen in the New Testament, particularly the book of Revelation. Here we are told that the Trinity will be opposed by the false trinity of the dragon, the beast, and the false prophet (Rev 12–13; 16:13; 20:10). Christ will be opposed by the antichrist (2 Thess 2:1–12; 1 John 1:18–23; 4:1–3; 2 John 7; Rev 13:1–8). The true church of those who bear the seal of God on their foreheads (Rev 7:1–8; 14:1–5) will be opposed by the false church of those who bear on them the mark of the beast (Rev 13:16–17; 14:9–11; 16:2; 19:20). The city of God will be opposed by the city of Babylon (Rev 17–18). The true testimony of God will be opposed by false prophesy (Rev 11:1–11; 13:11–18). And so on. In other words, the evil one will attempt to counter the true church and its true faith with a false church and a false faith. He will attempt to lead people away from worshipping Father, Son, and Holy Spirit by providing idolatrous substitutes for each of them.

---

[13] LW 4:236–37; 6:331; 7:121; 41:167–71.

[14] LW 4:235, 328; 8:133; 9:7; 12:360; 15:182–83; 16:331; 23:105; 27:161; 28:84–85; 52:162.

[15] LW 4:328; 39:191–92.

[16] LW 6:331; 7:121.

[17] LW 4:235–37, 328; 16:185.

[18] *Sermons on John* (1530–32), LW 23:279–81 = WA 33:445–48.

[19] *Lectures on Zechariah: The German Text* (1527), LW 20:233–35 = WA 23:567–69.

A TRIUNE-SHAPED HOLE

A final thought from Luther that suggests why idolatry should take this particular shape is that God has embedded the First Commandment into creation.[20] This includes our need for God, and the knowledge of God and his Law that he has written on our hearts. As weak and finite creatures, created for fellowship with God and dependence on him, we cannot escape our need for the triune God no matter how much we may want to. Nor can we erase the knowledge of God from our hearts. Sin and Satan can twist it, distort it, misdirect it, and suppress it, but not eliminate it.[21] Luther frequently refers to Romans 1 and 2 and says how the natural knowledge of God leads people into idolatry.[22] He writes, "If there had not been an inextinguishable knowledge of the divinity implanted in the minds of all men, idolatry would never have been found."[23]

When confronted with our needs we know there is a God, and we know we need a God to help us.[24] Yet just as the Jews in Jesus' day knew there is a God, but most of them did not recognize him standing before them, so by the light of fallen human reason we know there is a God but not his true identity.[25] Idolatry begins when we prefer our own opinions to the voice of the Holy Spirit, who reveals the true God to us through his Word. This means turning our natural reason into an idol by putting it in place of the Holy Spirit.[26] Then, when we grope in this false light for a god to help us in our need, we

---

[20] LW 40:96–97; 10:368. As Charles Arand notes, Luther did not regard the First Commandment as something God foists on us as an arbitrary imposition, but something he has built into creation in such a way that we cannot ignore it without doing violence to the very fabric of our being (Charles P. Arand, "Luther on the God Behind the First Commandment," *Lutheran Quarterly* 8 [Winter 1994]: 398–99, 407). One consequence of this is that the First Commandment pertains to both believers and unbelievers alike. This can be seen in Romans 1–3, where all people are held accountable for the failure to thank and honor the Creator, whether they are part of God's covenant people or not. Cf. Matt 5:45; Acts 14:17.

[21] *Commentary on Jonah: The German Text* (1526), LW 19:53–54 = WA 19:205–6.

[22] LW 9:54 = WA 14:588–89; LW 19:53–57 = WA 19:205–8; LW 3:117; 5:259–60; 6:113; 7:336; 22:148–59; 29:235; 40:96–97. This is the most natural interpretation of Romans 1 and 2, that the knowledge of God and his Law that he has written on every human heart does not lead people to God, but drives them to construct idols.

[23] Luther, *Commentary on the First Twenty-Two Psalms*, 2:45 = *Operationes in Psalmos* (1519–21), WA 5:392.37–38.

[24] LW 6:113; 7:336.

[25] LW 19:54–57 = WA 19:206–8; LW 3:117; 6:113.

[26] LW 1:149 = WA 42:112; LW 13:375; 14:202; 19:115; 31:350; 41:122; 52:107; cf. LW 9:53–54; 11:289; 16:160; 18:184.

inevitably grasp a second idol instead of the Father of all.[27] Furthermore, since we fail to obey the Law God has written on our hearts, our consciences accuse us. The light of nature reveals the problem, but not the solution through Jesus Christ. Therefore, unless we have taken to heart what God's Word says about the mercy he promises us in Christ, we flee from God in fear, and find a third idol to justify us and settle the Law's accusations.[28] In this way the natural knowledge of God drives people to create idols to supplant all three members of the Trinity.

A Systematic Way of Analyzing Idolatry

Once we realize that idolatry takes on this shape, we have a framework for analyzing idolatry and asking more probing questions about the idolatry of our society. Instead of only being able to recognize obvious idols, like money, sex, and power, that people trust in to satisfy their physical needs and desires, we will start to recognize more refined, spiritual idols. We will start to ask questions like, how do people in our society go about justifying themselves? how do they try to enlighten themselves? and on what basis do they attempt to relate to God?

Luther applies his question "What is it to have a God?" to every aspect of God's economy. He first asks what it means for us to have the Lord as our God in each area of life and then uses this as his criterion for identifying idols. I will follow this same pattern in dealing with Luther's thought. In each of the remaining chapters, I will deal with a different part of God's plan. I will begin by asking what Luther thinks it is to have the Lord as our God in this area of life. I will then explore what this teaches us about idolatry, and particularly the chief idol of the self. The central themes of these chapters are:

1. *The Idol of the Self and Providence.* God the Father is the one who provides us with all good things; all who think they can provide for their own creaturely needs apart from him are idolaters.
2. *The Idol of the Self and Love.* Our heavenly Father calls us to love him above anything else; all who love themselves more than him are idolaters.
3. *The Idol of the Self and Justification.* Jesus Christ must justify us sinners with a righteousness that is not our own; all who attempt to justify themselves are idolaters.

[27] *Commentary on Jonah: The German Text* (1526), LW 19:54–57 = WA 19:206–8; *Sermons on Deuteronomy* (1529), WA 28:609–11.

[28] LW 9:104 = WA 14:636–37; LW 7:336; 12:308–9, 378–79; 14:202; 16:249; 17:108; 22:148–59; 40:94; 51:17.

4. *The Idol of the Self and the Worship of God Incarnate.* No one can know or come to the Father except through his incarnate Son, who comes to us now through the means of the Gospel; all who devise their own path to God or worship of God apart from Christ incarnate are idolaters.
5. *The Idol of the Self and God's Word.* The Holy Spirit reveals God to us through his Word; all who bypass the Spirit-breathed Word and attempt to know God by means of their own reason are idolaters.
6. *The Idol of the Self and Repentance.* The Spirit must free us from our idols and create true faith in us; all who think they can produce true faith and its fruit without relying at all times on him are idolaters.

The first section of each chapter will provide a detailed summary of Luther's teaching. The next section will examine how this kind of idolatry is expressed in contemporary society. Then finally, in the conclusion to each chapter, I will make some suggestions for what this means for Christian proclamation. I will highlight how we can uncover the futility of this form of idolatry and then proclaim the gracious promises of God into this area of life.

Since Luther developed his theology of idolatry over against his understanding of the economy of salvation, the two cannot be understood in isolation from each other. Luther's theology of idolatry is only convincing to the extent that one accepts his account of God's plan. It is not possible within the scope of this book to defend a Lutheran understanding of this economy. I will therefore assume it as given and proceed to examine its implications for understanding idolatry. If you as a reader do not accept a Lutheran account of the economy of salvation at all points, my hope is that you will still find enough common ground to help you develop your own understanding of idolatry.

PART TWO

THE FIRST ARTICLE

Chapter Four

The Idol of the Self and Providence

When the Gospel first came to Papua New Guinea, many people were attracted to it because of the material blessings they thought it would bring. They saw the earthly wealth of the "white skins," and thought that if they adopted the white skins' religion similar wealth would flow their way. My mother taught at Asaroka Lutheran High School in the New Guinea highlands in the late 1960s, and remembers being impressed by an amiable and intelligent student who appeared to be a committed Christian. Then, after he graduated, he attended university in the capital Port Moresby, and subsequently held a senior position with the Papua New Guinean government as a development planner. Before long, she heard reports that he was going around the New Guinea highlands telling people that the Gospel was not what they needed. Instead, they needed development, which could bring them more blessings than the Gospel ever could. Evidently he had observed that Western culture has more than one God, and had switched his allegiance to the god he thought would be most successful in providing earthly things.

Such a transfer of confidence from God to some other provider gets to the heart of what Luther means by idolatry. In his Small Catechism, Luther explains the First Commandment by saying, "We should fear, love, and trust in God above all things."[1] This suggests three main features of idolatry: misplaced fear, misplaced love, and misplaced trust.

Of the three, Luther devotes the least attention to fear. When he deals with it he tends to treat it in conjunction with misplaced trust, instead of focusing on it as a separate issue. This makes sense, since confidence and fear are opposite sides of the same coin. Therefore I will not dedicate a separate chapter to fear, but will deal with this theme later in this chapter.

Luther spends more time focusing on misplaced love and misplaced trust. These are the two main ways we can turn ourselves into idols in relation to our Creator. First, we can love ourselves above everything else, so that we seek our own wellbeing above all, and use everything including God to serve our-

---

[1] SC I 2 = WA 30/1:354.

selves. Second, we can trust in ourselves above everything else, so that we rely on our own ability to secure the good things of life instead of trusting in the Lord to provide. In this chapter we will focus on trust, and in the next on love.

When Luther discusses idolatry in the Large Catechism he focuses exclusively on trust, and most of his examples are of idols that function in the domain of the First Article of the Creed. That is, they are things that we use as substitutes for the Creator and his work of providing for our earthly needs.[2] For instance, Luther talks about money, and how common it is to turn this into an idol by thinking that as long as we have money we do not need God, because our wealth will provide all we need. As we will see in subsequent chapters, Luther also speaks about the idolatry of misplaced trust in relation to the other Articles of the Creed. Yet idolatry that supplants our trust in the Creator's provision is the most obvious form of idolatry, and a good place to begin our discussion.

LUTHER'S TEACHING

For Luther, what does it mean to have God as our God in this area of our lives? It means to trust in our heavenly Father to provide us with all the good things we need for this earthly life. This means that all who think they can provide for their own creaturely needs without relying on him have put themselves in his place, and are idolaters. It is true that God frequently uses human labor and its fruits—such as science, technology, medicine, and economic development—to provide us with earthly blessings. Yet this is just one tool in his limitless toolbox, and does not belong in the place of God.

Luther's view of our Creator is not of a distant or abstract power who wound the world up but now leaves us to our own devices. Abstract powers and distant gods can be relativized and ignored, since in practical terms they leave us in the driver's seat. Instead, we have a personal Creator who is intimately involved with his creation, and cannot be evaded. Those with eyes to see encounter him in every moment of their lives.[3] Luther writes that "God himself is personally present in all things"[4] and is "wholly and entirely in all creatures and in every single individual being, more deeply, more inwardly, more present than the creature is to itself."[5]

---

[2] LC I 5–12, 18 = WA 30/1:133.17–134.17, 135.1–6.

[3] LW 28:180; WA 46:493–95; 49:423.10–12, 434.16–18; Oswald Bayer, *Martin Luther's Theology: A Contemporary Interpretation*, trans. Thomas H. Trapp (Grand Rapids, MI: Eerdmans, 2008), 106–12.

[4] *That These Words of Christ, "This Is My Body," Etc., Still Stand Firm against the Fanatics* (1527), LW 37:63 = WA 23:142.2–3.

[5] *That These Words of Christ Still Stand Firm* (1527), LW 37:60 = WA 23:136.32–33; cf. Acts 17:28.

This present God is constantly at work to give us his blessings. The so-called "laws of nature" do not operate by themselves, but are examples of his activity. He is simply so reliable in upholding his creation that we come to expect it and no longer regard it as miraculous. Luther says that the birth of each new life and the light of the sun are wondrous miracles, even if we do not recognize them as such.[6] In the same way God's mighty power is at work even when we are at work, since he must give us strength and skill and enable our labor to bear fruit. Luther writes,

> What else is all our work to God—whether in the fields, in the garden, in the city, in the house, in war, or in government—but just such a child's performance, by which He wants to give His gifts in the fields, at home, and everywhere else? These are the masks of God, behind which He wants to remain concealed and do all things.[7]

This means that in daily life, we are constantly dependent on God's good work to supply our every need and must live by faith in his provision. To think we can provide for ourselves, without at all times relying on him, is an idolatrous deception.

TRUSTING IN OUR WORKS = SEIZING GOD'S GLORY FOR OURSELVES

Luther stresses countless times that "works righteousness" stands at the heart of all idolatry, as we will see in chapter 6. Yet it is worth noting that for Luther, works righteousness is not merely an issue of salvation. It is not only when it comes to our redemption that we attempt to justify and establish ourselves on the basis of our works rather than trusting in God. Instead, this same perversion affects every aspect of our lives. Therefore when Luther explains the Creed in his catechisms he uses the language of justification in relation to every Article.[8]

When it comes to God's provision of earthly things, Luther stresses that this takes place "without any merit or worthiness in me."[9] He also emphasizes that none of us can own, preserve, or take credit for any of our temporal goods, but we must continually receive them as gifts from God.[10] Yet we act as if the world stands on our shoulders and is upheld by our deeds. We turn ourselves into idols by thinking that through our own strength and ingenuity we

[6] LW 1:53–54 = WA 42:40; LW 1:126 = WA 42:94–95.

[7] *Commentary on Psalm 147* (1530), LW 14:114 = WA 31/1:436.7–11.

[8] Bayer, *Martin Luther's Theology*, 95–100, 254.

[9] SC II = WA 30/1:365.2–3.

[10] LC II 16–21 = WA 30/1:184.14–185.9.

can secure all the things we need for this life. When we do this, we are making our own might our god and stealing God's glory for ourselves. Instead of giving thanks to him, we end up boasting that the things he has given us are our achievement.[11]

The following anecdote recorded by Mathesius Khumers illustrates Luther's attitude—that we are always beggars who live off of God's charity, though we rarely recognize it:

> Once, when Luther was traveling to Jessen to recuperate, along with Dr. Jonas, Veit Dietrich, and other table companions, though he himself did not have all that much, he gave alms to the poor there. Dr. Jonas followed his example, with the explanation: Who knows where God will provide the same for me another time! To which Luther replied with a laugh: As if your God has not provided it for you already.[12]

SEEING IS BELIEVING

Luther ties this tendency to trust in ourselves to our tendency to enthrone God's creatures in general as idols. He suggests that the reason it is so easy to worship the creature instead of the Creator is that God uses his creatures as masks of his activity. He uses the prince to provide us with protection. He makes plants and animals grow to provide us with food. He gives us joy through human companions. He provides us with our living through the work he has called us to do. When we have the attitude that seeing is believing, it is easy for us to put our confidence in these masks of God's provision, since they are all we see.[13] We then fail to recognize the true Giver who stands behind these masks and think that as long as we have these creatures, we have all we need. This means turning these creatures into idols.

Yet humans are the greatest of God's earthly creatures. Thus, trusting in the masks of God means trusting in ourselves more than anything, at least corporately if not individually. Furthermore, even when we turn creatures besides ourselves into idols, such as money or Mother Nature or other people, a certain self-confidence is likely to be involved. When we depend on our ability to acquire money, harness nature, win human favor, and acquire blessing from these creatures without God's provision, we have turned this ability into an idol.[14]

---

[11] LW 9:84–85 = WA 14:626; LW 2:125; 14:66–68; 16:215–16, 346–49; 19:115, 186–87; 21:216–17; 44:30–31.

[12] WA TR 4:140. Translated by Bayer, *Martin Luther's Theology*, 96.

[13] *Sermons on Deuteronomy* (1529), WA 28:607–14, 617–20; cf. LW 1:15.

[14] LW 9:96; 14:66–68; WA 28:612–14, 617–20.

MANIPULATING GOD

There is also a more subtle way in which we can place confidence in ourselves: by trusting in our ability to manipulate God or other "higher powers" for our own ends. We may acknowledge only one God. We may give God's name to other powers we see in the world like the sun, the moon, or fortune.[15] We may pile up many gods like Jupiter, Mars, and Venus.[16] For Luther it makes little difference. If we think this power can be made subject to our control we have an idol and not the true God, since the true God does not allow himself to be used in this way.[17] If we think God's favor can be bought, and we can use our works to coax him into blessing us instead of receiving everything by grace, then we have a false picture of God and have turned our power to manipulate him into an idol.[18]

TRUE FAITH TRUSTS IN GOD ALONE

The faith that God calls for has a completely different attitude. It trusts in the true God as the Giver of every good thing, gives all glory to him, and receives all of life as an ongoing miracle from his hand.[19] It realizes that all power belongs to him and not us, and that apart from him we can accomplish nothing. In his reflections on the Magnificat, where Mary praises Almighty God for turning the tables on the mighty of this world, Luther writes,

> Truly, in these words she takes away all might and power from every creature and bestows them on God alone. What great boldness and robbery on the part of so young and tender a maiden! She dares, by this one word, to make all the strong feeble, all the mighty weak, all the wise foolish, all the famous despised, and God alone the Possessor of all strength, wisdom, and glory. For this is the meaning of the phrase: "He who is mighty." There is none that does anything, but as St. Paul says in Ephesians 1: "God accomplishes all in all," and all creatures' works are God's works. Even as we confess in the Creed: "I believe in God the Father, the Almighty." He is almighty because it is His power alone that works in all and through all and over all. Thus St. Anna, the mother of Samuel, sings in 1 Samuel 2:9: "Not by might shall a man prevail." St. Paul says in

---

[15] LW 1:15; 4:236, 328; 20:170–71; WA 28:13.

[16] *Sermons on Deuteronomy* (1529), WA 28:609–11.

[17] David S. Yeago, "The Catholic Luther," in *The Catholicity of the Reformation*, ed. Carl E. Braaten and Robert W. Jenson (Grand Rapids, MI: Eerdmans, 1996), 18.

[18] LW 9:104; 38:106–7.

[19] Paul Althaus, *The Theology of Martin Luther*, trans. Robert C. Schultz (Philadelphia: Fortress, 1966), 110.

> 2 Corinthians 3:5: "Not that we are sufficient of ourselves to claim anything as coming from us; our sufficiency is from God." This is a most important article of faith, including many things; it completely puts down all pride, arrogance, blasphemy, fame, and false trust, and exalts God alone. It points out the reason why God alone is to be exalted—because He does all things. . . . For the word "mighty" does not denote a quiescent power, as one says of a temporal king that he is mighty, even though he may be sitting still and doing nothing. But it denotes an energetic power, a continuous activity, that works and operates without ceasing. For God does not rest, but works without ceasing, as Christ says in John 5:17: "My Father is working still, and I am working." In the same sense St. Paul says in Ephesians 3:20: "He is able to do more than all that we ask"; that is, He always does more than we ask; that is His way, and thus His power works.[20]

Luther outlines four ways God works to provide for his creation. He calls this God's fourfold rule. The first rule is when he works through his own mighty power without the cooperation of any creatures, such as when he gives his creatures life and provides them with their powers and skill. The second rule is when he works through his angels to guide and protect his creatures on earth. Often people attribute this protection to fate or good fortune, when really it is God's doing. His third rule is carried out by his preachers of the Gospel, who preach his Word outwardly and in this way bring his Holy Spirit, who works inwardly to change human hearts. His final rule includes the other earthly vocations, such as government and the rule of parents in the home. Through these callings he is at work to provide for our earthly needs.[21]

Luther then draws two implications from this. The first is that we should not despise the means through which God has chosen to work. We should not expect a heavenly miracle if we have refused to use the earthly means of assistance God has provided for us. To do so would be to put God to the test, and to demand that he provide for us in the manner of our choosing instead of in the manner he has chosen.[22] Yet the second implication is that we should not put our confidence in these earthly means but in God alone. To transfer the trust that belongs to God to these earthly things would be to turn them into idols. Therefore we should not be disturbed when the earthly things we need are lacking and God seems slow in answering our prayers, so that all we have

---

[20] *Commentary on the Magnificat* (1521), LW 21:328 = WA 7:574.3–34.

[21] *Lectures on Zechariah: The German Text* (1527), LW 20:169–72 = WA 23:511–14.

[22] LW 7:113–14; 9:74–75; 14:115; 28:347; 46:202–3; 76:370–71.

to cling to is his Word. Rather, we should trust in him to provide.[23] Luther writes, "God will save through the sword if it is at hand, and without the sword if it is not available. Hence, one must use things, but one must not trust in them. Only in God should one trust, whether that which you may use is at hand or lacking."[24]

This means that we cannot boast that we have earned the things God has given us through our labor. God does not need our help. He is quite capable of providing without it. In the usual course of daily life, he chooses to provide for us through our work. Therefore we should not despise the work he has called us to do, but do it with all our strength.[25] God honors us by allowing us to join him in his work.[26] He also uses our work as a means of restraining our sinful nature, and giving us opportunity to serve our neighbor.[27] If we refuse the honor of working with him, he will still carry out his work of caring for others, but threatens to withhold his blessings from us.[28] Yet although we can forfeit God's blessings by refusing to work, God does not give us anything because of our work, but simply because of his goodness.[29] Our work by itself creates or preserves nothing, for "Unless the Lord builds the house, those who build it labor in vain" (Ps 127:1).[30] Instead, our work is simply a matter of finding and collecting God's gifts.[31] When we believe otherwise, we transfer our trust from God to ourselves, and turn ourselves into idols.

CONSEQUENCES OF THIS IDOLATRY

This trust in human strength and earthly power has two inevitable consequences: futility and fear.

Anxiety vs. confidence. When we transfer our trust from God to his creatures, our fear gets displaced to his creatures as well. When our fear, love, and trust are in the Lord, he says, "Fear not" (Matt 10:28–31), and takes all our fears away. Yet without this confidence in him, our stance toward the rest of creation will always be fearful. Fear is the natural result of trusting in the uncertain things of this world, and performance anxiety flows predictably from trusting in our own unreliable performance.

---

[23] LW 9:70–71, 74–75; WA 28:612–13, 617–20.

[24] *Lectures on Deuteronomy* (1525), LW 9:75 = WA 14:617–18; cf. LW 76:369–70.

[25] *Exposition of Psalm 127, For the Christians at Riga in Livonia* (1524), LW 45:331 = WA 15:372–73.

[26] *Treatise on Good Works* (1520), LW 44:52 = WA 6:227.

[27] *Exposition of Psalm 127, For the Christians in Livonia* (1524), LW 45:326 = WA 15:367.

[28] LW 14:114–15; 44:52; 45:325–26.

[29] LW 9:96; 14:52–53; 45:326.

[30] *Exposition of Psalm 127, For the Christians in Livonia* (1524), LW 45:321–22 = WA 15:363.

[31] *Exposition of Psalm 127, For the Christians in Livonia* (1524), LW 45:326–27 = WA 15:368–69.

This may not always be apparent. When we rely on ourselves to provide for our needs, this leads to arrogance when things are going well. We then pat ourselves on the back for our diligence or wisdom. Yet when trouble comes this pride quickly turns to fear and dismay. We may try to stave off this fear with anxious toil, or shrink back from what we fear so that it paralyzes our actions. Yet these worries are in vain, since the future is in God's hands. Without his blessing and protection our toil can achieve nothing, but with it we have nothing to fear. Those who commit all things to the Lord will not be arrogant when things go well with them, since they will attribute this to the Lord's blessing and not themselves. Yet they will not be worried when trouble comes either. Instead, they will do their work with a happy heart and sleep at night without a burden of care, knowing that the Lord has promised to care for them and work all things together for their good.[32]

Ultimate futility vs. ultimate triumph. Idolaters have good reason to be anxious, since their idolatry is futile. Those who trust in human strength ultimately will come to ruin, and their idols will fail them when they need them most. Luther frequently talks about the futility of idolatry. He was fond of the German saying that it requires more toil to get into hell than into heaven.[33] Idols wear us out by demanding that we serve them, and then reward us badly by giving us misery and vexation, and failing us in our hour of need.[34] Yet the true God will care and provide for us, and those who live by faith in him will triumph over all adversities.[35]

This may not always be immediately apparent. Luther recognized that "God is a slow rewarder."[36] He writes, "God is patient and slow in carrying out both His promises and His threats."[37] In this way God trains us to live by faith in his Word. Since he delays in fulfilling his Word—including both his promises to provide for his people and his threats toward those who despise his aid—our present experience may seem to contradict it. The idolatrous flesh uses this as license to despise God's Word. It neglects both the threats and the promises, and looks to what its eyes can see. Faith on the other hand takes heed of God's threats and grasps hold of his promises, and is rewarded. In God's good timing he carries out his threats with full severity, and fulfills his

---

[32] LW 43:25–26; 45:321–34.

[33] LW 13:123; 17:110–11; 34:131.

[34] LW 16:17; 17:107, 109–11, 134–35, 401; 18:43–44, 50, 69–70; 19:20, 223–25; 20:164–65.

[35] Martin Luther, *Martin Luther's Complete Commentary on the First Twenty-Two Psalms*, trans. Henry Cole (2 vols.; London: W. Simpkin and R. Marshall, 1826), 1:21–22, 46, 130, 149, 454–57, 501–2; 2:225; LW 14:67–68; 45:319–20.

[36] Luther, *Commentary on the First Twenty-Two Psalms*, 1:489 = *Operationes in Psalmos* (1519–21) WA 5:307.29.

[37] *Lectures on Genesis* (1543–45), LW 8:202 = WA 44:726.33–34.

promises with great abundance, since his Word is sure.[38] This can be seen in human history. As the Old Testament shows us, those who despise God's threats may flourish briefly, but things never turn out well for them in the end.[39] Since God delays in carrying out his judgment, kingdoms may rise and flourish for a time through human wit and arrogance without giving heed to him. Yet even more swiftly they fall—and this not for lack of resources or manpower, but because their true watchman has withdrawn his protection.[40] Those who labor in unbelief to acquire wealth may find it. Yet it will then slip through their fingers. All their wealth will profit them less than the little in the hands of the righteous, who receive it with thankfulness and a carefree heart. Even if the wicked manage to hold on to wealth for a lifetime this will only lead to greater ruin as they go on blindly in their unbelief.[41] The righteous on the other hand may have to bear many crosses and suffer much for the sake of Christ. Yet they will not be deserted, even if they are a slain Abel or a swallowed Jonah.[42] Although they may go without for a time as they wait in faith for God to fulfill his promises, ultimately they lack no good thing, for it is impossible for God to forsake those he has promised to bless.[43] Therefore the watchword is "Wait a bit, wait a bit!"

Luther makes this thought the theme of a sermon on John 16:

> A little while, and you will see me no longer; and again a little while, and you will see me. . . . Truly, truly, I say to you, you will weep and lament, but the world will rejoice. You will be sorrowful, but your sorrow will turn into joy. When a woman is giving birth, she has sorrow because her hour has come, but when she has delivered the baby, she no longer remembers the anguish, for joy that a human being has been born into the world. So also you have sorrow now, but I will see you again, and your hearts will rejoice, and no one will take your joy from you. (John 16:16, 20–22)

Luther writes that these words apply not only to the apostles at the time of Jesus' crucifixion and resurrection, but to all Christians. We also see that the world has its season of joy and triumph, while we experience anguish and defeat as if God has hidden his face from us. Yet during these times we must not judge according to what we see and feel or we will be overwhelmed with

---

[38] *Lectures on Genesis* (1543–45), LW 8:199–204. = WA 44:724–28.

[39] *Preface to the Prophets* (1545), LW 35:267 = WA 11/1:5.

[40] *Exposition of Psalm 127, For the Christians in Livonia* (1524), LW 45:328–30 = WA 15:370–72.

[41] *Exposition of Psalm 127, For the Christians in Livonia* (1524), LW 45:327–28, 332 = WA 15:369, 373–74.

[42] *Preface to the Prophets* (1545), LW 35:267 = WA 11/1:5.

[43] *Lectures on Deuteronomy* (1525), LW 9:92–94 = WA 14:630–32.

misery. Instead, we must hold onto Jesus' promise, "A little while." Then we will endure until the great reversal takes place and we experience joy.[44]

CONCLUSION

Since God is the Giver of every good gift that we need for our earthly lives, he is the one we must trust to provide. The sinful human tendency is to trust in ourselves instead, and think that by our own work and ingenuity we can harness God's creatures and use them to supply what we need. This appears to make sense, since God normally uses these creatures as masks of his provision. Yet in reality, such efforts are futile. No creature can achieve anything without God's aid, whereas he can always find alternative means when he decides to provide.

In this chapter I have spent little time cataloguing idols like money and technology that we recruit in our efforts to provide for ourselves. The reason for this is that these idols are secondary. If one is torn down, another will spring up in its place, unless we first address the underlying spiritual dynamic that leads us to latch onto them in the first place. The only cure is to despair of our idolatrous trust in ourselves and to trust in the Lord.

CONTEMPORARY APPLICATION

As we have seen, Luther urges us to recognize our Creator as the source of every earthly blessing, so that we give all thanks to him and place all confidence in him as the only one who can provide for our earthly needs. In this light, the idolatry of our society is clearly evident, as more than anything our society places its hope in human potential.

THE FOCUS ON HUMAN ABILITY IN DOMINANT CONTEMPORARY SOCIAL NARRATIVES

This can be seen in the dominant narratives that shape American culture today. These narratives all place human beings center stage. In them we are the lead actors in a world that revolves around us and our achievements.

Christian Smith, a sociologist from Notre Dame, lists the following as some of the more significant narratives that have shaped contemporary American culture:

- The narratives of capitalism and socialism. These both place their hope in a particular human economic system to improve society.[45]

---

[44] Martin Luther, *Sermons of Martin Luther: The House Postils*, ed. Eugene F. A. Klug (3 vols.; Grand Rapids, MI: Baker Books, 1996), 2:85–95 = WA 52:283–89.

- The expressive romantic narrative, which celebrates the free expression of the human spirit.[46]
- The American experiment narrative, which lauds human freedom and democracy.[47]
- The narrative of liberal progress, which is a story centered on how noble human aspirations can be harnessed to make society more free and equal.[48]
- The narrative of scientific enlightenment and progress, which puts its hope in the power of human reason to improve our world.[49]
- Various postmodern narratives, which celebrate human freedom and choice and the power of the autonomous self to shape its own identity and values in positive ways.[50]
- The narrative of naturalism, which assumes that since there is no God or "superempirical order," we are free to direct our own fate.[51]
- The Christian narrative. This is the only religious narrative that has had a profound enough impact on American culture to warrant inclusion in this list as an effective challenge to all the human-centered narratives.[52]

Note how all these narratives, with the exception of the Christian narrative, center on human beings and their abilities. They are not stories about God or the gods, but instead focus almost exclusively on us. The focal point may be the human ability to construct more just or effective economic systems, the vital forces in human nature that need to be expressed, the value of a democratic political system, the power of human reason to improve human living conditions, or the power and freedom of human beings to create their own identities. It makes little difference. Human power takes center stage. Even the pursuit of material prosperity that is a central feature of the American dream is ultimately about the pursuit of human power. After all, what is "the almighty dollar" except a means of measuring and acquiring goods and

---

[45] Christian Smith, *Moral, Believing Animals: Human Personhood and Culture* (New York: Oxford University Press, 2003), 70.

[46] Ibid., 70–71.

[47] Ibid., 67–68.

[48] Ibid., 82–83.

[49] Ibid., 63–64, 67, 71.

[50] Ibid., 66–67, 88, 154–56.

[51] Ibid., 93–94, 98–106.

[52] Ibid., 67, 69.

services? That is, it is a means of gaining human services and the goods produced by human labor.

Stories like these, which focus on us and our abilities, certainly have their place within an overarching story that centers on God. Yet when such stories become the dominant narratives that shape our society, it tells us something about the inflated value we place on ourselves and our activity.

THE PRIVATIZATION OF RELIGION

Those who worship the true God are not immune from the power of these human-centered narratives. Instead, the temptation is to worship the Lord and our idols too. To do this we must limit God's authority over us in some way, by cutting him down to a more manageable size, relegating him to a conveniently remote region, stressing that he is an ineffable mystery, or consigning him to merely one sphere of life. As Charles Taber observes, this is particularly easy to do in a secular society, where religion has been isolated and relegated to a subordinate, auxiliary, private domain. This makes it easy for us to say "Yes, but" to God, and give the appearance of worshipping him, while our ultimate allegiance belongs to secular idols.[53] This privatization of religion means treating God as if he is irrelevant to the day-to-day affairs of this life, so that our idols have a field where they can reign supreme. Whenever we limit God's place in our lives to Sunday mornings and live like secular people the rest of the week, the problem is idolatry. We may still be looking to God for life hereafter, but when it comes to life in this world our confidence is more in ourselves and our ability to acquire earthly things.

TECHNICAL-RATIONAL CONTROL IN SOCIETY

One significant feature of modern industrial society has been the human attempt to exert technical-rational control over more and more areas of life. The sociologist Peter Berger writes,

> Modernity means (in intention if not in fact) that men take control over the world and over themselves. . . . In principle, there is the assumption that all human problems can be converted into technical problems, and if the techniques to solve certain problems do not as yet exist, then they will have to be invented. The world becomes ever more "makeable." This view of the world is essentially that of the engineer. First expressed in engineering proper, in the systematic manipulation of nature and of mechanics, it is carried over into multiple forms of social engineering (including politics), and finally

---

[53] Charles R. Taber, "God vs. Idols: A Model of Conversion," *Journal of the Academy for Evangelism in Theological Education* 3 (1987–88): 23–24, 26–27, 29.

> into engineering approaches to the most intimate areas of interpersonal experience (including psychology, qua engineering of the self).[54]

Despite the challenge postmodernism has made to the modern narrative of scientific enlightenment and progress, this feature of modern life remains unchanged. Our technological societies are still dominated by enormous efforts to control every area of life. As Berger points out, this is not just about technology, economic efficiency, and control of the means of production. It also extends to the social areas of life. Our society has Prozac to fix emotions, counseling to fix broken relationships, public relations experts to manage our political or corporate image, human resource departments to manage the people who work in our institutions, contraceptives, abortifacients, and IVF to control reproduction, urban planners to control the environments we live in, genetic modification to control the food we eat, education policies to ensure no child gets left behind, social welfare agencies to care for disadvantaged members of society, and although it may be popular to advocate small government our governments keep getting bigger, since it is also popular to demand that they control more and more things.[55]

From Luther's perspective, most of these things are neither good nor bad in themselves. On the one hand, it is possible to regard much of this work as faithful stewardship. God calls us to work to earn our living and to care for our neighbors, and in a highly complex society this will take complex forms. Yet on the other hand, it can be viewed as an idolatrous trust in human strength instead of in the Lord. So how can we tell the difference?

First, we can pay attention to Luther's dictum that our work in vocation must be established and guided by God's Word.[56] God calls us to work to care for our neighbors. He does not call us to work simply to accrue wealth, power, or pleasures for ourselves. When our efforts to control our world lead us to exploit the earth, exploit our neighbor, or transgress the bounds of God's Law, then we can be sure we have an idol. For instance, when our efforts to control our reproduction lead us to show a cavalier disregard for the lives of children in the womb, there is no doubt that we are serving an idol.

Second, when we become extremely anxious about our work,[57] and are unable to let go of it for long enough to spend time in God's Word or prayer,

---

[54] Peter L. Berger, *Pyramids of Sacrifice: Political Ethics and Social Change* (New York: Basic Books, 1974), 21.

[55] Cf. Craig M. Gay, *The Way of the (Modern) World, or, Why it's Tempting to Live as if God Doesn't Exist* (Grand Rapids, MI: Eerdmans, 1998), 33–36, 49–51, 71–72.

[56] LW 3:216–18; 4:103–7; 21:259–70; 37:363–65.

[57] See the data from Jean Twenge, reported in chapter 5, footnote 119, that indicates how anxiety is on the rise in contemporary American society.

or take our Sabbath rest, then we know we have an idol. In my parish ministry one of the most frequent excuses I hear from people for their slack church attendance is "We've been really busy, pastor." In most cases, this could be rephrased as "We've been off serving other gods." Luther writes regarding the Sabbath day that "our sinful nature is very unwilling to die and to be passive, and it is a bitter day of rest for it to cease from its works and be dead."[58] On the Sabbath day, God is at work while we rest and receive from him his gifts. This is an act of faith. It requires confidence that God is the one who creates life and not us, and therefore we can periodically cease our labor and leave things in his hands.[59] When we are unable to do this, this is the best evidence that we are in the grip of an idol that we think will give life, but in reality just wears us out by demanding our service 24/7. A Sabbath day of rest can be a bitter pill for the sinful nature, since it means letting go of our idols.

Technical-Rational Control in the Church

We should not think this is only a problem for people who labor in secular professions. In the Gospels we see our Lord constantly in prayer, particularly when he faced a big decision or crisis. He often stayed up late at night to pray, and he instructed his disciples to be people of prayer.[60] Many of the biblical saints also set us an example of fasting and prayer in times of need.[61] Yet all too often my experience of church life has been more like this: We face a problem, so we call a meeting. We pray for two minutes, and then plan and strategize for two hours. Maybe my experience is atypical—and certainly, I have experienced exceptions—yet my experience of the church is wide enough that I suspect it is not. If this is our standard way of managing the church, then in practical terms we have more faith in our planning and strategizing than in our Lord who answers prayer. The work habits of church leaders could also suggest the same thing, that as a group we place too much confidence in what our strength can achieve. It is worth noting that survey and

---

[58] *On Good Works* (1520), WA 6:248.26–27, cited in Oswald Bayer, *Theology the Lutheran Way*, ed. and trans. by Jeffrey G. Silcock and Mark C. Mattes (Grand Rapids, MI: Eerdmans, 2007), 92. I have followed Bayer's translation instead of the translation in LW 44:78. Bayer translates *leyden* (i.e., *leiden*) as "to be passive" rather than "to suffer." In Luther's day, *leyden* could mean to receive something or submit to something, just as "to suffer" could have this sense in old English (Alfred Götze, *Frühneuhochdeutsches Glossar* [5th ed.; Berlin: Walter de Gruyter, 1956], 149). Bayer has correctly observed that Luther is interpreting the Third Commandment at this point. He is not talking about pain and agony, but rather about ceasing from our work and permitting God to work.

[59] Bayer, *Theology the Lutheran Way*, 92–93.

[60] Luke 5:16; 6:12; 9:18, 28–29; 10:2; 11:1–4; 18:1–6; 21:36; 22:31–32; 39–46; 23:34, 46; John 17.

[61] Deut 9:25–29; 1 Sam 1:9–18; 7:5–11; 2 Kings 6:15–19; 19:14–19; 20:1–7; 2 Chron 7:12–15; 33:12–19; Ezra 10:1–6; Neh 1:4–11; Dan 9:1–23; Jonah 2:1–9; and all the Psalms of lament.

census data show that clergy are among the hardest working people in society.[62] Once again, this can be interpreted two ways. It could be a sign of faithful service and dedication to the Lord. Faithful service always requires crosses that vex our sinful nature, and long working hours may be one of them. Yet it could also be a sign that our work has become an idol, and we have allowed ourselves to think that we will build God's kingdom by the strength of our arms. The test is much the same as for work in any other vocation. Have we become so busy that we neglect our devotional life? Do we become so involved in our ministries that we neglect the other callings God has given us, such as our families and other relationships? Do we become so stressed and anxious that we can no longer find joy in our ministry, but are crushed by its burdens instead of being refreshed by periodically resting in the Lord? These are signs that we have come to trust in our own strength and not the Lord, so that although we preach about God's grace and power we are modeling something else.

A CHRISTIAN RESPONSE

Luther's call to trust in our heavenly Father as the source of every good gift—not only when it comes to our salvation, but also in our earthly lives—is a radical challenge to our modern Promethean age, with its idolization of human power. So how do we proclaim this message to people who are caught up in this idolatry?

The first step is to open people's eyes to its futility. As Luther points out, often this is not immediately apparent, since God is "a slow rewarder" and chooses to use human labor as a mask of his provision. Therefore the task of Christian proclamation is to uncover the futility of human self-confidence, in contrast with the reward that comes from trusting in the Lord.

One way to do this is to point to the personal toll this idolatry takes. As Luther points out, when we invest our confidence for success in life in the strength of our arms, there can be no end to our labor. Instead, we enslave ourselves to all kinds of activities that leave us exhausted. In addition, we will

---

[62] Figures from the 1991 census in Australia found that 55 percent of clergy worked 49 hours per week or more. This was higher than the 48 percent of medical doctors who worked this hard, and much higher than the national average for all employed people of just 15 percent. Of all denominations, Lutherans (who live by grace through faith!) had the hardest working clergy, with 67.2 percent working 49 hours per week or more (Australian Bureau of Statistics, *Australian Social Trends 1994,* ABS Catalogue No. 4102.0 [Canberra: Australian Bureau of Statistics, 1994], www.ausstats.abs.gov.au/ausstats/free.nsf/0/1CC597199AA4BD14CA257225 00049553/$File/41020_1994.pdf [accessed May 21, 2010], 195–96). In the US, a 1991 survey of pastors by the Fuller Institute of Church Growth found that 90 percent worked more than 46 hours per week (Maureen F. Dollard, Anthony Harold Winefield, and Helen R. Winefield, *Occupational Stress in the Service Professions* [London: Taylor & Francis, 2003], 312).

be anxious, as we worry about our performance and about all the things outside our control that could go wrong. The cure is not more anxious toil, but trust in the Lord.

Another way to do this is to wait until the idols start to fail, as eventually they will. Shortly after 9/11, I had lunch with a friend, and he told me how the attack on the World Trade Towers had filled him with fear. It made him think that if even America, with its enormous military, was not invulnerable to attack, then none of us were safe. If America could not defend itself, how much less could a little nation like Australia? In other words, he had put his confidence in Western military might, and this had proven to be an unreliable protector. This was an opportunity to talk to him about where true security comes from and how there is no security in this world except in the Lord.

Another approach is to reflect on the obvious limitations of human strength. The most helpful text here is the one Luther uses: "Unless the Lord builds the house, those who build it labor in vain. Unless the Lord watches over the city, the watchman stays awake in vain" (Ps 127:1). Yes, we can do remarkable things when the Lord chooses to bless us. Yet without the Lord's blessing, we can do nothing. Even unbelievers can see upon reflection how precarious life is and how fragile we are. One unforeseen misfortune, or one bout of ill health, and everything we have worked for comes crashing down. Furthermore, as mortal creatures our strength is short lived, and soon comes to an end. But if the Lord blesses us, we will be blessed, whether he chooses to work through our labor or through the many other means at his disposal.

Once people begin to see the futility of trusting in themselves, they are then able to hear the promises of God as good news: "Open your mouth wide, and I will fill it" (Ps 81:10). "Fear not, for I am with you; be not dismayed, for I am your God; I will strengthen you, I will help you, I will uphold you with my righteous right hand" (Isa 41:10). Scripture is full of such gracious promises, which have the power to lift the burdens and calm the fears that are the inevitable result of relying on ourselves to provide.

For those of us who confess that these promises are true, yet still struggle with the temptation to work nonstop as if everything depends on us, an important spiritual discipline is to practice Sabbath rest. That is, to stop our work at least one day a week and put all things in God's hands. This means crucifying our idol of self-reliance and putting into practice our faith in God's promises by saying, "Yes, there is much work that I have left undone, but today I will resign my attempts to control the universe and will trust in the Lord to provide."

CHAPTER FIVE

THE IDOL OF THE SELF AND LOVE

"What's in it for me?" This question governs virtually every business, social, and political interaction on our planet. It also governs how we deal with religion. It is so ubiquitous that we rarely reflect on what it reveals about us. Yet did God really create us to be so preoccupied with ourselves and our own wellbeing?

In the previous chapter we looked at the idolatry of trusting in ourselves instead of our Creator when it comes to providing for our earthly needs. In this chapter we will look at the idolatry of loving ourselves more than our Creator, as we strive to get the universe to revolve around us and our desires.

If God is God then the universe must revolve around him. Furthermore, if he is our God, then our lives must revolve around him, as our love for him governs our desires. Yet in our fallen state we love ourselves more than him and strive to "live as if we ourselves were God and lord of the earth."[1] That is, we try to use all things and even God for our own purposes,[2] as if the world should revolve around us and the things we want for ourselves.

LUTHER'S TEACHING

As we noted in chapter 2, Luther says that original sin has perverted human nature by making us curved in on ourselves. More than anything, this means that our love is turned inwards, in the sense that we always seek our own benefit in our dealings with God and his creatures.[3] Luther says that without faith and God's grace it is impossible for people not to seek their own advantage.[4] Instead of wanting the things that please God, they "are

---

[1] *Commentary on Psalm 147* (1530), LW 14:113 = WA 31/1:435.1–2; cf. 17:20; 31:10.

[2] LW 5:112; 17:17.

[3] Self-love in this sense is not the same as self-esteem. It is possible for us to love ourselves in the sense of pursuing our self-interest while at the same time despising ourselves for our failings.

[4] Martin Luther, *Martin Luther's Complete Commentary on the First Twenty-Two Psalms*, trans. Henry Cole (2 vols.; London: W. Simpkin and R. Marshall, 1826), 2:6 = WA 5:370.

continually turned in the direction of their own desires, so that they are unable not to seek the things of self."[5]

This self-centeredness is expressed not only in our dealings with created things, but also in our religion. As self-interested people, we are tempted to use God primarily as a means for obtaining blessings for ourselves. Luther rejected such an approach to religion as idolatrous. To think that God should revolve around us and our desires is to turn ourselves into idols, by loving ourselves more than him. It is also to turn him into an idol, by treating him merely as something to serve our ends.

Luther never denied that God serves human needs, or is the only one who is ultimately capable of fulfilling our desires. Yet he also recognized that God and his world do not revolve around us, and the true God calls us away from this self-centeredness. He therefore rejected religious eudemonism, the belief that the highest goal of religion is to advance us in our quest for personal happiness and well-being. His theology is therefore aptly called a Copernican revolution from the usual anthropocentric approach people take to religion.[6]

LUTHER AND EUDEMONISM

In order to see the radical nature of Luther's rejection of eudemonism it is worth comparing his position to that of St. Augustine, who cast a large shadow over the theology Luther inherited.

Augustine's eudemonism: Finding one's own good in God, the highest good. Augustine is an excellent example of an attempt to give a eudemonistic account of the Christian faith. As the Lutheran bishop Anders Nygren points out in his seminal work *Agape and Eros*, Augustine's understanding of love—which stands at the heart of his whole theology—is largely an attempt to baptize the eudemonism he found in the pagan philosophers. It is about distinguishing between enlightened and unenlightened self-interest and discerning where our true good lies.[7]

Like the Neoplatonic philosophers,[8] Augustine understood love primarily as desire.[9] It is therefore acquisitive—it seeks to satisfy its desire by acquiring

---

[5] *The Bondage of the Will* (1525), LW 33:176 = WA 18:709.14–15.

[6] I have borrowed this way of speaking about Luther's theology from Anders Nygren and Philip Watson, who both call Luther's theology a "Copernican revolution" from an anthropocentric to a strictly theocentric understanding of religion (Anders Nygren, *Agape and Eros,* trans. Philip S. Watson [New York: Harper Torchbooks, 1969], 681–84; Philip S. Watson, *Let God Be God!: An Interpretation of the Theology of Luther* [London: Epworth, 1947], 34–37, 73–96).

[7] Nygren, *Agape and Eros*, 476–503, 530, 538–48, 639.

[8] "Neoplatonism" is a modern term that is used to describe a philosophical tradition that dominated philosophical discourse in the Greco-Roman world from the time of its founder Plotinus in the middle of the third century AD until the middle of the sixth century. The Neoplatonists viewed themselves as heirs of Plato, but developed his thoughts in new directions

the objects of its desire. This means it is fundamentally self-interested. In the *City of God*, Augustine described fallen humanity as turned in on itself, and set love of self in opposition to love of God.[10] This sounds identical to Luther's statements about fallen human nature. Yet Augustine meant something different. He was not critiquing self-interest like Luther, but only self-sufficiency. Augustine simply assumed that love is self-interested.[11]

The problem as Augustine saw it is not that we humans are self-interested, but that we seek our self-interest in the wrong things. Instead of seeking our good in God, the highest good, we seek it in the lesser goods of this world. When he described human depravity as a matter of turning our love in on ourselves, he was not critiquing self-interest, but unenlightened self-interest. He was warning us against seeking our interest in ourselves, as if we can be our own highest good in a self-sufficient manner. He saw no problem with the pursuit of self-interest, as long as we do it in an enlightened way, by seeking it in God. Indeed, it was unusual for him to set love of self in opposition to love of God as he did in the *City of God*. His more common mode of speaking was to say that to love God is the best way to love oneself.[12] Augustine's whole theology is focused on identifying what is truly good for us, so we can pursue our self-interest in the most enlightened manner.[13]

---

by bringing them into creative dialogue with many other elements from the intellectual heritage and religious practice of their day. They regarded everything in the cosmos to be the result of a chain of emanations from the divine first principle known as "the One" or "the Good." From this, they concluded that all things in the cosmos reflect the goodness of the One, though they do so with increasing imperfection the further down they are on the chain of emanations, with spiritual things at the top and material things at the bottom. The goal of life for the Neoplatonists was to strive for perfection and happiness by fleeing from the concerns of the body and bringing the soul into closer alignment with the Good. They did this by cultivating desire for the Good through philosophical contemplation of it. Augustine was heavily influenced by Neoplatonic thought and incorporated many elements of it into his theology.

[9] Augustine, *Eighty-Three Different Questions*, 35.2; *City of God*, 14.7.

[10] Augustine, *City of God*, 14.13, 14.28.

[11] Nygren, *Agape and Eros*, 476–80, 501, 532–48; Matt Jenson, *The Gravity of Sin: Augustine, Luther and Barth on Homo Incurvatus In Se* (London: T & T Clark, 2006), 7, 15, 96.

[12] "We love ourselves so much the more, the more we love God" (Augustine, *The Trinity*, 8.8.12). "The Mind Loves God in Rightly Loving Itself; And If It Love Not God, It Must Be Said to Hate Itself. . . . He, therefore, who knows how to love himself, loves God; but he who does not love God, even if he does love himself,—a thing implanted in him by nature,—yet is not unsuitably said to hate himself" (Augustine, *The Trinity*, 14.14.18). "For it is impossible for one who loves God not to love himself. For he alone has a proper love for himself who aims diligently at the attainment of the chief and true good; and if this is nothing else but God, as has been shown, what is to prevent one who loves God from loving himself?" (Augustine, *On the Morals of the Catholic Church*, 1.26.48). Cf. Augustine, *Tractates on the Gospel According to St John*, 87.1; Nygren, *Agape and Eros*, 532–548.

[13] Nygren, *Agape and Eros*, 476–512, 532–48; Jenson, *The Gravity of Sin*, 17, 22–23, 25–28.

Augustine worked this out in terms of a Neoplatonic hierarchy of greater and lesser goods, with material things at the bottom, spiritual things at the top, and God as the highest good above all. This meant that he introduced a certain dualism between matter and spirit into his theology. It is true that he rejected Manichean dualism,[14] and recognized that since matter is created by God it must be good and not evil. Yet in a more subtle way he still devalued material things. He did not regard them as evil, but did regard them as "lesser goods" that are not worthy of the attention we give them. He did not consider the Pauline distinction between flesh and spirit to be a distinction between different human faculties, as if our spirits are good and our bodies are bad. Yet his view still yields a certain renunciation of material things. He regarded the struggle between flesh and spirit as a contest between two different orientations of the whole person. It is a struggle between *cupiditas*, the whole self as its desire is directed downwards to earthly and material things, and *caritas*, the whole self as its love is directed upwards to God. This means that although he did not say that material things are evil, he said that to turn toward them and love them inordinately is evil,[15] since this means diverting our attention away from God and higher spiritual things. This meant that Augustine, as well as much of the monastic tradition that followed his lead, regarded our love for the things of this world as the main obstacle that prevents us from loving God. He saw the call to love God as a call to flee earthly things, or at least not to become too attached to them, since they threaten to pull our devotion away from God, our highest good.[16]

Luther's rejection of eudemonism. Like Augustine, Luther also addressed the issue of human self-sufficiency. All his talk about our need to live by faith is directed against our deluded belief that we can be self-sufficient. Yet Luther was also keen to address our self-interest. He could see that the human problem is not simply that we need to direct more attention to God instead of trying to live without him. Rather, our human perversion reveals itself in our religious strivings as clearly as anywhere, since even when we seek God, we seek him for our own advantage. When we try to pull created

---

[14] The Manicheans were a religious group to which Augustine belonged for nine years, before his conversion to Christianity. The Manicheans saw the earth as a place of struggle between two coeternal Principles, the Father of Majesty who dwells in the realm of light, and the King of Darkness who dwells in the realm of darkness. They regarded human souls as particles of light that have been trapped in the darkness of the material world and need to escape. They therefore disparaged material things as inherently evil.

[15] Augustine, *City of God*, 12.6, 12.8.

[16] Nygren, *Agape and Eros*, 482–512; Jenson, *The Gravity of Sin*, 19–21; Dera Sipe, "Struggling with Flesh: Soul/Body Dualism in Porphyry and Augustine," *Concept* (2006), www.publications.villanova.edu/Concept/2006/Sipe.pdf (accessed April 29, 2010), 2–18.

things into our orbit it is bad enough. When we treat God as if he must revolve around us and our desires it is even worse.

For Luther, eudemonism cannot be Christianized, as Augustine attempts to do.[17] Instead, those who seek their own joy and self-interest will never find it. Even those who seek the joys of heaven will never enter if they seek it simply for their own benefit. Luther writes,

> The other error made by many who pray this petition [Thy kingdom come] is to think of nothing but their own eternal bliss. They suppose that the kingdom of God is composed of sheer joy and happiness in heaven. Inspired by their carnal sense and by their dread of hell, they seek only their own benefit and advantage in heaven. These people are unaware that God's kingdom consists of nothing other than piety, decency, purity, gentleness, kindness, and of every other virtue and grace; they do not know that God must have his way in us, that he alone must be, dwell, and reign in us. We must strive for that goal first and foremost. We are saved only when God reigns in us and we are his kingdom. We need not seek, desire, or pray for joy and happiness and all other desirable things, for they will all be ours when his kingdom comes. A good wine will naturally and inevitably produce joy and happiness when it is drunk. Even more, when grace and virtue (that is, the kingdom of God) are perfected, they result in joy and peace and bliss, and in every delight, naturally and surely and without our aid. Therefore, to turn our eyes away from false and selfish goals, Christ bids us to seek and to ask for God's kingdom itself and not for the fruits of the kingdom. Those people, however, begin at the far end and seek first that which should be last, meanwhile neglecting the first or valuing it solely because of the ultimate fruit. Consequently, they will receive nothing at all. They do not desire that which comes first, and therefore that which follows will not be theirs either.[18]

For Luther, to love God because he is *our own* highest good, and it benefits us to do so, is not what it means to "Love the Lord your God with all your heart." This reveals that Luther had a different understanding of love from Augustine. Instead of regarding love as the desire to acquire good things for oneself, he regarded it as that which "seeks not its own" (1 Cor 13:5),[19] but

---

[17] Nygren, *Agape and Eros*, 683, 726–27.

[18] *An Exposition of the Lord's Prayer for Simple Laymen* (1519), LW 42:41–42 = WA 2:98.29–99.10.

[19] LW 14:204; 17:198, 317; 21:339; 25:107, 352, 427, 505; 27:98; 28:328, 373; 29:227; 30:269, 304; 31:10, 41, 57; 37:201–2; 44:124, 248; 51:269–70.

seeks the good of the other without thought of self (Phil 2:4). If we only love those who love us, or are attractive to us, this is more an expression of self-interest than of love, and our kindness to them will cease as soon as it conflicts with our self-interest.[20] In the same way, if we only love God when he blesses us and gives us good things, this is more an expression of self-love than genuine love for God. [21] If we approach God with a "mercenary spirit," by only serving him because we expect some payout, we are idolaters as far as Luther is concerned.[22] We have made our fear of punishment or desire for reward our ultimate concern instead of God[23] and are trying to use him as an idol to serve our desires.[24]

Like Luther, Augustine also spoke about loving God for his own sake, rather than for the sake of any created enjoyments. Yet there is a subtle but significant difference between the two. For Augustine, the focus is still on us and our enjoyment. The issue is whether we enjoy God himself, or use him so that we may enjoy his creatures.[25] For Luther, the focus is not on us and our enjoyment. The issue is whether we love God simply because he is good, even when he hides his face from us so that we cannot enjoy him.[26]

Flesh and spirit: The whole self as it lives either by true faith or by idolatry. Luther works out his understanding of human love in terms of the Pauline distinction between flesh and spirit. This he sees as a distinction between true faith and idolatry. This also means a distinction between self-love and love of God. Like Augustine, he did not regard the flesh/spirit distinction to be a contrast between different faculties within the self, but a matter of how the whole self is oriented. For Luther, the flesh is the whole self—body, mind, and soul—as it is born in a natural way and curved in on itself through the corruption of original sin. He also refers to it as "the old self," "the old Adam," or "the sinful nature." This old self lives by a false faith, and is defined by its idolatry. The spirit, on the other hand, is the whole self as it is born again through the Holy Spirit, and is defined by what the Spirit

---

[20] *Heidelberg Disputation* (1518), LW 31:57 = WA 1:365; cf. Matt 5:46.

[21] Cf. Satan's accusation of Job, of only loving God out of self-interest (Job 1:9–11). The logic of the book of Job is that, if true, this is a serious indictment. Job is only vindicated because subsequent events demonstrate that the charge is not true.

[22] Luther, *Commentary on the First Twenty-Two Psalms*, 1:345–46; LW 14:295; 33:152–53; 21:319; 27:219, 332–33; 25:295.

[23] *Explanations of the 95 Theses* (1518), LW 31:201 = WA 1:599.

[24] *Lectures on Romans* (1515–16), LW 25:346 = WA 56:356–57.

[25] Nygren, *Agape and Eros*, 503–12.

[26] *Commentary on the Magnificat* (1521), LW 21:309–10 = WA 7:556–57.

plants in it, which is faith in Christ and holy desires.[27] When the Holy Spirit comes to dwell in someone and creates faith, this means a transformation of the whole person, eyes, ears, mouth, nose, body and soul,[28] as the whole person is sanctified and follows the Spirit's leading.[29] Thus even the body is made new. It is no longer an instrument for unrighteousness, but a living sacrifice given to God, a temple for the Holy Spirit, and a vessel God is preparing for resurrection (1 Cor 6:19; Rom 12:1). Yet the sinful nature resists this transforming work of the Spirit, so a struggle takes place between the two.

The sinful self loves itself above all things. The chief characteristic of our sinful nature according to Luther is self-interest. "The flesh seeks its own but not the things that are of God."[30] This does not simply mean that we seek earthly things instead of heavenly things, but rather that we pursue our self-interest in all things, regardless of whether they are physical or spiritual, in heaven or on earth. Indeed, those who live according to the sinful nature can be extremely religious. They are often outwardly pious and keep God's law. Yet the whole time they are looking at what they can gain for themselves. They are driven by things like fear of God's punishment, desire for human praise and other earthly benefits, and the hope that God will reward them.[31] Therefore, although they may keep God's law in an external manner, they do not genuinely love God or neighbor, since the love God calls for "seeks not its own" (1 Cor 13:5).[32] This sort of love comes only from the Holy Spirit.[33] Instead, beneath a veneer of external righteousness their real goal is to use both God and their neighbor for their own ends.[34] They treat God as an idol,

---

[27] WA 10/1.2:301.15–302.2; LW 11:522; 17:12; 21:x–xi, 303–6; 25:350–54; 27:87–91; 30:119; 33:288; Jenson, *The Gravity of Sin*, 66–71.

[28] *Admonition Concerning the Sacrament of the Body and Blood of our Lord* (1530), LW 38:107 = WA 30/2:603.

[29] *Commentary on the Magnificat* (1521), LW 21:303–7 = WA 7:550–54.

[30] *Lectures on Isaiah* (1527–30), LW 17:12 = WA 31/2:269.5–6; cf. LW 25:291, 313, 344–47; Luther, *Commentary on the First Twenty-Two Psalms*, 2:69–70.

[31] LW 21:155; 25:245–46.

[32] LW 14:204; 17:198, 317; 21:339; 25:107, 352, 427, 505; 27:98; 28:328, 373; 29:227; 30:269, 304; 31:10, 41, 57; 37:201–2; 44:124, 248; 51:269–70.

[33] LW 2:125; 9:68; 14:295; 25:350–52; Luther, *Commentary on the First Twenty-Two Psalms*, 1:23–25; 2:45, 48–55; 2:410 (sic). There is an error in the pagination in vol. 2 of this edition of Luther's *Commentary on the First Twenty-Two Psalms*. Pages 261–308 have been incorrectly numbered 381–428. Then on page 309, the correct pagination resumes, so that 381–428 are eventually repeated. Throughout this book, the pages that have been incorrectly labeled 381–428 will be marked (sic) to distinguish them from the pages that have been correctly labeled 381–428.

[34] LW 9:297; 13:186; 17:160; 18:221, 244; 20:271.

and their stomachs are their real gods.[35] Luther calls such people rebels under the appearance of obedience and fear of God.[36] They are,

> impure and perverted lovers, who are nothing else than parasites and who seek their own advantage in God, neither love nor praise His bare goodness, but have an eye to themselves and consider only how good God is to them, that is, how deeply He makes them feel His goodness and how many good things He does to them. They esteem Him highly, are filled with joy and sing His praises, so long as this feeling continues. But just as soon as He hides His face and withdraws the rays of His goodness, leaving them bare and in misery, their love and praise are at an end. They are unable to love and praise the bare, unfelt goodness that is hidden in God. By this they prove that their spirit did not rejoice in God, their Savior, and that they had no true love and praise for His bare goodness. They delighted in their salvation much more than in their Savior, in the gift more than in the Giver, in the creature rather than in the Creator. For they are not able to preserve an even mind in plenty and in want, in wealth and in poverty; as St. Paul says (Phil. 4:12): "I know how to abound and how to suffer want."[37]

This means that the true test of faith is the cross.[38] Idolaters despise the cross.[39] Those who follow the prudence of the flesh may praise God when all is going well, but quickly turn from him when tribulation comes.[40]

This self-interested self cannot simply be reeducated to be more enlightened in its self-interest. Salvation from the flesh does not mean training it to seek higher, spiritual pleasures and goods instead of lower, earthly goods, so that it becomes a more refined Epicurean. Instead, the flesh is at its worst when it seeks after spiritual things. Therefore it must die. The old Adam with its assertion of "I," "Me," and "Mine" must be put to death so that no "selfdom" remains.[41] Therefore Luther can say that true love of self is hatred of self,[42] that is, to despise self-seeking.

---

[35] LW 18:391; LW 9:54–55; 18:57, 394–95; 20:237.

[36] *Lectures on Romans* (1515–16), LW 25:244 = WA 56:258.

[37] *Commentary on the Magnificat* (1521), LW 21:309–10 = WA 7:556.25–557.5.

[38] By "the cross," Luther means the suffering that God lays upon the Christian. Luther's views on the cross of the Christian will be addressed more fully in chapter 9.

[39] Luther, *Commentary on the First Twenty-Two Psalms*, 1:213.

[40] *Lectures on Romans* (1515–16), LW 25:295 = WA 56:308.

[41] This language comes from *A German Theology* (*Theologia Germanica* 13–14), which did not originate from Luther's pen. Yet Luther gave it his endorsement and expressed similar thoughts

The spirit loves God's "bare" goodness. In contrast, the new self that is born again through the Holy Spirit has a completely different orientation from the old sinful nature. Instead of its love being curved in on itself, it is directed to God and neighbor. When Luther talks about contempt of self,[43] and calls self-love a great and grievous sin,[44] he is advocating contempt for the sinful self with its self-preoccupation. The cure for this self-love is not to wallow in self-loathing. That is just another form of self-focus. Instead, the cure is to despise the self-preoccupied self by forgetting about oneself, to stop looking at oneself and start looking to Christ.[45] Unlike the flesh, the new self is not wrapped up in itself, but has been taught by God's Spirit to forget about self so it can genuinely seek the good of the other.[46] It does not need to be coerced with rewards or punishments, since God has instilled in it a new love that delights in God for his own sake and does his will freely.[47] Since it has died to self-will and is alive to God's will, it keeps God's law simply because it is good, without self-interest.[48] Its love does not turn sour when it faces hardships. Instead, it endures these with patience, trusting that even when God brings us the cross he is good.[49] It says to Christ, "I seek not Thine, but Thee; Thou art to me no dearer when it goes well with me, nor any less dear when it goes ill."[50] Since it regards God as the highest good to which nothing can compare, it loves him even when everything else is taken away.

The spirit delights in God's will and loves all creatures for his sake. For Luther, God's call for us to love him above all else does not mean we should despise or forsake his creatures.[51] This brings us to a crucial difference between Augustine and Luther. For Augustine the greatest obstacle that prevents us from loving God is our love for created things, and love for God always means a certain detachment from created things. For Luther, the chief obstacle to our love for God is our love for ourselves, and this same obstacle prevents us from loving our neighbor. Therefore, when the Spirit leads us to die to our self-love and to love God as we ought, this also renews our love for

---

throughout his career. Note for instance how he describes the baptismal life in his Small Catechism (SC IV 12 = WA 30/1:382.6–383.2).

[42] *Lectures on Romans* (1515–16), LW 25:382, 512 = WA 56:392, 516–17.

[43] LW 7:183; 31:84.

[44] LW 26:297; 28:327; 36:203; 43:21; 45:118.

[45] LW 9:70; 14:169; 31:15.

[46] LW 25:512–13; 27:355–56; 35:67; 52:35–36.

[47] LW 1:93–94 = WA 42:71; 31:358–62; 9:68–69; 22:144–45.

[48] LW 14:295; 21:319; 25:292, 346–47; 33:152–53.

[49] LW 5:319–20; 12:374; 14:295; 22:144–45; 25:295–96, 347.

[50] *Commentary on the Magnificat* (1521), LW 21:311 = WA 7:557.36–37.

[51] *Lectures on Deuteronomy* (1525), LW 9:69 = WA 14:610.

neighbor. We are finally free to genuinely seek the good of our neighbor without self-interest getting in the way. Not only this, but the Spirit teaches us to delight in God's will. This means showing our love for God by loving and serving those around us as he commands,[52] and by receiving his gifts with thanksgiving.[53] For Luther, to flee from worldliness or carnality does not mean giving up earthly things through monastic renunciation. Instead, "If the Lord has given one a wife, one should now hold on to her and enjoy her."[54] Luther taught that Christians should embrace all sorts of earthly activities, such as loving one's spouse, rearing children, honoring parents, and obeying the magistrate, as spiritual activities.[55] Worldliness is defined by covetousness and anxious striving to acquire for ourselves things that God has not deigned to give us, as if possessing these things is of ultimate importance. Fleeing from worldliness, therefore, means accepting what God has given with contentment and thanksgiving without striving to go beyond the bounds of what he has prescribed.[56] It does not mean renouncing the good things of God's creation, but rather refusing to turn them into idols.

The value of Luther's insight can be seen from the following anecdote. One of my fellow pastors in Australia is an adult convert to the church. When he first began to take an interest in Christianity, one thing in particular held him back. He thought, "If I become a Christian, I will have to put God first in my life and my wife second, and I love her too much to do that." Yet in the end, he found the Gospel so exciting that he became a Christian anyway. His wife then noticed a difference in the way he treated her—he started treating her better than he ever had before. This impressed her so much that she decided she wanted to become a Christian too. This change in my friend's behavior makes perfect sense from Luther's perspective. When he no longer treated his wife as an idol, but as a gift of the true God, he was able to show her more love, not less. On the one hand, this can be explained through the work of the Holy Spirit, who produces love in our hearts. On the other hand, it has something to do with the nature of idolatrous love. Idolatrous love is an expression of the flesh, which always seeks its own interest in the object of its desire. It is therefore grasping, obsessive, and manipulative. When through faith we are enabled to treat the things of creation as just that—good things created by God, but not gods that we must possess and control as if our lives

---

[52] LW 7:315; 18:221; 20:271; 25:350–52; Luther, *Commentary on the First Twenty-Two Psalms*, 1:23–25; 2:45, 48–55, 410 (sic).

[53] LW 1:245; 13:366.

[54] *Lectures on Ecclesiastes* (1526), LW 15:30 = WA 20:36.14–15.

[55] *Lectures on Galatians* (1535), LW 26:216–17 = WA 40/1:347–48.

[56] *Lectures on Ecclesiastes* (1526), LW 15:8, 30 = WA 20:10–11, 35–36.

are at stake—then we are freed to seek their good without our self-interest constantly getting in the way.

Love as the Fruit of the Gospel. This kind of love that "seeks not its own" is a fruit of the Gospel. When we make idols of ourselves by thinking we have to provide for our own needs, we are doomed to constantly search and grasp for things to fill our needs. Yet when we learn through the Gospel to trust a gracious God, who cares for our needs out of pure generosity, he frees us from this concern. He's got our backs. We can leave it in his hands. We are then free to pursue God's will wherever it may lead.

Luther recognized early in his career that pure love for God means loving him for his own sake, without thought of ourselves.[57] Yet he experienced this as the crushing demand of the Law, which as sinners we are incapable of fulfilling.[58] Later he learnt to distinguish this demand of the Law that cannot justify us from the Gospel of Christ that does justify us.[59] However, this did not lead him to discard this call of the Law. Instead, he recognized that love for God and neighbor is something God works in us once we are already

---

[57] Luther's vision of what is entailed in the call to love God is shaped by his own reading of Scripture, as well as by various currents in medieval piety that focused on dying to self and self-will for the sake of following Christ and his will. One influence on him was a revival group from the fourteenth century called "The Friends of God." The Friends of God lived through a dark time when the Black Death was ravaging Europe and the Interdict of 1324 brought great turmoil to the church (Bengt Hoffman, "Introduction," in *The Theologia Germanica of Martin Luther*, trans. Bengt Hoffman [New York: Paulist Press, 1980], 3–5, 9). They focused on the renunciation of self and the mystical union between Christ and the believer. They consisted of both clergy and laity, and included Johann Tauler and "the Frankfurter," the anonymous author of a work both Luther and his father confessor Staupitz cherished (ibid., 2–9, 24). This work delighted Luther so much that in 1516 he published it as his very first publication, and then republished it in 1518 (ibid., 41–43). He called it *Eyn Deutsch Theologia* (now generally known by its Latin title, *Theologia Germanica*) and added a subtitle to describe its content: "the right understanding as to what Adam and Christ mean and how Adam must die within us and Christ must rise" (ibid., 41). *A German Theology* teaches that the essence of the fall is the assertion of "I", "Me", and "Mine" (*Theologia Germanica*, 2–5, 47), and that all who do not follow the light of Christ are turned in on themselves (ibid., 38). Therefore the old self with its "selfdom" and concern with self-will must die so that the life of Christ may dwell in us, and his will may become our will (ibid., 9–10, 13–14, 17–18, 20–26, 32–44, 47–53, 55–56). When his will becomes our will we forget about self and delight in freely following his call to love and serve his creatures (ibid., 21, 28, 30–31, 33, 44–45). Then we also find bliss and joy as a byproduct, since we have learned to concern ourselves only with that which is truly good, with God and his will (ibid., 9, 30, 44).

[58] *Lectures on Deuteronomy* (1525), LW 9:68 = WA 14:609.

[59] Luther says that to think we can be justified through our love for God instead of through God's love for us in Christ is to set up our love as an idol (*Lectures on Galatians* [1535], LW 26:398 = WA 40/1:605–6).

justified.[60] It is a fruit of the Gospel, which grows in those who recognize how kind God is to us.[61]

Thus in the final analysis Luther's rejection of Eudemonism is not antithetical to his view of God as the generous Giver of every good thing, but fits beautifully with it. Luther regarded God as so kindly and benevolent that he wants to freely give us every good thing, including blessings we cannot even imagine let alone expect or seek.[62] He is "an Almighty and exceedingly rich Bestower,"[63] who runs ahead of us with good things, even before we seek them. Before he created the first humans, he furnished the earth with rich gifts for their provision. Before we come to faith, he provides us with a Savior, who searches for us to draw us to himself.[64] Before we enter heaven, he prepares heavenly mansions for us filled with every kind of joy.[65] This is what frees us from constantly pursuing our interests. Indeed, Luther was so confident that God is good to us that he was even willing to regard the suffering God brings us as good.[66] Luther was not ignorant of those parts of Scripture that tell us to ask, seek, knock, pray, and present our needs to God. Yet he did not view this seeking as some arduous task we must perform, as if we must climb up to God in heaven (cf. Rom 10:6–8). God wants us to ask and seek, not because he is distant or reluctant to give, but so that we would learn to acknowledge him as the Giver.[67] He simply invites us to confess his generosity and grasp hold of the gifts he has readily placed at our disposal.

---

[60] Yeago, "The Catholic Luther," 18–26.

[61] LW 9:68; 26:217; 36:40–41; 44:30. In this there is a high degree of affinity between Luther and Bernard of Clairvaux, whom Luther held in the highest regard (WA 15:755.7–9; 20:746.15–19, 753.22–23; 46:782.21–24; 47:109.18–23; 50:471.1–5; LW 51:186; Franz Posset, "Bernard of Clairvaux as Luther Source: Reading Bernard with Luther's 'Spectacles,' " *Concordia Theological Quarterly* 54 [Oct. 1990], 282–84). In his treatise *On Loving God*, Bernard says that initially what attracts us to God is his benefits for us. Yet the more we realize how gracious and good he is the more we are moved by God's Spirit to love him for his own sake, so that we no longer serve him as slaves who are fearful of his punishment or as mercenaries who seek payment but as sons who serve out of love. The highest degree of love for Bernard is when we are moved only by love of God and his will, without any admixture of selfishness (Bernard of Clairvaux, *On Loving God*, VII–XV).

[62] "For since He gave us Christ, His only Son, the highest Good, He, through Him, also gives us all His good things, riches, and treasures, from which the angels in heaven derive all pleasure and joy" (*Sermons on First Peter* [1522], LW 30:24 = WA 12:280.12–14). Cf. LW 3:158; 6:158–59; 7:174–75; 9:69; 12:205; 21:328, 338; 25:351, 386; 27:47; 29:136; 42:89–90, 156; 44:50, 52, 59–60; 52:252; Eph 3:20.

[63] *Lectures on Genesis* (1538–42), LW 5:359 = WA 43:676.34.

[64] LW 24:148, 259; 35:374.

[65] LW 1:39; 45:48.

[66] We will explore this more fully in chapter 9.

[67] *The Sermon on the Mount* (1532), LW 21:143–45 = WA 32:417–19.

This frees us from constant concern regarding our needs. Even if something God has promised is lacking, we need not be concerned, but can wait patiently until he fulfills his promise.

Luther connects his discovery of the Gospel to a transformation in his understanding of love. The Gospel led him to see that God's love for us is primary, not our love for him.[68] Yet his love for us produces love in us for both him and our neighbor. Christian love does not originate in us, but comes from receiving God's love. Luther writes that deliverance from idolatry is something we receive passively as God's mercy transforms our will.[69] Likewise, Christian love is something we receive passively. By "passive" Luther means "receptive," not "inactive." As the power of God works in us it leads us to action, yet it does not originate in us, but must be received from outside. Luther likens the Christian to a tube. He receives God's love and blessings from above, and these then flow through him to his neighbor.[70]

The Gospel for Luther is not something that excuses our sin but then leaves us to wallow in it. Instead, God forgives us so that he may restore us to what he created us to be. Central to the good he wants for us is for us to recognize him as the highest and all-sufficient good, and to be genuinely in tune with him and his will. This means dying to our self-centered will. We are simply not created to have the world revolve around us. Luther's vision of the world, as God created it and is redeeming it to be, is not of us each striving individually for our own benefit. Instead, as God loves us and we love one another, everyone is cared for and our joy is multiplied through our life together.

THE FUTILITY OF IDOLATROUS SELF-LOVE: "FOR WHOEVER WOULD SAVE HIS LIFE WILL LOSE IT, BUT WHOEVER LOSES HIS LIFE FOR MY SAKE WILL FIND IT." (MATT 16:25)

Luther's thought is so antithetical to the usual human way of thinking that it is easy to misunderstand him. When Luther talks about dying to self-love and self-centered desires this does not mean he was a masochistic killjoy. He is not calling for the extinction of human desire, but rather its transformation through a radical shift in the center of gravity around which our lives revolve. The goal of his theology is for us to be swept up into the joy and beauty of life when it revolves around God as it ought, instead of the ugliness that results when we try to make it revolve around us. Yet Luther

---

[68] LW 54:442–43 = WA TR 5:210.

[69] *Lectures on Genesis* (1535–38), LW 2:246 = WA 42:437.

[70] WA 10/1.2:100.9–16. An English translation of this passage is given in Nygren, *Agape and Eros*, 735. Cf. LW 51:269–70; Rom 5:5; Gal 5:22.

recognized that this cannot take place without pain. Our idolatrous sinful nature fights tooth and nail to retain its place at the center of the universe. This must be put to death, and this is a painful process for us. Despite the pain, God makes us go through this process so that the new life Christ gives us can rise within us.

To put this another way, when God's Law is applied to our hearts, it demands that our love and our will be guided by what God calls good, not by what we find pleasing. Luther writes, "To love God is at the same time to hate oneself and to know nothing but God. We must make our will conform in every respect to the will of God. . . . So that we not only will what God wills, but also ought to will whatever God wills."[71] This means we are called to love and desire God's will even if it means suffering for the sake of God or neighbor, or giving up something we deeply desire. For the new creature of God, born in us through the Holy Spirit, these two things become one thing, since God's will is pleasing to us. Yet Luther took seriously how much we struggle against the sinful nature in this life, and how completely God's will goes against the grain for the sinful nature. Therefore it is not safe to be guided by what seems pleasing to us, even as redeemed people. We must be guided by God's Word, even when it does not appear good. Only God's Word can teach us to distinguish what is good from what is an idolatrous illusion.[72]

In rejecting eudemonism Luther is not teaching a new asceticism or advocating misery as a virtue. He had no time for those who impose on themselves self-chosen crosses,[73] or think God is pleased when they flee happiness and make themselves gloomy. Instead, he taught that when God gives us happiness or any good thing we should receive it with thanks.[74] He was not teaching that desire must be quenched in the Christian, or we should cultivate a Stoic apathy,[75] but rather that we must be filled with new, holy desires that faith and the Spirit bring.[76] He was not denying that God is the highest good, or that those who find him receive every good thing.[77] What he was denying is that we are able to recognize that God is the highest good while

---

[71] *Disputation Against Scholastic Theology* (1517) Theses 95 and 97, LW 31:15 = WA 1:228.

[72] "For idolatry is recognized only through the word of God" (*Lectures on Genesis* [1535–38], LW 2:250 = WA 42:440.14).

[73] LW 4:22; 7:113–14; 17:49–50, 294; 20:261–62, 329–30; 22:55; 30:109–10; 40:81; 43:165, 183–84; 51:198–99.

[74] *Lectures on Ecclesiastes* (1526), LW 15:30 = WA 20:10–11, 35–36.

[75] *Lectures on Genesis* (1543–45), LW 7:315 = WA 44:533.

[76] "For in those who have been baptized a new light and flame arise; new and devout emotions come into being, such as fear and trust in God and hope; and a new will emerges" (*Lectures on Galatians* [1535], LW 26:352–53 = WA 40/1:540.30–32). LW 9:69; 14:294–97; 27:139–40.

[77] LW 9:69; 12:205; 21:338; 25:351, 386; 27:47; 29:136; 30:24; 42:156; 44:50, 52; 52:252.

we are wrapped in the idolatry of our sinful nature.[78] He saw that we cannot truly rejoice in God while we are still fixated on ourselves and our inborn desires. True happiness comes to those who delight in God and his will so that his will becomes their will regardless of what it means for them.[79] Therefore true life and joy must be found on the far side of the death of the sinful self and the resurrection of the new. The sinful self that strives after its own interest without concern for God's will must die,[80] and Christ must rise within us. Life is not to be obtained by trying to grasp it for ourselves, but by giving it up for the sake of Christ. Joy is not to be found by pursuing it for ourselves, but by receiving it as a gift from him. Luther therefore had a deep sense that God brings about our good through a great reversal. While we are still intent on serving the idol of the self and seeking our own joy we will not find it. Instead, God gives joy to those who learn to deny themselves and follow Christ wherever he leads. Luther writes that a person

> cannot have more good than God has given him, even if he seeks it. Man does indeed seek beyond what God has done, but he does not find. God has given happiness, and you seek for more happiness but you will not find it. For no one can add even a particle to the works of God. If the Lord God has decided something, you will not add anything to it. When the heart is filled with happiness, it is not able to be sad, and vice versa. Thus God determines everything, so that you may learn to be content with what He has offered and will use even that moderately; then your joy will be in the Lord.[81]

This means that all our attempts to grasp happiness for ourselves are futile, since joy is a gift of God's Spirit that involves trusting in the Lord and contenting ourselves with his will (Gal 5:22–24). This is worth spelling out in more detail. For Luther, true joy involves the following:

Thankfulness and contentment. In his lectures on Ecclesiastes Luther reflects on how joy is a gift of God that eludes those who try to grasp it for themselves. He concludes that joy comes from being satisfied with God's Word and work, and receiving his gifts with thanksgiving and contentment. The restless, anxious yearning and striving of the sinful nature cannot lead to joy, since the sinful nature is always coveting what it does not possess. It does not thank God for the things it has or stop to enjoy them, but vexes itself with many troubles as it tries to heap up more—more riches, more glory, more

---

[78] LW 2:124–25; 7:177; 22:134; 25:240; 36:180; Luther, *Commentary on the First Twenty-Two Psalms*, 1.21–22, 78.

[79] LW 14:297–98 = *Operationes in Psalmos* (1519–21), WA 5:34–36.

[80] *Lectures on Ecclesiastes* (1526), LW 15:29–32 = WA 20:35–38.

[81] *Lectures on Ecclesiastes* (1526), LW 15:121 = WA 20:141.21–28.

honor, more fame. It cheats itself of the blessings it has in the present by uselessly troubling itself about a future it cannot control. Instead of appreciating what it has, it is constantly seeking after things it cannot attain, or, even if it does attain them, that it does not enjoy, since it soon despises them and seeks after something else. As wealth increases, so does greed. The more honor or power someone receives, the more she covets.[82] Luther gives the following examples. A man is alone and craves a wife, but when he finds one he quickly becomes bored with her. People with healthy eyes rarely stop to take pleasure in them or to reflect on what a good gift of God they are. Yet if they lost them, they would give great treasure to get them back. Julius Caesar and Alexander the Great toiled mightily for power, but when they achieved it were not satisfied, but perished striving for more.[83] Luther concludes that these examples demonstrate that,

> What sinners heap up belongs to the pious [cf. Eccl 2:25–26], because only they use it with thanksgiving and joy, even when they have very little. The impious, on the other hand, for all their anxiety and trouble, do not even use it. In short, the pious truly possess the whole world, because they enjoy it with happiness and tranquility. But the impious do not possess it even when they have it.[84]

The joy of serving God through serving one's neighbor. Furthermore, daily work is painful and tedious for the sinful nature, since it does not delight in pleasing God or serving its neighbor. Instead, it cares more about its own leisure. The flesh is particularly reluctant to work at tasks that are low and despised in the eyes of the world. This makes much of life distasteful, since our vocations force us to serve our neighbor if we are to live. In contrast, the Holy Spirit places in the believer a new heart that delights in expressing its love for God by doing those things that are pleasing to Him, and finds joy in showing love to its neighbor through acts of service.[85] Such love is only drudgery for the old self, not the new.[86] This brings new joy into daily work. For the believer it is "a laudable and happy thing to imitate the example of Christ in His deeds, to love one's neighbors, to do good to those who deserve evil, to pray for one's enemies, and to bear with patience the ingratitude of those who requite good with evil."[87] Even if the work God calls us to do is as

---

[82] *Lectures on Habakkuk: The German Text* (1526), LW 19:187 = WA 19:385.

[83] LW 15:7–8, 10–11, 47–48; 19:187; cf. LW 14:47–53.

[84] *Lectures on Ecclesiastes* (1526), LW 15:48 = WA 20:57.36–40.

[85] LW 26:133; 30:88; 35:374–75; 46:241; 52:38–39.

[86] Marc Kolden, "Luther on Vocation," *Word and World* 3 (Fall 1983): 389.

[87] *Lectures on Galatians* (1535), LW 26:247 = WA 40/1:389.29–31.

menial as hauling manure, the Christian can do this with honor and joy, knowing it is pleasing to God and beneficial for one's neighbor.[88]

Delighting in the Lord as the highest good, even in trials. The deepest joy in the Christian life comes from the Gospel itself. Luther writes that "faith in Christ makes life happy, even though we may fall at times [into sin]."[89] This is because Christ says, " 'Your sins are forgiven.' "[90] This experience of God's graciousness leads us to love him, and to trust him in the midst of our troubles. It also gives us the joy of a peaceful conscience. This is something the anxious striving of the sinful nature cannot acquire for itself. Therefore it can never have deep peace and joy, since "there can be no joy, no peace, but in a pure conscience."[91]

In addition, the Gospel produces in us the ability to delight in God's Law, so that all of God's Word becomes pleasing to us. In his comments on Psalm 1, "Blessed is the man who walks not in the counsel of the wicked . . . but his delight is in the law of the Lord," Luther concludes that this delight in God's Law is the secret to happiness.[92] Only those who have faith in Christ can do this. Even when we live by faith our sin still clings to us, so only Christ delights in God's Law perfectly.[93] We on the other hand "must through a humble faith in Christ pray . . . that the desire be sent down from heaven."[94] This desire for God's Law is not natural to us, but "as the Heavenly Father plants and cultivates, and transplants us out of Adam into Christ, it is conferred on us from heaven."[95] Since fallen human nature is inclined to evil, unbelievers can at best carry out the Law in an external manner out of fear of punishment or hope of reward. Inwardly they will hate the Law.[96] This means that life for them will be unpleasant, since God's Law and the consequences of breaking it confront us constantly in his creation.[97] Yet when through faith our desire becomes one with God's will "as love unites the lover with the beloved," then we will also "taste how good, sweet, pure, holy, and wonderful is the Word of God, the greatest good."[98] When God and his will become our

---

[88] LW 4:285; 21:266.

[89] *Lectures on Isaiah* (1527–30), LW 16:152 = WA 31/2:108.6–7.

[90] *Lectures on Isaiah* (1527–30), LW 16:153 = WA 31/2:108.7.

[91] Luther, *Commentary on the First Twenty-Two Psalms*, 1:169 = *Operationes in Psalmos* (1519–21), WA 5:119.29–30. Cf. 1:264; LW 16:152; 17:110–11; 18:44; 34:131.

[92] LW 14:287, 297 = *Operationes in Psalmos* (1519–21), WA 5:26–27, 34–35.

[93] LW 14:295 = *Operationes in Psalmos* (1519–21), WA 5:33.

[94] LW 14:297 = *Operationes in Psalmos* (1519–21), WA 5:35.26–27.

[95] LW 14:300 = *Operationes in Psalmos* (1519–21), WA 5:37.26–27.

[96] LW 14:295 = *Operationes in Psalmos* (1519–21), WA 5:33.

[97] LW 14:287 = *Operationes in Psalmos* (1519–21), WA 5:26–27.

[98] LW 14:297 = *Operationes in Psalmos* (1519–21), WA 5:35.4–7

highest joy, then our desire "will be elevated over all creation."[99] We will then be able to withstand all kinds of hardships that would shatter the blessedness of other people.[100]

Luther concludes that the blessedness and prosperity of the righteous in this life is a hidden prosperity. It is hidden under troubles and persecutions, but is experienced by those who have faith.[101] When God is our Lord, this gives us an inner confidence and joy that can sustain us even when outwardly we are troubled. When we have the peaceful conscience that flows from sins forgiven, a delight in God's will and abundant goodness, and the knowledge that he will care for us and sustain us even when all other things are taken away, then we can bear all burdens easily. We can be confident, bold, and courageous, even when others despise us or troubles assail.[102]

Conclusion

The nature of sinful human beings is to love themselves more than God and all things, and to use all things including God as a means to serve their own desires. This ultimately leads to frustration, when God and his world do not confirm with our sinful desires, and we discover our inability to furnish ourselves with joy. God on the other hand calls us to love him and his will without thought of ourselves. When we die to ourselves in this way, the surprising result is that we find joy as a byproduct, as we discover that God and his will are good.

Contemporary Application

"Look out for number one." Find some "me time." Learn to love yourself. These are often touted as the recipe for happiness in our society. But do we really need any encouragement? And has this philosophy really produced the happiness it promises?

Luther challenges us to see this kind of self-interest for what it is, a natural expression of the sinful nature and an exercise in idolatrous futility. Despite all our efforts, we cannot make God and his world revolve around us and our self-centered desires. Our attempts to do so only lead to frustration and misery. Instead, it is when we learn to forget about ourselves by delighting in the Lord and his will that we discover the joy and beauty of life as God created it to be.

---

[99] LW 14:297 = *Operationes in Psalmos* (1519–21), WA 5:35.2.

[100] LW 14:297 = *Operationes in Psalmos* (1519–21), WA 5:35.

[101] LW 14:298–99, 304 = *Operationes in Psalmos* (1519–21), WA 5:36–37, 41.

[102] LW 9:111–13; 26:133; 35:374.

OUR FUNDAMENTAL SELF-INTEREST

It is not hard to gather empirical evidence from contemporary society for the pervasive nature of human self-love. As the theologian Langdon Gilkey points out, politicians, advertising people, lawyers, police officers, and economists all know that people act out of self-interest with great predictability, and devise their policies on the basis of this knowledge.[103] Or as the Duke psychologists Michael and Lise Wallach point out, the vast majority of clinical and experimental psychologists need no convincing that humans act out of self-interest. The far more difficult task is to convince them—as the Wallachs try to do—that human beings can also be genuinely altruistic.[104]

In his book *Shantung Compound*, Gilkey relates his experience as a prisoner in a Japanese internment camp during World War II. This experience dramatically revealed to him the self-interest at the heart of human nature. Gilkey was raised on modern liberal assumptions about the goodness of human nature, and came into the camp convinced that old ideas about "fallen existence" and "original sin" were outdated. He thought people were basically moral and rational, and in a crisis their innate goodness would come shining through. What he discovered was that under the pressure of living with little more than they needed to survive the veneer of easy virtue and generosity fell away to reveal a deeper self-interest. While the prisoners still showed good humor and concern for one another, this rarely extended to genuine sacrifice, such as sharing precious commodities like food and living space in more than a token way.[105]

One anecdote Gilkey tells to illustrate this involves a violent dispute that broke out when the American Red Cross delivered to the camp 1,550 packages filled with food and other valuable supplies. The Japanese commander decided that each of the 1,450 prisoners would receive one package, except for the 200 Americans, who would each receive one and a half. Yet most of the Americans were convinced that since the packages came from America they should each receive seven and a half packages while the rest of the prisoners received none. They protested so loudly that the commander decided to withhold all the packages until he received a ruling from Tokyo (where his superiors decided that each prisoner should receive 1 package, with the remaining 100 going to other camps). What stunned Gilkey was not only the callousness of his compatriots toward their fellow prisoners,

---

[103] Langdon Gilkey, *Shantung Compound: The Story of Men and Women Under Pressure* (New York: Harper and Row, 1966), 93–95.

[104] Michael and Lise Wallach, *Psychology's Sanction for Selfishness: The Error of Egoism in Theory and Therapy* (San Francisco: W. H. Freeman, 1983), 1–29, 196–225.

[105] Gilkey, *Shantung Compound*, 89–95.

but also that few of them could recognize their attempts to hoard the packages as selfishness. The vast majority had no difficulty coming up with rationalizations for why they had a moral right to this wealth. Incidents such as this convinced Gilkey that people remain moral enough to be hypocritical, and to concoct excuses for their selfish behavior. Yet this just reveals that we are so thoroughly bent toward serving our own welfare that we enlist reason, religion and morality in this endeavor. This means we are hardly able to recognize our selfishness, let alone to extricate ourselves from it.[106]

THE CULTURE OF ME

One trend a number of scholars have observed in contemporary American society is a rise in narcissistic behaviors and attitudes. People on average have become more focused on the pursuit of their desires and less constrained by moral concerns or by loyalty to other people. A generation ago, Philip Rieff spoke about the rise of "therapeutic man," who lives for bread and circuses, and for his own subjective wellbeing.[107] He predicted in 1966 that religion would not disappear in the future but would be pressed into the service of therapeutic man, who desires to be pleased rather than saved. Religion would therefore not focus on right doctrine but on doctrines that amount to permission for people to live as they please.[108] As we will see when we look at the National Study of Youth and Religion,[109] this prediction has proven remarkably insightful. Likewise, in 1978 Christopher Lasch observed that American culture was becoming increasingly narcissistic.[110] Thirty years later, the research psychologists Jean Twenge and Keith Campbell had no difficulty amassing data to back up this claim.[111] They concluded that since Lasch wrote

---

[106] Ibid., 96–116.

[107] Philip Rieff, *The Triumph of the Therapeutic: Uses of Faith After Freud* (Wilmington, DE: ISI Books, 2006), 1–65, 199–223.

[108] Ibid., 19–20.

[109] See pages 81–83.

[110] Christopher Lasch, *The Culture of Narcissism: American Life in an Age of Diminishing Expectations* (New York: W. W. Norton, 1978), 3–51.

[111] For instance, they report on data from 16,275 college students who filled out the Narcissistic Personality Inventory between 1979 and 2006. This measures narcissistic traits on a sliding scale. They found that by 2006 two thirds of students scored above the 1979–85 average, a 30 percent increase in just over 20 years (Jean M. Twenge and W. Keith Campbell, *The Narcissism Epidemic: Living in the Age of Entitlement* [New York: Free Press, 2009], 30–31). They also report on a study conducted by the National Institutes of Health that asked a representative sample of over 35,000 Americans if they had ever experienced the symptoms of Narcissistic Personality Disorder during their lifetimes. This is the more extreme, clinically diagnosable form of narcissism. They found that 6.2 percent of Americans had suffered from NPD at some point in their lives, but this included just 3.2 percent of those over 65 and a massive 9.4 percent of those in their twenties (ibid., 35–36).

The Culture of Narcissism, narcissism has grown in American culture in ways Lasch could never have imagined.[112]

One key characteristic of narcissism, as described by modern psychology, is that it involves an inflated view of one's self that bears little relation to one's actual abilities or achievements.[113] We will talk about this aspect of narcissism in the next chapter when we talk about self-justification. For now, we will focus on the other key characteristic of narcissism, self-absorption. When Lasch talks about the growing narcissism in American society, he focuses largely on the tendency for people to live simply for themselves and their subjective feelings of wellbeing. This leads them to act out on their impulses and desires with little thought of any loyalty to anything or anyone beyond themselves.[114] Twenge and Campbell draw attention to the sense of entitlement that goes with narcissism. Narcissists tend to think they are entitled to have everything they want. They will frequently use other people to get what they want or explode with rage when they do not get it, with little concern for those they hurt along the way.[115]

This trend in contemporary society toward unrestrained narcissism does not prove that people today are more self-interested than people in previous ages who showed more discipline and restraint.[116] From Luther's perspective, it may just mean that people have become more crass and obvious in their Epicureanism. Yet it does make the self-interest of human nature more evident and reveals to us some of the consequences of trying to construct our lives around the pursuit of our desires.

Luther predicts that the unrestrained pursuit of our own peace and happiness will not lead to peace and happiness. This prediction has been borne out in contemporary society. As Elisabeth Lasch-Quinn wrote in 2006, "We embrace a gospel of personal happiness, defined as the unbridled pursuit of impulse. Yet we remain profoundly unhappy."[117] Twenge and Campbell refer to narcissism as "the fast food of the soul." It tastes great in the short term, but in the long run has dire consequences.[118] Twenge adds the following subtitle to her book *Generation Me: Why Today's Young Americans Are More Confident, Assertive, Entitled—and More Miserable Than Ever Before.* She reports on data that shows that rates of depression, suicide, and anxiety have all

---

[112] Ibid., 4.

[113] Ibid., 19–20.

[114] Lasch, *The Culture of Narcissism*, 6–13.

[115] Twenge and Campbell, *The Narcissism Epidemic*, 19–20, 196–97, 230–43.

[116] Cf. Lasch, *The Culture of Narcissism*, 32.

[117] Elisabeth Lasch-Quinn, introduction to *The Triumph of the Therapeutic: Uses of Faith After Freud*, by Philip Rieff (Wilmington, DE: ISI Books, 2006).

[118] Twenge and Campbell, *The Narcissism Epidemic*, 259.

increased dramatically among young Americans in the last few decades.[119] This rise in misery in our society has coincided with the rise in narcissistic attitudes and the unbridled pursuit of our desires. This does not prove that one has caused the other, but it is extremely suggestive. If giving free reign to our desires was supposed to make us happy and carefree, it has not succeeded. The Prozac-soaked minds of the twenty-first century support Luther's contention that this is not the path to joy.

Christianity That Reflects This Focus on Personal Wellbeing

This idol of self-interest is also evident among people who confess faith in the triune God. All too often, they try to combine faith in God with this idol. Luther suggests that "Satan readily lets God be the Lord of hosts, the God of Israel, some little deity, and he permits Him to be enthroned above the cherubim, but that he should be God alone, this Satan opposes."[120] The constant struggle for the Old Testament prophets was not simply to get the Israelites to worship the Lord, but to get them to worship him alone, rather than thinking they could worship other gods as well (e.g., 1 Kings 11:1–8; 18:21; Jer 7:9–10). The situation is no different today. For instance, according to the 2008 Pew Forum on Religion and Public Life, more than three quarters of Americans claim membership in a Christian denomination,[121] and 39 percent claim to attend worship services at least once a week.[122] Yet a 2005

---

[119] Twenge reports that of Americans born before 1915, only 1–2 percent had a major depressive episode during their lifetimes, even though they lived through the great depression and two world wars. Today the figure is more like 15–20 percent, although some studies put the figure closer to 50 percent, and the rate is higher among young people. One 1990s study showed that 21 percent of teens between 15 and 17 had already experienced major depression (Jean M. Twenge, *Generation Me: Why Today's Young Americans Are More Confident, Assertive, Entitled—and More Miserable Than Ever Before* [New York: Free Press, 2006], 105). In 2002 alone, 8.5 percent of Americans took an antidepressant at some time (ibid., 106), and in 2003, 16.9 percent of high school students admitted they had seriously considered committing suicide in the past year (ibid., 108). Some people have suggested that one factor in this rise in depression rates is an increase in the rate at which it is reported. Yet researchers have concluded that the trend is too large and consistent across studies for this to be the primary factor (ibid., 105–6). Twenge also collected data on thousands of college students and children aged 9–17 who completed measures of anxiety between the 1950s and 1990s. She found that the average college student in the 1990s was more anxious than 85 percent of students in the 1950s and 71 percent of students in the 1970s. With children the trend was even more dramatic. The change was so large that normal children in the 1980s reported higher levels of anxiety than child psychiatric patients in the 1950s (ibid., 107).

[120] *Lectures on Isaiah* (1527–30), LW 16:317 = WA 31/2:235.4–6.

[121] Pew Forum on Religion and Public Life. "U.S. Religious Landscape Survey: Religious Beliefs and Practices: Diverse and Politically Relevant." June 2008. religions.pewforum.org/pdf/report2-religious-landscape-study-full.pdf (accessed Jan. 28, 2010), 110.

[122] Ibid., 117.

survey by the Barna Group found that only 15 percent of Americans considered faith in God to be their highest priority in life, including only 23 percent of those who attend Protestant churches. Despite this, when pastors were asked to estimate how many of their people saw their faith as their highest priority, the average pastor put the figure at 70 percent. These results show that 85 percent of the American population and 77 percent of people who attend Protestant churches are self-confessed idolaters, and most pastors are out of touch with the scale of the problem.[123] Therefore the challenge for the church is not merely to understand the idolatry of the surrounding culture so we can proclaim the Gospel into this culture. The challenge is also to resist this idolatry ourselves, so it does not constantly undermine our faith and our ministry. Only then can we denounce the idols of our culture without hypocrisy, and show people a genuine alternative.

Moralistic therapeutic deism. At the top of the list of idols in our culture is the pursuit of personal happiness. This is not only true for those outside the church. The same is true for those inside. The vast majority of religious believers in America are convinced that the purpose of religion is to serve their own wellbeing.

This is one of the major findings of the National Study of Youth and Religion, the most comprehensive study of religion and spirituality among young Americans ever undertaken. This study looked at the religious beliefs and practices of American teenagers in 2002–2003, and then followed up with the same group of people five years later when they were young adults. It involved both a nationwide survey to gain quantitative data, and hundreds of face-to-face interviews to provide a qualitative picture to go along with this data.[124] One of the most significant findings of this study is that although the vast majority of young Americans identify themselves as Christians, this is not the creed that most of them espouse when asked to articulate for themselves the content of their faith. Instead, the dominant religion among young Americans, including those who regularly attend Christian congregations, is what the researchers call moralistic therapeutic deism.[125] The researchers found that although many young Americans are worshipping members of a religious tradition—evangelical Protestant, mainline Protestant, Catholic,

---

[123] Barna Group, "Surveys Show Pastors Claim Congregants Are Deeply Committed to God But Congregants Deny It!" Jan. 10, 2006, www.barna.org/barna-update/article/5-barna-update/165-surveys-show-pastors-claim-congregants-are-deeply-committed-to-god-but-congregants-deny-it (accessed Jan. 28, 2010).

[124] Christian Smith and Melinda Lundquist Denton, *Soul Searching: The Religious and Spiritual Lives of American Teenagers* (New York: Oxford University Press, 2005), 6–7, 292; Christian Smith and Patricia Snell, *Souls in Transition: The Religious and Spiritual Lives of Emerging Adults* (New York: Oxford University Press, 2009), 3–4.

[125] Smith and Denton, *Soul Searching*, 162–71; Smith and Snell, *Souls in Transition*, 154–56.

Jewish, Mormon, Hindu, or whatever—they have mostly failed to absorb the substantive content of the historical tradition to which they belong. Instead, they have replaced it with moralistic therapeutic deism. Some elements of their faith tradition are usually mixed in, but without these elements changing the core content.[126] Furthermore, the study found that most of these young people learnt this faith from their parents or other adults who modeled it for them.[127] Therefore it is safe to assume that it is not only the dominant religion among this age group, but is also widely popular in the American population as a whole. The researchers outline the creed of moralistic therapeutic deism as follows:

1. A God exists who created and orders the world and watches over human life on earth.
2. God wants people to be good, nice, and fair to one another, as taught in the Bible and by most world religions.
3. The central goal of life is to be happy and to feel good about oneself.
4. God does not need to be particularly involved in one's life except when God is needed to resolve a problem.
5. Good people go to heaven when they die.[128]

In subsequent chapters we will look at the moralistic and deistic elements of this creed. For now we will focus on its therapeutic aspect.

The researchers found that when young people were asked to talk about their faith, they made few references to the traditional content of the Christian faith, such as sin, repentance, grace, forgiveness, salvation, the triune God, faith, or love for God and neighbor. Instead, their words focused on personal happiness, feeling good about oneself, and feeling personally satisfied and fulfilled.[129] The researchers conclude that the primary purpose of moralistic therapeutic deism is to provide therapeutic benefits to its adherents. They write,

> This is not a religion of repentance from sin, of keeping the Sabbath, of living as a servant of a sovereign divine, of steadfastly saying one's prayers, of faithfully observing high holy days, of building character through suffering, of basking in God's love and grace, of spending oneself in gratitude and love for the cause of social justice, etcetera. Rather, what appears to be the actual dominant religion

---

[126] Smith and Denton, *Soul Searching*, 163–67, 171.

[127] Ibid., 166, 170, 261; Smith and Snell, *Souls in Transition*, 155, 285.

[128] Smith and Snell, *Souls in Transition*, 154. By permission of Oxford University Press, USA.

[129] Smith and Denton, *Soul Searching*, 167–68.

> among U.S. teenagers is centrally about feeling good, happy, secure, at peace. It is about attaining subjective well-being, being able to solve problems, and getting along amiably with other people.[130]

The god of moralistic therapeutic deism is a god who makes few demands that might prevent us from doing what we want. Indeed, he cannot be demanding, since his job is to solve our problems and make us feel good about ourselves. When he fails to deliver his promised therapeutic benefits we have the right to feel grumpy with him.[131] As one sixteen-year-old mainline Protestant boy complained in his interview, "Well, God is Almighty, I guess. But I think he's on vacation right now because of all the crap that's happening in the world."[132] Or as one fourteen-year-old conservative Protestant boy said, "God is an overall ruler who controls everything, so like, if I'm depressed or something and things aren't going my way I blame him."[133]

This suggests an obvious reason why an outward profession of Christianity often does not result in a transformed life. Those who have co-opted Christ's name in service of the idol of personal happiness are still shaped by the same primary commitment as the secular people around them. Therefore we have no reason to expect their lives to look much different.

Extrinisic vs. intrinsic faith. Just as narcissistic self-interest has not yielded greater wellbeing for society as a whole, it has not yielded greater wellbeing for religious people either. This has been shown by psychology of religion studies that examine the difference between an "intrinsic" and an "extrinsic" faith. People with an intrinsic faith treat their faith as a supreme good in its own right, whereas those with an extrinsic faith use it primarily as a means for gaining other things, such as social standing, interpersonal connections, self-justification, and personal therapeutic benefits. These studies have found that an intrinsic faith correlates positively with measures of mental health, but an extrinsic faith correlates negatively. Those with an intrinsic faith on average demonstrate more self-control, greater personal adjustment, a greater sense of wellbeing, more emotional stability, less neurosis, less fear of death, and less anxiety than the rest of the population. The reverse is true for those with an extrinsic faith, who score worse in these categories than the irreligious.[134] This suggests that Luther's distinction

---

[130] Ibid., 163–64. By permission of Oxford University Press, USA.

[131] Ibid., 164–65.

[132] Ibid., 165.

[133] Ibid., 165.

[134] Eva Jonas and Peter Fischer, "Terror Management and Religion: Evidence That Intrinsic Religiousness Mitigates Worldview Defense Following Mortality Salience," *Journal of Personality and Social Psychology* 91 (2006): 554–55.

between loving God for his own sake and using him for personal gain is highly significant even in terms of earthly benefits. Those who seek first the kingdom of God by loving him above all else are likely to reap additional rewards even in this life. But those who try to use God to serve the idol of their own earthly wellbeing are likely to learn the hard way that such attempts are counterproductive, since the true God refuses to serve our idols.

The church that panders to the idol of the self. So what part has the church played in the rise of moralistic therapeutic deism? Is it merely that the church has failed to communicate the content of the faith effectively enough, so that people have formed their own view of God based on the messages of the culture and their own idolatrous hearts? Or has the church actively contributed to the rise of this faith?

This is a question each church has to ask for itself, since the church is too diverse to paint all congregations or denominations with the same brush. Yet a case can be made that several trends in contemporary Christianity in America have contributed to this therapeutic mind-set.

One trend has been the use of human-centered psychology to inform pastoral practice. E. Brooks Holifield, professor of American church history at Emory University in Atlanta, has chronicled trends in pastoral care among American Protestant clergy from the early seventeenth century until the end of the 1960s.[135] He contends that over this time the focus of conversations between pastors and their parishioners shifted from repentance and otherworldly salvation to psychological wellbeing and self-realization.[136] He tries to identify the ideal that shaped pastoral care in different periods of America's history, and suggests that this ideal shifted from self-denial to self-love, from self-love to self-culture, from self-culture to self-mastery, and from self-mastery to self-realization.[137] Holifield then suggests that this transition in

---

[135] E. Brooks Holifield, *A History of Pastoral Care in America: From Salvation to Self-Realization* (Eugene, OR: Wipf and Stock Publishers, 1983), 11–13.

[136] Ibid., 11, 355–56.

[137] Ibid., 12, 351. Twenge and Campbell point out that self-actualization, at least as Abraham Maslow defined it, means reaching one's full potential, and includes sharing one's benevolence and sympathy with other people. Maslow placed self-actualization at the apex of his hierarchy of needs and believed it was extremely difficult to achieve. Yet one rung below it on his hierarchy he placed self-esteem, which is much easier to achieve. Twenge and Campbell then note that as the human potential movement evolved from the 1960s into the '70s and beyond the notion of self-actualization was eclipsed by the much easier concept of self-esteem. Now self-actualization is rarely discussed, but talk about self-esteem is everywhere (Twenge and Campbell, *The Narcissism Epidemic*, 60). Perhaps if Holifield had continued his account past the '60s he would have included another category, self-esteem.

the attitudes and practices of Protestant clergy has played a significant hand in the rise of the therapeutic culture Rieff describes.[138]

L. Gregory Jones, the dean of Duke Divinity School, observes that when the church adopts the therapeutic mind-set, and tries to translate the Gospel into psychological categories, it loses the eschatological focus of the Gospel. The therapeutically focused church easily adopts language and practices that sound like the Gospel—community, confession, brokenness, compassion, acceptance, forgiveness, peace, healing, and so on—but distorts them all, treating their psychological impact as if it is the primary thing instead of merely a side benefit. So sin becomes psychological brokenness, instead of rebellion against a God who will judge us on the last day. Forgiveness becomes a means for restoring our emotional wellbeing, instead of the means by which God builds his eschatological community. Pastoral care becomes psychological healing, instead of conformity to Christ's image by the power of his Spirit. In this way God, as well as the true hope of the Christian life in the world to come, fades into the background.[139]

Another trend in contemporary Western Christianity has been to focus on people's felt needs as the hook for getting them into church. For instance, Rick Warren, a popular author and leader in the church growth movement, encourages evangelism focused on people's felt needs.[140] He suggests that if a church is to be successful in evangelism, every sermon should begin with the felt needs of the unchurched to attract their attention and draw them into the biblical message.[141] He also suggests that this was Jesus' approach to evangelism. He writes, "People crowded around Jesus because he met their needs—physical, emotional, spiritual, relational, and financial. He did not judge some needs as being 'more legitimate' than others."[142] "Whenever Jesus encountered a person he'd begin with *their* hurts, needs, and interests."[143]

---

[138] Holifield, *A History of Pastoral Care in America*, 12, 16.

[139] L. Gregory Jones, "The Psychological Captivity of the Church in the United States," in *Either/Or: The Gospel or Neopaganism*, ed. Carl E. Braaten and Robert W. Jenson (Grand Rapids, MI: Eerdmans, 1995), 102–12.

[140] In this, Warren is by no means alone. For example, Christian A. Schwarz, head of the Institute for Natural Church Development in Germany, proposes eight "quality characteristics" that he claims—if they are all present in a congregation to a sufficiently high degree—will guarantee that the congregation will grow numerically (Christian A. Schwarz, *Natural Church Development: A Guide to Eight Essential Qualities of Healthy Churches* [St. Charles, IL: ChurchSmart Resources, 2000], 40–41). One of these quality characteristics is "need-oriented evangelism," which focuses on the questions and needs of non-Christians (ibid., 34–35).

[141] Rick Warren, *The Purpose Driven Church: Growth Without Compromising Your Message and Mission* (Grand Rapids, MI: Zondervan, 1995), 293–96.

[142] Ibid., 219.

[143] Ibid., 197.

When Warren says this, he overlooks all the Gospel stories in which Jesus refused to give people what they were seeking, or directed them away from their felt needs to what he judged to be truly important. For instance, when a man asked him, "tell my brother to divide the inheritance with me," Jesus refused, and instead responded with a lesson on the dangers of covetousness and the importance of seeking true treasure in heaven (Luke 12:13–34). It is not hard to multiply such examples.[144] In fairness to Warren, he tries to counterbalance his statements by saying that the felt needs of seekers should not drive the church's agenda,[145] and God calls us to live for his purposes rather than our own self-actualization.[146] Yet Warren virtually admits that this is a bait and switch. He suggests that it does not matter how selfish our motives are when we ask Christ to save us, since he can change our motives later.[147]

If we are to judge by the prevalence of moralistic therapeutic deism within the American population, people have done a better job of swallowing the bait than the church has done of effecting the switch. The problem with need-oriented evangelism is that one of the greatest needs we have is to be less focused on our own needs. Need-oriented evangelism plays on some half-truths. The Gospel does ultimately fulfill our deepest needs. In addition, Christ calls us to love our neighbors and to care for their earthly needs, and this can help to win a hearing for the Gospel. Yet at the same time the Law addresses our preoccupation with our own needs, and calls us to die to our sinful self-focus. It is true that Jesus went around caring for the needs of others. Yet he never tried to effect a bait and switch. Instead, when he called people to follow him he was completely upfront that this means counting the cost (Luke 14:25–33), dying to oneself, bearing a cross (Matt 16:24–25), taking last place (Mark 10:35–45; Luke 14:7–14), and surrendering our attachment to earthly wellbeing for the sake of God's kingdom (Matt 6:19–33; 10:34–39; John 16:33). The potential danger with need-oriented evangelism is that, taken to an extreme, it can muddy the distinction between Law and Gospel, and present people with a false gospel focused on the fulfillment of the felt needs of their sinful nature.

This becomes especially clear when it comes to a third trend in American Christianity, the prosperity gospel. Popular preachers such as Joel Osteen have proclaimed a gospel of self-esteem and earthly success. Osteen tells us

---

[144] E.g., Matt 12:38–42; Mark 10:17–22, 35–45; Luke 9:57–62; 10:38–42; John 6:15.

[145] Warren, *The Purpose Driven Church*, 79–80.

[146] Rick Warren, *The Purpose Driven Life: What on Earth Am I Here For?* (Grand Rapids, MI: Zondervan, 2002), 17–18.

[147] Warren, *The Purpose Driven Church*, 219.

that we cannot love others until we love ourselves.[148] Therefore we must learn to like ourselves by refusing to listen to accusing voices,[149] speaking works of affirmation to ourselves to build up our self-esteem,[150] having confidence in ourselves,[151] and regarding ourselves as champions.[152] Then we can live the lives of victory and prosperity in every area of our lives that God wants for us,[153] since "God didn't make you to be average. God made you to excel."[154] This is a message the idolatrous flesh can readily accept.

At first glance these errors appear difficult to avoid, since they all play on half-truths. Surely it is legitimate to talk about the psychological benefits of the Gospel? After all, as Luther emphasizes, the New Testament frequently speaks about the peace and assurance the Gospel brings to hearts and minds. Surely it is legitimate to talk about the Gospel as the answer to human need? How else can we present it in its sweetness? And surely it is legitimate to talk about acceptance and victory in Christ? Yet two dangers need to be avoided. The first is that Law and Gospel become blurred into each other instead of being properly distinguished. This is what Osteen does when he runs two messages into each other: we can accept ourselves because of God's mercy in Christ, and we can accept ourselves because God has made us to be star performers.[155] The second danger is that the eschatological message of salvation gets distorted into a message of earthly success and prosperity here and now. The prosperity God intends for us cannot sidestep repentance or the death of the self-focused sinful nature, nor can the "little while" that Luther saw as so important to faith be forgotten.[156] Otherwise we are pandering to the idolatrous sinful nature, which wants immediate gratification, instead of dying and living by faith. When Christianity has baulked on these two issues it has contributed to the rise of the therapeutic mind-set. This in turn ultimately leads to misery, not joy.

---

[148] Joel Osteen, *Become a Better You: 7 Keys to Improving Your Life Every Day* (Large print ed.; Detroit: Thomson Gale, 2007), 176.

[149] Ibid., 153–88.

[150] Ibid., 189–206.

[151] Ibid., 207–26.

[152] Ibid., 189.

[153] Joel Osteen, *Your Best Life Now: 7 Steps to Living at Your Full Potential* (New York: Time Warner Book Group, 2004), 82–90.

[154] Ibid., 82.

[155] Osteen, *Become a Better You*, 153–226.

[156] See chapter 4, pages 51–52.

Are People Really That Selfish?

As we have seen, it is not hard to accumulate evidence that fallen human beings are self-interested. Yet is it really true that they *always* act out of self-interest as Luther asserts? The most obvious challenge to Luther's view are examples of altruism among non-Christians. Such examples are not hard to find. For instance, one of the best-known humanitarians in my home country is an eye doctor called Fred Hollows, who was honored as Australian of the Year in 1990.[157] When Dr. Hollows realized that many people in impoverished countries around the world were needlessly going blind from treatable diseases like trachoma and cataracts, he dedicated his life to giving the gift of sight to these people. This meant travelling to many of the poorest and most remote regions of the world to treat people who could never afford to pay for his services. Yet Dr. Hollows is someone who turned his back on the Christian faith of his youth, and died a self-professed atheist.[158] So does Luther's view of the ubiquitous egoism of unbelievers really hold up when confronted with people like Fred Hollows?

I contend that it does, for two reasons. First, Luther had no difficulty acknowledging that humans in their fallen state can exhibit what he calls civic righteousness. They can be kind and virtuous in their outward dealings with other people.[159] Second, when he talks about ubiquitous self-interest he is not saying that this always displays itself in a crass and obvious manner. He is not saying there is no such thing as natural human sympathy or affection, or that people in their fallen state have no genuine concern for the welfare of anyone but themselves. What he is saying is that those who are outside of Christ will ultimately use even the noblest things of which we humans can boast for self-serving purposes.

Luther says that whatever the saints do is sanctified, even when they fall into sin, and that God works all things together for their good, even their failings. For instance, when they fall into sin, this teaches them humility, and leads them to cry to God for help, so that in this way their faith is increased. Yet the opposite is also true. "With the crooked Thou dost show Thyself perverse."[160] Luther interprets this to mean that for the ungodly even their good works and greatest gifts work together for them for evil, since they misuse God's gifts. They do not use their good works to glorify God, but

[157] Fred Hollows Foundation, "About Fred," www.hollows.org/AboutFred/ (accessed May 18, 2010).

[158] Joe Hildebrand, "Fred Hollows Remembered at Ceremony in Bourke," *The Daily Telegraph*, Feb. 11, 2008, www.dailytelegraph.com.au/news/nsw-act/a-vision-well-remembered/story-e6freuzi-1111115519873 (accessed May 18, 2010).

[159] LW 26:4; 27:219–20; 33:270; 35:385; 46:99–100; WA 2:43–44.

[160] Ps 18:26, as cited in LW 3:335.

instead take credit for themselves, and thereby become more proud, self-secure, and inclined to act like their own little gods.[161]

One way to unpack this further is to consider the work of Robert Spitzer, the Jesuit priest and former president of Gonzaga University. Spitzer has examined the long tradition of Western philosophy to learn what some of the greatest human minds have regarded as the path to happiness and fulfillment.[162] On the basis of this study he identifies four levels of things that bring satisfaction into our lives. This scale moves from the lowest level, which brings gratification that is immediate and often quite intense but is shallow and short lived, up to the highest level, where satisfaction may not always be so intense but is deeper and more lasting.[163]

The first level is basic physical stimulation.[164] I see the hamburger, I eat it, and it gives me pleasure.

The second is ego gratification. When we win, achieve our goals, or gain power, admiration, or popularity, it makes us happy.[165] I crush you on the tennis court, or I succeed in business, and it feels good.

Unlike level one and two, which involve basic, obvious, tangible gratification, level three and four deal with the intangibles of life. They involve seeking after transcendent goods, which Spitzer refers to as Love, Truth, Goodness, Beauty, and Being.[166]

Level three involves looking for the good beyond the self and contributing to the world around us because we want our lives to make a positive difference. It involves things like love and service toward others and striving for a better world in which there is more love, truth, justice, beauty, and so on.[167] Spitzer refers to the work of Victor Frankl, a psychologist who survived the Nazi concentration camps. Frankl observed that there were two basic groups among his fellow prisoners. One group could find no reason to live

---

[161] *Lectures on Genesis* (1538–42), LW 3:333–36 = WA 43:114–16. In the case of Fred Hollows, a third factor is also involved—the impact of Christianity in shaping Western values. For example, the actions of Fred Hollows would neither have been found nor valued among pre-Christian Romans.

[162] Robert J. Spitzer, Robin A. Bernhoft, and Camille E. De Blasi, *Healing the Culture: A Commonsense Philosophy of Happiness, Freedom, and the Life Issues* (San Francisco: Ignatius Press, 2000), 58–62; Robert J. Spitzer, "Toward a Philosophy of the Pro-Life Movement: Personhood, Rights, and 'Purpose in Life,'" Jan. 27, 2006, The Maclaurin Institute, www.maclaurin.org/mp3_group.php?type=MacLaurin+Campus+Lectures (accessed Jan. 17, 2008).

[163] Spitzer, Bernhoft, and De Blasi, *Healing the Culture*, 61–62, 65.

[164] Ibid., 64–66; Spitzer, "Towards a Philosophy of the Pro-Life Movement."

[165] Spitzer, "Towards a Philosophy of the Pro-Life Movement."

[166] Spitzer, Bernhoft, and De Blasi, *Healing the Culture*, 62.

[167] Spitzer, Bernhoft, and De Blasi, *Healing the Culture*, 62, 65, 77, 91.

apart from level one or two gratification, and since this was all taken away from them in the camps they fared poorly. Many staked all their hopes on the Allies liberating them by Christmas, and when this did not happen they gave up and died.[168] The other group found a higher reason to live outside themselves, such as "If I get out of here I'll never let this happen again" or "I've got to find my kids" or "this other prisoner needs my help." These tended to survive, and often went on to do great things.[169]

Spitzer then contends that we still end up dissatisfied when we are forced to settle for the limited measure of goodness, truth, love, beauty, and being that can be found in earthly things. Instead, we yearn for absolute knowledge, and unconditional love, and perfect justice and beauty, and being that is absolutely solid. This drives the artist or philosopher or scientist or lover or social activist to seek continually for more beauty or truth or love or justice. The final level of happiness comes when we stop trying to extract these transcendent goods from the imperfect things of this world and seek after Truth itself, Love itself, Goodness itself, Beauty itself, and Being itself. For Spitzer, this means seeking for God.[170]

The purpose of this excursus is this. When Luther speaks about human self-interest, we should not assume that he is merely talking about crass self-interest, such as one finds at level one and two in Spitzer's scheme. He is also talking about the highest, most refined, and most spiritual kinds of self-interest.

In order to make the case that humans do not always act out of self-interest, Michael and Lise Wallach make a distinction between "trivial" and "non-trivial" self-interest. They suggest that egoism is trivial and really should not be called egoism, if we find happiness or pleasure from pursuing higher things like justice or the common good.[171] They then argue that such enlightened pursuits are the best way to serve our own psychological wellbeing.[172] This is an admission that these pursuits can be self-serving, even if the Wallachs do not think they deserve that label.

---

[168] Cf. Viktor Frankl, *Man's Search for Meaning* (New York: Washington Square Press, 1985), 97.

[169] Spitzer, "Towards a Philosophy of the Pro-Life Movement." This is Spitzer's summary of Viktor Frankl's book *Man's Search for Meaning*. In the first half of the book Frankl relates his concentration camp experiences. He observes that the prisoners needed a rich inner life, a firm grasp on their moral and spiritual selves, and a purpose to live for if they were to both survive and resist the degenerating influences of the camps (Frankl, *Man's Search for Meaning*, 55–64, 70, 83, 86–87, 90–101, 110–15).

[170] Spitzer, Bernhoft, and De Blasi, *Healing the Culture*, 94–95, 104–8; Spitzer, "Towards a Philosophy of the Pro-Life Movement."

[171] Wallach, *Psychology's Sanction for Selfishness*, 200–202.

[172] Ibid., 227–74.

This distinction between trivial and non-trivial egoism is significant when it comes to earthly matters. Our communities need more people who find joy in seeking the common good rather than merely their own individual good. Yet Spitzer treats this distinction as if it is also of value in our dealings with God, and that if we can just lift people's eyes from lower kinds of self-interest to higher and more refined types we can lead them to God.[173] Luther is more cautious of absolving self-interest by calling it trivial, at least when it comes to our standing before God. Our concern should be God's will, not self-interest.

Yes, God's will has many benefits for us. In particular, God wants us to rejoice in the benefits he has for us in Christ and the Gospel. Yet this means coming at the issue from a wholly different direction. Only the sinful nature has self-interest as its primary guiding light. For Luther there is no smooth path of self-interest leading to God. Instead, pursuing enlightened self-interest while still in a state of rebellion against God will just make us more secure Pharisees. For Luther, the height of self-interest is self-justification. Luther did not consider unbelievers to be brute beasts who only seek crass pleasures. He acknowledged that they still have moral and spiritual concerns, and can do noble things, since they retain some knowledge of God's Law in their consciences. Yet one of the most powerful spiritual concerns we all have is for justification. Therefore unless we live by faith in Christ, even when we do noble things our self-interested rebellion against God is revealed, since instead of giving him credit, we use our good works to justify ourselves before him. This leads us into the topic of the next chapter.

A CHRISTIAN RESPONSE

Luther's exposure of the idolatrous nature of human self-interest provides a radical challenge to our therapeutic culture of me. It also challenges the church's efforts to baptize this self-interest and pander to the sinful nature. So how can we avoid this trap, and proclaim the Christian message winsomely without feeding this idolatry?

One part of the answer is to resist the temptation to promise earthly blessings that God does not promise. Such false promises only feed the desires of the sinful nature. Instead, we should imitate Jesus by directing people to "lay up for yourselves treasures in heaven" (Matt 6:20). The sinful nature is impatient of such delay, but those who have learned to content themselves in the Lord will wait patiently.

Another part of the answer is to expose the futility of the self-interested and self-directed pursuit of happiness. We can preach about the futility of trying to get the universe to revolve around us and our desires, and the misery

[173] Spitzer, Bernhoft, and De Blasi, *Healing the Culture*, 104–17.

that results when we try to force it to do so. We can teach that true joy is found not in selfishly pursuing our own interests, not even in a spiritual way, but instead in forgetting about ourselves and delighting only in the Lord and his will.

This is a lesson I learned the hard way. I left home when I was seventeen, and did not get married until I was thirty. In between I had many lonely years, including a number of years where I lived alone and worked alone as a sole pastor. During this time I prayed long and hard that God would provide me with a wife, but instead all my dating ended in disappointment. I began to worry that maybe God's answer was no, and that I would end up alone for the rest of my life. Then one day, as I reflected on the story of the woman at the well in John 4, I realized that I had turned my hope of finding a wife into an idol. I had allowed myself to think that unless I found a wife I would not have a happy and fulfilled life. Like the woman at the well, I was seeking satisfaction in earthly relationships, when Jesus alone was the font of living water who could quench my thirsting soul. I had been trying to use him to give me what I really wanted—a wife—when what I needed was to content myself in him and whatever he willed for me, knowing that he could satisfy me and do me good no matter what my relationship status. From then on, I continued to pray for a wife, but without the same anxiety, since I had determined in my mind to embrace the single life if this was God's will. When I did find my wife some time later, I had been released to receive her as a woman and not an idol.

This means that to a certain extent, the church must resist the call to be "relevant." Yes, we need to do our best to communicate the Gospel in such a way that it relates to people and their lives, and yes, the Gospel is always relevant, whether people recognize it or not. Yet what the average person on the street wants, and therefore regards as "relevant," is a god who will give them what they want and fulfill the narcissistic desires of their sinful nature. Instead of pandering to this, we need to help people see how boring and fruitless it is to be thinking about ourselves and our own needs and desires all the time. As Phillip Cary, professor of Philosophy at Eastern University, argues, it is far more interesting to take our eyes off ourselves and focus them on something outside ourselves that is beautiful and good irrespective of its benefit to us. What we want is to direct people's eyes away from themselves to the God who is beautiful and wondrous, so that, like the bride whose thoughts are occupied by her bridegroom, they begin to long for news of their beloved.[174]

---

[174] Phillip Cary, *Good News for Anxious Christians: 10 Practical Things You Don't Have to Do* (Grand Rapids, MI: Brazos, 2010), 157–74.

The only way to do this is to preach the Gospel, and in this way to direct people's eyes to the God of the Gospel who is beautiful and true and good. In a sense, belief in the Gospel could be called self-interested, since it is of utmost benefit to us to believe. Yet it is not self-seeking. It is not about the pursuit of self-interest, but about receiving the promises of the God who has pursued us to provide us with every good thing by grace—without the aid of our efforts to strive for what we want or need.

The one form of self-interest Luther never critiques is delight in the benefits God has promised to us in Christ and the Gospel. This makes perfect sense from the perspective of his theology. On the one hand, if we love God above all things, we will delight in his will for us; and central to his will is that we delight in Christ and the Gospel. On the other hand, only the Gospel can create in us true, unselfish love for God and neighbor and release us from our enslavement to the pursuit of our desires. Far from feeding the selfishness of the sinful nature, the Gospel is the only thing that can enable us to love in a selfless way. When all we know of God is the Law, our serving him will invariably be self-interested, since we will inevitably try to buy his blessing with our good deeds. In contrast, the Gospel stirs in us genuine love for God and releases us to do his will simply because we love him and regard his will as good.

Part Three

The Second Article

Chapter Six

The Idol of the Self and Justification

Justification is something we all engage in all the time. How can we look at ourselves in the mirror, and live with our flaws and failings? How can we look other people in the eye and hold our heads up high in our dealings with them? When others say that we are in the wrong, how can we satisfy our desire to be in the right? These are just extensions of the deeper question of how we sinners can stand before God and find favor in his sight.

For Luther, it is Christ who must justify us sinners with a righteousness that is not our own.[1] This is what it means to have the true God as our God in this area of our lives. When we instead seek to justify ourselves, we set up our presumed righteousness as an idol in his place.[2]

One form of self-justification should be familiar to anyone with even a limited knowledge of Reformation teaching, and that is the self-righteousness of those who strive to win God's approval through their good works or religious piety. While it appears very pious to engage in all kinds of activity aimed at winning God's favor, for Luther this is the height of impious idolatry, since it puts the human self in Christ's place. Since this is the main form of self-justification that Luther attacks, and it is still prevalent today, I will spend some time addressing it. Yet I won't spend overly long on it, since works-righteousness has received extensive treatment in Protestant literature, and examples of it are easy to identify. Instead, I will spend the majority of this chapter focusing on two things that are less obvious.

The first is that works-righteous legalism is not the only strategy people can adopt in their quest for self-justification. Luther also identifies a second strategy, that of the antinomians,[3] who attempt to justify themselves by

---

[1] LW 12:328, 367, 390; 16:120; 22:157; 31:297, 299.

[2] LW 9:104; 13:374–75; 14:202; 16:249, 262–63; 17:401; 18:167; 22:456; 26:257–59; 27:88; 31:350; 51:17.

[3] *Nomos* is the word for "law" in Greek, so an antinomian is someone who is anti the Law. The antinomians with whom Luther contended tried to exclude the teaching of God's Law from the church, as if it is possible to teach the Gospel without the Law as its backdrop.

denying or silencing God's Law instead of trying to keep it. Unless we recognize antinomianism for what it is, an attempt at self-justification, we will fail to discern the mechanism by which enormous numbers of people try to justify themselves, and thus convince themselves they have no need for Christ.

The second is that it is not just religious people who attempt to justify themselves before God and his Law. So do secular people. At first glance this may seem absurd, since thoroughly secular people do not even acknowledge that there is a God. Nevertheless, they are still answerable to God's Law, and on some level they know this and feel compelled to deal with this knowledge. As Luther concludes from Romans 1 and 2, there are no true atheists in the world, since God has imprinted a natural knowledge of himself and his Law on the human heart. Luther writes,

> Such a light and such a perception is innate in the hearts of all men; and this light cannot be subdued or extinguished. There are, to be sure, some people, for instance, the Epicureans, Pliny, and the like, who deny this with their lips. But they do it by force and want to quench this light in their hearts. They are like people who purposely stop their ears or pinch their eyes shut to close out sound and sight. However, they do not succeed in this; their conscience tells them otherwise. For Paul is not lying when he asserts that they know something about God, "because God has shown it to them."[4]

This means that even thoroughly secular people cannot escape the voice of conscience, which tells them they stand condemned by God and need to be justified before him. They have to deal with this guilty knowledge in some way.

The material from psychology in the second half of the chapter can help us to reflect on what self-justification looks like for people today. It also challenges us to consider that what often appears to be a secular activity—justification before the court of human opinion regarding mundane matters—cannot be separated from justification before God. Those who know they have been justified by God can say, "It is God who justifies. Who is to condemn?" (Rom 8:33–34). They may still seek human approval, yet without the same compulsive need, since this should now be a secondary rather than a primary issue for them. Yet those who have no secure knowledge of God's approval will be compelled to seek approval from other sources. Then, even if they obtain it, they will not be able to silence the nagging knowledge that this is not enough, since God is watching and his higher Law stands over their lives. Therefore their need for justification will have no end, and we would expect to

---

[4] *Commentary on Jonah: The German Text* (1526), LW 19:53–54 = WA 19:205.35–206.6.

see in them a compulsive need for validation. This is ultimately a need for God's approval, even though they seek to fulfill it in the secular domain.

This compulsive drive to seek justification is well-documented in psychology and cannot be explained purely in terms of the desire to secure human favors by winning human approval. Often our attempts at self-justification achieve the opposite. As we try to pass the buck, show why our victims deserve the abuse we give them, or demonstrate why we have the moral high ground over others, we often do more to aggravate others than to win their favor. For instance, when something goes wrong in my household, my sinful tendency is to want to blame my wife or children even when I am at fault. Yet what do I gain from this? It doesn't win me favor with them, but only leads to fights. Or, as we will see when we look at terror management theory, people feel more compelled to justify themselves when they are confronted with the knowledge that they will die than at other times. Yet why should this be the case? What good is human approval in the grave? This only makes sense if people are ultimately trying to justify themselves before a higher court of judgment.

LUTHER'S TEACHING

Whereas justification through Christ lies at the heart of true faith, self-justification lies at the heart of idolatry. Luther writes that "Whoever falls from the doctrine of justification is ignorant of God and an idolater,"[5] and "the opinion that we are justified by works apart from faith is the source of all idolatry."[6]

Luther introduces this theme in the Large Catechism, where he writes,

> Beside this, there is also a false worship and extreme idolatry, which we have practiced up to now. This is also still common in the world. All churchly orders are founded on it. It concerns the conscience alone, which seeks help, consolation, and salvation in its own works. The conscience imagines it can wrestle heaven away from God and thinks about how many requests it has made, how often it has fasted, celebrated Mass, and so on. Upon such things it depends and boasts, as though unwilling to receive anything from God as a gift. For it wants to earn or merit heaven with abundant works. The conscience acts as though God must serve us and is our debtor, and we are His liege lords. What is this but reducing God to an idol—

[5] *Lectures on Galatians* (1535), LW 26:395 = WA 40/1:602.12–13.

[6] *Lectures on Isaiah* (1527–30), LW 17:114 = WA 31/2:351.20. Cf. LW 17:17, 21–23, 107; 16:263; 20:332; 54:340; Martin Luther, *Martin Luther's Complete Commentary on the First Twenty-Two Psalms*, trans. Henry Cole (2 vols.; London: W. Simpkin and R. Marshall, 1826), 2.179.

> indeed, an apple god—and elevating and regarding ourselves as God? But this point is a little too clever and is not for young pupils.[7]

What Luther regarded as too clever for children he treated at greater length when addressing adults. Luther returned to this theme repeatedly throughout his career and touched on it in virtually all his biblical commentaries after his evangelical breakthrough.[8] He also addressed it in *The Freedom of the Christian*,[9] his *Treatise on Good Works*,[10] and numerous other places.[11] He continually reiterated that

> Whoever seeks righteousness apart from faith and through works denies God and makes himself into God. This is what he thinks: "If I do this work, I shall be righteous. I shall be the victor over sin, death, the devil, the wrath of God, and hell; and I shall attain eternal life." Now what is this, I ask you, but to arrogate to oneself a work that belongs to God alone, and to show that one is God?[12]

REJECTION OF THE LADDER OF MERIT

For Luther, Christ alone must be our Savior. He writes that

> mercy must be alone. It allows nothing to be joined with it in which a person may hope at the same time. For that would be for the feet to spread apart and limp between two ways, and like the Samaritans to foolishly worship God and an idol at the same time. No one can worship God except by a pure and undivided faith in his mercy alone. Otherwise we will not sing and give thanks to God alone, but

---

[7] LC I 22–23 = WA 30/1:135.17–27.

[8] LW 1:14, 149; 4:68, 159, 165, 171, 235–39; 9:53–54, 104; 12:322, 378–79, 389; 13:174–75; 14:33–34, 168–69, 202, 348; 16:14–15, 78, 229, 249, 262–63; 17:16–17, 21–24, 107–14, 162, 401, 412; 18:4, 9–10, 167, 255; 19:55–56, 115; 20:332; 22:152, 154–55, 456; 26:257–59, 395–401; 27:87–90; 29:48–49; 30:246; Luther, *Commentary on the First Twenty-Two Psalms*, 2:52, 117, 122, 179; WA 5:390.34–39; 40/3:357.5–11, 358.13–17, 359.6–9.

Judging by Luther's own comments (*Preface to Luther's Latin Writings* [1545], LW 34:336–37 = WA 54:185–86), as well as by the contents of his writings, I regard his evangelical breakthrough to have taken place no earlier than at some time during his lectures on Romans, so that his earliest lectures on the Psalms and much of his work on Romans are prior to it.

[9] *The Freedom of the Christian* (1520), LW 31:350 = WA 7:54.

[10] *Treatise on Good Works* (1520), LW 44:29–33 = WA 6:209–12.

[11] E.g., LW 36:216–17; 38:106–7; 44:319–20; 51:17; 54:340, 436.

[12] *Lectures on Galatians* (1535), LW 26:258 = WA 40/1:405.15–19.

> also to our idol, which has cooperated with him. God forbid such a thing as this![13]

Luther therefore rejected the semi-Pelagian strand of the theology he inherited, and insisted that our redemption cannot be a self-salvation project in any way. The conventional wisdom of many of his theological forebears was that in order to be saved a person must choose "to do what is in him."[14] In other words, "Do your best and God will do the rest." Luther rejected all such suggestions that we can contribute toward our salvation, and taught instead that we must be saved by grace alone.[15]

By itself, this was not particularly radical. Augustine and Aquinas had also taught that we must be saved by grace alone. What was truly revolutionary was that Luther also taught that we must be saved by faith alone.[16] This meant rejecting the Catholic doctrine of merit, and the Augustinian and Thomistic understanding of grace that stands behind it. For Augustine and Aquinas saving grace involves infused grace: that is, an infusion of God's power that enables us to love him and ascend to him through our meritorious deeds.[17] As far as Luther is concerned, this still makes salvation a human achievement. It still depends on our works. Such a view fails to distinguish justification and sanctification, and puts justification

---

[13] *Operationes in Psalmos* (1519–21), WA 5:390.34–39. Author's own translation.

[14] *Facere quod in se est.* This maxim was taught by William of Occam, Bonaventura (E. G. Schwiebert, *Luther and His Times: The Reformation from a New Perspective*, [St. Louis: Concordia, 1950], 167–69; LW 25:497), Gabriel Biel (Gabriel Biel, "The Circumcision of the Lord," in *Forerunners of the Reformation: The Shape of Late Medieval Thought Illustrated by Key Documents*, ed. Heiko Oberman [Philadelphia: Fortress, 1981], 170; Schwiebert, *Luther and His Times*, 169; Heiko Augustinus Oberman, *The Harvest of Medieval Theology: Gabriel Biel and Medieval Nominalism* [Durham, NC: Labyrinth, 1983], 53, 128–45), Duns Scotus, Jean Gerson, and by Luther's fellow Augustinians in the monastery in Erfurt, Johannes von Paltz and Johannes von Staupitz. While many, like Gerson, Paltz, and Staupitz, tried to minimize how much we humans can contribute and maximize the merits of Christ, they still regarded some human contribution as necessary to salvation (Berndt Hamm, "Volition and Inadequacy as a Topic in Late Medieval Pastoral Care of Penitents," in *The Reformation in the Context of Late Medieval Theology and Piety: Essays by Berndt Hamm*, ed. Robert J. Bast [Boston, MA: Brill, 2004], 88–127).

[15] LW 12:341–42; 25:497; 26:173–74; LW 33.

[16] Luther, *Commentary on the First Twenty-Two Psalms*, 2:114 = WA 5:444.

[17] "Accordingly, even the life eternal, which is surely the wages of good works, is called a grace of God by the Apostle. . . . We are, therefore, to understand that even man's merited goods are gifts from God, and when life eternal is given through them, what else do we have but 'grace upon grace returned'?" (Augustine, *Enchiridion* 28.107).

Thomas Aquinas, *Summa Theologica*, 2[1].109.3–10, 2[1].114.1–9; Thomas Aquinas, *On Charity*, trans. Lettie H. Kendzierski [Milwaukee: Marquette University Press, 1960], 22; Nygren, *Agape and Eros*, 513–14.

beyond our reach because of the sin that still clings to us. For Luther, a Christian may grow in the sanctified life, but only as one who has already been justified and united with Christ through faith.[18] Any suggestion that we are justified on the basis of our love for God or neighbor or our newness of life—regardless of whether these things are infused into us by God or not—is to replace Christ with an idol.[19]

Many scholars have characterized the medieval path of salvation as a human ascent to God via the ladders of virtue, speculation, and mysticism. God has done his bit to give us the help we need, but now we must do our bit to ascend to him via the paths he has provided.[20] Luther rejects all such attempts to climb up to God in this way as futile. He insists instead that the only ladder between us and heaven is Christ and his Word, to the exclusion of all human works, merits, and speculation.[21] He writes,

> the pope also has his own ladder and his own path leading to heaven. Each monastic order has its own way of ascent too; the Franciscans want to be saved by their rules, and the Augustinians want to go to heaven by theirs. . . . But the only way, ladder, and bridge for ascending into heaven is Christ, the Son of man, who is the only one ever to ascend into heaven. Any other way, ladder, or bridge is invented and dreamed up, yes, useless and vain. . . . The Turks say: "Whoever observes the Koran ascends into heaven." The Jews claim: "Whoever keeps the Law of Moses has a way of ascending into heaven." The pope declares: "Whoever obeys me ascends into heaven." There is no end or limit to the variety of methods. But they all prescribe heavenward journeys on which the travelers will break their necks.[22]

This is because,

---

[18] *Lectures on Galatians* (1535), LW 27:68–71 = WA 40/2:87–90.

[19] *Lectures on Galatians* (1535), LW 26:398 = WA 40/1:606.

[20] Anders Nygren gives examples of this in the theology of Augustine, pseudo-Dionysius, the Monastic Rule of Benedict, John Climacus, Maximus the Confessor, John Scotus Erigena, Dante's *Divine Comedy*, Aquinas, Bonaventura, and Bernard of Clairvaux (Nygren, *Agape and Eros*, trans. Philip S. Watson [New York: Harper Torchbooks, 1969], 512–32, 576–637); Irving Singer finds additional examples in Hugh and Richard of St Victor (Irving Singer, *The Nature of Love: Plato to Luther* [New York: Random House, 1966], 173–74, 189–92). Cf. Hamm, "Volition and Inadequacy," 89–90; Robert Norman Swanson, *Religion and Devotion in Europe, c. 1215 – c. 1515* (Cambridge, UK: Cambridge University Press, 1995), 195.

[21] LW 1:13–14; 3:274–77; 5:197, 215–24, 249–50; 6:104; 17:326; 22:200–209, 305–6, 329–36, 366–68; 23:55–56, 80, 102; 24:48; 26:30; 29:111; 40:147; 43:54–55; 44:319; WLS 1160–61 (3715).

[22] *Sermons on John* (1537–40), LW 22:330, 334 = WA 47:58.6–10, 21–25; 61.36–39.

> The whole lot of them are seeking heaven with lamps that have no oil [Matt. 25:1–13]. In other words, they seek heaven by means of their own works. Without their own works they expect nothing of God, for this is what their way of life and their vows teach them. But a Christian man ascends to heaven by virtue of the works of another, and that other is Christ.[23]

In chapter 8, we will discuss the paths of speculation and mystical experience by which people attempt to come to God. In this chapter we will look at the ladder of works.

WORKS RIGHTEOUSNESS: SELF-JUSTIFICATION THROUGH KEEPING (A VERSION OF) THE LAW

The most obvious way to justify ourselves is to claim that we keep the Law. Luther calls this making an idol of our righteousness,[24] and worshipping the work of our hands.[25] It involves denying Christ who redeems us,[26] setting ourselves up in his place,[27] and making ourselves equal to God, since he alone is righteous.[28]

Luther was convinced that works-righteousness was not only a feature of the church of his day, but also of Judaism, Islam, pagan idolatry, and human life in general.[29] Our sinful nature hates to have its sins exposed and hear that its righteousness is nothing before God.[30] It clings instead to the belief that we can do something to measure up.

This involves a false picture of God's Law. Since none of us is genuinely righteous apart from Christ, if we want to convince ourselves that we are righteous we must tailor God's Law to suit ourselves.[31] This can be done in the following way:

---

[23] *The Judgement of Martin Luther on Monastic Vows* (1521), LW 44:319 = WA 8:618.28–31.

[24] LW 4:148–49; 9:104; 14:202, 438; 16:249; 17:107–8; 36:217; 51:17.

[25] LW 4:165; 18:255.

[26] LW 14:34; 36:216–17.

[27] LW 4:68; 26:257–59; Luther, *Commentary on the First Twenty-Two Psalms*, 2:117.

[28] *Operationes in Psalmos* (1519–21), LW 14:348 = WA 5:73.

[29] LW 17:22–23; 22:330; 26:395–96; 27:88; 29:48–49; Luther, *Commentary on the First Twenty-Two Psalms*, 2:115–16, 229.

[30] Luther, *Commentary on the First Twenty-Two Psalms*, 2:417–18 = *Operationes in Psalmos* (1519–21), WA 5:657.

[31] *Lectures on Isaiah* (1527–30), LW 16:14 = WA 31/2.9.

First, omit the chief work of God's Law, the First Commandment, since this excludes self-righteousness and can only be fulfilled through faith in Christ.[32]

Second, focus on outward works, and forget that the Law is spiritual and goes right to the heart.[33]

Third, focus on a few works while ignoring the rest. As Luther writes,

> The repentance of the Papists, Turks, Jews, and all infidels and hypocrites is similar in all aspects. . . . It consists in experiencing sorrow and doing satisfaction for one or more actual sins, in then being secure regarding other sins or original sin. . . . their repentance is partial and temporal, only about some sins in some part of life.[34]

Finally, focus on self-chosen works instead of the works God commands. Luther writes that those who are self-righteous annul God's commands so they can set up their own.[35] This is because the works and worship of God mortify the sinful nature and only appeal to the eyes of faith.[36] In contrast, the works we choose nourish the sinful nature,[37] which loves to dress up its idolatry with an outward show of piety and works that glitter in the eyes of the world.[38]

External religion. One common form of works-righteousness is external religion. People perform some religious duty and then feel very holy, while despising the actual commands and promises of God.[39]

Many of the outward acts of worship people perform are neither good nor bad in themselves. What makes them idolatrous is the opinion attached to them—that one can be justified through them. Luther writes,

> Superstition and idolatry would not be idolatry and superstition if being sanctified and cleansed were not added. God has no objection

---

[32] LW 26:257; cf. LW 44:29–33; 4:68–69; John 6:29.

[33] LW 9:63, 71, 75–76, 102, 260.

[34] Martin Luther, *Solus Decalogus Est Aeternus: Martin Luther's Complete Antinomian Theses and Disputations*, ed. and trans. Holger Sonntag (Minneapolis, MN: Lutheran Press, 2008), 229 = WA 39/1:345.16–29.

[35] LW 17:17; 22:367.

[36] *Admonition Concerning the Sacrament of the Body and Blood of Our Lord* (1530), LW 38:106–8 = WA 30/2:602–4.

[37] Luther, *Commentary on the First Twenty-Two Psalms*, 2:161–62 = *Operationes in Psalmos* (1519–21), WA 5:474.

[38] LW 16:185 = WA 31/2:130.2–3; LW 9:165 = WA 14:668.11–13.

[39] LW 27:31, 59, 61, 221.

> if the papists are shaved and anointed to the point of wearing out the barbers, or whether they eat this or that. But when they add sanctification and trust, this God cannot put up with.[40]

Luther regarded monastic observances as a perfect example of this kind of idolatry. He therefore picked up Isaiah's mockery of heathen idolatry and applied it to them. A heathen takes a piece of wood. He burns half as fuel for his fire. With what is left he makes an image to appease his god (Isa 44:13–20). A Franciscan takes a rope. He uses one part to tie up his wagon. He ties the rest around his waist to win God's favor.[41] Luther continues,

> To wear the cowl is not yet idolatry . . . but to attach the name and form of justification to that cowl, this is an idol. In itself fasting is not idolatry, but the opinion attached to it is idolatry. If anyone does not put his trust in these works but simply does them, he does not sin.[42]

Often idolatrous religion is an imitation of godly worship in some way, since the devil and his followers ape the true God. Yet they despise the kernel and admire the husk. They imitate the outward forms but remove the Gospel and faith in Christ.[43] Luther uses the example of the Lord's Supper, which Christ instituted, but which the pope made into idolatry by removing the promise of the Gospel and turning it into a meritorious human work.[44] Therefore Luther says that all false religion is *ex opere operato*,[45] and that every *opus operatum* is idolatrous.[46] Idolaters all try to please God by the mere performance of some work, apart from faith in God's promises through Christ.

Luther does not conclude from this that we should discard external things. If Christ has commanded us to baptize with water, celebrate the Lord's Supper by eating and drinking, or perform other outward acts like honoring our parents, then we must do them. Yet we should pay particular attention to the words and promises God has attached to them, and this is where our faith

---

[40] *Lectures on Isaiah* (1527–30), LW 17:412 = WA 31/2:582.4–8.

[41] *Lectures on Isaiah* (1527–30), LW 17:22–23, 112–13 = WA 31/2:277–78, 349–50.

[42] *Lectures on Isaiah* (1527–30), LW 17:23 = WA 31/2:278.18–21.

[43] LW 4:235–38; 15:183; 16:14–15, 331; 44:29–33.

[44] *Lectures on Genesis* (1538–42), LW 4:236–37 = WA 43:304–6; cf. LW 13:314; 23:207; 35:91, 101; 36:148; 39:168.

[45] "By the performance of the work." Luther here is referring to the belief that God's grace can be obtained by the mere performance of some religious rite or action (such as participation in the mass), without faith in Christ. An *opus operatum* is the work performed.

[46] LW 54:436 = WA TR 5:198.

must reside.[47] If we forget God's promises, we will not rid ourselves of idolatry even if all physical idols are taken away. We might remove the idols from before our eyes, but not from our hearts. Instead, we will be like the Pharisees and Sadducees, who had no gods of wood or stone, yet set up many idols in their hearts as they tried to justify themselves.[48]

This involves a false picture of God and of ourselves. Those who think they can justify themselves through their works have a false picture of themselves. They reject God's verdict on them, that they are sinners, and thus in effect charge God with lying.[49]

Self-righteous people also have a false picture of God. The true God is gracious. He gives his favor as a gift. He gives to all people and receives nothing in return. Yet those who seek to earn his favor deny that he is merciful and turn him into a huckster whose favor must be bought.[50] They picture him as an angry judge who must be appeased by their works.[51] One imagines a god who has regard for his rope.[52] Another dreams up a cowled god, who wants to save anyone who wears a cowl.[53] Others think God will reward them for their fasting, chastity, or labor, and that without these God will give them nothing.[54] Thus they all make him out to be a liar, by refusing to believe his promise of salvation through Christ.[55] They then fashion and shape him according to their own opinions, as if they are the creators and he is the creature. They imagine a god who will bless them for their petty self-chosen deeds, though no such god exists.[56]

ANTINOMIANISM: SELF-JUSTIFICATION THROUGH SILENCING THE LAW

The second way we can attempt to justify ourselves is to adopt the strategy of the antinomians, who deny or silence God's Law.

As Luther contends, antinomianism is driven by the sinful nature, which does not want to die through repentance, but wants to indulge its desires

---

[47] *Lectures on Isaiah* (1527–30), LW 17:113 = WA 31/2:350.

[48] *Lectures on Zechariah: The German Text* (1527), LW 20:332 = WA 23:651.

[49] LW 4:159; 14:168.

[50] LW 4:68; 9:53–54; 12:322, 389; 13:374–75; 17:24; 18:9–10; 19:115; 38:106–7; 44:30–31; 54:340; Luther, *Commentary on the First Twenty-Two Psalms*, 2:52, 389–90 (sic).

[51] LW 17:108 = WA 31/2:345–46; 22:365–66.

[52] *Lectures on Isaiah* (1527–30), LW 17:112–13 = WA 31/2:349–50.

[53] LW 1:14; 17:16–17, 22.

[54] LW 17:162; 19:55–56; 22:152, 154–55; 29:49; 30:246.

[55] *The Freedom of the Christian* (1520), LW 31:350 = WA 7:53–54.

[56] LW 9:54; 12:378–79; 17:16–17, 22, 24, 107–9, 112–13; 18:9–10; 29:49; 30:246; 38:106–7; Luther, *Commentary on the First Twenty-Two Psalms*, 2:119, 122.

instead.[57] The sinful nature cannot receive the righteousness that comes from God's Spirit.[58] Yet although it is not righteous, it does not want to admit it. It hates to have its conscience burdened or its pretend righteousness denounced.[59] Therefore it reacts in anger when its sins are rebuked.[60]

Antinomians often try to silence the Law in the name of God's mercy.[61] Yet they want mercy without repentance.[62] Thus they show that they despise God's mercy, and are without faith, since genuine faith casts out love of sin.[63] Luther's final verdict on those who use the Gospel as a license to sin is that they are worse idolaters than the Papists.[64]

Antinomianism is really a form of the righteousness of the Law. Antinomians do not want to be justified by God's mercy, but want to establish a righteousness of their own. Therefore they cannot accept that the Law condemns them, and try to silence any law that challenges their presumption of virtue. They want their sins approved, not forgiven, and spring to their defense. Therefore Luther suggests that antinomians are self-righteous and proud of their own sanctity.[65]

This point needs to be stressed. Luther does not charge antinomians merely with lawlessness;[66] he charges them also with self-righteousness. He calls antinomianism "an alien and new way of teaching justification,"[67] and recognizes that it is really a strategy for self-justification. For "when sin is ignored, a false innocence is presumed."[68]

We noted earlier that Luther regarded the repentance of all who are outside of Christ to be the same. They all practice partial repentance by

---

[57] LW 3:221–24, 240; 4:50–51, 63, 241–42, 404–5; 54:308; Luther, *Antinomian Theses and Disputations*, 375.

[58] Luther, *Commentary on the First Twenty-Two Psalms*, 2:230 = *Operationes in Psalmos* (1519–21), WA 5:518.

[59] LW 1:169; 3:221, 223; 4:49–50; 22:389–90; Luther, *Commentary on the First Twenty-Two Psalms*, 2:230.

[60] LW 3:221, 281.

[61] LW 3:222; 4:49–52, 241–42, 404–5; 41:113, 147; 54:308; Luther, *Antinomian Theses and Disputations*, 237.

[62] LW 3:222–24, 240; 4:241–42, 404–5; 41:113–14, 147; Luther, *Antinomian Theses and Disputations*, 237.

[63] LW 4:405; 22:389; 26:155.

[64] *Lectures on Galatians* (1535), LW 27:51 = WA 40/2:64; cf. Luther, *Antinomian Theses and Disputations*, 53.

[65] LW 1:169; 3:239–40, 314; 4:49–53; 22:389; Luther, *Antinomian Theses and Disputations*, 375.

[66] Although he talks about this too, stressing how God's Law is needed to restrain chaos and anarchy (LW 22:389; 54:233, 248; Luther, *Antinomian Theses and Disputations*, 373]).

[67] Luther, *Antinomian Theses and Disputations*, 41 = WA 39/1:360.14.

[68] Luther, *Antinomian Theses and Disputations*, 137 = WA 39/1:348.19–20.

repenting of some sins, while remaining secure regarding the rest. Luther made this assertion in a disputation against the antinomians. This means he was lumping antinomians together with legalists. We noted earlier how no legalist can actually keep God's Law. They all change it to suit themselves. They commend themselves for keeping certain laws, but are antinomians regarding the rest.[69] Indeed, the more they try to justify themselves through the Law the more they hate it. Its demands wear them out, and they hate God's true, spiritual Law, since it convicts them.[70] Antinomians on the other hand can never expel the Law. At one point Luther says that the antinomians are worse than the Papists, since the Papists teach a partial repentance, whereas the antinomians teach none at all.[71] Yet Luther also recognized that try as they might, antinomians can never get rid of the Law. It always creeps back in. They cannot remove it because it is written on the heart and cannot be erased.[72] Therefore both antinomians and legalists end up with a partial law, designed to justify themselves.[73]

This desire to justify ourselves means that the knowledge of God's Law in our conscience can actually drive us to commit evil. When this knowledge is not combined with faith in the Gospel of Jesus Christ, it leads people to commit all kinds of sins against the truth in an attempt to silence its accusing voice.[74] Therefore the Law increases the trespass (Rom 5:20; cf. SA III ii 2)—not because the Law is evil, but because the human will is perverse.[75]

This involves a false view of God and of ourselves. The antinomians with whom Luther had to contend had a lot to say about Christ and his grace. Yet Luther said they had neither Christ nor his grace, but rather an idol.[76]

---

[69] Tae Jun Suk notes that in his Galatians commentary Luther treats legalism and antinomianism as two sides to the one coin (Suk, *Luther's Concept of Idolatry*, 72). He accuses the papists and the sectarian fanatics of trying to impose "a yoke of slavery" (Gal 5:1) while at the same time setting aside God's true Law and wanting to use their "freedom as an opportunity for the flesh" (Gal 5:13; LW 27:8, 52–54).

[70] Luther, *Commentary on the First Twenty-Two Psalms*, 2:414, 417 (sic).

[71] Luther, *Antinomian Theses and Disputations*, 235, 237 = WA 39/1:352.

[72] Ibid., 233; LW 47:110–11, 113.

[73] Cf. SD V 1.

[74] For a helpful contemporary reflection on this point, see J. Budziszewski, *The Revenge of the Conscience: Politics and the Fall of Man* (Dallas: Spence Publishing, 1999), 20–35; and J. Budziszewski, *What We Can't Not Know: A Guide* (Dallas: Spence Publishing, 2003), 139–60.

[75] Luther, *Commentary on the First Twenty-Two Psalms*, 2:417–18 (sic) = *Operationes in Psalmos* (1519–21), WA 5:559.

[76] *Lectures on Galatians* (1535), LW 27:51 = WA 40/2:64; *Lectures on Genesis* (1538–42), LW 3:336 = WA 43:116.

They spoke about God, Christ, faith, Law, grace, and so on, but understood these as much as a parrot understands his "hello."[77]

Antinomians want to eliminate the fear of God and his judgment,[78] so they can feel secure without repenting.[79] One way to do this is to adopt a distorted view of ourselves, and claim that we are already so holy and pleasing to God that we do not need to repent.[80] Maybe we think our sin is nothing—so trivial that God will not be bothered by it.[81] Maybe we think that some physical prerogative such as ancestry, circumcision, fasting, pilgrimages, or wearing a cowl makes us so holy that we are above God's Law and guaranteed his favor.[82] Maybe we dream that we are still as righteous as Adam was in paradise,[83] or as the elect will be in heaven. Since sanctification in us is never complete in this world,[84] Luther says that the only people for whom the teaching of the antinomians is relevant have already been taken from this life.[85]

The other way to eliminate the fear of God is to reject the biblical picture of a holy God who hates evil and cannot ignore injustice, and replace him with a lenient or distant god who does not judge human sin.[86] Luther at one point suggests that antinomians hope "the devil is across the ocean and God is tucked in our pocket."[87] They think God is tame or indulgent, and we have nothing to fear from him or the devil. At another point Luther suggests that all secure sinners—in whose ranks he includes the antinomians—give no thought to God and his Word when they are engrossed in sinning. They act as if he does not see what they are doing, but is asleep, blind, dead, impotent, far away, or non-existent.[88]

Since they eliminate the fear of God, antinomians also eliminate Christ.[89] Those who eliminate the condemnation of the Law eliminate our need for a Savior.[90] Those who belittle the disease belittle the cure.[91] Satan knows very

---

[77] Luther, *Antinomian Theses and Disputations*, 375 = WA 39/1:358.31–32.

[78] *Lectures on Genesis* (1538–42), LW 4:241–42 = WA 43:308–9.

[79] LW 3:222, 239–40, 314; 22:389; 41:114; 47:119.

[80] LW 3:225; 4:49–50, 52, 237–43; 54:233–34.

[81] *Lectures on Genesis* (1538–42), LW 4:240 = WA 43:308.

[82] LW 4:49–50, 52, 237–43.

[83] LW 54:308, 233–34.

[84] Luther, *Antinomian Theses and Disputations*, 43, 245 = WA 39/1:361, 356.

[85] Luther, *Antinomian Theses and Disputations*, 243–45 = WA 39/1:355–56.

[86] *Lectures on Genesis* (1538–42), LW 3:220–21 = WA 43:33.

[87] *Against the Antinomians* (1539), LW 47:114 = WA 50:473.40; cf. LW 47:11, 19.

[88] *Lectures on Genesis* (1535–38), LW 2:219–22 = WA 418–19.

[89] Luther, *Antinomian Theses and Disputations*, 247, 249 = WA 39/1:357.

[90] Ibid., 57, 137; LW 47:110–13.

well that the Law cannot be erased from our hearts, nor can its consequences be removed from our lives apart from Christ. Yet Christ can be taken away from us, and this is the devil's goal. The diabolical purpose at work is to accustom people to ignore the Law so they do not flee to Christ.[92]

In addition to eliminating any need for Christ's redemption, antinomians also eliminate the new life in Christ that the Holy Spirit works in us. Luther says that although the antinomians teach about Christ, grace, forgiveness, and redemption, when they preach Christ against the Holy Spirit it is evident that they have no Christ.[93] Those who have the Spirit are taught by him to despise their sin and love God's will instead.[94] Antinomians on the other hand have clearly rejected the Spirit since they do not struggle against the sinful nature.[95] When they separate Christ from the sanctifying work of the Spirit in this way, they proclaim a new, false Christ. They have forgotten that Christ purchased us so that his Spirit might transform us into new people who live for righteousness. They therefore take Christ away at the same time as they proclaim him![96] They may use the name of Christ, but their Christ is an idol who justifies sin instead of sinners.

THE CONSEQUENCES OF SELF-JUSTIFICATION

Try as we might to justify ourselves, the idols we establish for this purpose all fail to make us righteous or win for us God's approval.

Enduring guilt. Since no idol can atone for sin, or take our guilt and shame away, they leave us under God's wrath. Though idolaters try to cast out fear, they have everything to fear, since God will judge them and they will perish.[97] The self-confidence of those who try to justify themselves must be destroyed or they will never be saved.[98]

Unstable conscience. This inability to eradicate guilt means that idols cannot give us a peaceful conscience. Instead, the conscience they deliver is

---

[91] Luther, *Commentary on the First Twenty-Two Psalms*, 420–21 = *Operationes in Psalmos* (1519–21), WA 5:659.

[92] LW 47:110–13; cf. Luther, *Antinomian Theses and Disputations*, 139, 373; Luther, *Commentary on the First Twenty-Two Psalms*, 420–21.

[93] *On the Councils and the Church* (1539), LW 41:113–15 = WA 50:599–600.

[94] LW 41:143–44; Luther, *Antinomian Theses and Disputations*, 37, 45, 139, 141, 239, 245, 247, 249.

[95] LW 4:241–42; 41:113–14, 145–47.

[96] *On the Councils and the Church* (1539), LW 41:113–15, 145–47 = WA 50:599–600, 626–27.

[97] LW 2:223–25; 3:222–24, 278–82; 4:63, 158–59, 241–42, 404–5; 12:322; 14:348; 16:106; 17:110, 116; 18:39, 167, 308; 20:236, 239–40; 22:158, 389–90; 23:121; 27:80; Luther, *Commentary on the First Twenty-Two Psalms*, 2:167, 239–40.

[98] *Lectures on Genesis* (1538–42), LW 4:53 = WA 43:173.

unstable.[99] Luther writes, "By the works of the law, men either become proud and presume, or else, they fall into despair and hate God."[100] The same project of self-justification can lead to either pride or despair, or both, as the conscience vacillates between the two.

Those who justify themselves feel proud and secure when things go well. They are arrogant toward God and look down on other people.[101] Luther says that those who feel secure based on the Law are impenitent and contemptuous of God.[102] All their righteousness is a sham designed to honor and lift up themselves.[103] Indeed, "a self-righteous person is a thief of the divine glory and also an idolater, because he lays claim to God's glory for himself."[104]

Yet this pride can easily turn to dismay. The righteousness of the Law provides no genuine security. The same people quickly become despondent, discouraged, and despairing as soon as things go badly, or they experience God's wrath, or they cannot assuage the conviction of sin.[105] Just like self-righteous pride, this despair is a form of impenitence. It is blasphemy against the Holy Spirit, a denial of his compassion, and a refusal to give up the goal of self-justification.[106]

Hypocrisy. Self-justification always leads to a hypocritical pretense of righteousness rather than the real thing.[107] Even when people strive to keep certain parts of God's Law, this Law can only change the works, not the doers of the works.[108] Only the Gospel can change our hearts so we keep God's Law from the heart, with love for God and neighbor. The Law by itself can convert

---

[99] LW 9:291; 12:164; 17:162; 18:254–55; 20:235; 22:158; 29:49; Luther, *Commentary on the First Twenty-Two Psalms*, 2:415 (sic).

[100] Luther, *Commentary on the First Twenty-Two Psalms*, 2:390 (sic) = *Operationes in Psalmos* (1519–1521), WA 5:543:24–25; cf. Luther, *Antinomian Theses and Disputations*, 27.

[101] LW 9:273; 19:57; 21:217; Luther, *Commentary on the First Twenty-Two Psalms*, 2:414–15 (sic).

[102] Luther, *Antinomian Theses and Disputations*, 235 = WA 39/1:352.

[103] LW 3:336; 9:54; 14:34; 17:162; Luther, *Commentary on the First Twenty-Two Psalms*, 2:390 (sic), 2:419.

[104] *Lectures on Isaiah* (1527–30), LW 17:162 = WA 31/2:387.31–32; cf. 44:319–20.

[105] Luther, *Commentary on the First Twenty-Two Psalms*, 2:413–15 (sic); LW 1:169–72; 2:222–23; 12:378–79; 16:160–61; 17:109–10; 19:57; Luther, *Antinomian Theses and Disputations*, 33, 35 = WA 39/1:345.16–346.29.

[106] Luther, *Antinomian Theses and Disputations*, 235 = WA 39/1:352.22–27; LW 4:68–69; 16:14–15.

[107] LW 20:237–38; 29:49; 39:192; 44:33–34; Luther, *Commentary on the First Twenty-Two Psalms*, 2:413–15 (sic).

[108] Luther, *Commentary on the First Twenty-Two Psalms*, 2:391 (sic) = *Operationes in Psalmos* (1519–21), WA 5:544.

the hand but not the heart.[109] It therefore makes people hypocrites. Though they perform works outwardly, they do them reluctantly, or with a view to their own advantage, without the love and affection that comes from the Spirit.[110] Since their righteousness is a sham, they live a lie and sin in secret.[111]

Entitlement rather than gratitude. Far from producing genuine love for God, self-justification breaks down all thankfulness toward him by breeding a sense of entitlement.[112] If God's favor can be bought, and we have paid our dues, then God owes us. We are like taxpayers. We have rights. So how dare he bring misfortune upon us![113]

Luther observes that if we justify ourselves, we will condemn God. If we consider our will to be holy, we will condemn his as unholy whenever it conflicts with ours. In particular, we will charge him with injustice when trouble comes upon us. Yet if we condemn ourselves as sinners, we will justify God. Only then will we recognize that any hardship he brings upon us is less than we deserve, and any good he gives us is unmerited kindness.[114]

Exhaustion. All that the idol of self-righteousness can ultimately do for its devotees is make them weary and anxious. Luther calls self-righteous people "the devil's martyrs."[115] They sacrifice all their strength seeking to justify themselves, only to inevitably fail.

Luther gives two reasons why this idol exacts great toil from those who follow it. First, like all idols, the idol of self-righteousness is based on deception, and "a lie requires much labour and care to make it appear like truth."[116] Second, the works of the Law have no end for those who seek to be justified by them. They can never forgive sins or deliver a quiet conscience. Therefore those who seek to be justified by them keep piling up more in the vain hope that eventually they will have enough.[117]

---

[109] Ibid., 2:410 (sic); *Commentary on Psalm 2* (1532), LW 12:87 = WA 40/2:304.

[110] Luther, *Commentary on the First Twenty-Two Psalms*, 2:22, 228–29, 407–9 (sic).

[111] LW 16:229; 35:372–73.

[112] Cf. Karen Horney, *Neurosis and Human Growth: The Struggle Toward Self-Realization* (New York: W. W. Norton, 1950), 40–63; Jean M. Twenge and W. Keith Campbell, *The Narcissism Epidemic: Living in the Age of Entitlement* (New York: Free Press, 2009), 19–20, 196–97, 230–43.

[113] Cf. Timothy Keller, "Smashing False Idols: Gospel Communication," 2007, The Evangelists Conference, www.evangelists-conference.org.uk/2F014-02GospelCommunication.mp3 (accessed Sept. 15, 2009)

[114] Luther, *Commentary on the First Twenty-Two Psalms*, 1:18, 80, 86, 159–63, 205; 2:33–34, 192, 234–39, 427–28 (sic).

[115] *Lectures on Isaiah* (1527–30), LW 17:110, 112, 299 = WA 31/2:348.14, 349.16, 491.1.

[116] Luther, *Commentary on the First Twenty-Two Psalms*, 2:121 = *Operationes in Psalmos* (1519–21), WA 5:448.34–35.

[117] LW 17:110–12, 116; 20:235; 26:406; 33:288–89; Luther, *Commentary on the First Twenty-Two Psalms*, 2:121–24, 415 (sic), 417 (sic).

SUMMARY

Luther writes, "For peace of conscience they 'multiply idols' to themselves."[118] He teaches that whenever people are without faith in Christ's justifying work they will inevitably be driven by guilt to create idols, in the false hope that these will justify. This involves two basic strategies: self-justification by attempting to keep the Law, and self-justification by attempting to silence the Law. In practice, both strategies end up at the same point: self-justification through tailoring the Law to excuse our sins and commend our works. This is a highly unstable enterprise, since it is based on self-deception regarding both the true content of God's Law and our standing before him. It leads to arrogance while this deception holds, but despair when the cracks appear.

CONTEMPORARY APPLICATION

If Luther's assessment of the human condition is accurate, then we should expect to see fallen people engaged in a never-ending quest for self-justification, driven along by a guilty conscience that knows God's Law but can find no rest from its accusations apart from Christ.[119] In the remainder of this chapter I will highlight some ways in which this is evident in our society.

THE PERVASIVENESS OF SELF-JUSTIFICATION

In the culture of Papua New Guinea in which I lived as a child, the wisest leaders in the church and the community knew that in order to resolve any conflict it was necessary to provide one's opponent with the opportunity to save face. If an opponent was backed into a corner from which they could not escape without losing face, they would turn and fight like a cornered dog and the conflict would drag on interminably. Yet if they were given the opportunity to back down without being shamed the conflict could often be resolved. This wisdom, distilled from much practical experience, reveals how desperately people seek to be justified.

A similar form of cultural wisdom is present in Western society, which has learnt from psychologists that self-esteem is an essential component in mental and emotional wellbeing. A whole range of psychologists, from Carl Rogers to Abraham Maslow, Fritz Perls, and Erich Fromm, has regarded lack

---

[118] Luther, *Commentary on the First Twenty-Two Psalms*, 2:124 = *Operationes in Psalmos* (1519–21), WA 5:450.10.

[119] Note Oswald Bayer's discussion of justification as something that we are under compulsion to engage in, and is therefore "being done always and everywhere" (*Living by Faith: Justification and Sanctification*, trans. Geoffrey W. Bromiley [Grand Rapids, MI: Eerdmans, 2003], 1).

of self-esteem to be one of the most basic human problems.[120] From the perspective of Luther's theology this diagnosis is accurate. People do have a deep-seated need to be justified, so they can hold their heads up instead of hanging them in shame. Luther would disagree with the remedy that modern psychologists usually prescribe. He would have no time for the suggestion that we should redouble our efforts to justify ourselves, either by reducing the demands we place on ourselves (i.e., trying to silence the Law), or by constantly affirming ourselves and trying to excel (i.e., trying to measure up before the Law). Despite this, he would whole-heartedly agree with the diagnosis.

The description of self-justification from social psychology. The human process of self-justification has been described in detail in recent decades by social psychologists. The first step is to pass the buck and blame everyone but ourselves for our moral failures. As the social psychologist David Myers points out, we look in vain for anyone to take responsibility for atrocities such as My Lai or Auschwitz.[121] Then, if we cannot disown our actions, we try to justify them instead. The psychologist Karl Menninger writes, "Every slayer finds reasons for making his particular violation an exception, a non-crime if not a non-sin. Hitler had his reasons for killing the Jews. Custer had his reasons for killing the Sioux. Our military men had reasons for killing the Viet Cong soldiers, and the Viet Cong had their reasons for killing ours."[122]

In the previous chapter we noted Langdon Gilkey's observation of how his compatriots in the internment camp found ways to rationalize their selfish behavior. This same tendency to rationalize has been observed in experimental psychology. Elliot Aronson, one of the leading researchers of the phenomenon known as cognitive dissonance, says it is more accurate to refer to humans as rationalizing animals than rational animals.[123] Cognitive dissonance theory suggests that when people's behavior challenges what they want to believe about themselves—that they are moral and rational—they will find ways to rationalize this behavior to remove the dissonance.[124]

---

[120] Terry D. Cooper, *Sin, Pride, & Self-Acceptance: The Problem of Identity in Theology & Psychology* (Downers Grove, IL: InterVarsity, 2003), 8–10.

[121] David Myers, *The Inflated Self: Human Illusions and the Biblical Call to Hope* (New York: Seabury Press, 1981), 22.

[122] Karl Menninger, *Whatever Became of Sin?* (New York: Hawthorn Books, Inc., 1973), 14.

[123] Elliot Aronson, "The Rationalizing Animal," in *Psychology is Social: Readings and Conversations in Social Psychology*, ed. Edward Krupat (2nd ed.; Dallas: Scott, Foresman and Co., 1982), 76.

[124] Ibid., 81.

Many experiments have confirmed this phenomenon. One finding is that before people make a decision they look for as much information as possible about the different alternatives, but after they have made a decision they only look for confirmation that they have made the right decision, while minimizing or ignoring disconfirming evidence. So for instance, a person who has just built a home on the San Andreas Fault will be far less receptive to information about the danger of earthquakes than a person who is merely renting, since acknowledging the validity of this evidence could call into question the wisdom of the investment.[125]

Another finding is that people shift their views of others and of the boundary between right and wrong to justify their behavior. For instance, in one experiment children were asked about their attitudes to cheating. Then they were put in a competitive situation in which it was impossible to win without cheating. After the competition their attitudes to cheating were retested. Those children who had cheated had now become more lenient in their attitudes to cheating, while those who resisted the temptation had become more strict.[126] This agrees with Luther's contention that people fit the Law to their works.

Still another finding is that people routinely justify their cruelty by blaming their victims. In experiments where subjects are induced to inflict cruelty on others, before long they start to convince themselves that their victims are stupid or mean or deserve the cruel treatment in some way. Ironically, the more they think of themselves as kind, the more they can be induced to denigrate their victims, since they need an excuse for their cruelty if they are to maintain their self-image.[127]

David Myers, in agreement with Freud, suggests that the most powerful justifications are moral and religious. He points out how prayer services were held in support of the Hiroshima bombing crew and the white-ruled government of South Africa, and how the most common way to refer to the distinction between whites and blacks in seventeenth-century slave owning America was to speak of Negroes and Christians.[128]

This human tendency to justify ourselves is so pervasive that it is evident not only when it comes to matters of great moral importance, but also in very mundane settings. This is what social psychology experiments have uncovered—a tendency to distort our perceptions of ourselves and others in self-justifying ways in all kinds of everyday situations. Psychologists call this the self-serving bias.

---

[125] Ibid., 77–78.

[126] Ibid., 79.

[127] Ibid., 80–81.

[128] Myers, *The Inflated Self*, 28–29.

One way this manifests is in our attribution of causality. We tend to take credit for our successes yet blame others or circumstances for our failures. For instance, students who receive a good mark on an examination tend to accept it as a good measure of their abilities, whereas students who receive a poor mark tend to criticize the exam as unfair. Or if I win at Scrabble it is because of my verbal dexterity, but if I lose it is because I received a Q but no U.[129] Or in group tasks, the members of the group all want to claim responsibility for the performance of the group when it succeeds, but not when it fails.[130]

Another way the self-serving bias manifests is called the "above average effect". When rating ourselves we tend to overrate our abilities and the contributions we make to society. For instance, one survey of American high school seniors found that 60 percent rated themselves in the top 10 percent when it came to their ability to get along with others, and 25 percent rated themselves in the top 1 percent. Or in marriages, both partners tend to overestimate how much they contribute toward supporting the household, while underestimating how much their partner contributes, so that both are likely to think that they are doing more than their fair share.[131]

This is all evidence that self-justification is part of the standard human *modus operandi*. And if we are all such nice, intelligent, easy to get along with people, who make such outstanding contributions to society, why would we need Christ?

Self-justification in terror management theory. A more recent development in social psychology, which provides more evidence of our tendency to justify ourselves, is the experimental research project spawned by Terror Management Theory.

TMT is based on the premise that we humans must all have a belief system that promises us immortality of some kind, or else the fear of death would overwhelm us. The logic of TMT is as follows. All people know that sooner or later they will die, whether they like it or not. This causes immense anxiety. Nevertheless, few people are crippled by this fear, since we have a defense mechanism against it: our belief systems that promise us immortality. These may include religious beliefs that promise real immortality, or secular beliefs that promise some kind of surrogate immortality. We may hope to live on through an earthly legacy that will survive our death, such as our children, our work or creative achievements, the ideals for which we have fought, the people we have helped or inspired, or the nation we love. Such things

---

[129] Ibid., 21–22.

[130] Ibid., 21, 25–26.

[131] Ibid., 22–27.

convince us that our lives have a greater significance that will live on, and this helps us to cope with our approaching death.[132]

This premise has led to a testable hypothesis, that when we are confronted with death we will assuage our fear by: (1) seeking to bolster our immortality-promising beliefs; and (2) seeking to bolster our self-esteem, or the belief that we measure up according to the standards of our beliefs and can therefore expect to cash in on their promised rewards.[133]

This hypothesis has been rigorously tested and confirmed.[134] The experiments involve calling death to the participants' conscious or subconscious attention, and then seeing if this sparks a "worldview defense" in comparison with a control group.[135] For instance, when a group of judges were reminded of death and then asked to set bail for a case, on average they set bail nearly ten times as high as the control group. This was the expected outcome according to TMT, since it was assumed that judges would cherish the belief that they are serving the greater good by upholding law and order. Therefore, when confronted with death, they would reaffirm this commitment by getting tough on the bad guys.[136] Other experiments found that reminding people of death makes them express more patriotism, less openness toward those who criticize their country, less acceptance of those who challenge their religious views, more aggression toward those who challenge their political views, less willingness to treat icons such as an American flag or a crucifix with disrespect, more willingness to give money to charity, more self-esteem bolstering behavior, and so on.[137] Yet people who already have high self-esteem were found to be less affected by reminders of death.[138] So were those with an

---

[132] Jonas and Fischer, "Terror Management and Religion," 553; Tom Pyszczynski, Sheldon Solomon, and Jeff Greenberg, *In the Wake of 9/11: The Psychology of Terror* (Washington DC: American Psychological Association, 2003), 11–27, 83–84; Sheldon Solomon, Jeff Greenberg, and Tom Pyszczynski, "The Cultural Animal: Twenty Years of Terror Management Theory and Research," in *Handbook of Experimental Existential Psychology*, ed. Jeff Greenberg, Sander L. Koole, and Tom Pyszczynski (New York: Guilford Press, 2004), 13–20.

[133] Jonas and Fischer, "Terror Management and Religion," 553; Solomon, Greenberg, and Pyszczynski, "The Cultural Animal," 20–21.

[134] Jonas and Fischer, "Terror Management and Religion," 554; Pyszczynski, Solomon, and Greenberg, *In the Wake of 9/11*, 37–92; Solomon, Greenberg, and Pyszczynski, "The Cultural Animal," 24.

[135] Jonas and Fischer, "Terror Management and Religion," 556; Pyszczynski, Solomon, and Greenberg, *In the Wake of 9/11*, 45–46, 52–53; Solomon, Greenberg, and Pyszczynski, "The Cultural Animal," 20–21.

[136] Pyszczynski, Solomon, and Greenberg, *In the Wake of 9/11*, 45–47.

[137] Ibid., 47–54, 71–81; Solomon, Greenberg, and Pyszczynski, "The Cultural Animal," 21–23.

[138] Pyszczynski, Solomon, and Greenberg, *In the Wake of 9/11*, 38–44, 81–82; Solomon, Greenberg, and Pyszczynski, "The Cultural Animal," 22–23.

intrinsic religious faith.[139] Evidently people with high self-esteem or an intrinsic faith feel less need to justify themselves and their beliefs than the rest of the population.

The literature on TMT is couched in secular terms and assumes a materialistic, Darwinian framework. Yet the empirical evidence supports Luther's view of the world equally well. When confronted with death, we cling to our gods and try to justify ourselves before them, hoping they will protect us from what we fear. Yet the proud feel more secure in this endeavor, and people of faith feel less need of it. This suggests one reason for why idols so easily gain a powerful hold on the human heart: we desperately need something to calm our fears, including above all our fear of death. Indeed, TMT was developed to explain why people's worldviews have such a powerful emotional hold on them.[140] As the book of Hebrews tells us, Christ came to "deliver all those who through fear of death were subject to lifelong slavery" (2:15). And what does our fear of death enslave us to if not the idols that we hope will give us life?

Low self-esteem or pride? So what should we make of these findings that show the pervasiveness of human attempts at self-justification? Do they prove that we humans are proud and egotistical? Or do they prove that we are compensating for a deeper insecurity and lack of self-esteem?

According to Luther, we should expect that both are true. When we attempt to establish a righteousness or worth of our own apart from Christ we are engaged in an egoistic enterprise, and become proud whenever we think we are succeeding. Yet this is a highly insecure endeavor. It means living in a fool's paradise, which we can only maintain through much self-deception. Therefore it involves the constant danger that reality will break through and plunge us into despair.

The St. Louis psychologist Terry Cooper comes to a remarkably similar conclusion by approaching this question from the perspective of psychology. Cooper notes how both theologians and psychologists are divided over the question of whether pride is the basic human problem, or whether outward

---

[139] Jonas and Fischer, "Terror Management and Religion," 564. See chapter 5, page 83 for the distinction between intrinsic and extrinsic faith.

The vast majority of the religious participants in this study were Christians (ibid., 557, 560, 562). Therefore one could expect that one component of their faith was the Gospel of Jesus Christ. The study was only designed to test the difference between an intrinsic and extrinsic faith, not to test whether the doctrinal content of a person's creed makes any difference. If one adopts Luther's perspective, one would expect that a faith that centers on the Gospel of Jesus Christ (including belief in a genuine resurrection!) would do more to allay the fear of death than a religion of the Law. This has not been examined by psychologists as far as I know, but would make an interesting study.

[140] Pyszczynski, Solomon, and Greenberg, *In the Wake of 9/11*, 11–12; Solomon, Greenberg, and Pyszczynski, "The Cultural Animal," 13–14, 25–26.

manifestations of pride simply conceal a more fundamental insecurity. Theologians like Augustine and Reinhold Niebuhr, and psychologists such as Sigmund Freud, Ralph Greenson, Paul Vitz, and David Myers, have contended that pride is the basic problem. Psychologists such as Carl Rogers, Erich Fromm, Abraham Maslow, and Fritz Perls have suggested the opposite, that lack of self-esteem is the real problem. In this they have been backed up by popular preachers such as Harry Emerson Fosdick, Norman Vincent Peale, and Robert Schuller.[141] Cooper then suggests that both sides are right and both are wrong, since pride and low self-esteem are not opposites, but two sides of the same coin. To show how this is the case he draws on the work of the psychoanalyst Karen Horney, and suggests that what she describes in neurotic patients is simply a more pronounced case of what takes place in us all.[142]

Horney suggests that both pride and self-contempt in neurotic patients are products of what she calls "the pride system."[143] She writes that "Pride and self-hate go inseparably together; they are two expressions of the one process."[144] Horney suggests that neurosis develops when people are confronted with their anxieties about life and their own sense of inadequacy, yet instead of facing this fear head on, or building up self-confidence through real achievements or genuine character development, they enlist their imagination to produce a fantasy about themselves.[145] This means projecting an ideal image of themselves in place of their real selves. They then try to live up to the demands of this idealized self, and to convince themselves and others that this is who they are.[146] They do this through heroic feats of rationalization.[147] Yet the larger the gap between their ideal self and their real self, the harder it is to maintain this illusion. Therefore the more grandiose the image, the more contemptuous they become of their real self, since the more it holds them back from what they imagine themselves to be.[148]

This attempt to construct an ideal image of oneself is an egoistic enterprise, even if it does not always appear egotistical. Horney suggests that a person's ideal image may be quite self-effacing.[149] For instance, a person with a deep need for acceptance from others may think of themselves as a saint or a martyr. They may go to extraordinary lengths to comply with other people

---

[141] Cooper, *Sin, Pride, & Self-Acceptance*, 7–20.

[142] Ibid., 112–47.

[143] Horney, *Neurosis and Human Growth*, 110–11.

[144] Ibid., 109.

[145] Ibid., 86–91.

[146] Ibid., 17–39, 86–91.

[147] Ibid., 22, 94.

[148] Ibid., 86–154.

[149] Ibid., 214–58.

and never upset them. Yet this is just as egoistic as a person who projects an image of strength, and has a win-at-all-costs mentality. Both are trying to live up to an ideal of perfection they can never ultimately attain.[150] This fits perfectly with Luther, who talks about how our sinful nature is so perverted that we even take pride in our humility.[151]

What Horney describes in neurotic patients, Luther says takes place within us all, unless we despair of the attempt to justify ourselves and grasp hold of Christ. Since we are sinners, self-justification always involves constructing a perception of ourselves that does not match the true state of our character or behavior. It therefore shares one of the leading characteristics of narcissistic neurosis, an inflated and unrealistic view of oneself.[152] The attempt to justify ourselves always means constructing a false image of ourselves that we imagine to be true, and leads to an inability to look at our true selves without despairing. This false image is an idol, a phony that supplants Christ. Only in Christ can we face who we truly are, in all the depths of our sin, and still hold our heads up because of what he has claimed us to be.

Summary. Luther suggests that all who are outside of Christ—Jews, Muslims, hypocritical Christians, the irreligious, and even genuine Christians when they fail to live in accordance with their confession of faith in Christ—will all attempt to justify themselves in one way or another. Indeed, they must, since they are driven by a knowledge of how God's Law accuses them. This means that even those who are not overtly religious, and only appear to be concerned with human approval for the sake of this earthly life, are on a more fundamental level trying to justify themselves before God. When contemporary psychologists describe exactly what Luther predicts—an unstable combination of pride and insecurity that produces all kinds of self-justifying behavior—we should recognize this for what it is. It is the idol of the self at work, which wants to displace Christ and establish its own worth apart from him.

Self-Justification through Keeping the Law: "Moralistic Therapeutic Deism"

It is now time to consider some examples in our society of the two major strategies of self-justification that Luther identifies. We will begin with self-justification through keeping the Law.

Much of what passes as Christianity in contemporary society is better described as moralism in a Christian guise. It is more focused on good morals

[150] Ibid., 18–26; Cooper, *Sin, Pride, & Self-Acceptance*, 112–47.

[151] LW 16:263, 332–33, 346–47; Luther, *Commentary on the First Twenty-Two Psalms*, 2:424–25 (sic).

[152] Twenge and Campbell, *The Narcissism Epidemic*, 19–20.

than salvation through faith in Christ. It therefore follows the path of self-justification through keeping the Law.

As we noted in the previous chapter, one of the findings of the National Study of Youth and Religion is that the de facto dominant creed in America is moralistic therapeutic deism. As the name suggests, this is a form of legalism. The majority of young people in America, as well as the adults who taught them this faith, believe that the primary purpose of religion is to instill morals,[153] and teach people how to be nice, kind, pleasant, respectful, responsible, and successful.[154] Then, since they think that all religions are primarily about teaching morality, they conclude that all religions are basically the same.[155] Furthermore, they conclude that religion is non-essential for performing its central role, since they think people can distinguish right from wrong and live good lives without religion. So religion may be useful for teaching children, but once someone has learned what they need to know they can graduate and leave it behind. Some people may decide they still need it to keep them on track, but that is just their own lifestyle choice.[156]

Since moralistic therapeutic deism is common among churchgoers of all denominations, the researchers write,

> Viewed in terms of the absolute historical centrality of the Protestant conviction about salvation by God's grace alone, through faith alone and not by any human good works, many belief professions by Protestant teens, including numerous conservative Protestant teens, in effect discard that essential Protestant gospel.[157]

Later they write,

> A significant part of Christianity in the United States is actually only tenuously Christian in any sense that is seriously connected to the actual historical Christian tradition, but has rather morphed into Christianity's misbegotten stepcousin, Christian Moralistic Therapeutic Deism. This has happened in the minds and hearts of many individual believers and, it also appears, within the structures of at least some Christian organizations and institutions. The language, and therefore the experience, of Trinity, holiness, sin, grace, justification, sanctification, church, Eucharist, and heaven and hell

---

[153] Smith and Denton, *Soul Searching*, 124–27, 136, 155, 163, 167–68, 171; Smith and Snell, *Souls in Transition*, 82–83, 145–49, 154–56.

[154] Smith and Denton, *Soul Searching*, 163.

[155] Smith and Snell, *Souls in Transition*, 82, 145–48.

[156] Ibid., 82–83, 148–49; Smith and Denton, *Soul Searching*, 155–56.

[157] Smith and Denton, *Soul Searching*, 136. By permission of Oxford University Press, USA.

appear, among most Christian teenagers in the United States at the very least, to be supplanted by the language of happiness, niceness, and an earned heavenly reward.[158]

This finding is backed up by the 2008 U.S. Religious Landscape Survey by the Pew Forum on Religion and Public Life. This survey found that the majority (52 percent) of people in America who identify themselves as Christians believe that at least some non-Christian religions can lead to eternal life.[159] This should be expected if large numbers of people think religion is primarily about morality, since non-Christians can be moral too. This was another finding of the same study, that of all the people in the United States who call themselves Christians there are more who think that salvation depends at least partly on our good works than who believe in salvation through faith in Christ alone.[160] Looking through Luther's eyes, this tells us that the idol of self-righteousness is alive and well.

Self-Justification through Silencing the Law

The second strategy for self-justification that Luther identifies is to silence the Law. This is just as evident in contemporary society as self-justification through keeping the Law.

Moral relativism in society. It is impossible to get a handle on ethical discourse in our society without grappling with the basket of views and attitudes that go by the name of moral relativism. By moral relativism people usually mean the belief that moral norms are not fixed for all people in all times and places, but change according to individual or cultural beliefs and circumstances. To count as moral relativism, this must be more than just a recognition that circumstances should be taken into account when it comes to applying moral norms. Instead, it involves the belief that the norms themselves are not fixed, but ever changing.[161]

---

[158] Ibid., 171.

[159] Pew Forum on Religion and Public Life, "Many Americans Say Other Faiths Can Lead to Eternal Life," pewforum.org/docs/?DocID=380 (accessed Jan. 29, 2010).

[160] The study found that of all the people in the U.S. who are affiliated with a religion, 91 percent are Christians (not including Mormons and Jehovah's Witnesses). Yet when asked what determines if a person receives eternal life, only 17 percent of religious people said faith in Jesus Christ. 29 percent said a person's actions, 10 percent said a combination of beliefs and actions, 13 percent said belief in God or other generic beliefs, 21 percent either didn't believe in eternal life, didn't know, or refused to answer the question, and 10 percent gave other answers (Pew Forum, "Many Americans Say Other Faiths Can Lead to Eternal Life").

[161] In judicial law, there is a distinction between a crime that is *malum prohibitum*, evil because society prohibits it, and one that is *malum in se*, evil in itself. Moral relativism denies this distinction, and reduces all evils to the level of *malum prohibitum*. I don't know of any educated

If, like Luther, we accept what the book of Romans says about the natural law, thoroughgoing moral relativism cannot be lived out consistently. Try as we might to expel the demands of God's Law we cannot succeed, since God has built his Law into the fabric of creation, and it does not change along with our changing culture or our changing whims. So despite the rhetoric of moral relativism, this Law always sneaks back in. This is what we see in our society, that moral relativism is accompanied by a new brand of legalism.

This can be seen in every level of society: in popular attitudes, in academia, in the highest level of public life, and in the church. For the sake of brevity, I will restrict my comments to popular attitudes and the church.[162]

First we will look at popular attitudes. A 2002 survey by the Barna Group found that 64 percent of adults and 83 percent of teens agreed with the statement that moral truth always depends on the situation, as opposed to 22 percent of adults and only 6 percent of teens who said there are unchanging moral absolutes. Even among born again Christians,[163] just 32 percent of adults and 9 percent of teens said they believed in moral absolutes.[164] However, this result was contradicted by the 2008 Pew Forum's Religious Landscape Survey. It found that 78 percent of respondents agreed with the statement, "There are

---

person who denies that certain norms are *malum prohibitum*, and change from one society to another. The question is whether all norms can be reduced to that level.

[162] Two places to go for a discussion of relativistic moral theory within the academy, and how it masks certain moral commitments that it doesn't openly acknowledge, are Iris Murdoch, *Existentialists and Mystics: Writings on Philosophy and Literature*, ed. Peter Conradi (New York: Penguin, 1999), 59–75; and Charles Taylor, *Sources of the Self: The Making of the Modern Identity* (Cambridge, MA: Harvard University Press, 1989), 3–32, 53–107, 317–40, 495–521. For an assertion of the right of the individual to construct their own morality by the U.S. Supreme Court—a body that could never live out such a creed—see United States Supreme Court, *Planned Parenthood of Southeastern Pennsylvania et al. v. Casey, Governor of Pennsylvania, et al.* 505 U.S. 833 (1992), supremecourtus.gov/opinions/boundvolumes/505bv.pdf (accessed Jan 29, 2010), 851; and Budziszewski, *What We Can't Not Know*, 22–23. For another example of moral relativism in American public life, and a discussion of how this reveals a degenerate form of natural law, see Joseph Biden, "Opening Statement, Senator Joseph R. Biden, Chairman of the Judiciary Committee Hearing on the Confirmation of Clarence Thomas to be an Associate Justice to the U.S. Supreme Court," Sept 10, 1991, www.gpoaccess.gov/congress/senate/judiciary/sh102-1084pt1/6-21.pdf (accessed May 12 2009), 8–20; and Phillip E. Johnson, "Nihilism and the End of Law," *First Things* (March 1993), www.firstthings.com/article.php3?id_article=5101&var_recherche=natural+law (accessed May 14, 2009).

[163] Defined as those who claim to have made a personal commitment to Jesus Christ that is still important in their life today, and believe that when they die they will go to heaven because they have confessed their sins and accepted Christ as their savior. Respondents were not asked to describe themselves as "born again."

[164] Barna Group, "Americans Are Most Likely to Base Truth on Feelings," Feb 12, 2002, www.barna.org/barna-update/article/5-barna-update/67-americans-are-most-likely-to-base-truth-on-feelings (accessed Jan 28, 2010).

clear and absolute standards for what it right and wrong."[165] Evidently the result depends on how the questions are asked. Yet this conflicting result makes sense when one considers the results obtained by the more sophisticated questioning involved in the National Study of Youth and Religion. This study found that young people in America are very conflicted when it comes to the question of whether there are moral absolutes or not.

On the one hand, most teens and young adults in America have a strong ethos that forswears judging any ideas or people that may be different.[166] They believe that everyone has the right to choose what is right for themselves, and that criticizing anyone for their choices is intolerant and unloving. This means that most of them react negatively to words such as commitment, duty, faithfulness, obedience, calling, obligation, accountability, and responsibility, since they judge such things to be coercive, and antithetical to the sovereign freedom of the individual.[167] On the other hand, the same people often draw clear moralistic lines and make decisive judgments on certain matters of right and wrong, which they regard as self-evident to any reasonable person. Statements like, "Well, obviously you shouldn't hurt someone else," or "It's totally wrong to have sex with someone you don't really care about," are commonplace.[168] Furthermore, their moral relativism does not stop them from being moralistic therapeutic deists, who assume that the purpose of religion is to inculcate an ethic of niceness, which they think is not relative but common to all religions.[169] So the researchers conclude that in practice they "continually seesaw, with little self-awareness that they are doing so, between their individualist Jekyll and moralistic Hyde selves, incapable of reconciling their judgments with their anti-judgmentalism, and so merely banging back and forth between them."[170] In practice, most of them end up adopting an ethic of pragmatic consequentialism, guided by the silver rule of "don't hurt others," yet without much ability to analyze or defend what they are doing apart from saying "it feels right to me."[171]

What we see here is not genuine moral relativism, but an attempt to construct a new morality by grasping certain tenets of God's Law and using them to trump the rest. It is what Luther says the self-righteous always do: keep one

---

[165] Pew Forum, "U.S. Religious Landscape Survey: Beliefs and Practices," 61.

[166] Smith and Denton, *Soul Searching*, 144; Smith and Snell, *Souls in Transition*, 48–53.

[167] Smith and Denton, *Soul Searching*, 143; Smith and Snell, *Souls in Transition*, 49.

[168] Smith and Denton, *Soul Searching*, 144; cf. Smith and Snell, *Souls in Transition*, 46–47.

[169] Smith and Snell, *Souls in Transition*, 82–83.

[170] Smith and Denton, *Soul Searching*, 144–45. By permission of Oxford University Press, USA.

[171] Smith and Snell, *Souls in Transition*, 47, 51–52, 292–94. By permission of Oxford University Press, USA.

or two laws with self-righteous zeal, so they can feel secure about their neglect of the rest.[172]

The political and ethical philosopher J. Budziszewski accurately describes what is going on when he talks about "cannibalizing the conscience." Since the conscience is powerful and inescapable, we cannot simply ignore it, or invent a new morality out of thin air. If we want to suppress our conscience, we need something equally powerful to do it, and the only thing that fits the bill is the conscience itself. Although in reality the different tenets of the Law are in harmony with each other, if we twist them it becomes possible to use one to oppose another. The Nazis stilled their consciences regarding their murder of the Jews by vilifying their victims, so they could carry out the slaughter in the name of retributive justice and the greater good. In a similar way, Communist regimes have excused all kinds of injustice in the name of ending human need. Likewise, people in Western society today attack the institution of marriage in the name of love, promote homosexual marriage in the name of fairness, and justify the murder of children in the womb in the name of compassion for women and respect for their freedom.[173] This is the best way to understand moral relativism in contemporary society. As a number of scholars have pointed out, proponents of moral relativism frequently defend it in the name of certain moral commitments that are apparently not relative, such as benevolence, tolerance, understanding, humility, a respect for human freedom, or love.[174] This reveals moral relativism to be an attempt to justify the neglect of certain virtues by silencing them in the name of others.

The false gospels of inclusivity and affirmation within the church. While the belief that moral norms are relative is more common among non-Christians and nominal Christians than among committed Christians, it is still prevalent among regular church attenders.[175] Indeed, something very similar to moral relativism has become the reigning view in many segments of the church.

---

[172] The Canadian philosopher Charles Taylor hints at this phenomenon when he suggests that the contemporary Western world has espoused certain goods, such as freedom and benevolence, yet has failed to recognize that these goods do not stand alone, but belong together with a plurality of other goods that we should be pursuing (Taylor, *Sources of the Self*, 495–521).

[173] Budziszewski, *What We Can't Not Know*, 186–90.

[174] E.g., Murdoch, *Existentialists and Mystics*, 65–74; Smith, *Moral, Believing Animals: Human Personhood and Culture* (New York: Oxford University Press, 2003), 88, 155–56; Taylor, *Sources of the Self*, 321–40; Oswald Bayer, "Law and Freedom: A Metacritique of Kant," in *Freedom in Response: Lutheran Ethics: Sources and Controversies*, trans. Jeffrey F. Cayzer (New York: Oxford University Press, 2007), 154–55; Smith and Denton, *Soul Searching*, 144.

[175] Pew Forum, "U.S. Religious Landscape Survey: Religious Beliefs and Practices," 61–63; Smith and Snell, *Souls in Transition*, 264–65; Barna Group, "Americans Are Most Likely to Base Truth on Feelings."

William Abraham, professor of theology at Southern Methodist University in Texas, contends that inclusivism is the working ideology of many churches today, particularly "mainline" churches like his own United Methodist Church. Abraham correctly identifies inclusivism as a new form of moralism. He suggests that this ideology began with the legitimate quest to eliminate racism and patriarchal domination, yet has now expanded beyond all bounds as it seeks out new victims to liberate and new oppressors to castigate. He suggests that the result, at least in his own denomination, has been that the oppressed have claimed the moral high ground and used it to become the oppressors. As a result, people now constantly walk on eggshells, wondering when they will become the next target of the thought police.[176] This is an example of the phenomenon described above. A legitimate virtue, in this case a desire to bring justice to the oppressed, has been espoused with self-righteous zeal, to the extent that it has been blown out of all proportion and used to trump other virtues.

This new moralism becomes even worse when people confuse it with the Gospel. Philip Turner, former dean of Berkeley Divinity School at Yale, suggests that the current division over homosexual marriage and ordination within his own Anglican Communion is ultimately not about ethics. Instead, the split is between those who teach a Gospel of redemption and those who espouse a gospel of acceptance or inclusivity instead. The old Gospel focused on forgiveness. It called for repentance and faith, and led to holiness of life. In contrast, the new gospel teaches that God simply affirms us for who we are, and dispenses with God's judgment on sin and his call to repentance. It therefore does away with his forgiveness, since there is no longer anything to forgive.[177]

David Yeago, professor of Systematics at the Lutheran Theological Southern Seminary in South Carolina, argues that something similar is happening within worldwide Lutheranism. In the past the church proclaimed a Gospel that focused on the forgiveness of sins and liberation from the condemnation of the Law. Now many are proclaiming a new gospel that liberates us not merely from the condemnation of the Law, but from the Law altogether. This new gospel treats the Law as oppressive because it is law, not because we are disobedient and stand condemned by it. Instead of teaching what Luther taught, that Christ liberated us so that we may learn to love God's Law and

---

[176] William J. Abraham, "Inclusivism, Idolatry and the Survival of the (Fittest) Faithful," in *The Community of the Word: Towards an Evangelical Ecclesiology*, ed. Mark Husbands and Daniel J. Treier (Downers Grove, IL: InterVarsity, 2005), 131–38.

[177] Philip Turner, "An Unworkable Theology," *First Things* 154 (June/July 2005): 10–12; cf. Abraham, "Inclusivism, Idolatry and the Survival of the (Fittest) Faithful," 140.

live in harmony with his will,[178] it encourages people to discard the Law instead.[179] This is simply antinomianism.

If the current debates in the church about homosexuality were simply about how to interpret God's Law, they would be far less serious. Ultimately they are debates about the Gospel, not the Law. The permissive stance that many churches are taking over sexual ethics is being defended in the name of the Gospel. This is not the true Gospel, but a perverted gospel that justifies sin instead of justifying sinners by offering us affirmation instead of forgiveness. As Luther tells us, the struggle against antinomianism is ultimately a struggle to preserve the Gospel, not the Law. Antinomianism is a strategy for self-justification. It is about establishing a righteousness of our own by silencing the accusing voice of the Law. This does away with the need for Christ. It is "another gospel," and is even more pernicious than the false works-righteous gospel that Paul confronted in Galatia. As Luther notes, works-righteous people usually leave some room for repentance and forgiveness. The antinomians do away with them altogether. If the current debates in worldwide Christendom were merely about sexual ethics, they could possibly be resolved. Yet when our sexual liberation is proclaimed in the name of the Gospel it must divide the church, since the church can only have one Gospel. Any other gospel is self-righteous idolatry.

A CHRISTIAN RESPONSE

Richard Keyes tells a story that illustrates why the idolatry of self-justification is such a big problem for the church. He tells of a letter Sigmund Freud wrote to James Putnam, a professor of neurology at Harvard. In this letter Freud wrote, "I have no dread at all of the Almighty. If we ever were to meet I should have more reproaches to make to Him than He could to me. I should ask Him why He had not given me a better intellectual equipment, and He could not complain that I had not made the best use of my supposed freedom."[180] So in one step Freud justified himself and condemned God, by blaming God for his inherited sins and failings. As a result, he felt no need for Christ. If a Christian had said to him at that moment, "Mr. Freud, I have good

[178] E.g., LW 14:287–300; 26:352–53; Luther, *Antinomian Theses and Disputations*, 141, 245 = WA 39/1:350.3–6, 356.3–24.

[179] David Yeago, "Gnosticism, Antinomianism, and Reformation Theology: Reflections on the Cost of a Construal," *Pro Ecclesia* 2 (Winter 1993): 38–46.

[180] Ernest Jones, *The Life and Work of Sigmund Freud*, ed. and abr. Lionel Trilling and Steven Marcus (New York: Basic Books, 1961), 375–76. This is loosely quoted in Richard Keyes, "Giving a Word Back," www.bethinking.org/what-is-apologetics/giving-a-word-back.htm (accessed Nov. 17, 2006). The exact quote and its source was obtained through correspondence with Keyes.

news for you, that Jesus died to bring you forgiveness for your sins," this would have been a solution to a non-problem as far as Freud was concerned.[181]

As C. S. Lewis points out, once people no longer have a sense of their own sinfulness, they start to act as if God is on trial and not them.[182] They start to think that they are entitled to God's blessings, so that they lose all gratitude for the good things God gives them. Instead of being grateful, they act as if God has done them a great injustice when he fails to bless them the way they think they deserve. Then, instead of feeling any need for God's forgiveness, they act as if they hold the high moral ground, and lose all gratitude for Christ.[183]

On the one hand, the response the church needs to make to this is quite simple. We need to proclaim God's true Law, that exposes us as sinners, rather than a law that we have altered to justify ourselves. Then we need to proclaim the true Gospel of the forgiveness of sins, not a false gospel that excuses our sin as if it is okay.

On the other hand, this is a difficult art. In particular, we need to avoid a simplistic preaching of Law and Gospel that people can co-opt for the purpose of justifying themselves. Instead, we need to be able to challenge the idolatry of self-justification head on through a focused proclamation of Law and Gospel. This means that we need to be alert to how this idolatry manifests itself in our society, so that we can expose it for what it is.

One contemporary theologian who has thought through the practical implications of this better than most is Timothy Keller, pastor of Redeemer Presbyterian Church in Manhattan and professor of practical theology at Westminster Theological Seminary in Philadelphia. Keller, like Luther, identifies two strategies for self-justification. He characterizes these as the paths of religious legalism and irreligious rebellion. He then argues that at essence the two are the same, since both are idolatrous attempts at self-salvation. Religious legalists try to keep all the rules, hoping that God will bless them.[184] Irre-

---

[181] Keyes, "Giving a Word Back."

[182] C. S. Lewis, *God in the Dock: Essays on Theology and Ethics*, ed. Walter Hooper (Grand Rapids, MI: Eerdmans, 1970), 243–44.

[183] "The glory of God cannot be declared unless the baseness and vileness of man be declared at the same time. Nor can we preach forth God as true, righteous, and merciful, unless we at the same time set forth men as liars, sinners, and miserable" (Luther, *Commentary on the First Twenty-Two Psalms*, 2:389 (sic) = *Operationes in Psalmos* [1519–1521], WA 5:542.38–40). Cf. 2:215–16, 427–28; LW 22:157–58.

[184] Keller, "Smashing False Idols: Gospel Communication"; Timothy Keller, "Smashing False Idols: Gospel Realisation," 2007, The Evangelists Conference, www.evangelists-conference.org.uk/1F014-01GospelRealisation.mp3 (accessed Sept. 15, 2009); Timothy Keller,

ligious rebels try to write their own rules, hoping to bless themselves. In the process they end up as legalists, just with a different law. Keller says that people in New York City today are every bit as legalistic as the Pharisees, since they all live for their achievements and seek in them their sense of self-worth.[185] One pursues money. Another pursues artistic expression. Still another pursues relationships and family. Since they turn these into ultimate things and seek their ultimate validation in them, they become enslaved to serving them and the laws that govern them.[186] This puts enormous demands on them, and punishes them without mercy if they fail to measure up.[187]

Keller contends that such an understanding of idolatry is critical in proclaiming Law and Gospel, or judgment and salvation, in society today. This is for two reasons. The first is that the more that moral relativism permeates our society, the less people respond when the Law is preached in moral terms. When Keller first went to Manhattan as a church planter in 1989, he attempted to use the evangelism tools he had been trained in such as D. James Kennedy's *Evangelism Explosion*. These tools all basically followed the same approach. They began by telling people they were sinners who broke God's rules, and therefore needed Jesus. He found this approach had little impact on most people. They were far more likely to say, "Well, I don't have the same view of the rules as you do," than to acknowledge their sin. Yet as soon as he started talking about sin using the conceptual structure of idolatry he started getting traction. Once he started telling people that sin is not so much about doing bad things as it is about taking good things and making them into ultimate things, they could see that what he said applied to them. He could then show them that they had become enslaved to something that could never give

---

"Talking About Idolatry in a Postmodern Age," April 2007, www.stevekmccoy.com/keller-idoaltry.pdf (accessed March 4, 2010).

[185] Timothy Keller, "How the Cross Converts Us," 2007, Christian Life Conference (Second Presbyterian of Memphis, TN), www.2pcmedia.org/get.php?web=2007-01-19_How_the_Cross_Converts_Us.mp3 (accessed Sept. 15, 2009); Timothy Keller, "How the Cross Changes Us," 2007, Christian Life Conference (Second Presbyterian of Memphis, TN), www.2pcmedia.org/get.php?web=2007-01-19_How_the_Cross_Changes_Us.mp3 (accessed Sept. 15 2009); Timothy Keller, *Counterfeit Gods: The Empty Promise of Money, Sex, and Power, and the Only Hope that Matters* (New York: Dutton Adult, 2009), 40, 72–78.

[186] Timothy Keller, "The Grand Demythologizer: The Gospel and Idolatry," April 20, 2005, The Gospel Coalition, thegospelcoalition.org/resources/video/The-Grand-Demythologizer-The-Gospel-and-Idolatry (accessed March 3, 2010).

[187] Timothy Keller, "Reaching the 21st Century World For Christ," 2005, The Gathering, thegathering.com/gws/media/_mp3/2005/2005-Tim%20Keller-Reaching%20The%2021st%20Century%20World%20For%20Christ.mp3 (accessed Sept. 15, 2009).

them the satisfaction and validation they sought, and how Christ could set them free.[188]

The second reason why an understanding of idolatry is crucial for proclaiming the Gospel today is that only when we deal with sin in terms of idolatry do we have a profound enough view of sin to be able to deal with both irreligious rebellion and legalistic religion at the same time. If we talk about sin in terms of breaking God's rules, it is easy to see why rebellious people like the younger son in the story of the prodigal son stand condemned, but not so easy to see why legalistic people like his brother also stand condemned. Since the default mode of the human heart is self-justification, when people hear us calling them to repent and believe in Jesus they naturally assume that we are preaching some form of legalistic piety: kiss up to God and do what he says and he will forget your past and bless you. Yet many people in our society have already been burnt by older brother Christianity and want nothing to do with it. Only when we clearly teach that legalistic religion and irreligious rebellion are both futile attempts at self-salvation will many people be able to see that we are preaching a third way, the way of the Gospel.[189]

Such self-salvation projects are futile. They are futile before God, and they are futile at delivering a peaceful conscience on earth. This was driven home for me recently with one of my parishioners, a woman who has been in and out of mental hospital with mood swings so severe that she frequently attempts suicide when she is low. Once when she was down she told me how her psychologists try to treat her depression. Their strategy is to boost her self-esteem. They ask her to identify things she likes about herself, and then repeat these as mantras to prevent her from feeling down about herself. For a short time this strategy will help her to pick up and feel fantastic, but before long something will go wrong that will remind her of her flaws so that she comes crashing down once more. I then explained to her that this is what attempts at boosting self-esteem are wont to do. They produce swings between pride and despair, because we are incapable of providing a stable foundation for our own sense of worth. The only cure is to come to terms with the reality that we are all deeply flawed, and need our worthiness to be grounded not in ourselves but in Christ our Savior. This immediately made sense to her, and has proven to be a step on the road to healing.

---

188 Keller, "Smashing False Idols: Gospel Communication"; Keller, "Smashing False Idols: Gospel Realisation."

189 Keller, "Smashing False Idols: Gospel Communication"; Keller, "Reaching the 21st Century World For Christ."

Chapter Seven

The Idol of the Self and the Worship of God Incarnate

Finding God on Earth

If God is in heaven and we are on earth, then how can we know him? Now that God has banished the fallen human race from walking and talking with him face to face, how can we worship him, and seek refuge in him in all our needs? And since God's transcendent greatness surpasses all we can know or think, how can we relate to him? The pagans sought to put a face to God and locate him within our physical world by creating cultic images. If we reject this approach to God, then how do we locate him and seek his face?

Luther's answer is that we cannot do any of these things unless God gives himself to us in a way we can handle. He does this in Christ incarnate, who is "God with us." In Christ, God has come down from heaven to earth to make himself known to us and available to us, so that our faith can grasp hold of the true God and his benefits.[1] Furthermore, Christ is not a God who was with us two thousand years ago but is with us no longer now that he has ascended into heaven. Instead, he continues to come and dwell in the midst of his people through the means of the Gospel (Matt 28:20; John 14:23). It is this incarnate mediator between God and humankind who now provides the down-to-earth focal point for Christian faith and worship.[2]

Luther took seriously the fact that idolatry is something that was first defined in the cultic domain. It is true that he regarded idolatry as ultimately a matter of the faith in one's heart, and since this faith spills out and affects all

[1] As Melanchthon wrote in his 1521 *Loci Communes*, a work Luther praised most highly, "to know Christ means to know his benefits" (Philip Melanchthon, "Loci Communes Theologici," in *Melanchthon and Bucer*, Library of Christian Classics, ed. Wilhelm Pauck [Louisville, KY: Westminster John Knox, 2006], 21). Cf. LW 26:287–88; 30:29–30, 152.

[2] Every time the New Testament refers to Christ as the mediator, it is within the context of worship (1 Tim 2:5; Heb 8:6; 9:15; 12:24).

of life it is a much larger issue than merely what cultic rites we observe. Yet it would be wrong to assume that Luther ever divorced faith from concrete acts of worship. The worship rites we observe reveal more than anything what Luther calls "incarnate faith,"[3] faith not in the abstract but as it is lived out in real life. We misread Luther if we fail to see that he centers his discussion of idolatry in what we actually do in our *cultus*. Do we seek to get in touch with God by going on a pilgrimage to a holy site, buying an indulgence, joining a monastery, praying to the saints, or engaging in other self-invented acts of piety? Or do we get baptized, listen to the preaching of the Gospel, confess our sins and receive forgiveness in Christ's name, go to the Lord's Supper, and pray to the Father in the name of his Son? That is, do we seek to worship God in our own way? Or do we worship him in the way that he has prescribed for us, by looking to his incarnate Son, who comes to us now in the means of the Gospel that he has instituted?

Luther's theology of worship is inseparable from his theology of the incarnation. This should come as no surprise, since a central question we must answer in any discussion on worship is how the gap between God in heaven and his worshippers on earth can be bridged. Luther is more than anything a theologian of the incarnation. In his hymn *A Mighty Fortress*, Luther says of Jesus Christ, "there is no other God."[4] This is not a throwaway line, or a denial of the Trinity in favor of some sort of Christomonism, but a statement about the importance of the incarnation. If we will not know and worship God as he comes down to earth in Christ, but instead attempt to climb up to him through our self-invented piety, we will never find the true God, but only an idol of our imagination.

LUTHER'S TEACHING

The Lutheran liturgical scholar John Kleinig traces the foundation for Luther's theology of worship back to a sermon on John 6:51, in which he comments, "If you want to have God, then mark where He resides and where He wants to be found."[5] Luther then tells us where this is: in Jesus Christ who is present with us through the Gospel.[6]

---

[3] *Lectures on Galatians* (1535), LW 26:264–68 = WA 40/1:414–18; cf. LW 2:77, 266–27; 21:205; 22:393; 35:370.

[4] "Er heist Jhesu Christ, der Herr Zebaoth, Und ist kein ander God" (WA 35:456). Cf. LW 3:338; 5:50; 12:101, 352; 14:103; 15:305; 17:86; 19:80; 22:368, 463; 23:124, 246, 366; 24:98, 403; 26:29; 38:46, 82, 258, 309; 41:165; WA 25:94.5–19; 35:456; See also 1 John 5:20, "He is the true God and eternal life."

[5] *Sermons on John* (1530–32), LW 23:121 = WA 33:187.18–21. Cited in John Kleinig, "Where is your God? Luther on God's Self-Localisation," in *All Theology Is Christology. Essays in Honor of*

TRUE WORSHIP IS WORSHIP THROUGH FAITH IN JESUS CHRIST

Luther contends that the only way we can worship the true God, and thereby fulfill the First Commandment, is through faith in Jesus Christ. Luther observes that the Old Testament prophecies and their New Testament fulfillment apply the First Commandment to Christ. The First Commandment tells us to worship God alone. Yet Scripture then points us to the Lord's anointed, and tells us to worship him. Christ has now fulfilled the worship God established through Moses (Col 2:16–17; Heb 8–10), so the Bible now transfers our worship from these ceremonies to Christ.[7] Luther writes,

> the worship of God [*cultus Dei*] is now the adoration of this King, not the ceremonies of Moses, the pope, monks, heathen, or Turks. That means laying hold of this King and believing He is the Son of God, who suffered for us and rose again; moreover, acknowledging Him in reverence, accepting His Word, believing, and doing everything through faith in Him, to His glory, so that everything may take place, as Paul says, "in the name of Jesus" (Col. 3:17).[8]

Luther spells this out in most detail when he reflects on the theology of the incarnation in John's Gospel. In particular, he uses Jesus' words in John 14,

> "I am the way, and the truth, and the life. No one comes to the Father except through me. If you had known me, you would have known my Father also. From now on you do know him and have seen him." Philip said to him, "Lord, show us the Father, and it is enough for us." Jesus said to him, "Have I been with you so long, and you still do not know me, Philip? Whoever has seen me has seen the Father." (John 14:6, 9)[9]

From this Luther concludes that whenever we form our own picture of God or path to God we grope blindly and grasp an idol instead of the true God, since only Christ can reveal God to us and enable us to come to him.[10]

David P Scaer, ed. Dean O. Wenthe et al. (Fort Wayne, IN: Concordia Theological Seminary Press, 2000), 118.

[6] *Sermons on John* (1530–32), LW 23:120–21 = WA 33:185–87.

[7] LW 12:285–89; 14:277; cf. 13:325; 15:313.

[8] *Commentary on Psalm 45* (1532), LW 12:289 = WA 40/2:595.20–25.

[9] LW 22:494; 23:53–54, 90; 345–46; 24:56–59, 65; cf. 2:49; 3:297; 12:84–85; 15:311–12; 16:55; 17:386; 30:222, 285–86.

[10] LW 22:366–68; 23:55–56, 80; 19:53–57; cf. Matt 11:25–27; John 1:9; 8:12; 10:1–16; 12:35–36; 14:6; 15:5; 1 John 2:23; LW 29:111; 43:54–55; 52:57–61. Luther fleshes this out by drawing on

Luther also reflects on John 1:14–18, and concludes that although it is possible to have a "legal knowledge" of God apart from Christ, true "evangelical knowledge" comes only through Christ. Through natural reason we can know something of the Creator's power, and the Law he has embedded in nature. Yet this partial knowledge is not yet true knowledge, since it does not give us any certain knowledge of God's attitude toward us, nor enable us to come to him. Instead, it leads people to fabricate idolatrous works and worship in the hope that these will please him. Those who devise their own worship based on natural reason always fall into some kind of futile works righteousness. What we need if we are to have fellowship with God is the evangelical knowledge that comes through Christ. We need to see the face of Jesus, who reveals to us God's mind and his true plan of salvation. Then we will look into God's face and see into his heart, and know that he is kind and friendly and wants to save us through Christ.[11]

The devil does not want us to have this knowledge of Christ or be saved through him, so he rages against this article of the faith.[12] Luther writes,

> I have also noticed that all error, heresy, idolatry, offense, misuse, and evil in the church originally came from despising or losing sight of this article of faith in Jesus Christ. And if one looks at it correctly and clearly, all heresies do contend against this dear article of Jesus Christ, as Simeon says of him, that he is "set for the fall and rising of many in Israel, and for a sign that is spoken against" [Luke 2:34]. . . . St. John also gives no other or more certain sign for

---

many other pictures from John. Just as the Jews were commanded not to worship on every hilltop or under every tree, but only at the mercy seat in Jerusalem, so Christ is our temple and mercy seat. Only through him does God promise to forgive sins and answer prayer (LW 22:248–50, 366–67; 23:120–21; 24:23–24; cf. John 1:14; 2:21; Rom 3:25; Heb 2:17; 1 John 2:2; 4:10; LW 17:61; 19:80; 26:273; 27:64; 30:223; 31:64; 37:364; 51:277–86; Martin Luther, *Martin Luther's Complete Commentary on the First Twenty-Two Psalms*, trans. Henry Cole [2 vols.; London: W. Simpkin and R. Marshall, 1826], 2:208–9). Christ is Jacob's ladder, who has opened heaven through his incarnation, and ushers us into God's presence (LW 22:200–203, 207–9; cf. John 1:51; LW 5:217–24). In no other way can we climb up to God, neither by works nor by wisdom (LW 22:328–335, 366–68; 23:55–56, 80; 24:48; cf. 5:223; 26:30; 29:111; 43:54–55). Christ is the bread of life who must feed us, the fountain of life who must give us drink if we are to live (LW 22:135; 23:55–56; John 4:13–14; 6:35–51). He is the road, bridge, and doorway to heaven, the leader who must guide us through the dark, and the lamp that must light the way (LW 22:305–6; 23:56, 319–21; 24:48; cf. John 8:12; 10:9, 14–16; 14:6; LW 29:111; WLS 1160–61 [3715]).

[11] *Sermons on John* (1537–40), LW 22:135, 149–59 = WA 46:653–54, 666–74; LW 24:59–61, 97–99; cf. 3:276–77; 12:84–88; 29:211.

[12] LW 22:332, 368; 24:62.

> recognizing false and anti-Christian spirits than their denial of Jesus Christ [2 John 7].[13]

Therefore Luther concludes that if we want God and not an idol, we must be immune to every message that induces us to seek God or salvation somewhere else apart from Christ, no matter how wise, clever, or lofty it may be.[14] We must conclude,

> I must and will hear or see no work, no worship of God, no spirituality, no holy life other than that of this Man Christ, or that which He transmitted to the apostles, and the apostles, in turn, transmitted to the preachers. When I hear these, I hear Christ Himself; and when I hear Christ, I hear the Father.[15]

> I know of no other God in heaven or on earth than of this One, who talks to me and treats me as I see Christ doing.[16]

When Luther says there is no God apart from Jesus Christ he is not denying any part of trinitarian theology, but rather asserting that Christ is the point at which we gain access to the whole Trinity. Through Christ we gain access to the Father, since he is the perfect image of the Father and reveals the Father to us.[17] Through Christ we also gain access to the Holy Spirit, since he is the font of the Holy Spirit,[18] who alone pours out the Spirit on us.[19] Thus he enables us to be truly spiritual people, who are renewed in God's image.[20]

TRUE WORSHIP IS WORSHIP THROUGH CHRIST'S HUMANITY

When Luther stresses that we must find and worship God in Christ and nowhere else, he specifically means the incarnate Christ who has come down to earth for us. Luther pulls together much New Testament material to establish this point. The New Testament calls Jesus' body the new temple of

---

[13] *The Three Symbols or Creeds of the Christian Faith* (1538), LW 34:207–8 = WA 50:267.14–20, 23–26; cf. 24:320.

[14] *Sermons on John* (1537–40), LW 22:487–89 = WA 47:195–97; *Sermons on John* (1537), LW 24:22–24 = WA 45:480–83; *Sermons on John* (1537–40), LW 22:494 = WA 47:202.5–7; cf. 12:84–87; 44:318–19.

[15] *Sermons on John* (1537), LW 24:70 = WA 45:524.23–27; cf. Matt 17:5; John 5:19; 7:16.

[16] *Sermons on John* (1537), LW 24:62 = WA 45:517.10–12.

[17] LW 12:47–48; 15:339; 22:19–20; 34:220–21; 38:275; cf. 2 Cor 4:4; Col 1:15; Heb 1:3.

[18] *Sermons on John* (1537–40), LW 22:134–35, 487–89 = WA 46:652–54; 47:195–97.

[19] *Lectures on Galatians* (1535), LW 27:131 = WA 40/2:168.

[20] LW 1:60–65, 68, 339–40; 2:141; 22:285–90; 26:352–53, 356–57; 27:139–40; 31:89, 358–59; 34:140, 177; cf. Rom 8:29; 1 Cor 15:49; 2 Cor 3:18; Eph 4:20–24; Col 3:10; 1 John 3:2.

God, where we must go to find him (John 1:14; 2:19–21).[21] It says that the man Jesus shares in all the glory and properties of God, since in him the whole fullness of God dwells bodily (Col 2:9).[22] It tells us that the Holy Spirit dwells in him fully (John 3:34),[23] and that this man is God and Lord over all (John 1:18; 1 John 5:20).[24] Luther emphasizes that we must say with Paul, "I decided to know nothing among you except Jesus Christ and him crucified" (1 Cor 2:2). This means going to the child on Mary's lap and the man on the cross, and knowing that in him are hidden all the treasures of the godhead.[25] It means seeking salvation nowhere else,[26] and recognizing that when we see the man Jesus we see God himself,[27] even if only the eyes of faith can recognize this fact.[28]

When Luther emphasized that we must know God through Jesus' humanity, he was specifically objecting to speculation about God in his majesty. Luther repeatedly charged scholastic theologians like Gerson, as well as other reformers like Zwingli, Schwenckfeld, Carlstadt, and Oecolampadius, with neglecting Christ's humanity and trying to gain speculative access to his divinity, as if they were able to exalt themselves to heaven or gain direct access to God.[29] In contrast, he asserted that only when we hold onto Christ's humanity will his true divinity become manifest.[30] When Oecolampadius said to him at the Marburg colloquy, "You should not cling to the humanity and the flesh of Christ, but rather lift up your mind to his divinity," Luther replied, "I do not know of any God except him who was made flesh, nor do I want to have another. And there is no other God who could save us, besides the God Incarnate."[31]

---

[21] *Sermons on John* (1537–40), LW 22:248–50 = WA 46:760–63.

[22] LW 5:224; 12:87–88; 22:487–89, 494; 26:30.

[23] *Sermons on John* (1537–40), LW 22:487–89 = WA 47:195–97.

[24] *Commentary on Psalm 8* (1537), LW 12:101 = WA 45:209–10.

[25] *Lectures on Genesis* (1538–42), LW 3:276–77 = WA 43:73; Col 2:3.

[26] *Sermons on John* (1537–40), LW 22:489, 494 = WA 47:197, 202.

[27] LW 15:308–10; 5:222; 12:101.

[28] LW 22:203–4; 24:59–60. Cf. Luther's beautiful reflections on how the angels of God bow before the lowly baby in the manger, since this One who is so far beneath them is at the same time so far above them (*Lectures on Genesis* [1538–42], LW 5:218–21 = 43:579–81).

[29] LW 3:276; 12:49; 23:101–2; 26:28–30; 38:46, 82; 54:22.

[30] *Sermons on John* (1530–32), LW 23:101–2 = WA 33:154–55.

[31] Hermann Sasse, *This Is My Body: Luther's Contention for the Real Presence in the Sacrament of the Altar* (Adelaide, South Australia: Lutheran Publishing House, 1977), 203. Sasse's account of the dialogue at Marburg is a reconstruction based on several different eyewitness accounts.

The reason why speculations about God in his majesty are useless is that God has decided that he wants us to know him through the incarnation alone. Luther writes,

> The humanity is that holy ladder of ours, mentioned in Gen. 28:12, by which we ascend to the knowledge of God. Therefore John 14:6 also says: "No one comes to the Father but by Me." And again: "I am the Door" (John 10:7). Therefore he who wants to ascend advantageously to the love and knowledge of God should abandon the human metaphysical rules concerning knowledge of the divinity and apply himself first to the humanity of Christ. For it is exceedingly godless temerity that, where God has humiliated Himself in order to become recognizable, man seeks for himself another way by following the counsels of his own natural capacity.[32]

Those who try to investigate God's majesty apart from Christ's humanity are seeking things they cannot know. God in his majesty is hidden from them. Therefore instead of gaining true knowledge, they end up weaving fantasies about a god they have invented for themselves. Since they are sinners, if they were to encounter God in his glory they would discover that he is a raging fire who must consume them. Only Christ incarnate reveals the true God to us in his mercy, and prepares us to meet him in glory on the last day.[33] Therefore Luther concludes,

> Whenever you are concerned to think and act about your salvation, you must put away all speculations about the Majesty, all thoughts of works, traditions, and philosophy—indeed, of the Law of God itself. And you must run directly to the manger and the mother's womb, embrace this Infant and Virgin's Child in your arms, and look at Him—born, being nursed, growing up, going about in human society, teaching, dying, rising again, ascending above all the heavens, and having authority over all things. In this way you can shake off all terrors and errors.[34]

For

> In Him alone is salvation, grace, and life. Whatever you think about God aside from Him is vain speculation and mere idolatry.[35]

---

[32] *Lectures on Hebrews* (1517–18), LW 29:111 = WA 57:b99.3–10.

[33] LW 16:55–56; 17:330–31; 26:28–30, 39.

[34] *Lectures on Galatians* (1535), LW 26:30 = WA 40/1:97.28–98.13.

[35] *Commentary on Psalm 2* (1532), LW 12:88 = WA 40/2:305.21–22.

TRUE WORSHIP IS WORSHIP THROUGH THE GOSPEL

The Christ that Luther is speaking of is not any Christ we might imagine, but the Christ who comes to us now through the Gospel.[36] It is not sufficient that Christ came down from heaven to earth at one place and time. If we are to receive him now he must also come to us. This he does in the Gospel. Luther theology of the incarnation is always closely tied to his theology of the Word and the Sacraments, the means through which Christ descends to us now. We cannot grasp Christ directly as he once walked the streets of Galilee or as he now dwells in glory in heaven. Instead, we must grasp him sacramentally, as he comes to us in the Gospel, hidden under the form of created things.[37]

Luther regarded the incarnation as paradigmatic for all God's dealings with us this side of eternity. Just as God has come to us under the covering of Jesus' humanity, so he always deals with his people on earth not in majesty, but covered by external words, works, signs, and images.[38] In biblical times he came to his people under the external coverings of the tabernacle, the ark with its mercy seat,[39] the pillars of cloud and fire,[40] a voice from heaven, a dove

---

[36] Cf. Tae Jun Suk's working definition of idolatry for Luther as "any worship apart from faith in Christ who is revealed in the Word" (Tae Jun Suk, *The Theology of Martin Luther between Judaism and Roman Catholicism: A Critical-Historical Evaluation of Luther's Concept of Idolatry* [Ann Arbor, MI: UMI Dissertation Services, 2001], 126–27).

[37] For Luther, the Gospel is always sacramental. It doesn't just tell us about Christ, but brings Christ and his blessings to us. He writes: "All the words and stories of the gospels are sacraments of a kind, sacred signs by which God works in believers what the histories signify. Just as baptism is the sacrament by which God restores us; just as absolution is the sacrament by which God forgives sins, so the words of Christ are sacraments through which he works salvation. Hence the gospel is to be taken sacramentally, that is, the words of Christ need to be meditated on as symbols through which that righteousness, power, and salvation is given which these words themselves portray. . . . We meditate properly on the gospel, when we do so sacramentally, for through faith the words produce what they portray. Christ was born; believe that he was born for you and you will be born again. Christ conquered death and sin; believe that he conquered them for you and you will conquer them" (*Sermon on Christmas Day* [1519], WA 9:439, 442. Translated in John Kleinig, *Grace upon Grace: Spirituality for Today* [St. Louis: Concordia, 2008], 101–2).

[38] Luther, *Commentary on the First Twenty-Two Psalms*, 2:208; LW 1:11; 2:45–48; 3:274–75; 24:67–71. Luther continually stresses that we are not able to receive God in his majesty. Not only is God in his infinite majesty beyond the level of our comprehension, so that we cannot understand him unless he condescends to meet us at our level, but as sinners we cannot look at God's face unveiled without being consumed by his wrath against sin (LW 1:11–14, 309; 2:46–48; 3:275–76; 4:61; 6:128–29; 16:55–56; 22:157; 24:65, 67; cf. Ex 33:18–20; Rom 11:33–34; 2 Cor 3:7–4:6).

[39] Luther, *Commentary on the First Twenty-Two Psalms*, 2:208; LW 1:11, 309; 2:46.

[40] LW 1:11, 309; 2:46.

descending from heaven,[41] his appearances in human form, his words in human language,[42] and ultimately through his incarnate Son.[43] Today he still comes to us under external coverings, as Christ and his Spirit come to us through the Word, Baptism, the Lord's Supper, Absolution,[44] and in people who believe and proclaim the Gospel.[45]

This means that Luther's Christological emphasis should not be played off against his emphasis on God's written, proclaimed, and enacted Word. The two belong inseparably together. Luther says, "We do not separate, or differentiate between God and His Word or ministry, given to us through Christ. . . . By no means should we become so foolish as to sever and separate God, Christ, and His Word from one another."[46] When Christ's servants proclaim and enact the Word he gave them and the Sacraments he instituted, we hear him speaking and see him at work.[47] The Word and Sacraments are like pipes that draw water from the spring of Christ.[48] For Christ has "put himself into the word."[49] God "wraps Himself up in Baptism, in absolution, etc.,"[50] and through blessing, preaching, and the Sacraments he descends to speak to us.[51] So wherever people receive these gifts in faith they can be assured that Christ is present with them, together with the Father and the Spirit.[52] Therefore it is no surprise that just as Luther calls Christ the image of the Father, he also calls God's Word, Baptism, the Lord's Supper, and Absolution "divine images" and the "tabernacle of God" through which we come to see and know and meet with God.[53]

---

[41] *Lectures on Genesis* (1535–38), LW 2:45 = WA 42:294.

[42] LW 4:61; 43:200.

[43] LW 2:45, 48–49; 3:275–77; 24:68–71.

[44] Luther, *Commentary on the First Twenty-Two Psalms*, 2:209; LW 1:11, 309; 2:46, 48; 3:275; 6:128–29; 24:67–71.

[45] LW 22:202–4, 488–89; 23:56; 24:70; cf. SA III 4.

[46] *Sermons on John* (1537), LW 24:67 = WA 45:522.3–5, 20–21.

[47] *Sermons on John* (1537), LW 24:66–67, 70–71 = WA 45:521–22, 524–25.

[48] *Sermons on John* (1537), LW 24:70–71 = WA 45:524–25.

[49] *The Sacrament of the Body and Blood of Christ—Against the Fanatics* (1526), LW 36:343 = WA 493.21; cf. LW 52:46.

[50] *Lectures on Genesis* (1535–38), LW 1:11 = WA 42:10.6.

[51] *Lectures on Genesis* (1538–42), LW 5:197 = WA 43:564; *Sermons on John* (1537–40), LW 22:202–3 = WA 46:712.

[52] *Sermons on John* (1537–40), LW 22:209 = WA 46:718–19; cf. John 14:23.

[53] *Lectures on Genesis* (1535–38), LW 2:47 = WA 42:295.4; *Lectures on Genesis* (1538–42), LW 4:179 = WA 43:265.8–11; cf. LW 6:172–73; 52:46.

Luther is quite clear that we cannot have Christ apart from the Gospel.[54] He writes,

> How, then, do we have Christ? After all, he is sitting at the right hand of the Father; he will not come down to us in our house. No, this he will not do. But how do I gain and have him? Ah, you cannot have him except in the gospel in which he is promised to you.[55]

Yet when we have this Gospel, we can be certain that we have Christ:

> When you open the book containing the gospels and read or hear how Christ comes here or there, or how someone is brought to him, you should therein perceive the sermon or the gospel through which he is coming to you, or you are being brought to him. For the preaching of the gospel is nothing else than Christ coming to us, or we being brought to him. When you see how he works, however, and how he helps everyone to whom he comes or who is brought to him, then rest assured that faith is accomplishing this in you and that he is offering your soul exactly the same sort of help and favor through the gospel. If you pause here and let him do you good, that is, if you believe that he benefits and helps you, then you really have it. Then Christ is yours, presented to you as a gift.[56]

For Luther, the created means through which God comes to us are indispensable. Just as we must refuse to worship any God apart from the one who gives himself to us in the man Jesus Christ, so we must not worship a Christ we dream up for ourselves, or any of the false christs presented to us by the devil.[57] Instead, our faith in Christ must be enclosed within God's Word and fixed to the external signs of favor God has given us. Otherwise we will be tossed around by every wind of doctrine, and wander away to serve some idol of our own speculation.[58]

TRUE WORSHIP IS WORSHIP THAT GOD HAS INSTITUTED

Luther had one simple justification for directing all this attention to Christ, and that is that God tells us to do so. Luther regarded a Christocentric

---

[54] Paul Althaus, *The Theology of Martin Luther*, trans. Robert C. Schultz (Philadelphia: Fortress, 1966), 35.

[55] *Two Sermons Preached at Weimar* (1522), LW 51:114 = WA 10/3:349.17–21; cf. John 14:23.

[56] *A Brief Instruction on What to Look for and Expect in the Gospels* (1521), LW 35:121 = WA 10/1:13.19–14.7.

[57] LW 30:251–58, 285–88; cf. Matt 24:23–24; 1 John 2:18–24; 4:1–6; 2 John 7–9.

[58] Luther, *Commentary on the First Twenty-Two Psalms*, 2:208–9; LW 6:128–29.

approach to worship to be the necessary consequence of his more general principle: that we cannot know or worship the true God unless he shows us how. Luther teaches that the root cause of all idolatry is that people ignore what God has prescribed in his Word and presume to devise their own means of approaching him.[59] Thus they engage in the self-chosen religion condemned by Jesus and the apostle Paul (Matt 15:6–9; Col 2:23).[60]

Luther spells this out at length when he discusses idolatry in his "Preface to the Prophets" in the Luther Bible. There he proposes the following rule:

> *Gottesdienst*[61] without God's Word is *Teuffelsdienst* [worship of the devil]. In contrast, let everyone see to it that he is certain his *Gottesdienst* has been instituted by God's Word, and not invented by his own pious notions or good intentions. Whoever engages in *Gottesdienst* to which God has not borne witness ought to know that he is worshipping not the true God but an idol that he has concocted for himself.[62]

Luther wastes little time attacking the obvious idolatry of those who worship false gods and have no intention of worshipping the God of Israel. Instead, he focuses nearly all his attention on those who think they are worshipping the God of Israel, but worship him in their own self-chosen way. This, Luther contends, is no different from worshipping a false god. It means acting like we are the creators who can shape God according to our thoughts and intentions,[63] as if he must conform to us by delighting in whatever acts of piety we choose.[64] Luther says this is equivalent to inventing a new god, since the real God does not accommodate himself to our opinions in this way.[65]

Luther illustrates this by pointing to the Old Testament. God commanded the Jews to worship him only at the mercy seat in Jerusalem, yet they chose to worship in every place that pleased them.[66] King Jeroboam led the way. He

---

[59] LW 1:159; 2.284, 356; 8:230; 16:160; 17:16–17; 18:184; 19:11; 20:332; 24:327–28; 27:87–90; 35:270–73; 51:327; 52:90–92. This fits with the common Jewish interpretation of idolatry, that idolatry is not only a matter of worshipping the wrong God, but also of attempting to worship the right God in the wrong way, and thus committing the sin of *avodah zarah*, or "nonprescribed cult" (Louis Isaac Rabinowitz, "Idolatry," in *Encycopaedia Judaica* [New York: Macmillan, 1971], 8:1229–31; cf. Exod 30:9; Lev 10:1; 16:2; Num 3:4; 26:61; Deut 12:13–14).

[60] *Lectures on Zechariah: The Latin Text* (1526), LW 20:76 = WA 13:612; LW 16:244–46.

[61] Literally "divine service." This is the usual term in the Luther Bible for worship.

[62] *Preface to the Prophets* (1545), LW 35:273 (translation altered) = WA DB 11/1:15.13–16.

[63] LW 1:149; 17:17; 9:54; 40:60–61; 52:84–85.

[64] LW 19:11; 36:147.

[65] *Commentary on Jonah: The German Text* (1526), LW 19:55–56 = WA 19:207–8.

[66] LW 22:366–67; 24:24; 35:269–70.

invented his own place and manner of worship because he was afraid of the political implications of his people going up to worship in Jerusalem, the capital of his political rival. Thus he became an idolater, though he had no intention of defecting from the God who brought Israel out of Egypt.[67]

Luther found even more examples in the church of his day.[68] The Papal church taught that God must be worshipped by fasting, observing holy days, praying to the saints, and performing other works commanded by the Pope, while faith in Christ was set aside.[69] Likewise, it taught that the mass is a sacrifice, though God's Word teaches that Christ has been sacrificed once for all.[70] Furthermore, the monks thought they could worship God through their cowls, ropes, tonsures, bare feet, and holy orders, though no word of God has established such worship. Therefore Luther says they create a false god, since they imagine a god who can be reconciled through such self-chosen works.[71] The Sacramentarians like Zwingli reasoned that Christ is not present in the Lord's Supper since he is up in heaven, despite Christ's promise.[72] Therefore Luther says that all these people are idolaters, since they give up the Word and worship God according to their own thoughts.[73] For "it is idolatry to establish worship [*cultum*] as a result of one's own choosing and not as the result of a command of the Lord."[74] When people do this, they "shape God according to their own worship,"[75] as if he must bless whatever they choose.

Luther observes that whenever people depart from what God has instituted and fashion their own worship, this is inevitably some form of self-righteousness. Since natural human reason knows nothing of Christ or the Gospel, it concludes that one must become godly and enter God's kingdom through good works, and devises works accordingly. Yet God's Word teaches that one becomes godly and a member of his kingdom through faith in Christ.[76] Therefore the true God will only be found by the hungry soul who "relies on the words and seeks God nowhere but in the Christ who lies in the manger, or wherever He may be—on the cross, in Baptism, in the Lord's Supper, or in the ministry of the divine Word, or with my neighbor or brother."[77]

---

[67] LW 17:17; 35:269, 272; 1 Kings 12:28.

[68] LW 35:270, 272–73.

[69] LW 22:367–68; WA 28:610–20; LC I, 11, 22 = WA 30/1:134.7–12, 135.17–26.

[70] *The Misuse of the Mass* (1521), LW 36:147 = WA 8:493.

[71] LW 1:14; 17:17; 19:55–56; 22:22, 152, 154–55.

[72] LW 23:80; 30:258.

[73] LW 1:149; 12:48–49; 17:108.

[74] *Lectures on Genesis* (1535–38) LW 2:284 = WA 42:465.

[75] *Lectures on Isaiah* (1527–30), LW 17:16–17 = WA 31/2:273.2–3.

[76] LW 1:11, 14–15; 17:16–17; 22:55–56, 368–69; 23:55–56; 24:229–30; 52:58–60.

[77] *Sermons on John* (1530–32), LW 23:56 = WA 33:81.37–42.

THE SELF-LOCALIZING GOD

As we have noted, central to Luther's theology of worship is his conviction that we only have access to the transcendent God where he chooses to make himself immanently available to us. John Kleinig describes this theology of God's self-localization in the following way:

> As he [Luther] reworked his Catholic heritage evangelically . . . he repeatedly reflected on the apparent localisation by God of himself at the temple in Jerusalem. He, as it were, took up the ancient taunt of the pagan idolaters against the Israelites for their lack of idols and asked himself: 'Where is your God?' His answer was that the process of divine self-localisation, which had begun in the Old Testament, culminated in the incarnation of our Lord. In the man Jesus God localised himself once and for all far more physically and completely than any pagan god in any statue.[78]

Luther insists that although God is infinite and fills all things, he is not present in the same way in every place. Only in clearly defined places does he give people full access to himself.[79] It is one thing for God to be present in creation, and another for him to be present for us in such a way that we can grasp hold of him.[80] In the Old Testament, he did not choose to make himself available to his people on every hilltop or under every tree, but only where he chose to put his name and promised to be present in blessing (Exod 20:24; Deut 12:5–14). Likewise, he now makes himself available to us in the body of the man Jesus, who in turn comes to us in the Word, the water, the bread and the wine of the Gospel. Just as he once made himself available in the created tabernacle and temple, so now he is available in his new temple, Jesus' created body.[81] Thus if we want to find God we do not turn our eyes upwards to heav-

---

[78] Kleinig, "Where is your God?" 117.

[79] "Although he is present in all creatures, and I might find him in stone, in fire, in water, or even in a rope, for he certainly is there, yet he does not wish that I seek him there apart from the Word, and cast myself into the fire or the water, or hang myself on the rope. He is present everywhere, but he does not wish that you grope for him everywhere. Grope rather where the Word is, and there you will lay hold of him in the right way. Otherwise you are tempting God and committing idolatry" (*The Sacrament of the Body and Blood of Christ—Against the Fanatics* [1526], LW 36:342 = WA 19:492.19–25). Cf. LW 37:214–30.

[80] *The Babylonian Captivity of the Church* (1520), LW 37:68–69 = WA 23:150–52.

[81] The main passages in which Luther develops this theme of God's self-localization are LW 1:94–95, 248–50, 309, 330; 2:284–86; 3:108–10, 163–64, 168–69; 4:178–83; 5:241–51; 6:127–29, 265–66; 12:352; 13:33–37; 19:44–45, 79–80; 23:120–25, 128–30; 35:268–70; 37, 68–69; WA 16:530f; 25:94; 25:236f; WA 40/3:51–57, 335–39, 399–443. See also Luther's discussion on three possible modes of presence in LW 37, 214–30, parts of which are quoted in SD VII, 93–103.

en toward the infinite God in his glory, nor do we turn our eyes inwards to find the spiritual God within. Instead, we turn our eyes outwards to the particular external things in which the infinite God has chosen to become locally present, and the transcendent God has made himself available within his creation.

LUTHER IN CONTRAST TO OTHER APPROACHES TO WORSHIP

Luther's answer to where we must look to find God distinguishes him from pagan idolaters, Roman Catholics, and the Reformed. His assertion that we can only know and worship God through Jesus Christ is obviously a rejection of all non-Christian theology and worship. Yet by itself this assertion is relatively uncontroversial in Christian circles. All orthodox Christian theology places Christ at the center of God's revelation and at the heart of Christian worship. What is more controversial is the way Luther identifies Christ so closely with the means of the Gospel. This sets him at odds with both Catholics and the Reformed.

Luther and pagan idolatry. Luther is in full agreement with pagan idolaters that God can make himself available within sacred places or holy things within creation. The point of disagreement is over the question "What places, and which things?" Luther's incarnational, sacramental theology is highly specific. It is not some theory about created things in general, and how they serve as vehicles of the divine. Instead, it is an assertion that God has chosen particular places and things as the means by which he comes to us to bless us.[82] The error of pagan idolatry as far as Luther is concerned is not that pagans try to worship God by means of created things, but that they use self-chosen things instead of the things God has designated in his Word. The difference between the worship before the ark in the temple in Jerusalem and the worship before the golden calves at Bethel and Dan is not that one employed visible, created things and the other did not. They both did. Instead, it is that one was instituted by God whereas the other was not. This means that God had attached himself and his blessing to the one and not the other.[83]

To help us see Luther's position clearly we should note the contrast between Luther and Calvin on this point. For Calvin, one key problem with pagan idols is that they are physical and visible. He writes, "We must cling to

---

[82] Phillip Cary, professor of philosophy at Eastern University in Pennsylvania, characterizes the medieval theology of the sacraments, as well as Luther's theology that grew out of it, as a piety of the external and the particular. He contrasts this with the spirituality of the Augustinian tradition, in which the things that really count are always inward and universal (Phillip Cary, *Outward Signs: The Powerlessness of External Things in Augustine's Thought* [Oxford: Oxford University Press, 2008], vii).

[83] LW 9:81; 17:17; 22:366–67; 24:24; 35:268–73; 36:259; 40:87–88.

this principle: God's glory is corrupted by an impious falsehood whenever any form is attached to him. . . . God's majesty is sullied by an unfitting and absurd fiction, when the incorporeal is made to resemble corporeal matter, the invisible a visible likeness, the spirit an inanimate object, the immeasurable a puny bit of wood, stone, or gold."[84] To prove this point he appeals to various passages of Scripture that censure or mock pagan idolaters for worshipping inanimate objects (Ps 115:4, 8; 135:15; Isa 41:29; 44:9–20), or for thinking that God can be compared to an image of metal or stone created through human imagination and skill (Deut 4:15–16; Isa 40:18; 41:7; 45:9; 46:5; Acts 17:29).[85] Yet as far as Luther is concerned, these passages do not prove Calvin's point. The problem he sees in these passages is not that the pagan idols are visible and physical, but that they lack divine institution. This means they also lack God's Spirit. Luther contends that these passages condemn not just physical images made of wood or stone, but any pictures we form of God apart from his Word, including mental images.[86] To Luther's way of thinking, the prophets are right to mock pagan idolaters for worshipping blocks of wood. Yet the problem is not that the wood is physical, but that the worshippers lack the Word. A block of wood apart from the Word is just a block of wood, just as water apart from the Word is only water.[87] Only when God's Word is attached to a physical thing can it be God-bearing and life-giving.[88]

Luther's response to pagan idolatry is ultimately christological. If we are to worship God only in the place where he tells us he has descended to meet us, then we must worship him through Christ. This is most obviously the case now that Christ has come in the flesh, and says, "No one comes to the Father except through me" (John 14:6). However, Luther also considered Christ to be the focal point of Israel's worship in the Old Testament. He saw this worship—from the serpent Moses placed on the pole to the sacrifices offered in the temple—as a covering for the pre-incarnate Christ who was already with Israel, and as a sign pointing to the incarnate Christ who was to come.[89] Luther suggests that God forbad the people of Israel from making any other images or worshipping before them since this would divert them from Christ,[90] the only mercy seat at which we can grasp hold of God.[91]

---

[84] Calvin, *Institutes of the Christian Religion* [1559], 1.11.2.

[85] Calvin, *Institutes of the Christian Religion* [1559], 1.11.2–4.

[86] LW 9:58; 17:21–22, 37–39, 59, 107–14, 140–41.

[87] Cf. Luther's treatment of Baptism in the Small Catechism (SC IV 9–10 = WA 30/1:381.6–11).

[88] LW 17:113; 36:341.

[89] LW 15:313; cf. 1 Cor 10:4, 9; Col 2:16–17; Heb 10:1.

[90] *Commentary on Psalm 2* (1532), LW 12:87–88 = WA 40/2:305; cf. Paul J. Achtemeier, "Gods Made with Hands: The New Testament and the Problem of Idolatry," *Ex Auditu* 15 (1999): 58–59.

This is a profound critique of pagan idolatry. It gets to the heart of the function cultic images played in the pagan worship of the ancient Near East. The purpose of cultic images was to function as mediators between the gods in heaven and their worshippers on earth. The key characteristic of these images was not that they visibly resembled their gods. Sometimes they were thought to do so, but in other cases they were only intended as symbols of the deity or as focal points for the presence of the transcendent god. Examples of the latter include standing stones, open-air sanctuaries, or empty chariots pointing to an invisible god.[92] Instead, what was important about them was that they were believed to be physical vessels in which the spirit of a god was believed to dwell so that they functioned as representatives of that god on earth and a means by which people could gain access to the god.[93] In other words, when humans construct such images they are attempting to bring about an incarnation, to bridge the gap between heaven and earth by bringing the power and presence of the gods down to earth in a tangible way. Thus pagan cultic images directly challenge Christ's place in the economy of salvation. Therefore the best rationale for forbidding them is that they are counterfeits of the real incarnation.

Luther and Roman Catholicism. Much of Luther's attack on idolatrous worship is directed against Roman Catholicism. Luther attacked all of the following as idolatrous: works of supererogation such as fasting and holy orders;[94] indulgences;[95] pilgrimages to see holy relics or sites;[96] the cult of the

---

[91] LW 17:61; 19:80; 22:248–49, 366–67; 23:120–21; 24:23–24; 26:273; 27:64; 30:223; 31:64; 37:364; 51:277–86; Luther, *Commentary on the First Twenty-Two Psalms*, 2:208–9.

[92] Tryggve Mettinger, *No Graven Image?: Israelite Aniconism in Its Ancient Near Eastern Context* (Stockholm: Almqvist and Wiksell International, 1995), 18–35. Many scholars who have studied the iconography of the ancient Near East have concluded that Jeroboam's golden calves were intended this way, not as visible depictions of God, but as depictions of the steed on which the invisible God rode. This would make them analogous to the ark of the covenant, the visible throne of the invisible God (Tryggve Mettinger, "The Veto on Images and the Aniconic God in Ancient Israel," in *Religious Symbols and Their Functions*, ed. Haralds Biezais [Uppsala, Sweden: Almqvist and Wiksell International, 1979], 21–22; Othmar Keel and Christoph Uelinger, *Gods, Goddesses, and Images of God in Ancient Israel,* trans. Thomas H. Trapp [Minneapolis: Fortress, 1998], 192; Mettinger, *No Graven Image?*, 19).

[93] Rabinowitz, "Idolatry," 8:1232–33; John F. Kutsko, *Between Heaven and Earth: Divine Presence and Absence in the Book of Ezekiel* (Winona Lake, IN: Eisenbrauns, 2000), 57–61; G. K. Beale, *We Become What We Worship: A Biblical Theology of Idolatry* (Downers Grove, IL: IVP Academic, 2008), 64–70.

[94] LW 1:14; 17:17; 5:259–60; 19:55–56; 22:22, 51, 152, 154–55, 367–68; 35:406; WA 28:610–20; LC I, 11, 22 = WA 30/1:134.7–12, 135.17–26.

[95] LW 4:179; 8:230; 22:51; 31:201; 34:16–17; 35:406; 41:222, 237.

[96] LW 4:130; 34:16–17; 35:406; 39:241–43; 40:92; 48:339–42; SA II 2.11–24.

saints;[97] the Mass when it is turned into a meritorious human work;[98] and any other act of worship, from the observance of holy days to the erecting of religious images, if it is done without the Gospel in the belief that it will earn merit with God.[99] Luther's key criticism is that although the Papal church claims to teach Christ, it effectively denies him. This is because it denies that Christ alone is our righteousness, and replaces Christ's merit with self-invented human works.[100]

When Luther objects to worship practices invented by the Catholic Church without God's Word, his objection is the same as his objection to pagan worship. Although the worshippers have pious intentions and think they are worshipping God, their worship is not God pleasing. Instead, it is directed to an idol, since they are looking for God in the wrong place. By seeking God in their human speculations,[101] their monastic rules and observances,[102] their pilgrimages to Rome and Santiago,[103] their altars and chapels,[104] their fasts,[105] their alms,[106] their indulgences, their sacrifices for the dead,[107] their pope,[108] their traditions and ceremonies,[109] and their saints,[110] they have lost sight of the one place God wants to be found, in the Gospel of Christ.

Luther agreed with his Catholic opponents that God makes himself available to us in concrete things on earth. The point of contention was over the question "In what things in particular?" Unlike many of the other Reformers, Luther never attacked the Catholic Church for its sacramentalism per se, or for its use of visible, created things in worship. He never denied the sacramental power of Baptism, the Lord's Supper, or Absolution. He simply objected that much of the sacramental system of the Catholic Church had insufficient basis in God's Word, and that even the genuine Sacraments had been twisted

---

[97] LW 1:179; 8:203; 17:378; 24:22, 74, 369; 36:299–300; 41:204; 43:211; 44:32; 47:45–46; WA 28: 611, 615–20; SA II 2.25–28.

[98] LW 13:314; 23:207; 27:89; 28:86; 34:31; 35:91, 101; 36:142, 148, 288; SA II 2.1–11.

[99] LW 9:82; 35:270–73; 51:84.

[100] LW 22:451; 30:252–53, 285–86.

[101] WA 40.3:335–39; LW 6:128–29.

[102] WA 40.3:51–57; LW 3:109, 168; 4:180–82; 5:247; 6:127; 23:121, 128–30.

[103] LW 3:107–9; 4:179–80; 5:247; 6:128–29.

[104] LW 4:179; 6:127.

[105] *Lectures on Genesis* (1535–38), LW 3:168 = WA 42:668; LW 23:121.

[106] *Lectures on Genesis* (1535–38), LW 3:168 = WA 42:668.

[107] *Lectures on Genesis* (1538–42), LW 4:180 = WA 43:266.

[108] *Lectures on Genesis* (1538–42), LW 5:244 = WA 43:597.

[109] *Lectures on Genesis* (1538–42), LW 5:245–47, 251 = WA 43:598–600, 602.

[110] *Sermons on John* (1530–32), LW 23:128 = WA 33:199; WA 28:607–20.

so that the promise of the Gospel attached to them had been obscured.[111] Luther's goal was never to draw his opponents' attention away from physical things to spiritual things, or from earth to heaven, but rather from self-invented things to the God-ordained place of worship in Christ and the Gospel.

Luther and the Reformed. The controversy between Luther and the Reformed theologians of the sixteenth century was also about the place of worship. Yet here there was not basic agreement that God can make himself available to us in particular places or things within creation. For the Reformed, God gives us signs within creation that point us to the God who transcends all created things. This is not the same as giving himself to us through created things. Luther and the Reformed agreed that true worship of God is worship through faith in Jesus Christ. The disagreement was over the question of where we find Christ. Do we find him here on earth in particular, external, created things? That is, do we find him in the means of the Gospel? Or is the Gospel a sign that does not actually give us Christ, but directs us to find Christ elsewhere, either in heaven or in our hearts?

Phillip Cary articulates the difference between Luther and the Reformed when he writes,

> For Luther the Gospel is not, as the old Protestant saw it, like one beggar telling another beggar where to get bread. That would mean the minister's job is to instruct people in how to meet the conditions necessary for salvation—how to get from here to where the true bread is. Instead, for Luther the gospel is one beggar simply giving another beggar the bread of life.[112]

For Luther, the Gospel gives us Christ. For the Reformed, it directs us to find him somewhere else.

Both Luther and the Reformed were convinced that the worship of their day had become idolatrous, and their efforts to rid the church of this idolatry were central to their respective reform projects. However, they tended to operate with different guiding principles regarding what is idolatrous and what is not.[113] As we have seen, Luther's guiding concern was that our faith and

---

[111] For a full treatment of this subject, see *The Babylonian Captivity of the Church*, particularly LW 36:18–92.

[112] Phillip Cary, "Why Luther is not quite Protestant: Logic of Faith in a Sacramental Promise," *Pro Ecclesia* 14 (Fall 2005): 461.

[113] At this point, the analysis of John Maxfield is superior to that of Carlos Eire. Eire gives an excellent portrayal of the Reformed theologians of the sixteenth century, and their actions and motivations in their war against idolatry. Yet Eire's treatment of Luther is more superficial. He tends to write Luther off for his failure to share the Reformed outlook, instead of trying to understand him on his own terms. He portarys Luther as half-hearted in his battle against

worship life be grounded in the promises of God and the means of salvation he has instituted for us in the Bible. This includes such physical things as the sacraments and the death and resurrection of Christ. The Reformed on the other hand were convinced that God's transcendence over all created things must be preserved at all costs lest we fall into idolatry. Carlos Eire, professor of history and religious studies at Yale, identifies what he calls a "hermeneutic of transcendence" in the Reformed war against idolatry. That is, they had a metaphysical outlook that drew sharp boundaries between matter and spirit, and stressed to a high degree God's transcendence over all finite earthly things. Their basic assumption was that it is impossible for the infinite, invisible, spiritual God to be too closely associated with any finite, visible, physical thing.[114] Thus they concluded that our worship must be centered on things that are "spiritual" in the sense of non-visible and non-material. This led them to ban religious images. It also led them—at least from Luther's perspective—to fight against the created means of salvation that God has instituted.

First, let us look at how these different guiding principles led to a different stance regarding religious images. Luther's position was that no part of the Law of Moses, including the ban on images, is directly binding on Christians, since we are no longer people of the old covenant but are under a new covenant through Christ. He writes, "We will regard Moses as a teacher, but we will not regard him as our lawgiver—unless he agrees with both the New Testament and the natural law."[115] Furthermore, he observes that even under the old covenant images were only banned if people worshipped them. He therefore concludes that religious images by themselves are not a problem for Christians, but only become a problem if people attach an idolatrous opinion to them by worshipping them or trusting in them. To ban them, when God has not banned them, would therefore not be a blow against idolatry. Instead, it would be to engage in a self-chosen work. This would itself be an expression

---

idolatry, since although he warned people against a works-righteous approach to images he didn't join the Reformed in banning images or spiritualising the Sacraments (Carlos M. N. Eire, *War Against the Idols: The Reformation of Worship from Erasmus to Calvin* [Cambridge: Cambridge University Press, 1986], 2–3, 28, 55). Maxfield delves more deeply into Luther's thought, and shows that he was absolutely committed to fighting idolatry throughout his career. The difference between him and the Reformed was not the result of any lack of commitment from either side, but rather a different view of what is and is not idolatry (John A. Maxfield, "Martin Luther and Idolatry," in *The Reformation as Christianization: Essays on Scott Hendrix's Christianization Thesis*, ed. Anna Marie Johnson and John A. Maxfield [Tübingen: Mohr Siebeck, 2012], 141–68).

[114] Eire, *War Against the Idols*, 1–3, 7–8, 24, 28, 31–36, 40–41, 43–44, 47–62, 66, 69, 72–73, 77–78, 84–87, 91–93, 98, 168, 171, 173, 177–80, 184–89, 197–98, 200–201, 205–33, 311–13, 318.

[115] LW 35:165; cf. LW 9:79–81; 35:164–68; 40:92–98; Matt 12:1–12; John 5:16; 7:22–23; 9:14–16; Col 2:16–17; Acts 10:1–11:18; 15:1–29; 1 Cor 8:1–13; Gal 2:1–14; 4:10–11; 5:1–13; Phil 3:2–3; Heb 8:1–13; James 2:10.

of idolatry if people believed that God required such self-chosen acts of devotion.[116] In contrast, the general Reformed attitude was that the Old Testament ban on cultic images expresses an eternal truth about God's nature. It teaches that he is transcendent over all visible, physical things, and that it demeans his majesty to be associated with such things.[117] Therefore they applied this piece of Old Testament ceremonial law to Christians in a broad brush manner,[118] and treated sacred images as inherently idolatrous regardless of whether people worship them or not.[119]

These same guiding principles led to different views of the Sacraments. If it demeans God's majesty to be associated with any physical thing, then what about the Sacraments? The basic Reformed opinion was that the rejection of idolatry also entails a rejection of the church's sacramental system. Although they retained Baptism and the Lord's Supper, they spiritualized them. They interpreted them symbolically, and denied that God or his power can be present within the elements. For instance, Zwingli insisted that external things such as the external Word or Sacraments can have no saving effect on the soul, nor can they be vehicles of the Spirit, since God cannot be bound to any created thing.[120] Even Calvin, who attributed more power to the Sacraments than most of the Reformed, still treated them as visible pledges that God

---

[116] LW 9:81–82, 85; 35:268–70; 36:259–60; 40:85–88, 90–91, 99; 51:79–81, 84. Cf. Louis Isaac Rabinowitz, editor-in-chief of the *Encyclopedia Judaica*, who asks why certain cultic images were commanded in the Old Testament—such as the cherubim above the ark and on the walls and doors of the temple—whereas others were forbidden. He concludes that there is no satisfactory explanation except that God has commanded some and forbidden others (Rabinowitz, "Idolatry," 8:1229–31).

[117] Eire, *War Against the Idols*, 1–3, 7–8, 24, 28. 31–36, 40–41, 43–44, 47–62, 66, 69, 72–73, 77–78, 84–87, 91–93, 98, 168, 171, 173, 177–80, 184–89, 197–98, 200–201, 205–33, 311–13, 318. Randall C. Zachman, *Image and Word in the Theology of John Calvin* (Notre Dame, IN: University of Notre Dame Press, 2007), 58–59, 78, 231; Calvin, *Institutes of the Christian Religion* [1559], 1.11.1–3; 4.17.19; John Calvin, *John Calvin's Sermons on the Ten Commandments*, ed. and trans. Benjamin W. Farley (Grand Rapids, MI: Baker, 1980), 66; John Calvin, "Short Treatise on the Holy Supper of our Lord and Only Saviour Jesus Christ," in *Calvin: Theological Treatises*, ed. J. K. S. Reid (Louisville, KY: Westminster John Knox, 2006), 159, 166.

[118] Eire, *War Against the Idols*, 24, 56, 58, 92, 226; cf. Zachman, *Image and Word in the Theology of John Calvin*, 3; Calvin, *Institutes of the Christian Religion* [1559], 1.11.2, 1.11.13.

[119] Eire, *War Against the Idols*, 13–17, 59–60, 205–16, 225–28; Calvin, *Institutes of the Christian Religion* [1559], 1.11.5–7, 1.11.13.

[120] Huldrych Zwingli, *Huldreich Zwinglis Sämtliche Werke*, ed. Emil Egli et al., Corpus Reformatorum 88–101 (14 vols.; Zürich: Theologischer Verlag, 1982–91), 2:110; 3:263, 761, 787; 5:622, 626; Huldrych Zwingli, *Huldreich Zwingli's Werke*, ed. Melchior Schulero and Johannes Schultess, (7 vols.; Zürich: Friedrich Schulthess, 1830–41), 4:10, 13, 37, 284; 6.1:569; Gottfried W. Locher, *Zwingli's Thought: New Perspectives* (Leiden, The Netherlands: E. J. Brill, 1981), 12–13, 56, 180, 225–27.

would perform the thing signified through the parallel operation of his Spirit, rather than as vehicles of divine power or presence per se.[121] Calvin calls it a great error "to think that a hidden power is joined and fastened to the Sacraments by which they of themselves confer the graces of the Holy Spirit upon us, as wine is given in a cup ... They do not bestow any grace of themselves."[122] Indeed, we must "place no power in creatures ... neither ought our confidence to inhere in the sacraments, nor the glory of God be transferred to them. Rather, laying aside all things, both our faith and our confession ought to rise up to him who is author of the sacraments and all things."[123] Calvin enacts this view in his liturgy of the Lord's Supper, in which he writes,

> Let us lift up our spirits on high where Jesus Christ is in the glory of His Father, whence we expect Him at our redemption. Let us not be fascinated by these earthly and corruptible elements that we see with our eyes and touch with our hands, seeking Him there as though He were enclosed in the bread or wine. Then [only] shall our souls be disposed to be nourished and vivified by His substance, when they are lifted up above all earthly things, attaining even to heaven, and entering the kingdom of God, where He dwells. Therefore let us be content to have the bread and wine as signs and witnesses, seeking the truth spiritually where the word of God promises that we shall find it.[124]

Thus we can see that even for Calvin, the most sacramental of the major Reformed theologians, we are not to seek God in the Sacrament, but above it. His basic assumption is that even when God institutes created means, the real action must be elsewhere: never in the bread or wine or Word, but always beyond these things in God. This is not a mediating position between Luther and Zwingli, but a clear rejection of Luther's sacramental realism as an idolatrous fixation with created things. Calvin makes this clear in a letter to Bucer,

---

[121] Calvin, *Institutes of the Christian Religion* [1559], 4.17.5–6, 4.17.9–37; Calvin, "Short Treatise on the Holy Supper of our Lord," 163, 165; John Calvin, "The clear explanation of sound doctrine concerning the true partaking of the flesh and blood of Christ in the Holy Supper: to dissipate the mists of Tileman Heshusius," in *Calvin: Theological Treatises*, ed. J. K. S. Reid (Louisville, Kentucky: Westminster John Knox, 2006), 263–64, 267–68, 270, 276–78, 287, 289, 298, 301, 308–9, 314; John Calvin, "Confession of Faith concerning the Eucharist," in *Calvin: Theological Treatises*, ed. J. K. S. Reid (Louisville, Kentucky: Westminster John Knox, 2006), 168; Zachman, *Image and Word in the Theology of John Calvin*, 306–13, 323–42.

[122] Calvin, *Institutes of the Christian Religion* [1559], 4.14.17.

[123] Ibid., 4.14.12.

[124] John Calvin, *Writings on Pastoral Piety*, trans. and ed. Elsie Anne McKee (Mahwah, NJ: Paulist Press, 2001), 133.

in which he writes, “What else is the adorable sacrament of Luther but an idol set up in the temple of God?”[125]

In complete contrast, Luther regarded a high view of the Sacraments as essential if we are to avoid idolatry. That is, he regarded the rejection of Christ’s sacramental presence with us as a rejection of the incarnate Christ that must inevitably lead to idolatry.[126] He states this in his commentary on 1 John, where he reflects on how the spirit of the antichrist will deny that the Son of God has come in the flesh (1 John 2:18–23; 4:1–3). Luther applies this to the “fanatics” and “Sacramentarians” and calls them “antichrists in part.”[127] He does not call them antichrists in full like the papists, since they do not deny the merits of Christ.[128] Nevertheless he writes,

> He, however, who denies Christ in one place denies Him everywhere. Thus those who say: “It is not Christ who has His body in the bread and His blood in the wine” do not have Christ. Indeed, they have an idol of their hearts. For they deny the chief attribute of the divinity, namely, the presence of Christ. . . .
>
> The spirit of the Sacramentarians denies grossly that Christ came in the flesh when they say that Christ’s “flesh profits nothing” (John 6:63), likewise that the spirit must do everything, that Baptism amounts to nothing. . . . Christ has flesh, but in it there is the full Divinity. God has offered Himself to us in Christ. Christ came into the flesh to be with us in Baptism and at the Holy Supper. Every spirit who is at pains to teach that Christ does everything through the sacraments is of God, is glad to hear about Christ, and gives thanks. For he understands that Christ is his and that He came in the flesh. Therefore this has been stated emphatically: Behold, this is the test of a spirit, whether he is of God or of the devil.[129]

Luther is being unfair here, by focusing on this one area of the Christian life where the Reformed deny Christ’s presence, while ignoring the many ways they confess him. Nevertheless, we should not dismiss Luther’s comments without attempting to understand the rationale behind them. Luther’s concern is that the Sacramentarians “convert Baptism, faith, and the Lord’s Sup-

---

[125] John Calvin, *Letters of John Calvin,* vol. 2, ed. Jules Bonnet (Philadelphia: Presbyterian Board of Publication, 1858), 234.

[126] LW 1:149; 8:133; 12:48–49; 17:108; 23:157, 187–88; 37:130–31.

[127] *Lectures on First John* (1527), LW 30:252, 287 = WA 20:669.28, 730.24.

[128] *Lectures on First John* (1527), LW 30:252 = WA 20:669.

[129] *Lectures on First John* (1527), LW 30:258, 286 = WA 20:682.37–40, 727.36–728.24, 728.35–37.

per into nothing but Law and commandment."[130] For Luther, the Sacraments are Gospel, and the Gospel is sacramental. If we say that the means of the Gospel do not actually deliver Christ and his grace to us, then they are not Gospel. Instead, they are laws that teach us how to express our piety or vainly direct us to climb up to God. And if the means of the Gospel are not Gospel, then we have no Gospel. Nor do we have Christ, since we can only grasp hold of Christ sacramentally through the Gospel and not with some self-invented law. Luther writes,

> The Anabaptists claim that Baptism is nothing if one is not previously sanctified. They do not want to acquire holiness through and from Baptism, but by their piety they want to make Baptism holy and wholesome. As I see it, this is to lose the Cornerstone completely and to be justified, not through the grace of Christ in Baptism but through one's own self, so that Baptism gives nothing, creates nothing, brings nothing. Instead, we bring and give everything to Baptism beforehand, so that it is nothing but an unnecessary symbol by which one is supposed to be able to recognize such pious folk. . . . The fanatics do the same thing with their Sacrament, which does not sanctify or bring grace but shows and demonstrates how blessed and holy they are without the Sacrament.[131]

Luther never responded directly to Calvin's view of the Lord's Supper, which is that Christ is truly offered to us, provided that by faith we climb up to him in heaven. Yet it is doubtful that this departure from the Zwinglian position would have improved matters much in Luther's mind. This still leaves us in the position of having to climb up to God, rather than simply receiving him as he climbs down to us. Christ bids us to look to the Sacrament, "given for you for the forgiveness of sins." Calvin invents a new law and bids us to look to heaven instead.

Even more serious as far as Luther is concerned is the Reformed understanding of Christ's incarnation. This can be seen most clearly in Luther's debates with Zwingli. Zwingli tried to draw a sharp line between the infinite, spiritual Son of God and the finite, physical Son of Man. Although he said there is only one person of Christ, he refused to draw the necessary conclusions from this. He went on to treat the two natures as if they are two persons who can still act independently of each other, like Siamese twins instead of one integrated person. This is because he denied that the attributes and actions of each nature must be applied to the whole person of Christ in fact, not

[130] *Sermons on John* (1530–32), LW 23:99 = WA 33:150.24–26.

[131] *Commentary on Psalm 117* (1530), LW 14:39 = WA 31/1:257.10–18, 21–23.

just as a figure of speech.[132] Luther replied that this produces "a kind of Christ after whom I would not want to be a Christian."[133] That is, this refusal to acknowledge the true unity of the person of Christ produces a false Christ, an idol.

The most crucial issue was that Zwingli insisted that only the human nature suffered and died, and the divinity did not share in this suffering.[134] Luther recognized, as did the early church in the case of Nestorius,[135] that this turns Christ's death into something that is merely human and has no power to save us.[136] Yet many other problems result from such attempts to divide Christ. For instance, Zwingli asserted that Christ was only referring to his divine nature when he said, "I am the way, the truth, and the life," and "whoever has seen me has seen the Father."[137] For Luther, this leaves us speculating fruitlessly about the naked God in his majesty, instead of knowing him in his incarnation. Furthermore, Zwingli insisted that at the ascension Christ's hu-

---

[132] Huldrych Zwingli, "Friendly Exegesis, that is, Exposition of the Matter of the Eucharist to Martin Luther, February 1527," in *Huldrych Zwingli Writings*, Vol. 2, translated by H. Wayne Pipkin (Allison Park, PA: Pickwick Publications, 1984), 319–36; cf. LW 15:341–43; 28:265–67; 37:212–13; 41:101–4.

[133] *Confession Concerning Christ's Supper* (1528), LW 37:209 = WA 26:320.8–9.

[134] Zwingli, "Friendly Exegesis," 321, 324.

Calvin also refused to say that God truly shared in the sufferings of Christ on the cross so that the merits of his death were divine merits and not merely human merits (Calvin, *Institutes of the Christian Religion*, 2.14.2, 2.17.1, 4.17.30; John Calvin, *Commentaries on the Book of the Prophet Jeremiah and the Lamentations*, trans. and ed. John Owen [Grand Rapids, MI: Eerdmans, 1950], xviii–xix [from dedicatory epistle to commentary on Jeremiah]).

[135] Cyril of Alexandria, *On the Unity of Christ*, trans. John Anthony McGuckin (Crestwood, NY: St. Vladimir's Seminary Press, 1995), 70, 132; Cyril of Alexandria, "The Third Letter of Cyril to Nestorius," in *Christology of the Later Fathers*, ed. Edward R. Harvey (Louisville, KY: Westminster John Knox, 2006), 351, 354; Second Council of Constantinople, "The Anathemas of the Second Council of Constantinople (Fifth Ecumenical)," in *Christology of the Later Fathers*, ed. Edward R. Harvey (Louisville, KY: Westminster John Knox, 2006), 379–81; Third Council of Constantinople, "The Statement of Faith of the Third Council of Constantinople (Sixth Ecumenical)," in *Christology of the Later Fathers*, ed. Edward R. Harvey (Louisville, KY: Westminster John Knox, 2006), 383–84; Philip Schaff and Henry Wace, eds., *The Seven Ecumenical Councils*, Nicene and Post-Nicene Fathers, Second Series, Vol. 14 (Grand Rapids, MI: Eerdmans, 1982), 217–18.

[136] LW 28:264–65; 37:209, 231; 41:103–5.

[137] Zwingli, "Friendly Exegesis," 325. Although he shared some of Zwingli's tendency to divide the two natures, Calvin was more sensible than Zwingli at this point, and recognized that the human nature is an essential part of God's revelation of himself to us in Christ. (John Calvin, *Calvin's Commentaries: The Gospel According to St. John and the First Epistle of John*, trans. T. H. L. Parker, ed. David W. Torrance and Thomas F. Torrance [Grand Rapids, MI: Eerdmans, 1961], 149 [commentary on John 17:22]; Zachman, *Image and Word in the Theology of John Calvin*, 262.)

man nature ascended into heaven in such a way that it is now absent from the earth, and that his promises of his ongoing presence with his disciples apply only to his divine nature.[138] As far as Luther is concerned, this robs us of Christ, since there is no Christ who is not incarnate.[139] Instead, we must believe that he is with us in the bread and wine at his table, and even in the dungeon, in torture, and in death. Otherwise we are robbed of Christ where we need him most.[140]

Luther and God's transcendence. From a Lutheran perspective, the hermeneutic of transcendence is an alien imposition on Scripture that results in a one-sided reading of it.[141] It latches on to those parts of Scripture that speak about God's transcendence, but can never fully account for all the "incarnational" elements in Scripture, where the transcendent God makes himself present and available to his people through created things.

Luther's willingness to acknowledge that God has bound himself to created means does not mean he was any less convinced of God's transcendence than the Reformed. Quite the opposite. It was his belief in God's almighty power that led him to assert that if the Creator chooses to join himself to part of his creation, and to unite the infinite with the finite by becoming incarnate, he is able to do so.[142] If he decides to join himself to words spoken in human

---

[138] Zwingli, "Friendly Exegesis," 325–35.

[139] *Confession Concerning Christ's Supper* (1528), LW 37:207, 218–19 = WA 26:317, 332–3.

[140] *The Sacrament of the Body and Blood of Christ—Against the Fanatics* (1526), LW 36:342–43 = WA 19:492–93; cf. LW 22:209.

[141] Eire calls this a scripturally based metaphysics (*War Against the Idols*, 3). Yet he also observes that most of these reformers were influenced by the Platonism of humanists like Erasmus (ibid., 28, 31–36, 200, 231). In the case of Calvin, possible sources of Platonic influence include Erasmus and the other sixteenth century humanists, Calvin's favorite church father Augustine (Charles Partee, "The Soul in Plato, Platonism, and Calvin," *Scottish Journal of Theology* 22 [Sept. 1969]: 294), and Calvin's own reading of Plato (Zachman, *Image and Word in the Theology of John Calvin*, 15–17). Charles Partee argues persuasively that Calvin cannot be called a Christian Platonist in the strong sense (Partee, "The Soul in Plato, Platonism, and Calvin," 287, 294–95). He regarded the study of Scripture under the guidance of the Holy Spirit as the only source of doctrine, and his goal was to develop a biblical theology, not some fusion of faith and philosophy. Nevertheless, he did use philosophy selectively as an aid to the study of the Scriptures (Charles Partee, *Calvin and Classical Philosophy* [Leiden, Netherlands: E. J. Brill, 1977], 13–22), and often argued on the basis of Scripture and "common sense." For Calvin, "common sense" had the flavor of French humanism. As Quirinius Breen points out, Calvin was already well into his twenties and a seasoned humanist by the time he came to evangelical faith. This means that the mind-set of French humanism, including its Platonic elements, was already ingrained, and it would have been almost impossible for him to leave it completely behind (Quirinius Breen, *John Calvin: A Study in French Humanism* [Grand Rapids, MI: Eerdmans, 1931], 146). The influence of Platonism is therefore one possible explanation for the spiritualizing tendency in Calvin's theology, and in Reformed theology in general.

[142] *Lectures on Genesis* (1538–42), LW 5:219–20 = WA 43:579–80.

language, put himself into the bread at the Lord's Table, wrap himself in Baptism and Absolution, and break into the human soul to dwell there, these things are not beyond his ability.[143] If he chooses to bind himself to concrete promises, this is not us binding him, but him choosing to bind himself, and he is free to do so. If we say that he must obey the preconceived metaphysical limits our human minds place upon him, and cannot do the things he has told us he has done in his Word, then we are placing a human limit on him. In response to Zwingli's assertion that God could not be contained within the physical elements of the Lord's Supper, Luther wrote,

> There is no need to enclose him here, as this spirit dreams, for a body is much, much too wide for the Godhead; it could contain many thousand Godheads. On the other hand, it is also far, far too narrow to contain one Godhead. Nothing is so small but God is still smaller, nothing so large but God is still larger, nothing is so short but God is still shorter, nothing so long but God is still longer, nothing is so broad but God is still broader, nothing so narrow but God is still narrower, and so on. He is an inexpressible being, above and beyond all that can be described or imagined.[144]

In other words, human metaphysical rules, or the limits of the physical universe such as time and space, do not apply to an almighty God. Nor do they limit what he is capable of doing in and through the man Jesus Christ. Instead of using human rules like these to figure out what God is like or has done, we must be guided by God's Word.

Luther also rejects the Reformed notion that God's heavenly glory would be debased if he came to us through created things. He argues instead that God's glory is revealed most in his willingness to enter into our world and the lowest depths for us. When Oecolampadius argued that it would demean Christ to be present in the elements on the altar, Luther replied,

> According to Oecolampadius' wisdom, it is true, Christ has no other glory than to sit at the right hand of God on a velvet cushion and let the angels sing and fiddle and ring bells and play before him, and to be unconcerned with the problem of the Supper. But according to the faith of us poor sinners and fools, his glory is manifold, when his body and blood are present in the Supper . . . it is a glory and praise of his inexpressible grace and mercy that he concerns himself so profoundly with us poor sinners and shows us such gracious love and goodness, not content to be everywhere in and around, above

---

[143] LW 1:11; 23:165–77; 26:356–57; 36:343; 37:207.

[144] *Confession Concerning Christ's Supper* (1528), LW 37:228 = WA 26:339.36–340.2.

> and beside us, but even giving us his own body as nourishment . . . Now, we poor fools hold that glory appears when someone shows his virtue, mercy, and goodness to others. For anyone to permit himself to be glorified and served by others is a mean sort of glory, not a divine glory. Therefore one might do well to take the fanatics to school to learn what glory means. . . . Meanwhile, you do not see that if your conclusion were good and convincing, I also would brag and boast that the Son of God was not born of a woman, as the heathen bragged against SS. Cyprian and Augustine. Why? Because it is not glorious for God to be born from the frail body of a human. Again, it is not glorious for Christ to be led by the devil out of the wilderness to [the pinnacle of] the temple and the high mountain, therefore it did not happen. Again, it is not glorious that he was crucified, therefore it did not take place! . . . But the glory of our God is precisely that for our sakes he comes down to the very depths, into human flesh, into the bread, into our mouth, our heart, our bosom.[145]

SUMMARY

For Luther there are only two options. Either we can know and worship God through Christ, or we can form our own faulty picture and vain worship of God apart from Christ. Yet since we can only grasp hold of Christ as he comes to us sacramentally in the Gospel, to worship God through Christ means the same thing as to worship him through the created means of the Gospel. Far from it being demeaning to God's heavenly majesty for him to be present in the flesh, God is glorified above all by his presence with us in the incarnation and in the Gospel. When we separate God from the Gospel, we detract from his glory by turning him into a false god, who must be served by our self-invented laws and acts of worship.

CONTEMPORARY APPLICATION

IDOLATRY: RELIGION APART FROM CHRIST

The most obvious implication of Luther's teaching is that any worship, faith, or spirituality that is not centered in Jesus Christ is idolatrous. All such piety involves a distorted knowledge of God instead of the true knowledge that comes through Jesus Christ. It also lacks divine power, since it grasps hold of a dead idol instead of the living God.

---

[145] *That These Words of Christ, "This Is My Body," Etc., Still Stand Firm Against The Fanatics* (1527), LW 37:70–72 = WA 23:155:15–19, 32–36, 157.2–7, 19–25, 30–32.

What sort of God is it that you do (or do not) believe in? The goal of Christian proclamation is not to direct people to a generic god, but to a very specific God, the God who reveals himself to us in Jesus Christ. No other version of God will do. If Luther and the New Testament are to be believed, on some level all people know there is a God (Rom 1:19; 2:15). The problem is what people do with this knowledge, and how they suppress it, twist it, and distort it so that they can create their own god. This suggests that the greatest challenge for Christian proclamation is not to prove to people that there is a God, even if in some cases it may be necessary to uncover this buried knowledge or refute the rationalizations people use to suppress it. The greater challenge is to give people an accurate picture of God in contrast to all the false pictures that abound. This means proclaiming Christ and allowing him to dethrone all idols.

Many people whose view of God is not shaped in a significant way by Christ still believe in a transcendent god of some kind. Yet such a god can never save them. Those who do not know God through Christ can only have a legal knowledge of God, not an evangelical one. A legal knowledge of God makes God unbearable unless his teeth are pulled in some way, since his Law crushes and condemns us unless we are in Christ. One such toothless tiger is the god of moralistic therapeutic deism, a benevolent but distant and undemanding god.[146] Such a god is too much of a lightweight for us to need a Savior to deliver us from his wrath. Thus it should be no surprise that even those moralistic therapeutic deists who call themselves Christians place little importance on the doctrine of Christ.[147]

Such a view of God, as too harmless to be anything other than benign, should never be mistaken for the Gospel. The resultant god is an idol who will fail people on the last day. Even before that happens, he will fail those who are more sensitive to the weight of God's Law and his curse upon creation. One such person is Tom, an atheist I met a few years ago. Tom told me he did not believe in God, but that if God did exist and ever showed up, he would spit in his face, and hoped the U.S. President would call out the military to fight him to the death. At one stage Tom had been a churchgoer. Then his son developed schizophrenia, and Tom concluded that if God exists he must be malicious to bring this disease on his son. He decided he would rather live in a world where such tragedies are thrown up by the blind forces of nature than a world run by a tyrant from whom there is no escape. Another person like this

---

[146] Christian Smith and Melinda Lundquist Denton, *Soul Searching: The Religious and Spiritual Lives of American Teenagers* (New York: Oxford University Press, 2005), 164–65.

[147] Smith and Denton, *Soul Searching*, 136, 167–68; Christian Smith and Patricia Snell, *Souls in Transition: The Religious and Spiritual Lives of Emerging Adults* (New York: Oxford University Press, 2009), 145–48.

was Charles Darwin. He was too aware of the cruelty in this fallen creation to be convinced by facile talk about how it all comes from the hand of a benign Creator. This was one significant force that drove him to deny that God has given the world its present form and to attribute it to natural forces instead.[148] Likewise, when the modern Darwinist Richard Dawkins dismisses the God of the Bible as a malevolent bully, and uses this to justify his atheism,[149] he is expressing sensitivity to the reality that God is a cruel tyrant to those who view him outside the lens of Christ. The true God is not a god who is so tame that we need not fear him, but a God whose wrath against human sin and curse upon creation has been overcome in Christ.

This suggests that the great challenge for Christian proclamation—even when addressing atheists who purport to have no belief in any God—is to address people's idolatrous legal knowledge of God with an evangelical knowledge of him. For many people this will involve addressing their false belief that they can worship God apart from Christ. For some it will mean addressing the legal knowledge of God that is the suppressed binary opposite of their atheism.

Vacuous spirituality. Many people in contemporary society think they can be spiritual without Christ.[150] This amounts to a belief that the gap between God and us is small enough that we can cross it on our own.

For Luther it is quite clear that all such spirituality lacks divine power, since only through the man Jesus do we have access to the triune God.[151] Therefore any spirituality that we claim apart from Christ must be either an expression of the human spirit or the product of an evil spirit. It is therefore carnal, worldly, or perhaps even demonic, but not spiritual in a biblical sense.

This has the obvious implication that this spirituality will fail a person on the last day. Yet it will also guarantee that a person will fail to achieve whole-

---

148 Cornelius G. Hunter, *Darwin's God: Evolution and the Problem of Evil* (Grand Rapids, MI: Brazos, 2001), 9–18, 127–43.

149 Richard Dawkins, *The God Delusion* (Boston: Houghton Mifflin, 2006), 31.

150 For instance, a 1998 survey in Australia found that 74 percent of respondents said they believed in a higher power of some kind and two thirds said that a spiritual life was important to them, yet only 35 percent said they believed in a personal God (Peter Kaldor et al., *Build My Church: Trends and Possibilities for Australian Churches*, NCLS Research [Adelaide, South Australia: Openbook Publishers, 1999], 8–9). Likewise, in a Gallup Poll in the United States in 2003, almost a third of respondents chose to define spirituality without any reference to God or a higher authority, but rather as "a calmness in my life," "something you really put your heart into," or "living the life you feel is pleasing" (George H. Gallup Jr., "American Spiritual Searches Turn Inward," 2003, www.gallup.com/poll/7759/Americans-Spiritual-Searches-Turn-Inward.aspx [accessed July 27, 2010]). These results suggest that in the minds of many people spirituality has little or no connection to the doctrine of Christ.

151 Cf. Matt 3:11; John 7:39; 14:6–17, 26; 15:26; 16:13–14; Acts 2:38; Rom 5:1–5; 8:1–16; 1 Cor 6:17, 19; 12:3; Gal 3:1–5, 14; 4:6; Eph 2:18; Heb 10:19–22; 1 John 4:2–3.

ness and spiritual wellbeing in the present. As we noted earlier, Luther defines a human being as *hominem iustificari fide*,[152] one whom God created to live by faith. This means that faith is absolutely central to our humanity, so that we need faith in Jesus Christ to be truly human. Only through Christ, the perfect image of God,[153] can God's image be renewed in us so that we are restored to what God originally created us to be.[154] Christ needs to pour out on us the Holy Spirit, to work faith in us and to remake us in Christ's image, until our transformation is finally completed on the last day.[155] In this way we put on Christ and become little "christs" to one another.[156]

This helps us make sense of the words of the Psalmist, that those who make and worship idols become like them: blind, deaf, dumb and lifeless (Ps 115:4–8; 135:15–18). This is God's judgment on idolatry, and it is not an arbitrary judgment. Instead, God is enforcing the natural consequences of idolatry (Isa 6:9–10). We have been created to be filled by God's Spirit. He is the one who gives us eyes to recognize God, ears to hear his Word, lips to praise his name, and believing hearts that do his will. He is the one who fills us with life and vitality, and defines us by making us to be like Christ.[157] Pagan idols were intended to give their worshippers access to the gods and their spirit. Modern religions and spiritualities attempt to do the same. Yet only Christ can bring us the true God and his Spirit. If we replace Christ with some idol, we will be filled and defined by a very different spirit. This will be either an evil spirit that is destructive and death dealing, or the human spirit, which has been defiled by sin and has no independent life of its own. Thus we will be blind and dead to God and his life-giving power, and our lives will be devoid of the kind of vitality God intends for us.[158]

IDOLATRY: CHRISTIANITY APART FROM THE GOSPEL

A more subtle form of idolatry occurs when people claim the name of Jesus Christ, but separate this name from the Gospel. For Luther, this effectively means denying Christ. Since this form of idolatry is harder to identify than when Christ is denied outright we will spend more time examining it.

---

[152] *Disputation Concerning Man* (1536), WA 39/1:176, thesis 32.

[153] LW 1:224; 12:47–48; 15:339; 22:13, 19–20; 34:220–21; 38:275; cf. Col 1:15; 2 Cor 4:4; Heb 1:3.

[154] LW 1:61–68, 90, 142, 338–40; 22:30, 285; 31:358–59; 34:177, 194; 39:177, 194; Luther, *Commentary on the First Twenty-Two Psalms*, 1:261; Col 3:10; Eph 4:20–24; 1 Cor 15:49; Rom 8:29; 1 John 3:2.

[155] LW 1:65, 68, 338; 2:141; 34:140.

[156] LW 26:352–53; 31:367–68.

[157] LW 1:64–65; 22:285–90; 26:431; 27:139–40.

[158] Cf. Luther's treatment of Isa 44:9 and Ps 115:5 at LW 17:107–8 = WA 31/2:345–46.

Anonymous Christians. One attempt to separate Christ from the Gospel is the teaching on anonymous Christians proposed by the Jesuit theologian Karl Rahner. On the one hand, Rahner affirms that salvation is through Christ alone. On the other hand, he says that people who follow their conscience but do not explicitly believe in Christ can still be saved. He holds these two things together by proposing that there must be anonymous Christians, people who are saved through Christ even though they do not explicitly know him or the Gospel.[159] Rahner's views were endorsed by the Second Vatican Council in the document *Lumen Gentium*, which asserts that those who follow their conscience and strive to live a good life can be saved without any explicit knowledge of Christ.[160]

Rahner and *Lumen Gentium* declare a salvation that is supposedly in the name of Christ, yet has been divorced from the proclamation of the Gospel. Luther explicitly rejects such ideas. He asserts that God's Old Testament people should not be compared to pagans who do not know the Gospel, since from the earliest times they had explicit Gospel promises to which they could cling.[161] He rejects Zwingli's suggestion that upright pagans could be saved, and says that although God is wont to gather for himself believers from among heathen people, such as Ruth the Moabite and Rahab the Canaanite and Jethro the priest of Midian, this does not take place without the Word of Christ.[162]

---

[159] Karl Rahner, *Karl Rahner in Dialogue: Conversations and Interviews 1965–82*, ed. Paul Imhof and Hubert Biallowons, translation ed. Harvey D. Egan (New York: Crossroad, 1986), 135.

[160] "Finally, those who have not yet accepted the Gospel are related to the people of God in various ways. There is, first, that people to whom the covenants and promises were made, and from whom Christ was born in the flesh (see Rom 9:4–5), a people in virtue of their election beloved for the sake of the fathers, for God never regret his gifts or his call (see Rom 11:28–29). But the plan of salvation also includes those who acknowledge the Creator, first among whom are the Moslems: they profess to hold the faith of Abraham, and together with us they adore the one, merciful God, who will judge humanity on the last day. Nor is God remote from those who in shadows and images seek the unknown God, since he gives to everyone life and breath and all things (see Acts 17:25–28) and since the Saviour wills everyone to be saved (see 1 Tim 2:4). Those who, through no fault of their own, do not know the Gospel of Christ or his church, but who nevertheless seek God with a sincere heart, and, moved by grace, try in their actions to do his will as they know it through the dictates of their conscience—these too may attain eternal salvation. Nor will the divine providence deny assistance necessary for salvation to those who, without any fault of theirs, have not yet arrived at an explicit knowledge of God, and who, not without grace, strive to lead a good life" (Second Vatican Council, "Lumen Gentium," paragraph 16, in *Vatican Council II: Constitutions, Decrees, Declarations—The Basic Sixteen Documents*, ed. Austin Flannery, [Northport, NY: Costello, 1995], 21–22).

[161] *Sermons on John* (1537–40), LW 22:70 = WA 46:596; Gen 3:15.

[162] *Lectures on Genesis* (1543–45), LW 8:135–36 = WA 44:678–79; cf. LW 14:9; 33:281; 54:57. The closest Luther comes to saying that someone who has not heard the Gospel could be saved is when he suggests that the prayers and longings of Christian parents to bring their children to

Sacramental absence and reflective faith. A more subtle separation between Christ and the Gospel takes place in Reformed theology. This is due to a weak sacramental theology.

Luther is sometimes unduly harsh in his treatment of the Reformed. He overstates the case when he says that anyone "who denies Christ in one place denies Him everywhere."[163] Without doubt the Reformed preach the Gospel, proclaim forgiveness in Christ's name, baptize in the name of the triune God, and so on. In this way, they bring Christ to people regardless of what theories they hold about what they are doing. Nevertheless, it is still true that theories that separate Christ's presence and forgiveness from the external means of the Gospel have the danger of undermining the Gospel, and directing us to look elsewhere to find assurance of salvation and of God's presence with us.

Luther accused the Reformed of denying Christ's presence with us by denying his presence in the means of grace.[164] Five centuries later John Jefferson Davis, an American evangelical from Gordon-Conwell Seminary, laments that contemporary evangelical worship lacks much sense of God's presence.[165] From Luther's perspective, this is the expected outcome of Reformed theology. Davis prescribes a renewed focus on Christ's presence in the Lord's Supper as a remedy for this malaise.[166] With this, Luther would wholeheartedly agree. However, the understanding of Christ's presence that Davis prescribes is Calvinistic rather than Lutheran. He insists that Christ is not physically present in the elements, but spiritually present through the bond the Holy Spirit creates between Christ and the believer.[167] From a Lutheran perspective, this is not strong enough medicine for at least two reasons. First, Calvin rejects simple faith in Christ's word—"This is my body, this is my blood"—and replaces it with a speculative theory about how Christ can be physically absent yet spiritually present. Speculative theories cannot bring Christ to us or anchor our faith the way Christ's promise can. Second, on a Calvinistic understanding Christ's presence cannot be guaranteed for all who come to the altar. Instead, only those who ascend to Christ by faith commune

---

Baptism might be accepted by God as efficacious for salvation if the children die before they can be baptized. Yet even here Luther is not saying that some kind of faith or works or piety apart from the Gospel could be saving, but rather that the parents might be able to save their children through the faith the parents have in Christ and the Gospel (*Comfort for Women who have had a Miscarriage* [1542], LW 43:247–50 = WA 53:205–8).

[163] *Lectures on First John* (1527), LW 30:258 = WA 20:682.37–38.

[164] *Lectures on First John* (1527), LW 30:258 = WA 20:682.

[165] John Jefferson Davis, *Worship and the Reality of God: An Evangelical Theology of the Real Presence* (Downer's Grove, IL: IVP Academic, 2010), 7–12.

[166] Ibid., 113–70, 203–6.

[167] Ibid., 12, 34–35, 94–95, 109–10, 116, 128, 164, 203–5.

with Christ.[168] Furthermore, Calvin asserts that "there is no communion of the flesh of Christ except a spiritual one, which is both perpetual and given to us independently of our use of the Supper."[169] This means that our own faith is the necessary and sufficient condition for communing with Christ, whereas the external means of the Sacrament are neither necessary nor sufficient. This automatically shifts our attention away from the Sacrament to the faith and piety we can have apart from the Sacrament, since this alone can guarantee Christ's presence with us.[170]

Philip Cary refers to this kind of "faith in our own faith," as "reflective faith." He regards this as characteristically Reformed, and contrasts it with the "unreflective faith" of Luther. Both Luther and the Reformed agree that we are saved by faith alone. Yet Cary suggests there is a subtle disagreement over the nature of this faith, and whether to some extent faith must be its own object. He illustrates this with the following syllogisms. First, the Reformed syllogisms:

Major Premise:	Whoever believes in Christ is saved.
Minor Premise:	I believe in Christ.
Conclusion:	I am saved.[171]

Or else:

Major premise:	Christ promises Absolution of sins to those who believe in him.
Minor premise:	I believe in Christ.
Conclusion:	I am absolved of my sins.[172]

This results in a reflective faith. In order to know if I am saved, I need to look into my own heart and know that I have faith and therefore meet this condition of salvation. Therefore to some extent my faith must always be based on itself, not just on God's promise.

What enables Luther to avoid such "faith in my own faith" is his sacramental theology. That is, he does not merely operate with the general promise of the Gospel, but also the specific promise of the Gospel "for me" in the Sacraments.[173] Luther's understanding of the Sacraments is that in them Christ

[168] Calvin, *Institutes of the Christian Religion* [1559], 4.17.5, 4.17.31–33.

[169] Calvin, "The clear explanation of sound doctrine concerning the true partaking of the flesh and blood of Christ in the Holy Supper," 295.

[170] Cf. *Commentary on Psalm 117* (1530), LW 14:39 = WA 31/1:257.

[171] Cary, "Why Luther is not quite Protestant," 450.

[172] Ibid., 458.

[173] Ibid., 452–61.

literally addresses the individual recipients and promises them forgiveness and salvation. Therefore when I go to receive the Sacraments he promises salvation "for me."[174] This means that the logic works differently:

Major premise:	Christ told me, "I baptize you in the name of the Father, Son and Holy Spirit."
Minor premise:	Christ never lies but only tells the truth.
Conclusion:	I am baptized (i.e., I have new life in Christ).[175]

Likewise:

Major premise:	Christ says, "I absolve you of your sins in the name of the Father, the Son and the Holy Spirit."
Minor premise:	Christ never lies but only tells the truth
Conclusion:	I am absolved of my sins.[176]

Furthermore, I must believe this, otherwise I am calling Christ a liar when he makes this promise to me. For Luther, faith in Christ is equivalent to faith in Baptism, Absolution, and so on. It means believing that Christ speaks the truth when he says, "I baptize you."[177]

This promise still calls for faith. A person can reject this salvation and call God a liar, and in that case will not receive what God promised. Yet Luther contends that the promise remains true: God has given me salvation whether I accept it or not. It is like money deposited in a bank in my name. It is mine whether I believe in it or not, or ever benefit from it by withdrawing it. It is not as if the money is withdrawn and given to someone else if I refuse to accept it. Since this gift is unconditional, I am free to have faith in the promise given to me, without needing to reflect on whether my faith is sufficient to make the promise mine.[178] Thus faith depends entirely on the promise, rather than the promise depending on faith. Luther writes,

> There is quite a difference between having faith, on the one hand, and depending on one's faith and making baptism depend on faith, on the other. Whoever allows himself to be baptized on the strength of his faith, is not only uncertain, but also an idolator who denies Christ. For he trusts in and builds on something of his own,

---

[174] Ibid., 458; *The Sacrament of Penance* (1519), LW 35:17 = WA 2:717–19.

[175] Cary, "Why Luther is not quite Protestant," 451.

[176] Ibid., 458.

[177] Ibid., 457–59; *The Sacrament of Penance* (1519), LW 35:13–17 = WA 2:717–19.

[178] *The Keys* (1530), LW 40:367 = WA 30/2:498–99; Cary, "Why Luther is not quite Protestant," 460–61.

> namely, on a gift which he has from God, and not on God's Word alone.[179]

Here we can see how Luther regarded faith that reflects back on itself to find assurance as a subtle form of idolatry that takes the focus off of Christ and his Word and puts it back on the self. For Luther, the faith of the Christian is not interested in itself and its own experience and feeling. Instead, it is wholly captivated by Christ and his promise of salvation.

This is related to the way Luther deals with the question of predestination. In his Genesis commentary, Luther wrote what he intended to be his final word on this subject.[180] Here he makes a distinction between the hidden God and the God revealed in the Gospel. He cautions people against trying to search out the hidden counsels of God rather than contenting themselves with God as he is proclaimed in the Gospel. He writes,

> For God did not come down from heaven to make you uncertain about predestination, to teach you to despise the sacraments, absolution, and the rest of the divine ordinances. Indeed, He instituted them to make you completely certain and to remove the disease of doubt from your heart, in order that you might not only believe with the heart but also see with your physical eyes and touch with your hands. Why, then, do you reject these and complain that you do not know whether you have been predestined? You have the Gospel; you have been baptized; you have absolution; you are a Christian.[181]

Since for Luther we find God in the Gospel itself, rather than above or beyond it, this is a perfectly natural way to deal with the problem of predestination. How do I know that God has made me the object of his saving plans? He has baptized me. He has absolved my sins. He has preached to me the Gospel. When he does so he means what he says. This is all I need to know. Luther is not dodging the question of predestination, but answering it based on what God has revealed "for me" in the Gospel. This word tells me that God is well disposed toward me and is not secretly plotting to damn me for all eternity, unless I dare to doubt it and call God a liar. This word revealed in the Gospel trumps any speculations about God's hidden counsels.[182]

Yet for a person like Calvin, who does not believe that the real action is ever in the external efficacy of the Word or the Sacraments but always in the

---

[179] *Concerning Rebaptism* (1528), LW 40:252 = WA 26:164.40–165.5.

[180] *Lectures on Genesis* (1538–42), LW 5:42–50 = WA 43:457–63.

[181] *Lectures on Genesis* (1538–42), LW 5:45 = WA 43:460.4–11.

[182] *Lectures on Genesis* (1538–42), LW 5:49 = WA 43:462.

more fundamental eternal decree of God to which they point, this will always appear like an evasion of the real issue.[183] Without a sacramental theology, the Gospel gives us nothing more than a general promise to the elect, and we need some other means of determining whether we are among the elect to whom it applies. Calvin expressly denies that the Gospel by itself can provide this proof of election.[184] Instead, we must also look for the inner call of the Spirit to assure us that we are among the elect.[185] Calvin still says that we should seek from the Word of the Gospel assurance of salvation. Yet by this he does not mean that the words themselves give a firm promise "for me," but instead that we should look for this word to produce in us an inward call.[186] It is this inward call that Calvin says cannot deceive us and is the ultimate sign that we will be saved on the last day.[187]

This has led to a tendency in Reformed theology to include the experience of faith as part of the content of faith. My faith must look not only to the promise of the Gospel but also to some inner call in my heart before I can know I am saved. If all that one is looking for is simple assent that the Gospel promises are true, this would be okay. Yet Calvin is looking for more than this. He is looking for an inner assurance that I am among the elect, which in his view no outer word of Christ can tell me. Calvin intensifies the problem further by distinguishing between those who have true faith and can never fall away, and those who appear to have faith but can fall away.[188] This has led later generations of Calvinists to ask themselves whether they have true faith, or only apparent faith. Since the Gospel cannot tell them this, they have to look for signs in themselves that their faith is genuine. This has led many to look for things like their experience of inner renewal and holiness or their personal conversion experience as signs of election.[189]

When people do this their faith is not looking to the Gospel alone to find assurance of salvation, but also to their own faith or holiness. This is not how Luther teaches justification by faith. He urges us to look away from ourselves and to direct all our attention to Christ and his promises. It sounds like Luther's theology, since salvation is still "by faith alone." Yet since the object is not Christ's promise alone, this is not "faith alone" in the Lutheran sense. The minute the object of our faith is our own faith, then faith becomes a new inward Protestant work that corresponds to the outward works of Catholi-

---

[183] Cf. Calvin, *Institutes of the Christian Religion* [1559], 3.21.3–4.

[184] Ibid., 3.24.1.

[185] Ibid., 3.24.2–3.

[186] Ibid., 3.24.4–8.

[187] Ibid., 3.24.2–3.

[188] Ibid., 3.24.7.

[189] Cary, "Why Luther is not quite Protestant," 475–81.

cism. In both cases, assurance of salvation is grounded in God's renewing work in us instead of Christ's promise for us, and in a subtle way the pious self takes the place of Christ as the focus of our confidence. That is, it becomes an idol.

The theology of abstractions. Another way of subtly undermining Christ and the Gospel is to resort to a theology of abstractions, which refuses to be tied to the concrete descriptions God gives us of himself.

Moshe Halbertal and Avishai Margalit, two Jewish philosophers who have coauthored a book on idolatry, note two basic ways of approaching the question of idolatry. The first is to accept the anthropomorphic metaphors the Bible uses to describe idolatry, and the anthropomorphic view of God this entails. The Bible uses two primary metaphors to convey why idolatry is such an unspeakable sin: idolatry is adultery against one's spouse, and idolatry is rebellion against one's Lord.[190] That is, it depicts idolatry as a sin that occurs in the context of an interpersonal relationship that demands loyalty. This means that God must be sufficiently personal like us for such an interpersonal relationship to be possible.[191] This is the approach Luther consistently takes to idolatry, to see it primarily as a violation of the interpersonal, covenantal relationship we have with God.[192]

The second approach is to look at idolatry in less biblical and more philosophical terms,[193] and to assert that God is the "wholly other," who must remain transcendent over all visible, physical, temporal, created, or earthly things. This turns the issue on its head, and makes anthropomorphism into the great enemy. According to this approach, if one is to avoid idolatry it is necessary to purify one's view of God from anthropomorphisms and other

---

[190] Moshe Halbertal and Avishai Margalit, *Idolatry*, translated by Naomi Goldblum (Cambridge, MA: Harvard University Press, 1992), 9–36, 214–35.

[191] Ibid., 1, 9, 237–38.

[192] Although Luther recognized that God transcends any anthropomorphic description of him, he did not think it is possible for us to get beyond the earthly pictures God gives us of himself, nor did he think these pictures deceive us. At one point he comments that the anthropomorphites were unjustly condemned by Rome for speaking about God as if he has ears, eyes, arms etc. He thought no one should be condemned for holding to the descriptions God gives of himself in Scripture, nor can we improve on them. Instead, we can only grasp hold of God under the earthly wrappings in which he presents himself to us (*Lectures on Genesis* [1535–38], LW 1:14–15 = WA 42:12; LW 2:45–46).

[193] Halbertal and Margalit point out that this view of God has more in common with pagan philosophy than with the biblical picture of God. Instead of freeing us from idolatry, it is just as easy to view excessive abstraction as the path to creating an idolatrous philosopher's god in place of the God of Abraham, Isaac, and Jacob (Halbertal and Margalit, *Idolatry*, 134–35). It is the Greek philosophers such as Aristotle who insisted that the false god is the anthropomorphic one, and that God must be absolutely separated from the fluctuating life of the emotions and finite physical things (ibid., 238).

concrete elements (such as corporeality, locality, visibility, and emotion) through a process of abstraction.[194]

The problem with this is that if it is pursued consistently it rules out all contact between God and us, including all the contact outlined in the Bible.[195] Since we are creatures, there can be no contact between God and us that does not involve created things. Halbertal and Margalit point out that those who see an unbridgeable metaphysical gap between the Creator and his creation as the primary issue in idolatry usually do not stop with attacking visible images. Instead, the logic of their position tends to drive them to attack other concrete representations of God as well, including Scripture.[196] If God must remain so transcendent over his creation that it is impossible for him to present himself to us visibly, it is also reasonable to conclude that he cannot present himself in human language or conceptual frameworks, since these, too, are finite, created things. This leads not only to the avoidance of images but also to attempts to purify our thoughts concerning God so as to maintain his transcendence over all human thinking.

As we have seen, the Reformed have used this kind of metaphysical approach to the question of idolatry in their treatment of cultic images and the Sacraments. However, they never consistently apply this line of reasoning throughout their theology. For instance, Randall Zachman, professor of Reformation studies at Notre Dame, has conducted a thorough study of Calvin's attitude toward images, and demonstrates that Calvin had two arguments against cultic images. On the one hand, he argues that since God is incomprehensible, incorporeal, and invisible he cannot be represented visibly. On the other hand, he talks about the "living images," that God himself makes, and contrasts these with the false and "dead" images humans construct for themselves.[197] If this second line of thinking were followed consistently it would destroy the first, and vice versa. Once we start to admit that

---

[194] Ibid., 2–3, 109–12, 130–32, 238–39. This approach to idolatry is often justified through an appeal to Deut 4:15, "Since you saw no form on the day that the LORD spoke to you at Horeb out of the midst of the fire, beware lest you act corruptly by making a carved image for yourselves." On this basis people argue that it is either impossible or else demeaning for God to have an image. Yet this text never says that God cannot appear in visible form, but simply that he did not appear in this way to Israel. The numerous Old Testament passages that talk about people seeing God or his likeness suggest that it is possible for him to appear in visible form (e.g., Exod 24:11; 33:20; Num 12:8; Isa 6:1; Ezek 1:26), even if God generally does not allow sinful people to have the degree of exposure to him that sight permits (cf. Halbertal and Margalit, *Idolatry*, 45–47, 52–53, 239).

[195] E.g., Exod 13:21; 20:20–21, 24; 25:22; 29:38–46; 40:34–38; Lev 16:2; Deut 12:5; 31:15; John 1:14; 14:6–23.

[196] Halbertal and Margalit, *Idolatry*, 53–62, 239.

[197] Zachman, *Image and Word in the Theology of John Calvin*, 50–54; cf. 25–49, 257–61, 436–39.

God's almighty power enables him to cross the metaphysical divide between himself and his creation, the only relevant question becomes: Where and how has he chosen to do so? Calvin never resolved this tension in his thought.[198] Yet it is evident that he had enough faith in Scripture and God's revelation in Christ that he was only willing to push his assertion of God's transcendence so far and no further.

Contemporary scholars have not always been so circumspect. Instead, they have used God's transcendence over creation as a reason to attack Scripture and the doctrine of the Gospel and to promote an abstract view of God. For instance, it is not unusual today for those who hold to the doctrine of scriptural inerrancy to be accused of "Bibliolatry," that is, of worshipping the Bible instead of the God who stands behind it.[199] Others have pushed this a step further, and questioned whether God can be represented at all in human language. An example here is the Catholic theologian Nicholas Lash, who suggests that in order to avoid idolatry our doctrine should be regulative rather than descriptive. It should regulate how we are to speak about God, and how we are to behave, worship, and hope, but should not purport to give us a "fix" on God or his true nature, since he is a holy mystery who can never be brought into our world of images, narratives, and descriptions.[200] Likewise, the French philosopher and lay theologian Jacques Ellul stresses that God cannot be tied to any image, created thing, or concrete predication about him. He says that we should avoid not only visible images but also mental images. He attacks not only images but also human language, and suggests that we must renounce all biblical literalism or fixed doctrinal formulations if we are to avoid idolatry.[201]

In this he is simply pursuing the metaphysical approach to idolatry a few steps further than Calvin. Luther saw this as the logical conclusion of unqualified iconoclasm. He said that if the iconoclasts were absolutely serious that we must have no images of God, they should stop reading Scripture lest they

---

[198] Ibid., 53; cf. 40–41, 266–67, 305.

[199] E.g., Kurt W. Peterson, " 'The Spirit Gives Life, but the Letter Kills': Bible-olatry in American Protestantism," *Ex Auditu* 15 (1999), 120–22, 124–26; H. Richard Niebuhr, *Radical Monotheism and Western Culture, With Supplementary Essays* (New York: Harper & Brothers, 1960), 125; cf. 115.

[200] Nicholas Lash, *The Beginning and the End of "Religion"* (Cambridge, UK: Cambridge University Press, 1996), 49, 53, 88–90; Nicholas Lash, *Easter in Ordinary: Reflections on Human Experience and the Knowledge of God* (Charlottesville: University Press of Virginia, 1988), 276.

[201] Jacques Ellul, *The Humiliation of the Word*, trans. Joyce Main Hanks (Grand Rapids, MI: Eerdmans, 1985), 50, 62–63, 79–85, 91, 94–97, 105–8, 111, 183–92, 200–203; Jacques Ellul, *The Ethics of Freedom*, trans. and ed. Geoffrey W. Bromiley (Grand Rapids, MI: Eerdmans, 1976), 145–46, 156, 163, 166.

form a mental image of him.[202] Ellul's theology heads in this direction. However, he never follows this line of thought consistently, something he could not do without ceasing to be Christian. Instead, he tries to hold it in dialectical tension with God's use of the incarnation and the Scriptures. Yet this makes everything in his theology uncertain, since everything he asserts based on Christ and Scripture he then negates through his assertion of God's transcendence over all assertions.

Theologians such as Lash and Ellul see this as a virtue. They regard abstract or dialectical theology as necessary to prevent us from getting a "fix" on God or laying hold of him as a possession, and thereby asserting our mastery over him. This might be a cause for concern if the doctrine of Christ were of human devising, or if God were a petty idol who is so easily mastered. But if our doctrine is God-given, and in it we encounter the true and living God and not some idol, then we are the ones in danger of being mastered and not him.

In Luther's estimation, we need God to master us and fix our attention on Christ, or we will inevitably wander away to serve self-chosen idols. He regarded abstract theology, which speculates about God instead of being tied down by Christ and his Word, as every bit as idolatrous as the worship of gods of wood or stone. Far from taking God's transcendence too seriously, it does not take it seriously enough, and acts as if we can do what God cannot, and cross the gulf between him and us with our speculations. Then, through its refusal to hold to God as he encounters us in the specific doctrinal formulations of Christ and the Gospel, abstract theology leaves us at the mercy of our sinful selves and the deceptions of the devil. It leaves the field wide open for us to make up a faith of our own devising, focused on ourselves and whatever idols suit our fancy. As Charles Taber points out, if God is an "ineffable mystery," who does not encounter us in binding and concrete ways, then he cannot provide much of a challenge to the concrete, functional gods we pursue in day-to-day life.[203]

David Yeago observes that a form of abstract theology has been common among Protestants over the last century. This has been promulgated in the name of Luther and his distinction between Law and Gospel.[204] Yet this is not

---

[202] *Lectures on Deuteronomy* (1525), LW 9:82 = WA 14:622; *Against the Heavenly Prophets in the Matter of Images and Sacraments* (1525), LW 40:99–100 = WA 18:83–84.

[203] See chapter 4, page 54.

[204] Yeago draws examples of such theology from the work of theologians as diverse as Gerhard Forde (David S. Yeago, "Lutherans and the Historic Episcopate: Theological Impasse and Ecclesial Future," *Lutheran Forum* 26 [Nov. 1992]: 36–40), Werner Elert, Rudolph Bultmann, and Paul Tillich (David Yeago, "Gnosticism, Antinomianism, and Reformation Theology: Reflections on the Cost of a Construal," *Pro Ecclesia* 2 [Winter 1993]: 39–49). Yet his goal is not to critique the theology of any individual theologian in its entirety, but rather to identify a wider trend within theology (ibid., 45).

Law and Gospel as Luther understood them, but law and gospel divorced from their theological context and transformed into abstract dialectical principles: one of the letter that enslaves us to rules and other fixed forms, the other of the spirit that liberates us from the constraints of such order.

This new theology agrees with Luther that the Gospel liberates us from the oppressiveness of the Law, yet misconstrues how this takes place. For Luther, the Law is oppressive because of our situation in the larger theological context, not because the Law is oppressive in itself. The Law is oppressive not because it is inherently oppressive to conform to God's order, but because we are in rebellion against this order. We find the Law enslaving because of our sinful disorder and non-conformity to Christ. The Law condemns us, and in that sense is our enemy, because it condemns everything that is outside of Christ.[205] The solution is therefore faith in Christ that reunites us with him and brings us both forgiveness and renewal, so we begin to delight in God's Law and walk in his ways.[206] Yet much contemporary Lutheran and Protestant theology grounds the oppressiveness of the Law in the Law itself and its very nature as constraint or demand. The Law is oppressive simply because it is law and binds us to fixed forms. Under this construal, the gospel cannot mean a change in our situation in relation to an unchanging Law, so that we no longer stand condemned by it. Instead, the gospel can only be good news if it means putting an end to the Law altogether. Therefore this theology is necessarily antinomian. What is more, it is also necessarily Gnostic. Since this theology sees concrete forms as the problem, it is antithetical to the doctrine of the incarnation. Once form and order per se are equated with enslavement, then doctrine that binds us to a God who took particular incarnate form must also be enslaving, and the incarnate God must be an enslaving God. Under such a construal it makes perfect sense that the charge of legalism would be leveled against all who insist on fixed doctrine, including the doctrine of Christ.[207]

This turns Luther's theology completely on its head. For Luther, the Gospel cannot be separated from the doctrine of Christ with all its concrete shape and content. It is about the Son of God who is undialectically identified with the man born of Mary, who comes to bring God's undialectical grace to those caught in undialectical sin.[208] The Gospel as an abstract principle set in dialectical opposition to the Law is no Gospel at all. It is simply idolatry. The only Gospel that is worthy of the name is the one that reconciles and unites us with God in the concrete form of the man Jesus, as he comes to us in the particular

---

205 *Heidelberg Disputation* (1518), LW 31:41 = WA 1:354.

206 *Kasper Cruciger's Summer Postils* (1544), WA 21:458–59.

207 Yeago, "Gnosticism, Antinomianism, and Reformation Theology," 38–49.

208 Cf. Ibid., 47, 49.

means he has instituted.[209] It is this Gospel that must remain at the heart of all our worship and devotion if it is to be centered in the true God.

CONCLUSION: PROCLAIMING THE INCARNATE GOD

The incarnation of Jesus Christ is good news. It is good news that God has come down to earth to save us. It is good news that he became one of us. It is good news that he speaks to us in human language and relates to us in a human way. And it is good news that he comes to us through his Word and Sacraments with his grace and power. How wonderful it is that he does not leave us floundering, vainly speculating about him or groping for something to help us in our needs, but instead gives himself to us as a gift in this way!

The flipside to this good news is its exclusivity. God has provided us with one way of having access to him, through Christ and the means of the Gospel. Scripture tells us that Christ is the only one who opens up the way into God's presence (e.g., Heb 10:19–22). People take offense at this because they think they can devise their own worship of God or road to him with their own thoughts, feelings, or rituals. This is a temptation not only for non-Christians, but also for Christians, when we lose our focus on Christ and the Gospel.

This is something that is all too easy to do. On a number of occasions I have been involved in sorting out "worship wars" within the church. On more than one occasion I have listened to people's grievances, and heard them summarize their complaints with these words, "They won't let us worship God the way we want." Fortunately, what both sides want in these battles is usually centered on things like their preferred musical style, or the extent of lay involvement in worship, or the degree of flexibility with which we approach traditional liturgical forms. Generally no one is trying to get rid of the preaching of the Gospel. Nevertheless, people frequently become so fixated on such things that they will refuse to come to church or fracture the body of Christ if they do not get their way, even if the Gospel is still being faithfully enacted and proclaimed. If we do this we have lost our focus on the Gospel, and have instead made an idol out of worshipping God "the way we want," as if this is what makes worship worthwhile.

In situations like this, faithful ministry involves constantly refocusing people's eyes on the one essential thing, on Christ and the means of the Gospel through which he comes to us. This is where he wants to meet with us to bless us. With those who lose sight of this, we can gently expose the idolatrous futility of trying to grasp hold of God in some other way, and then proclaim the wonderful gift of our God incarnate, who comes to us wrapped in words and bread and wine and water.

---

[209] *Sermons on John* (1530–32), LW 23:129–30 = WA 33:201–2.d.

Part Four

The Third Article

Chapter Eight

The Idol of the Self and God's Word

A friend of mine, who went to seminary as a mature age student, had a moment of self-insight a couple of years into his seminary training. He realized that up to that point in his life he had been adjusting the Bible to fit with his reason, without even being aware of what he was doing. Whenever he came across something in the Bible that did not seem reasonable to him, he instinctively twisted it around to fit with what he thought was right. Then one day he suddenly realized that if the Bible is God's Word, he needed to adjust his thinking to fit with God's wisdom instead of the other way round. In other words, he became aware that he had made his reason into an idol, and needed to repent.

This kind of idolatry is rife in the Western world. Perhaps we still follow the wisdom of the Enlightenment, and think that we must subject all traditional authorities, including the Bible, to a process of methodological doubt, and only accept them if we can verify them according to the standards of our autonomous reason. Or perhaps we have succumbed to the pervasive relativism that has followed on the heels of the Enlightenment, and refuse to accept any truth claim unless it is "true for us." Either way it is our own thinking that reigns as master in place of God.

In this chapter we will look at idolatry in relation to Luther's view of God's Word as the light that must inform the human mind if it is to have an accurate understanding of God. In the previous chapter we began to look at Luther's view of the external word of the Gospel, and therefore we will be touching on some of the same ground. However, in the previous chapter the focus was on Christ, with the Word being relevant as the means by which Christ is sacramentally present with his church on earth. Now we will focus on the Word itself. In particular, we will focus on the Bible as the voice of the Holy Spirit that enlightens the human mind concerning the things of God and norms all our thinking about him.[1]

---

[1] For Luther, Scripture is authoritative for two reasons. The first is that it has authority because of its content, that is, the way it points us to Christ and brings Christ to us (see for instance

The chief idol Luther identifies in this area is human reason, or more particularly, human reason that refuses to be enlightened and regulated in this way. This enables us to understand Luther's ambivalent attitude toward human reason. On the one hand, he can praise it as God's gift.[2] On the other hand, he can spurn it as the devil's whore.[3] The way to reconcile these apparently contradictory statements is to be aware of Luther's distinction between the ministerial and magisterial uses of reason, or reason that is used as a servant versus reason that presumes to be the master. Reason functions as a good servant when it acts within its area of competency in the earthly domain, and when it is willing to be enlightened by God's Word in theological matters. Reason functions as a bad master when it sets itself above God's Word and presumes to be competent to deal with theological things on its own. When we use our reason this way, we elevate our wisdom above the wisdom God teaches us through his Spirit-given Word. Thus we turn our reason into an idol. Since reason is a great gift, its potential for abuse is also great, and it makes a particularly potent idol.

LUTHER'S TEACHING

Luther teaches that when humans attempt to know God by the power of their own reason—instead of allowing the Holy Spirit to instruct them through the Word—they fall into a two-fold idolatry. First, they turn their reason into an idol by putting it in the place of the Holy Spirit. Second, their reason then devises a false picture of God so that they end up worshipping a figment of their imagination instead of the true God. In this way, human reason can function both as an idol and as the source of other forms of idolatry.

David W. Lotz, "Sola Scriptura: Luther on Biblical Authority," *Interpretation* 35 [July 1981], 267–73, who argues—albeit one-sidedly—for this way of understanding Luther's view of scriptural authority). This is sometimes called the material principle. The second is that it has authority because of its nature as God's Word, composed under the inspiration of the Holy Spirit. This is sometimes called the formal principle. The two are not in conflict, and so should not be played off against each other. I have chosen to deal with the authority of Scripture under Pneumatology instead of Christology for the following reasons: (1) whenever Luther gives us a summary of his economy of salvation, such as in the Large Catechism or in his *Confession Concerning Christ's Supper*, he deals with the written and proclaimed Word under Pneumatology, emphasizing that it is the work of the Holy Spirit to publish the work of Christ (LC II 38–46; LW 37:366); and (2) when Luther defends the authority of Scripture in polemical contexts he usually does this on the basis of its inspiration (e.g., LW 24:109–110; 32:11; 36:135–37; 39:164–66).

[2] LW 34:137; 54:71; WA 40/3:612.31.

[3] LW 40:174–75, 216; 51:374; cf. LW 41:227.

LUTHER'S CONFIDENCE IN SCRIPTURE

In his published doctoral dissertation on Luther's view of Scripture, Mark Thompson, Principal of Moore Theological College in Sydney, notes that Luther's view of Scripture was profoundly connected to his view of God. He writes,

> He [Luther] was convinced that one could not tamper with the Scriptures without tampering with God. One could not describe the Scriptures as obscure without blaspheming God. Further, he insisted that the Scriptures had a vital role in what he saw as the basic structure of the Christian life: God addresses his people in human words and calls upon them to believe the words that he has spoken.[4]

The working assumption for everything Luther says about the idol of human reason is this conviction that the Scriptures are a clear and authoritative word addressed to us by God to which our reason should bow. While it is impossible to give a comprehensive account of Luther's view of Scripture within the scope of this chapter, the following themes are directly relevant to his thoughts on idolatry.

The inspiration of Scripture. Luther was convinced that the whole of Scripture is the Word of God who cannot lie.[5] In 1543, he wrote,

---

[4] Mark D. Thompson, *A Sure Ground on Which to Stand: The Relation of Authority and Interpretive Method in Luther's Approach to Scripture* (Carlisle, Cumbria, UK: Paternoster, 2004), 284. Luther never composed a dogmatic treatise on Scripture. He had no shortage of things to say on the topic, but his views need to be pieced together from comments scattered throughout his works. The above dissertation, completed under Alister McGrath at Oxford, is the best recent attempt to do this. Thompson not only gives a clear and comprehensive survey of the relevant material from Luther, he also deals with previous attempts. This means he is able to build on the strengths of previous research while responding to some of its weaknesses.

[5] Many scholars have tried to paint Luther as a proto higher critic, and to dispute that he held to a doctrine of plenary verbal inspiration. As evidence they produce a number of critical comments that Luther made regarding certain parts of Scripture, most notably the book of James. The problem with this view is that these critical comments are extremely rare, whereas statements from Luther in which he either asserts or implies that Scripture in its entirety is nothing less than the inerrant Word of God can be multiplied almost endlessly. Therefore a more balanced position is that these critical comments do not represent Luther's considered position on Scripture, but should be accounted for in other ways. For instance, Luther's comments on James can be viewed as candid wrestlings with this difficult part of Scripture that never crystallized into a final position or overturned Luther's fundamental confidence in the inspiration and inerrancy of Scripture. In particular, there is evidence that Luther toyed with the idea that James, being part of the antilegomena, was not a legitimate part of the canon, although he never came to a final conclusion in this regard (LW 34:317; 35:395–97; 36:118; 52:206). Thus his comments on James do not reflect his attitude toward the vast majority of the books in the canon that he was fully convinced were canonical. Thompson provides a detailed discussion of these issues, as well as a thorough response to those who dispute that Luther regarded the whole

> "No prophecy ever came by the impulse of man; but moved by the Holy Spirit, holy men of God spoke." [2 Pet 1:21] Therefore we sing in the article of the Creed concerning the Holy Spirit: "Who spake by the prophets." Thus we attribute to the Holy Spirit all of Holy Scripture and the external Word and the sacraments.[6]

The Danish Luther scholar Regin Prenter, among others, has argued that "to Luther the Word in its real sense is Christ,"[7] and that "When the living Christ himself is the Word, then the outward Word as such, whether we find it in the Bible, in the sermon, or in the sacrament, can never directly be identified with God's own Word."[8] This is hard to square with Luther's own statements on the matter, since Luther says the exact opposite, that both Christ and the written Word are God's Word:

> Holy Scripture is God's Word, written and spelled and formed in letters, just as Christ is the eternal Word of God veiled in human flesh.[9]

Furthermore, since Scripture is God's Word it cannot err and compels our allegiance:

> The saints could err in their writings and sin in their lives, but the Scriptures cannot err.[10]

> The Word is so irreproachable that not a single iota can err in the Law or the divine promises. For that reason we must yield to no sect, not even in one tittle of Scripture, no matter how much they clamor and accuse us of violating love when we hold so strictly to the Word.[11]

The clarity of Scripture. The conviction that Scripture is inspired and inerrant is not by itself sufficient to establish it as an authoritative guide for us. The message of Scripture must also be clear. If it is not, it cannot function as our guide, but must in practice give way to whatever interpreters or interpre-

---

of canonical Scripture as God's inerrant Word (Thompson, *A Sure Ground on Which to Stand*, 68–90, 112–46).

[6] *Treatise on the Last Words of David* (1543), LW 15:275 = WA 54:34–35.

[7] Regin Prenter, *Spiritus Creator*, trans. John M. Jenson (Eugene, OR: Wipf and Stock, 2001), 112. Used by permission of Wipf and Stock Publishers. www.wipfandstock.com.

[8] Ibid., 106.

[9] *Sprüche aus dem Alten Testament* (1541), WA 48:31.4–6.

[10] *Misuse of the Mass* (1521), LW 36:137 = WA 8:485.19–21; cf. LC IV 57; LW 1:122; 32:11; 52:49.

[11] *Commentary on Psalm 45* (1532), LW 12:242 = WA 40/2:531.30–34.

tations are able to illuminate it. Luther rejects any suggestion of this, and insists that Scripture is "in and of itself most certain, simple, and clear, its own interpreter, testing, judging, and illuminating everything else."[12]

The most obvious challenge to the clarity of Scripture is the empirical fact that the world is full of people who claim to follow the Bible, yet come to different conclusions regarding its message. Luther faced this challenge head on in his career, first when he was told to abandon his interpretation of Scripture in favor of the authoritative interpretation of the church, and then later when the Reformed challenged his right to take a stand on the words, "This is my body." In response, Luther asserted both the need and the right to take a stand on the clear words of God.[13] He defended this by reiterating the Bible's claims about itself, that it is a bright and clear light shining in a dark place.[14] He also appealed to the nature of Scripture as the Word of the Holy Spirit, who is wise and capable enough and knows his subject matter well enough to express himself clearly using the conventions of human language.[15] From this he concluded that any darkness that exists is in the hearts and minds of the interpreters, not in Scripture.[16] Furthermore, the way to dispel this darkness is to direct our attention to Scripture in preference to all human interpreters, who are always less clear than the text they purport to illuminate.[17] For,

> a man ought not to presume that he speaks more safely and clearly with his mouth than God spoke with his mouth. He who does not understand the Word of God when it speaks of the things of God, ought not believe that he understands the words of a man speaking of things strange to him. No one speaks better than he who best understands; but who understands the things of God better than God himself?[18]

Luther's conviction that Scripture is clear took on systematic importance for him. It guided his interpretation of Scripture, and helped him to see that many who claim to be interpreting Scripture are in reality evading its message. In particular, Luther makes the following two points in relation to the clarity of Scripture:

---

[12] *Assertion of all Articles* (1520), WA 7:97.23–24.

[13] Thompson, *A Sure Ground on Which to Stand*, 193–205.

[14] *Answer to the Hyperchristian, Hyperspiritual, and Hyperlearned Book by Goat Emser in Leipzig* (1521), LW 39:164 = WA 7:639.

[15] LW 19:152; 32:244; 33:93–94.

[16] LW 33:28.

[17] LW 32:11–12, 217; 39:164–65; cf. LW 31:266; Thompson, *A Sure Ground on Which to Stand*, 197–200.

[18] *Against Latomus* (1521), LW 32:244 = WA 8:118.

First, Christ is the key to understanding all of Scripture. An essential step in interpreting any text is to identify the author's central thesis. This then helps to make sense of the rest of the text. Luther was convinced that Scripture clearly tells us what its central thesis is: the Gospel of Jesus Christ.[19] Luther's conviction that Christ is the essential content of Scripture was not a critical principle he foisted onto Scripture from elsewhere and used to suppress other themes in Scripture. Rather, he regarded the Gospel of Christ as the central theme that is clearly taught in Scripture and makes sense of all its other themes: from the Law, which points us to our need for Christ, to the grace that we ultimately find in Christ. In this he was treating Scripture as a consistent and united whole.[20] He then asserts that those who fail to grasp this central message that is so clearly taught in Scripture cannot claim to understand anything in Scripture, since they have failed to see the light that illuminates the whole.[21]

The second point Luther makes is that if Scripture is clear, we should look for its meaning in the words of Scripture, not in extra-biblical sources. If we claim to be interpreting Scripture but cannot point to clear words of Scripture to establish our interpretation we are in reality evading Scripture. Luther encountered this with people like Cajetan and Eck, who asserted that the papal interpretation was correct while Luther's was false, yet could not show him from the words of Scripture why this was the case.[22] Luther identifies the following evasions:

- Simple laziness, an unwillingness to devote ourselves to Scripture and read it over and over again and compare one part to another until we develop enough familiarity with it that its meaning becomes clear to us.[23]

---

[19] Luther points to the following as proof that Scripture gives us the key to its own interpretation: Revelation 5 identifies the Lamb of God as the one who opens the scroll with the seven seals (Rev 5:1–10; LW 52:41–42, 205); Jesus said that he is the light of the world (John 8:12; LW 8:287), and that all of Scripture points to him (John 5:39,46; LW 10:6; 15:268; 35:122, 235); and Jesus preached himself from Scripture (Luke 24:25–27, 45–47; John 3:14; LW 15:268; 22:339; 35:123; 52:21, 171–72), as did his apostles, who explained how he fulfils and makes sense of the Old Testament (Acts 3:18–24; 17:2–11; Rom 1:1–2; 3:21; 1 Cor 15:3–4; 2 Cor 3:14–16; 1 Pet 1:10–12; LW 35:122–23, 235–36; 52:21–22, 172). If the Old Testament is ultimately about Christ, then how much more is the New!

[20] Thompson, *A Sure Ground on Which to Stand*, 152–83.

[21] LW 8:287–88; 15:268–69, 339; 16:92–93; 22:156–57, 366–68; 33:26; 35:132, 245–48; 52:205, 207; WLS 68–70 (199, 204–8), 80–83 (241, 248–50, 252–53), 98 (304).

[22] LW 31:266–67; 32:67–68; 44:133–34.

[23] LW 3:114; 33:27; 34:286; 39:163; cf. LW 45:363–64.

- Paying more attention to human interpretations and opinions—such as those of the church fathers, theologians, traditions, and councils—than to Scripture, and judging Scripture in the light of these instead of the other way round.[24]
- Claiming direct illumination from the Spirit, and using these private revelations to judge Scripture. Luther agrees that prayerful dependence on the Holy Spirit is essential for biblical study, yet stresses that the role of the Spirit here is to impress on our hearts and minds the words of Scripture, not to teach us something that is not contained in these words.[25]
- Importing thoughts and definitions from philosophy into Scripture, instead of carefully reading Scripture to see how it uses terms and ideas.[26]
- Obscuring the words by ignoring grammar and context, or by reading Scripture selectively, instead of reading each part in the light of the rest of Scripture.[27]
- Evading the natural meaning of the words by resorting to allegories and special pleading, or by inventing figures of speech where the context or articles of faith established elsewhere in Scripture do not demand them. Luther's belief that God wants us to understand him and therefore speaks clearly led him to eschew obscure or esoteric interpretations of Scripture and to prefer the simplest possible interpretation of any given passage.[28]

---

[24] LW 32:11–12, 217; 39:164–65; 41:19–27, 121–31.

[25] *Preface to the Wittenberg Edition of Luther's German Writings* (1539), LW 34:285–86 = WA 50:659.

[26] Holger Sonntag, who translated Luther's Antinomian Disputations into English, argues that Luther's approach to academic disputations at Wittenberg reveals his efforts to purge theology of philosophical definitions of God, humanity, righteousness, sin, etc., and to replace them with Scriptural ones. Although Luther clearly understood formal logic, and he and his students employed it in these disputations, Luther rarely bothered to correct his students' mistakes in logic. Instead, he focused most of his effort on ensuring that in their premises and conclusions they defined their terms in a biblical way instead of importing worldly definitions into theology (Holger Sonntag, "Translator's Preface," in *Solus Decalogus Est Aeternus: Martin Luther's Complete Antinomian Theses and Disputations*, ed. and trans. Holger Sonntag [Minneapolis, MN: Lutheran Press, 2008], 18–21). See also Erling T. Teigen, "The Clarity of Scripture and Hermeneutical Principles in the Lutheran Confessions," *Concordia Theological Quarterly* 46 (April–July 1982): 154, 158–59; LW 8:261; 12:310; 13:125; 34:137–39,142; 38:239.

[27] WA 2:361.16–20; LW 15:313; 19:42; 24:104; 27:29; 35:170–71; 37:242–43.

[28] LW 29:181; 33:162–63; 36:15–16, 30, 279–80; 37:211, 270; 39:165, 178; 40:157–58, 190.

It is only against the backdrop of this confidence in the clarity of Scripture and its ability to function as our guide that Luther's teaching on the idolatry of human reason makes sense.

REASON AS AN IDOL

Luther teaches that idolatry begins when we try to set up ourselves as teachers above God and his Word. In his Isaiah commentary, he writes,

> Last time I began to set forth the fountain and source of all idolatry, because our perversity refuses to be taught and formed but would rather teach and form God. . . . Summary: All idolatry comes from our wisdom, whereby we appear upright to ourselves and have no regard for what God commands.[29]

Luther agrees with Augustine that pride is "the mother of all heresies."[30] This is because the proud refuse to be taught by God.[31] Instead, they want to be considered learned themselves, and set themselves up as masters over God and his Word.[32] They elevate their own opinions to the heavens, and presume to be smarter than God.[33] They act as if they can correct God's Word, and thus "Everyone poses as God's teacher, and He must be everybody's pupil."[34] By disregarding God's Word and elevating their own thoughts above his, they turn themselves and their opinions into an idol they set in his place.[35]

When Luther talks about reason as an idol he is working with a broader view of reason than the narrow rationalism of the Enlightenment. Luther does not start with a theory about human reason and then construct a theory about idolatry on this basis. Instead, he starts with confidence in God's Word, and then when he sees how frequently human wisdom is opposed to this Word he rejects all such wisdom as idolatrous. Luther is not particularly concerned whether this reason is rationalistic or religious in nature. His concern is whether it is established by the Word or not. Therefore he makes little distinction between the natural theology of the scholastic theologians, the canons and traditions of the papacy, the opinions of the radical reformers, and the

---

[29] *Lectures on Isaiah* (1527–30), LW 17:17 = WA 31/2:273; cf. LW 52:59–60.

[30] Martin Luther, *Martin Luther's Complete Commentary on the First Twenty-Two Psalms*, trans. Henry Cole (2 vols.; London: W. Simpkin and R. Marshall, 1826), 1:180 = *Operationis in Psalmos* (1519–21), WA 5:126.37; cf. 54:378–79.

[31] *Church Postils* (1521–22), LW 52:59–60 = WA 10/1.1:205–7; cf. LW 12:309 = WA 40/2:323–25.

[32] LW 13:234; 16:95; 21:37; 23:51, 229–32; 51:387.

[33] LW 15:303; 23:208, 232, 252; 24:156; 25:167.

[34] *Sermons on John* (1530–32), LW 23:208–9 = WA 33:329; cf. LW 17:19–20; 23:79.

[35] LW 1:149 = WA 42:112; 13:375; 14:202; 19:115; 31:350; 41:122; 52:107; cf. LW 11:289.

religious convictions of heathens, Muslims, and Jews. Even though many of these claim divine inspiration, Luther treats them all as merely products of human reasoning, since their claims cannot be established by the Word. He writes,

> The Anabaptists, the Sacramentarians, and the papists are all idolaters—not because they worship stones and pieces of wood, but because they give up the Word and worship their own thoughts.[36]

When Luther attacks human reason, he is not suggesting that we should be unreasonable. Instead, he is fighting for a particular view of what counts as true reason when it comes to divine matters. Brian Gerrish, Distinguished Service Professor of Theology at Union Theological Seminary, suggests that Luther talks about human reason in three different ways that need to be carefully distinguished:

> (1) natural reason, ruling within its proper domain (the Earthly Kingdom); (2) arrogant reason, trespassing upon the domain of faith (the Heavenly Kingdom); (3) regenerate reason, serving humbly in the household of faith, but always subject to the Word of God. Within the first context, reason is an excellent gift of God; within the second, it is Frau Hulda, the Devil's Whore; within the third, it is the handmaiden of faith.[37]

It is reason in this second sense that concerns us in this chapter. Only when reason trespasses on the domain of theology and sets itself up in opposition to God's Word can it be idolatrous. Luther is happy to say that we should follow the light of natural reason when it comes to judging earthly things that fall within the area of human experience. What he has in mind here are those areas of earthly life where we have no word from God, such as how to build a house or bridle a horse or milk a cow.[38] Since reason as it operates in this

---

[36] *Lectures on Genesis* (1535–38), LW 1:149 = WA 42:112.

[37] B. A. Gerrish, *Grace and Reason: A Study in the Theology of Luther* (Oxford: Oxford University Press, 1962), 26; see also 10–27, 76–82. By permission of Oxford University Press.

[38] *Sermons on John* (1530–32), LW 23:84 = WA 33:127; cf. LW 1:143; 17:110; 23:84; 33:98–99; Gerrish, *Grace and Reason*, 12–17, 71–75. The following statement it typical: "It is necessary to make a distinction between God and men, between spiritual and temporal things. In earthly, human affairs man's judgment suffices. For these things, he needs no light but that of reason. Hence God does not in the Scriptures teach us how to build houses, to make clothing, to marry, to wage war, to sail the seas, and so on. For these, our natural light is sufficient. But in divine things, the things concerning God, and in which we must conduct ourselves acceptably with him and must secure happiness for ourselves, human nature is absolutely blind" (Martin Luther, *Sermons of Martin Luther: The Church Postils*, ed. J. N. Lenker, trans. J. N. Lenker et al. [8 vols.; Grand Rapids, MI: Baker Books, 1995], 6.319 = WA 10/1.1:531.5–13). However, we should note

domain may be wise or foolish but not idolatrous, it is irrelevant to our discussion in this chapter. It is reason as it operates in the domain of faith that concerns us here. In this domain Luther consistently distinguished between reason that sets itself up as master and judge over God's Word, and reason that humbly submits to the Word and uses the Word to direct its thinking.[39] He spurned the first while praising the latter.[40]

This should tell us that Luther's attack on reason was not driven by a belief that faith should be unreasonable, but rather by the conviction that in the realm of theology our reason must be informed by a higher wisdom or else it will judge falsely.[41] The question is: When it comes to our knowledge of God, will we make every thought captive to God's Word (2 Cor 10:5),[42] so that God

---

that for Luther all of earthly life is spiritual in some sense, since God is the Creator of all, and in all of life we are responsible to our Creator. Therefore Luther believed that even when it comes to earthly life reason has its deficiencies (Siegbert W. Becker, *The Foolishness of God: The Place of Reason in the Theology of Martin Luther* [Milwaukee, WI: Northwestern, 1999], 60–68). For instance, he writes: "He who knows God also knows, understands, and loves the creature, because there are traces of divinity in the creature. . . . But the godly alone observe this difference in the creatures. The ungodly have no knowledge of it; for they know neither God nor the creatures, far less their use" (*Lectures on Genesis* [1538–42], LW 4:195–96 = WA 43:276.27–28, 30–32).

"Thus our entire knowledge or wisdom is based solely on the knowledge of the material and formal cause, although in these instances, too, we sometimes talk disgraceful nonsense. The efficient and final cause we obviously cannot point out . . . Therefore let us learn that true wisdom is in Holy Scripture and in the Word of God. This gives information not only about the matter of the entire creation, not only about its form, but also about the efficient and final cause, about the beginning and about the end of all things, about who did the creating and for what purpose He created. Without the knowledge of these two causes our wisdom does not differ much from that of the beasts, which also make use of their eyes and ears but are utterly without knowledge about their beginning and their end" (*Lectures on Genesis* [1535–38], LW 1:124–25 = WA 42:93.19–22, 94.3–8).

[39] LW 14:15; 20:244; 23:51, 80–81, 84, 229; 24:109; 28:70; 34:208; 40:197; 51:379; 54:71.

[40] Luther asserts that "Reason, speech, and all gifts and created things are therefore different in believers and Christians than in unbelievers" (LW 54:184 = WA TR 3:106.9–10). This is because reason undergoes "regeneration through the Word" (LW 54:183 = WA TR 3:105.24). When asked in 1533 whether things like logic and the tools of arts and nature are useful in the study of theology, Luther replied that "good tools—for example, languages and the arts—can contribute to clearer teaching." Yet he then went on to distinguish the right use of these things—by those whose minds are illuminated by the Holy Spirit through the Word—from their frequent abuse (LW 54:71 = WA TR 1:191).

[41] "Our nature is so corrupt that it no longer knows God unless it is enlightened by the Word and the Spirit of God. How, then, can it love God without the Holy Spirit? It is true that there is no desire for anything that is unknown. Hence our nature cannot love God, whom it does not know; but it loves an idol and the dream of its heart" (*Lectures on Genesis* [1535–38], LW 2:124 = WA 42:349).

[42] LW 12:269; 23:230–31; 32:112.

becomes our teacher (Isa 54:13; John 6:45)?[43] Will we acknowledge that his thoughts are higher than our thoughts, and his ways than our ways (Isa 55:8–9)?[44] Will we concede that his wisdom turns ours into foolishness (1 Cor 1:18–25)?[45] Or will we set our thoughts above his and judge his Word on that basis?[46] When we do the latter, we turn our reason into an idol. We also become fools.[47] Far from acknowledging that this kind of reason is truly reasonable, Luther calls it "a blind fool,"[48] and urges us to "show the Holy Spirit the honor of conceding that He is smarter and wiser than we are."[49]

When Luther calls reason "the devil's whore," he is not merely using a colorful insult. Instead, he is making a theological point by picking up on the Old Testament contention that idolatry is spiritual adultery. He is saying that those who prefer human thinking to biblical wisdom are engaged in idolatry, since they have gone whoring after another teacher in place of Christ and his Word. In a sermon on 1 Peter in 1522, he says,

> Just as a virgin is physically pure and blameless, so the soul is spiritually blameless because of faith, through which it becomes the bride of Christ. But if it falls from faith into false doctrine, it must go to ruin. For this reason Scripture consistently calls idolatry and unbelief adultery and whoring, that is, if the soul clings to the teachings of men and thus surrenders faith and Christ.[50]

Likewise, in his Heidelberg disputation he stresses the need for the human mind to be wedded to Christ if it is to reason well: "Just as a person does not use the evil of passion well unless he is a married man, so no person philosophizes well unless he is a fool, that is, a Christian."[51]

---

[43] LW 17:243–45; 23:96–100; 36:151; 48:53–54.

[44] LW 9:54.

[45] LW 13:253; 26:227–28.

[46] LW 23:230–32; 38:257.

[47] LW 23:163, 165; 28:174.

[48] *The Sermon on the Mount* (1532), LW 21:260 = WA 32:515.

[49] *Sermons on John* (1537), LW 24:109–10 = WA 45:560; cf. 23:80.

[50] LW 30:26 = WA 12:282.19–24; cf. Ezek 6:9; 16:1–63, 23:1–49; Hosea 1–4; LW 9:214; 15:257; 24:309–10; 41:207–8, 218–20, 227. Tae Jun Suk and Philip Watson both suggest this interpretation of Luther's use of this expression, but fail to note this passage in which Luther himself supplies this interpretation (Tae Jun Suk, *The Theology of Martin Luther between Judaism and Roman Catholicism: A Critical-Historical Evaluation of Luther's Concept of Idolatry* [Ann Arbor, MI: UMI Dissertation Services, 2001], 46–49; Philip S. Watson, *Let God Be God!: An Interpretation of the Theology of Luther* [London: Epworth, 1947], 87–88).

[51] LW 31:41 = WA 1:355.4–5.

Luther's point is clear. He is saying that in spiritual matters the human mind cannot be autonomous.[52] God has created it to be wedded to Christ and his Word. When it refuses to listen to this Word, it does not think for itself, but rather prostitutes itself to a new master. It aligns itself with God's enemy, and falls captive to one deception of the devil or another. Therefore Luther urges us to have one bridegroom only. By this he means that we should listen to the voice of Christ alone, and not to any human teaching that takes his place.[53]

Luther charges every non-Christian religion with committing idolatry in exactly this way. He accuses them of mistaking human wisdom for divine wisdom by putting their own natural reason and knowledge of God in place of the Holy Spirit and his Word. Luther acknowledges that there is a natural knowledge of God implanted in every human heart. Yet he contends—in harmony with Romans 1—that this does not lead people to know the true God, but rather to construct idols (Rom 1:18–25).[54] Thus it is a poor substitute for the inspired Word.

Luther makes the same charge against all who claim to be Christians, yet teach their own doctrine instead of the doctrine contained in God's Word. Here he has in his sights both the Catholics, with their traditions and magisterium, and the left wing of the Reformation, with its rejection of scriptural teaching on matters such as Baptism and the Lord's Supper.[55]

Against the church of Rome Luther asserted that "all canons, laws, decretals, and councils are idolatry wherever they do not agree with the voice of the Bridegroom. Thus all human doctrine is idolatry."[56] In 1545, Emperor Charles V promulgated against Luther a set of theses that asserted papal infallibility and the authority of the church to compel belief without an express word of Scripture.[57] To this, Luther replied with some theses of his own:

1. Whatever is taught in the church of God without the Word is a godless lie.

2. If it is declared an article of faith, it is a godless heresy.

---

[52] Cf. LW 33:65–66.

[53] *Sermons on John* (1537–40), LW 22:452–53 = WA 47:166–67.

[54] LW 1:46–62; 2:250; 3:117; 4:145–46; 7:336; 9:52–54, 58; 9:130–31; 16:152, 160; 17:140, 157–58; 18:138, 184, 221; 19:11, 53–57; 20:10; 26:397, 399–401; 22:17–19; 27:87–90; 29:235; 52:58–60, 90–91; Luther, *Commentary on the First Twenty-Two Psalms*, 2:45.

[55] LW 1:229; 2:284, 355–56; 17:53; 19:11, 55–56; 27:87–90; 51:374–77 .

[56] *Sermons on John* (1537–40), LW 22:442 = WA 47:157; cf. LW 17:38–39; 22:430; 41:122, 130, 223, 311; 53:35; Luther, *Commentary on the First Twenty-Two Psalms*, 2.132.

[57] *Against the Thirty-two Articles of the Louvain Theologists* (1545), LW 34:350–51 = WA 54:419–21.

3. Whoever believes it is an idolater and worships the devil instead of God.[58]

Luther was not ignorant that both the papacy and the radical reformers claimed that they were guided by the Holy Spirit, and not merely following the dictates of their own reason. Yet Luther would not grant that they were taught by the Spirit when they departed from the external Word that the Spirit inspires. Instead, he accused them of mistaking their own foolish ideas for the voice of the Holy Spirit:

> Whatever ideas occurred to some fool, whatever he dreamed up, or whatever appealed to his fancy, was called an inspiration of the Holy Spirit. Everyone held his own thoughts to be the Holy Spirit and revelation.[59]

> But the devil's bride, reason, the lovely whore comes in and wants to be wise, and what she says, she thinks, is the Holy Spirit. . . . It walks about, cooks up fanaticism [*Schwärmerei*][60] with baptism and the Lord's Supper, and claims that everything that pops into its head and the devil puts into its heart is the Holy Spirit.[61]

Luther writes that while these "Enthusiasts" claim to be full of the Spirit, in reality they subject God's Word to the mastery of their own human spirits, as they doubt it and twist it and carve it up so that it comes out the way they think it should.[62] In opposition to all such claims to have direct access to the voice of the Spirit, Luther directs us to the external Word as the place where God has promised to grant his Spirit:

> Christ does not want to give you the right to run to and fro in search of the Spirit, to lose yourself in reverie and say: "I have this by inspiration of the Holy Spirit." Actually, it may be the devil who inspired you! Thus they alleged in the edict issued at the Diet of Augsburg: "The church is holy; therefore it follows that its proclamations are holy and given by inspiration of the Holy Spirit." Christ does not recognize such inspiration. He binds us solely to His Word. He does not want to see the Holy Spirit divorced from His

---

[58] *Against the Thirty-two Articles of the Louvain Theologists* (1545), LW 34:354 = WA 54:425.

[59] *Sermons on John* (1530–32), LW 23:174 = WA 33:274.

[60] *Schwärmerei* means "enthusiasm" in German. This is an expression Luther used for those who claim to have a direct hotline to God in their hearts, and use their own religious feelings to override God's written Word.

[61] *Last Sermon in Wittenberg* (1546), LW 51:374 = WA 51:126.

[62] *Sermons on John* (1530–32), LW 23:229–30 = WA 33:361–65; LW 33:90.

> Word. Whenever you hear anyone boast that he has something by inspiration of the Holy Spirit and it has no basis in God's Word, no matter what it may be, tell him that this is the work of the devil. Christ does not bind you to anything but His mouth and His Word. He does not want to leave you wandering aimlessly about; He wants you to hear His Word. He declares: "The words which I speak are spiritual. Therefore if you want to obtain the Holy Spirit, you must adhere to My words; for they are spirit and life."[63]

When Luther accuses his opponents of an idolatrous attachment to human reason, he is really accusing them of corrupting the Christian faith with the natural religion of humankind, and worshipping a philosophical god instead of the true God.[64] As a result, Luther says that the same basic faith is "common to all the heathen, the papists, the Jews, the Mohammedans, and the sectarians. . . . they all have the same reason, the same heart, the same opinion and idea."[65] Thus Luther agrees with contemporary pluralists that all

---

[63] *Sermons on John* (1530–32), LW 23:173 = WA 33:273–74; cf. 3:275–77; 12:287–88; 17:60–61, 243–44; 22:367–68; 23:229–30; 40:146–48; SA III 8.1–13. Luther's rule of thumb is that "God does not want to deal with us in any other way than through the spoken [literally: external] Word and the Sacraments. Whatever is praised as from the Spirit—without the Word and Sacraments—is the devil himself." (SA III 8.10 = WA 50:216.26–29) As a general rule he is scathing toward those who seek to know God by means of their own contemplations or spiritual experiences, or by seeking direct revelation from God, rather than by paying attention to the Word that God has already given in Scripture as the common possession of the church (LW 1:234–35; 3:274–75; 13:110–11; 25:287–88; 36:109; 54:112; cf. Gerhard O. Forde, "When the Old Gods Fail: Martin Luther's Critique of Mysticism," in *The Preached God*, ed. Mark C. Mattes and Steven D. Paulson [Grand Rapids, MI: Eerdmans, 2007], 56–68; Martin Luther, *Solus Decalogus Est Aeternus: Martin Luther's Complete Antinomian Theses and Disputations*, ed. and trans. Holger Sonntag [Minneapolis, MN: Lutheran Press, 2008], 87–91 = WA 39/1:345.22–23; Heiko A. Oberman, "Simul Gemitus et Raptus: Luther and Mysticism," in *The Dawn of the Reformation: Essays in Late Medieval and Early Reformation Thought* [Edinburgh: T & T Clark, 1986], 130–45). Does this mean that Luther was a complete cessationist, who could never admit the possibility of a person today receiving a direct revelation from God, as did the prophets of old? Not entirely. On a few occasions he does admit that this is possible. Yet when he does, he stresses three things: (1) Extreme care needs to be taken with all such revelations, since the devil can easily produce counterfeit signs and revelations; (2) all such revelations must be thoroughly tested (LW 9:129–30, 187–90; 18:109; 21:270–80), and if they cannot be tested then we should take the advice of Gamaliel and postpone judgment (LW 48:365–67); and (3) although such revelations may be helpful in providing us guidance in temporal matters, they are not necessary for our faith and cannot compare with what has already been revealed and attested in Scripture (LW 24:365–71). For a particularly instructive passage in which he gives a nuanced account of his view, see LW 3:166–67.

[64] *Lectures on Genesis* (1535–38), LW 2:124–25 = WA 42:349–50; LW 4:145.

[65] *Lectures on Galatians* (1535), LW 26:396 = WA 40/1:603; cf. Suk, *Luther's Concept of Idolatry*, 71–72, 228–29; Ingemar Öberg, *Luther and World Mission: A Historical and Systematic Study*, trans. Dean Apel (St. Louis: Concordia, 2007), 56.

religions are the same!—apart from the one true religion that has been revealed from heaven through Christ and his Word. The reason all other religions are fundamentally the same is that they all stem from the same source, the same idol: the natural reason of humankind, which people have put in place of Christ's inspired Word.

REASON AS THE SOURCE OF IDOLATRY

Not only does Luther regard it as idolatrous for us to elevate our thoughts above God's thoughts, he contends that whenever we do this it leads to further idolatry, since we then form a false picture of God. When we ignore God's Word and try to grasp God with our reason instead, we end up worshipping a false god that we have dreamed up for ourselves. Luther makes this point in his discussion of the fall in Genesis 3. He says that Eve fell into sin before she ate the fruit, since she set aside faith in God's Word and listened to a different teacher. The serpent's line of attack was to cast doubt on God's Word, and to encourage her to think about God and his will based on a different word than the one God himself had given. In this way, he presented to Adam and Eve a new god of his own invention without them even noticing. Our first parents took the bait by forming their impression of God apart from his Word. In the same way, whenever we attempt to deal with God on our own terms, apart from his Word, we slip into idolatry.[66]

So why is it inevitable that the portrait of God derived from human reason will diverge from the one God gives us in his Word? If a natural knowledge of God is available to us apart from the Word (Rom 1:18–25; 2:15), then why is it that the world does not know God through its wisdom (1 Cor 1:21)? Luther gives two main answers to this question. The first is that although human reason knows certain things about God, it does not know the most important thing about him, since it does not know the Gospel. The second is that the human mind is distorted by the sinful human will.

Natural human reason does not know the Gospel. Luther's main complaint about the natural knowledge of God is that it is impossible for us to know the Gospel in this way. Gerrish provides a helpful summary of Luther's thoughts on this point. He writes that the problem with general revelation for Luther is not that its content is false.[67] The problem is that it is partial and

---

[66] *Lectures on Genesis* (1535–38), LW 1:146–62 = WA 42:110–22.

[67] At one point Luther defines idolatry as "an erring notion or conscience devised about the true God" (*Lectures on Deuteronomy* [1525], LW 9:130 = WA 14:648). For Luther, idolatry is always more than just the projection of human desires or the product of human imagination. It always involves some genuine knowledge, as limited or as distorted as this knowledge may be (cf. Heinrich Bornkamm, *Luther and the Old Testament*, trans. Eric W. Gritsch and Ruth C. Gritsch, ed. Victor I. Gruhn [Philadelphia: Fortress, 1969], 48–55).

superficial, and therefore people draw false inferences from it. In particular, general revelation reveals God's power and justice, without revealing his grace in Jesus Christ. Reason concludes from God's power that it will be useful to have him on our side, and reason concludes from his justice that the way to get him onside is good works. It therefore leads people to construct a false eudemonistic and legalistic conception of religion.[68]

In the previous chapter we noted Luther's distinction between the "legal knowledge" of God that is available to natural reason, and the "evangelical knowledge" that only comes through Christ. Luther frequently asserts that human reason knows there is a God, and knows something of his power, law, and justice. Yet it does not know God's true identity, as the Father of Jesus Christ who wants to show us mercy through Christ. Therefore it gropes blindly after God and assigns divinity to the wrong object.[69] Moreover, since it does not understand the Gospel, it adopts a legalistic opinion regarding whatever god it chooses to worship.[70] It is this legalistic opinion that Luther regards as that common rationale behind every idolatrous religion:

> Whoever surrenders this knowledge [of God through the Gospel of Jesus Christ] must necessarily develop this notion: "I shall undertake this form of worship; I shall join this religious order; I shall select this or that work. And so I shall serve God. There is no doubt that God will regard and accept these works and will grant me eternal life for them. For He is merciful and kind, granting every good even to those who are unworthy and ungrateful; much more will He grant me His grace and eternal life for so many great deeds and merits!" This is the height of wisdom, righteousness, and religion about which reason is able to judge; it is common to all the heathen, the papists, the Jews, the Mohammedans, and the sectarians. . . . Therefore there is no difference at all between a papist, a Jew, a Turk, or a sectarian. Their persons, locations, rituals, religions, works, and forms of worship are, of course, diverse; but they all have the same reason, the same heart, the same opinion and idea. The Turk thinks the very same as the Carthusian, namely, "If I do this or that, I have a God who is favorably disposed toward me; if I do not, I have a God who is wrathful." There is no middle ground between human working and the knowledge of Christ; if this

---

[68] Gerrish, *Grace and Reason*, 100–103.

[69] WA 28:608–14; LW 7:336; 19:53–57.

[70] LW 1:149 = WA 42:112; 3:117–18; 4:119; 12:403–4; 19:11, 54–56, 115; 22:149–59; 23:55–56, 80; 26:113, 399–400; 27:87–88; 52:56–60, 107; LC II 66–68; Öberg, *Luther and World Mission*, 54–56.

> knowledge is obscured, it does not matter whether you become a monk or a heathen afterwards.[71]

As the above quote suggests, when Luther says that reason does not know the Gospel, this does not mean that it cannot know anything of God's undeserved kindness and mercy. Luther acknowledges that God's undeserved goodness is evident in creation,[72] and that natural reason can recognize that God is kind, gracious, merciful, and benevolent in a general sense.[73] Yet for Luther the Gospel is not some general notion regarding God's benevolence, but a firm promise through Christ that God's mercy is "for me." What reason lacks is such a promise regarding the extent of God's mercy. Therefore when the conviction of sin strikes, or trouble overtakes us and makes it appear as if God is against us, we easily doubt that he will be gracious to us.[74] Without any promise of mercy, the anxious conscience has no certainty, and seeks refuge in the Law.[75]

Natural human reason is distorted by the human will. The second reason Luther gives for why people do not know God through their reason is that the human mind has been corrupted by the sinful human will. Just as Paul says that idolatrous people wilfully suppress the truth (Rom 1:18–25), and seek out teachers to suit their own sinful passions (2 Tim 4:3), so Luther contends that "the ungodly world wants to be deceived."[76] Far from picturing fallen people as engaged in an unbiased quest for truth, Luther says that our sinful presumption causes us to deliberately distort the truth, so that we see God "through a colored glass"[77] instead of as he really is.

---

[71] *Lectures on Galatians* (1535), LW 26:396 = WA 40/1:603.

[72] SC II 2 = WA 30/1:365.2–3; cf. Matt 5:44–45; 6:26, 28–30.

[73] *Lectures on Genesis* (1538–42), LW 3:117 = WA 42:631–32; *Commentary on Jonah: The German Text (1526)*, LW 19:54 = WA 19:205–6.

[74] *Commentary on Jonah: The German Text (1526)*, LW 19:54 = WA 19:205–6; LW 29:235; Öberg, *Luther and World Mission*, 48–50; Gerrish, *Grace and Reason*, 15; cf. LW 12:403–4.

[75] One is reminded here of Islam, in which one of the 99 names for Allah is "the merciful one." Nevertheless, Islam remains a religion of the law. The reason for this is that Allah never binds himself to any promises of mercy, but always remains free. Therefore I can never count on him to be merciful to me, and am thrown back on the law as the only way to improve my chances with him (Jens Christensen, *Mission to Islam and Beyond: A Practical Theology of Mission* [Blackwood, South Australia: New Creation Publications, 2001], 276–80).

[76] *Lectures on Isaiah* (1527–30), LW 17:249 = WA 31/2:453; cf. LW 2:17, 19, 354; 18:221; 28:81; 41:127

[77] *Lectures on First John* (1527), LW 30:237 = WA 20:637; cf. LW 15:228; 17:108, 140; 51:282, 287; Bernhard Lohse, *Martin Luther: An Introduction to His Life and Work*, trans. Robert C. Schultz (Philadelphia: Fortress, 1986), 159–60.

Luther gives three main reasons why our sin leads us to distort our picture of God and turn him into an idol: our divine aspirations, our contempt for God's Law, and our contempt for the Gospel.

First, our proud self-will means that we do not want anyone telling us what to think, not even God.[78] Luther regarded this as more than just intellectual arrogance, but an expression of the divine aspirations of the sinful human will. In our sinful nature, we want to be gods, who have the godlike power to shape all things including God as we see fit. We want to be the creators and him to be the creature,[79] so that we can "adjust the plans and thinking of God to our plans and thinking."[80] Luther writes, "It is the nature of every ungodly man to mold God for himself and refuse to be molded by God."[81] Therefore people become "artificers who shape God according to their own design"[82] and "whittle God according to their purpose."[83]

Second, we willfully distort the knowledge of God because our sinful nature has no love for his Law. This is partly because it is too bound up in its love for created things to love God or pay attention to him.[84] It is also because it is unable to live up to the Law's demands, and feels condemned by it. Therefore it finds it oppressive and derives no joy from listening to it.[85] Instead of loving God and his will, its bad conscience causes it to flee from him in fear, supposing that he is not merciful and good but a judge and a tyrant.[86] As a result, those who live according to the flesh are unwilling to listen to God's Law as it really is. Instead, "They fit the words of the lips of God to their own works."[87] They invent their own law, and call whatever pleases them good.[88] Thus they call good evil and evil good.[89] If they do love some small part of

---

[78] Cf. *Lectures on Isaiah* (1527–30), LW 16:216 = WA 31/2:153–54; LW 20:10; 52:60

[79] *Lectures on Isaiah* (1527–30), LW 17:16–20 = WA 31/2:273–276; cf. Michael Parsons, "Luther on Isaiah 40: the Gospel and Mission," in *Text and Task*, ed. Michael Parsons [Waynesboro, GA: Paternoster, 2005], 69–70; Suk, *Luther's Concept of Idolatry*, 175.

[80] *Lectures on Deuteronomy* (1525), LW 9:54 = WA 14:589.6–7; cf. LW 17:108–9, 140; 19:11; 25:157.

[81] *Lectures on Isaiah* (1527–30), LW 17:16–17 = WA 31/2:273.1–2.

[82] *Lectures on Isaiah* (1527–30), LW 17:17 = WA 31/2:273.5–6.

[83] *Lectures on Isaiah* (1527–30), LW 17:17 = WA 31/2:273.6–7.

[84] *Lectures on Genesis* (1535–38), LW 2:124 = WA 42:349.

[85] LW 14:294–300, 310; 52:59–60, 107; Luther, *Commentary on the First Twenty-Two Psalms*, 2:20–27; 2:310–11; 2:417–18 (sic); cf. John Kleinig, *Grace upon Grace: Spirituality for Today* (St. Louis: Concordia, 2008), 97–98.

[86] *Lectures on Genesis* (1543–45), LW 7:336 = WA 44:549; LW 12:309 = WA 40/2:324.

[87] Luther, *Commentary on the First Twenty-Two Psalms*, 2:163.

[88] LW 12:308–9; 14:294–95; 20:10; 52:58–59; Luther, *Commentary on the First Twenty-Two Psalms*, 1:534–35.

[89] Luther, *Commentary on the First Twenty-Two Psalms*, 1:524–27, 581; Isa 5:20.

God's Law, it is not because they truly love God and his will, but because they think they can use it for their own advantage, such as by using it to justify themselves.[90]

Third, we deliberately distort the knowledge of God because our sinful nature despises the Gospel. When we live according to the flesh, we want to justify ourselves, and thereby glorify ourselves through our own righteousness instead of glorifying God by receiving righteousness from him. Those who are wrapped up in the sinful nature resent the Gospel, since it reveals their righteousness to be nothing.[91] Instead of rejoicing in the Gospel, they twist the Law to justify themselves, and invent works by which they imagine they can make themselves pleasing to God. Thus they worship an imaginary god who is pleased with their works, whom they have manufactured after the pattern of their works.[92] This then leads them to despise the Gospel even more, since as soon as they feel secure in their own righteousness they feel no need for the Gospel. Luther writes, " 'Here I am, for I am the Lord thy God, full of mercy.' . . . these words are but cold things, when they are sounded out of their place and season, (that is, before a soul that is secure and full)."[93]

This tendency of the human will to pervert revelation means that there is a kind of bibliolatry for Luther. It is not what many modern scholars call bibliolatry: the doctrine of verbal inspiration or inerrancy. Instead, it is to misuse Scripture to create an idol through which we attempt to justify ourselves. Just as God can be used for idolatrous purposes, so can his Word.

CONCLUSION

Luther's basic understanding of the genesis of idolatry is that the human desire to be like God leads fallen human beings to twist all knowledge of God and construct a false view of him, as one who allows them to be the sort of gods they want to be. They imagine a god who does not tell them what to think, but fits in with their views and opinions. They concoct a god that does not tell them how to behave, but approves of the same things they approve of. They dream of a god who is as pleased by their righteousness as they want him to be. Such a god is a tame god who does not threaten their aspirations to divinity. Such a view of God is only possible when people refuse to let God teach them, and set themselves up as teachers over him.

---

[90] LW 14:295; Luther, *Commentary on the First Twenty-Two Psalms*, 1:535–36.

[91] LW 9:54; 22:157–58; Luther, *Commentary on the First Twenty-Two Psalms*, 2:215–16, 310–11, 389 (sic), 417–18, 427–28.

[92] LW 9:54, 130–31; 17:16–20, 107–9, 140; 19:11; 51:281–82; 52:59–60, 107.

[93] Luther, *Commentary on the First Twenty-Two Psalms*, 1:564 = WA 5:351.15–16, 19–20; cf. LW 51:287.

Idolatry is therefore bound up with the effects of sin on the human mind. Luther's discussion of the limitations of general revelation should not blind us to his basic point of view, which is that unredeemed humanity is wilfully ignorant of God. Siegbert Becker, in his study of Luther's view of reason, summarises Luther's view accurately when he writes, "Luther held that the fault for man's failure to know God and to read the record correctly lies not at the doorstep of the revelation, whether in the works [general revelation] or in the Word [special revelation], but in the depravity of human nature."[94] The limitations of natural human reason do not excuse people of their failure to pay sufficient attention to the Word, or of the way they twist both special and general revelation to suit themselves. Humans may be blind, yet they are culpable for their blindness, since it results from their attempts to elevate their own wisdom, their own will, and their own righteousness above God's. To put it differently, idolatrous views of the God who transcends the self are primarily a product of the idol of the self.

This idol of the self can oppose the knowledge of God in a couple of ways. The first is when our idolatrous faith in our own natural reason leads us to think we have no need of God's Word and can neglect it. Luther counters this by calling us back to the Word, and insisting that if we are to know the true God we must rely on his instruction and not our wisdom. The second is when we attempt to master God's Word and twist it so it conforms to our ideas. Luther writes,

> What I have observed is this, that all heresies and errors in connection with the Scriptures have arisen, not from the simplicity of the words, as is almost universally stated, but from neglect of the simplicity of the words, and from tropes or inferences hatched out of men's own heads.[95]

Luther's call for us to return to the Word is grounded in the conviction that the Scriptures speak clearly and therefore can function as our teacher, rather than being "a waxen nose" that we mold to our own opinions.[96] Yet although the Scriptures are clear, they are not clear to us when we wilfully resist their message,[97] and interpret them through the colored lens of our own idolatry.[98] Therefore the human will needs to be converted if it is to receive

---

[94] Becker, *The Foolishness of God*, 26.

[95] *The Bondage of the Will*, LW 33:163 = WA 18:701.11–13.

[96] *Operationes in Psalmos* (1519–21), LW 14:338 = WA 5:66.

[97] LW 16:243; 19:152; 32:11–12; 33:25–29; 89–100; 39:163–65; Thompson, *A Sure Ground on Which to Stand*, 191–235.

[98] LW 17:108–9 = WA 30/2:345–46; LW 21:216–17; 23:240–41; 27:28–29; 30:237; 36:337; 37:20; 44:50; 51:281–82.

God's Word with true understanding. This primarily involves conversion to the Gospel. Only then will we embrace the central message of Scripture, love the true God and his will, and desist from our attempts to twist the biblical message in a vain attempt to justify ourselves and our rebellion. Luther writes,

> Thus all of Scripture, as already said, is pure Christ, God's and Mary's Son. Everything is focused on this Son, so that we might know Him distinctively and in that way see the Father and the Holy Spirit eternally as one God. To him who has the Son Scripture is an open book; and the stronger his faith in Christ becomes, the more brightly will the light of Scripture shine for him.[99]

How this conversion of the will takes place will be the subject of the next chapter.

CONTEMPORARY APPLICATION

Luther presents a challenge to all theology that starts "from below," and uses our own thoughts and experiences as its foundation.[100] For Luther, theology is a thoroughly theocentric activity.[101] Not only is God the subject matter of theology, but he must be the teacher. The Word of this teacher certainly intersects with the things of this world, and finds points of contact within the realm of creation that are accessible to the eyes and ears and minds of all.[102] It comes to us under the covering of created things, and speaks not only of heavenly things but also of earthly things, as it addresses us in our situation as earthly creatures. Yet it is still a word from above. The movement cannot be reversed. We cannot start with what we know of things below and work our way up to God.[103]

Luther's thought also presents a challenge to many types of theology that claim to be "from above," but are really "from below" as far as he is concerned. God has told us to pay attention to one particular Word "as to a lamp shining in a dark place" (2 Pet 1:19). This is the Word of the apostles and

---

[99] *Treatise on the Last Words of David* (1543), LW 15:339 = WA 54:88–89.

[100] Luther frequently speaks about the importance of experience in shaping our faith, and can even say that "experience alone makes the theologian" (LW 54:7 = WA TR 1:16). Yet as Oswald Bayer points out, when he says this he does not mean experience per se, but experience with the Word of God (Oswald Bayer, *Martin Luther's Theology: A Contemporary Interpretation*, trans. Thomas H. Trapp [Grand Rapids, MI: Eerdmans, 2008], 37). The truly Christian experience is experience that is shaped and informed by the Word, not experience that is put in place of the Word. See footnote 26 in chapter 9 for more on this topic.

[101] Cf. Watson, *Let God Be God!*, 88; Öberg, *Luther and World Mission*, 63, 70.

[102] LW 40:97; Watson, *Let God Be God!*, 84–85; Becker, *The Foolishness of God*, 28–29, 60.

[103] LW 26:28–30; 31:40, 52–53.

prophets that is centered in Christ and recorded in Holy Scripture. This Word is truly from above. Any other word that is not derived from this is from below, despite what anyone may claim.[104]

The purpose of this chapter is not to give a comprehensive account of Luther's approach to Scripture, or to respond to all the hermeneutical questions that confront us today. Instead, the purpose is to expose the epistemological root of all idolatry, the human presumption that we can deal with divine matters by ourselves without carefully heeding what God has to say. This presumption obviously affects unbelievers who have no intention of listening to Scripture. Yet it also affects people who acknowledge that Scripture is God's inspired Word, but nevertheless co-opt it to suit their own human thoughts or experiences. Indeed, most of Luther's thoughts on this subject were given in response to those who acknowledged the formal authority of Scripture, yet failed in practice to submit their thinking to it.

Formal Acknowledgement but Practical Neglect

A contemporary example of how a person can acknowledge Scripture's authority in theory yet fail to norm their thinking by it in practice is provided by the apologist Norman Geisler. As one of the drafters of the *Chicago Statement on Biblical Inerrancy* and the author of the recent book *Defending Inerrancy*,[105] Geisler has been a staunch defender of biblical inerrancy. Yet in

[104] This of course presupposes an established canon of Scripture. The purpose of this chapter is not to answer contemporary challenges to the biblical canon or to persuade people who are not already convinced that this canon is God's Word. As important a task as that may be, Luther never applied himself to it. This is not particularly surprising, given that he lived in a society in which the formal authority of Scripture was rarely questioned. Nevertheless it is possible to infer from Luther's general approach to Scripture how he would most likely have responded to such challenges if he had faced them. For instance, Luther always treats Scripture as a first principle, something you argue from not argue to, something that judges all human thoughts not the other way round. Secondly, he treats God's Word as its own best defense, since it alone has the power to create faith in human hearts. Therefore, if confronted with modern challenges to Scripture he would be likely to point primarily to the self-attesting power of God's Word, rather than relying on history or tradition or science or other authorities that can at best confirm the authority of Scripture, not establish it (for more on this, see chapter 9, including the section on apologetics). However, Luther never developed these thoughts in a systematic way, unlike later theologians who were inspired by him such as Calvin and the dogmaticians of Lutheran orthodoxy (Robert Preus, *The Inspiration of Scripture: A Study of the Theology of the 17th-Century Lutheran Dogmaticians* [St. Louis: Concordia, 1957], 88–118; Calvin, *Institutes of the Christian Religion* [1559], 1.7.4–5).

[105] R. C. Sproul, "Explaining Inerrancy: A Commentary," 1980, International Council on Biblical Inerrancy Foundation Series 2, 65.175.91.69/ICCP_org/Documents_ICCP/English/White_Papers/01_Biblical_Inerrancy_Paper.pdf (accessed Oct. 25, 2012), iii; Norman L. Geisler and William C. Roach, *Defending Inerrancy: Affirming the Accuracy of Scripture for a New Generation* (Grand Rapids, MI: Baker Books, 2011).

at least one key area his theology is shaped more by human reason than by God's Word.

One of Luther's strongest defenses of scriptural clarity comes in *The Bondage of the Will*.[106] Evidently Luther was convinced that Scripture is clear enough on this issue to settle the matter, and he marshalled much evidence from Scripture to demonstrate that the human will after the fall is in bondage to sin and can only be freed by God's mercy.[107] In contrast, Geisler has published a book in which he argues that the will of fallen and unredeemed people is not bound, but free to choose for or against God. Geisler's book is replete with Scriptural references and quotations, yet his arguments are rationalistic rather than scriptural. Indeed, his arguments bear an uncanny resemblance to those of Erasmus. His chief arguments are: (1) "ought implies can," (2) reward and punishment, praise and blame are unjust unless those who are rewarded or punished are free to merit it,[108] and (3) many church fathers teach free will.[109] He produces not one passage of Scripture to prove his chief contention, unless one first accepts his rationalistic premises that he expects us to accept without scriptural proof. That is, when he tries to demonstrate scriptural support for his position, his evidence consists of this: any time Scripture presents us with an "ought," or talks of praise or blame, or even talks of choice or will or faith,[110] he takes this as proof of his position.[111] He then runs through countless Bible passages that teach the opposite—that fallen human beings are in bondage to sin unless they are elected by God and liberated by God's grace[112]—and tries to find a gloss to get around every one of them.[113]

Two points are worth noting. The first is the way Geisler gives the appearance of scriptural argumentation by multiplying biblical citations, while his arguments are in fact derived from human reason. The second is the way he says that our salvation ultimately hinges on our free will decision, and not

---

[106] LW 33:24–28, 89–100 = WA 18.606–9, 652–59.

[107] LW 33:246–89 = WA 18:756–83.

[108] Norman Geisler, *Chosen But Free: A Balanced View of Divine Election* (Minneapolis, MN: Bethany House Publishers, 2001), 29–31; cf. LW 33:120–32, 141–44, 147–55.

[109] Ibid., 150–59.

[110] Here he is begging the question, and assuming that *choice* must mean free choice, *will* must mean free will, etc.

[111] Geisler, *Chosen But Free*, 33–35.

[112] Geisler does concede that we all need the aid of God's grace to overcome sin or move toward God (ibid., 30–31, 36–37). Thus he is not a full-blown Pelagian, merely a synergist. Yet he treats this grace as something that has been given to all people, believers and unbelievers alike, apart from the means of grace, so that in practical terms our salvation now hinges entirely on our free choice.

[113] Ibid., 58–96.

purely on God's mercy. Thus he ends up contending for human merit against the grace of God. To echo Luther's response to Erasmus, in this way he seeks to purchase God's favour more cheaply than Pelagius. Pelagius at least set the price of God's favour high, and insisted on great effort and many works. Geisler contends that it can be bought cheaply with a tiny act of human free will.[114] As Luther predicts, since Geisler starts by forming his picture of God on the basis of human reason and not the Word he ends up devising a form of self-justification.

RESULTANT DISTORTIONS IN OUR PICTURE OF GOD

Luther contends that whenever human thinking eclipses the Word we will end up distorting our picture of God in particular ways, as we remake God as we see fit. First, we will turn him into a tame god, one who does not threaten our purposes and desires, but can be manipulated to serve our ends. Second, we will adopt some kind of legalistic opinion concerning this god, and will fail to know the true God who wants to save us through the Gospel. It is therefore worth looking at a few examples of how idolatrous "theology from below"—that pays insufficient attention to God's Word while placing greater store in human thoughts, feelings, experiences, or traditions—distorts our picture of God in the way that Luther predicts.

Gods that resemble ourselves. Since at least the time of Xenophanes of Colophon—who observed in the fifth century BC that the Egyptians made their gods dark and snub nosed, whereas the Thracians made them red haired and blue eyed[115]—observers of religion have noted the tendency for humans to worship gods that resemble themselves. Recently a team of behavioural scientists led by Nicholas Epley from the University of Chicago decided to study this phenomenon empirically. They conducted a series of studies on religious believers in the United States, and confirmed that the subjects did indeed adjust their picture of God to bring him into alignment with themselves. The researchers asked the subjects to state what position they held on a range of issues (abortion, affirmative action, the death penalty, the Iraq war, marijuana legalisation, and same-sex marriage). They then asked them to state what position they thought God, Bill Gates, the average American, and George Bush would hold. The result was a strong correlation between the "Self" and "God" responses, and only weak correlations between the "Self" and any of the other responses. To eliminate the possibility that this strong correlation was due to the subjects trying to line themselves up with God, ra-

---

[114] LW 33:268 = WA 18:770. Geisler is fully cognizant of the fact that he is opposing *sola gratia*, since he openly confesses his synergism (Geisler, *Chosen But Free*, 241–43).

[115] Anthony Kenny, *An Illustrated Brief History of Western Philosophy* (Malden, MA: Blackwell Publishing, 2006), 5.

ther than lining God up with themselves, the researchers did further studies in which they manipulated the subjects' opinions on the issues in question. What they found was that this manipulation flowed on to the subjects' assessment of what God would think, without affecting their assessment of what other people would think in a significant way. Furthermore, brain scans of the participants showed that when they reasoned about God's thoughts they used similar mental pathways to when they reasoned about their own thoughts, but different pathways when they reasoned about other people. This suggests that they were reasoning about God egocentrically.[116] These results led the researchers to conclude that,

> Intuiting God's beliefs on important issues may not produce an independent guide, but may instead serve as an echo chamber that reverberates one's own beliefs. . . . People may use religious agents as a moral compass, forming impressions and making decisions based on what they presume God as the ultimate moral authority would believe or want. The central feature of a compass, however, is that it points north no matter what direction a person is facing. This research suggests that, unlike an actual compass, inferences about God's beliefs may instead point people further in whatever direction they are already facing.[117]

These results agree with Luther's contention that without a fixed compass outside ourselves in God's Word, we distort our picture of God in egocentric ways. We turn him into a tame god who doesn't challenge us, since he always agrees with what we think.

Making Christ in our image. This egocentric distortion of our picture of God extends to our picture of Christ. Stephen Prothero, chair of the Department of Religion at Boston University, has conducted a historical study that charts different portraits of Jesus that have achieved popularity in the American mind at different stages of U.S. history and among different segments of the population. He concludes that "Americans of all stripes have cast the man from Nazareth in their own image."[118]

Prothero chronicles how one generation of Americans after another has changed its portrait of Jesus to suit its own fancy. Under the influence of the Enlightenment, Deists, Unitarians, and biblical critics remade Jesus into an

---

[116] N. Epley, et al., "Believers' estimates of God's beliefs are more egocentric than estimates of other people's beliefs," *Proceedings of the National Academy of Sciences*, 106 (2009), www.pnas.org/content/106/51/21533.full.pdf+html (accessed 28 Nov. 2011), 21533–38.

[117] Ibid., 21533, 21537.

[118] Stephen Prothero, *American Jesus: How the Son of God Became a National Icon* (New York: Farrar, Straus and Giroux; London: Sandra Dijkstra Literary Agent, 2003), 7.

enlightened moral teacher and existentialist philosopher.[119] In the spirit of individual liberty of the early republic, the Calvinist God of the colonial era—centered on the sovereignty of the Father—looked too much like bad King George, and Calvinism steadily gave way to an Arminianism centered on Jesus.[120] In the popular revivals of the Second Great Awakening and the sentimentality of the early Victorian era, Jesus became gentle Jesus meek and mild, a sweet and somewhat feminized Savior.[121] During the progressive era, from the late nineteenth century through the World Wars, Jesus was made over in more masculine terms, as a manly fighter, a social crusader, a savvy business executive, and a dynamic leader and celebrity.[122] In more recent times, he has morphed from the alternative lifestyle dude of the "Jesus Freaks" in the hippie era to the rocking superstar of Contemporary Christian Music.[123] During the civil rights movements, African Americans embraced Jesus as a "black Moses;"[124] members of the Nation of Islam claimed him as a Black Muslim prophet;[125] "womanist" theologians claimed that the face of Jesus could be seen most clearly in African-American women;[126] while to the KKK he was a Klansman.[127] Mormons may have ditched the Christian creeds, but have embraced Jesus as their great white elder brother.[128] Even Jews and Hindus have gotten in on the act, the one claiming Jesus as a Jewish rabbi distinct from the Christian Christ,[129] the other depicting Jesus along the lines of a Hindu avatar.[130]

On the one hand, Prothero's study should tell us something of the richness of Christ. Most of the portraits Prothero describes latch onto a genuine characteristic of the biblical Christ, who is so multi-faceted that an enormous variety of people can find something in him to embrace. On the other hand, most of these portraits skew the biblical picture of Christ in some way, often to the point where it can no longer be called Christian in a biblical or creedal sense. Furthermore, if all we see in Jesus are those things that fit with our biases and preferences, he can never transform us. As Prothero comments, "In

---

[119] Ibid., 19–42.

[120] Ibid., 43–56.

[121] Ibid., 56–86.

[122] Ibid., 87–123.

[123] Ibid., 124–57.

[124] Ibid., 200–228.

[125] Ibid., 218–19.

[126] Ibid., 207–8.

[127] Ibid., 8, 299.

[128] Ibid., 161–99.

[129] Ibid., 229–66.

[130] Ibid., 267–90.

the United States, Jesus is widely hailed as the 'King of Kings.' But it is a strange sort of sovereign who is so slavishly responsive to his subjects."[131]

One of the movements Prothero examines is the higher biblical criticism spawned by the Enlightenment, with its various quests for the historical Jesus.[132] Prothero notes the critique of Albert Schweitzer and George Tyrell, that far from uncovering the real Jesus, scholars engaged in these quests tend to see their own reflections instead.[133] This critique is worth noting, since this same spirit is evident in many of the other movements that Prothero describes, a spirit that is willing to judge the biblical portrait of Christ as defective. Furthermore, higher biblical criticism remains extremely influential in contemporary academic theology.

The issue with higher criticism is not with scholarly or historical investigations of the Scriptures per se, nor with the different analytical tools that biblical scholars use. Rather, it is with the pre-commitments scholars bring to their work. Do they approach Scripture with "faith seeking understanding," or do they hold the veracity of its contents in doubt until their truth can be established with their own investigations? Is their purpose to understand the text, or to judge whether or not to believe it? When a clash occurs between Scripture and some other historical source or scholarly theory, which takes precedence? In other words, what is their highest authority? Where have they placed their faith? Or, more bluntly, who is their God?

The late Old Testament scholar James Barr argues that underlying the shift in biblical scholarship that took place at the time of the Enlightenment was a change in "the conditions under which people were prepared to believe."[134] He writes,

> By criticism, when used of theology, I mean this: that the establishment of theological truth does not take place by a mere passive acceptance of data given by the sources of revelation, but takes place through a critical and estimative weighing of these data. The theologian asks "Is this true? . . . What made the difference in the eighteenth century was not biblical criticism as such, but a more

---

[131] Ibid., 297.

[132] Ibid., 32–41.

[133] "Whatever Jesus was, He was in no sense a Liberal Protestant" (George Tyrell, *Christianity at the Cross-Roads* [London: Longmans, Green, and Co., 1910], xxi). "The Christ that Harnack sees, looking back through nineteen centuries of Catholic darkness, is only the reflection of a Liberal Protestant face, seen at the bottom of a deep well" (ibid., 44). See Prothero, *American Jesus*, 34; Albert Schweitzer, *The Quest of the Historical Jesus: A Critical Study of its Progress from Reimarus to Wrede*, trans. W. Montgomery (London: Adam and Charles Black, 1910), 4–6.

[134] James Barr, *Holy Scripture: Canon, Authority, Criticism* (Philadelphia: Westminster, 1983), 121. By permission of Oxford University Press.

> critical theological attitude to the sources of all belief, of which the Bible was first or at least central."[135]

Barr is right that during the Enlightenment there was a change in the conditions under which people were prepared to believe. Yet he is wrong in suggesting that for the first time people became genuinely critical toward sources of belief such as the Bible. The suggestion that people in the past were somehow "pre-critical," and simply received the data of revelation without questioning it, is false. If it were true, Luther would not have had to fight so hard for the primacy of scriptural authority. In every age there have been people who have adopted a critical stance toward Scripture, at least in practice, if not in theory. People have always judged the Bible in the light of their own thoughts and opinions, or by appeal to other authorities. Luther's struggle against this critical stance is evident in a letter to Hieronymus Dungersheim, one of his early Catholic opponents, in which he writes, "We want Scripture to be judge, you want to be judges against Scripture."[136] The issue is not whether we think critically or not, but what gets critiqued in the light of what? In other words, what is our highest authority? The truth behind Barr's comments is that people are now likely to use different authorities to judge the Bible than they did before. In Luther's day, people were likely to judge Scripture in the light of the philosophy of Aristotle, or the traditions of the Catholic Church, or their own religious experiences. In modern times, they are more likely to judge it based on their scientific or historical investigations. Yet the game remains the same. We are still trying to subject Scripture to one human authority or another, so that God becomes our pupil.

The result of this will be that we end up seeing in Jesus our own reflection. We will end up telling him who he must be, instead of allowing him to teach us about himself. Historical and scientific investigations will only reveal the kind of things that history and science can reveal—that is, human and earthly things—and they won't always reveal these with a high degree of certainty. The result will be a human and earthly Jesus, with our picture of him being uncertain, changing, and malleable enough for us to mold to our whims. The method will not allow us to rise above this to the true, unchanging, divine-human Son of God.

This also reveals why Christ can never be played off against Scripture, as many modern day Lutherans and Protestants are wont to do. If we do this we will quickly end up with a false christ, who constantly changes according to our whims. As we noted in the previous chapter, Luther's Christ is always the one proclaimed in the Bible, not some Christ we think we can have or know

---

[135] Ibid., 121. By permission of Oxford University Press.

[136] WA Br 2, 301:125.11–12.

apart from it. Therefore Luther warns against those who "delude the people by using the name of Christ."[137] He cautions us to "stick to the Word of God. Ignore every other word—whether it is devoid of Christ, in the name of Christ, or against Christ, or whether it is issued in any other way."[138] If we want to retain Christ, we must not import our own ideas into Scripture.[139] If we want to preach Christ faithfully, we must proclaim all the doctrines of Scripture.[140] If we want to know Christ, we must pay attention to his Word, lest the devil "mislead us through Christ himself,"[141] and we end up constructing a false Christ.[142] We saw in the previous chapter Luther's emphasis on Christ as the one who must show us what God is like. Yet the Scriptures are what we need if we are to know what Christ is like. Luther's emphasis on Christ and Scripture cannot be played off against each other. If one is lost, both are lost, and we are left with an idol.

THE GOD OF NATURAL THEOLOGY

Luther's attack on human reason can be legitimately construed as an attack on natural theology. It is not an attack on natural revelation per se. Luther asserts often enough that such revelation is genuine. The problem is what people inevitably do with natural revelation if they give insufficient attention to special revelation. The Swedish Luther scholar Ingemar Öberg summarizes Luther's position succinctly when he writes,

---

[137] *Sermons on John* (1530–32), LW 22:51 = WA 47:165.

[138] *Sermons on John* (1530–32), LW 22:51 = WA 47:165.

[139] "The cupidity of a greedy man is as nothing compared with a man's hearty pleasure in his own ideas. He then brings these fine ideas into the Scriptures, and this is devilishness pure and simple. . . . Then assuredly the true doctrine is soon lost, however willingly one preaches and willingly one listens. Then Christ is gone. Then they fall down before the devil on the mountain and worship him" (*Last Sermon in Wittenberg* [1546], LW 51:377 = WA 51:130.34–41).

[140] "We too teach nothing but Jesus crucified. But Christ crucified brings all these things with him" (*The Bondage of the Will* [1525], LW 33:71 = WA 18:638.24–639.1). "If they believed that it is the Word of God, they would not play around with it this way. No, they would treat it with the utmost respect; they would put their faith in it without any disputing or doubting; and they would know that one Word of God is all and that all are one, that one doctrine is all doctrines and all are one, so that when one is lost all are eventually lost, because they belong together and are held together by a common bond" (*Lectures on Galatians* [1535], LW 27:38 = WA 40/2:47.30–34).

[141] *Against the Heavenly Prophets in the Matter of Images and Sacraments* (1525), LW 40:134 = WA 18:116.

[142] Luther said of Karlstadt that "he constructs his own Christ" (*Against the Heavenly Prophets*, LW 40:135 = WA 18:117), by insisting that we must imitate the works of Christ, while paying insufficient attention to his words.

> Natural theology speculates about the divine majesty (*theologia gloriae*). Both within Christendom and in the heathen world, natural theology is characterized by rationalism, legalism, and moralism, by the Law and self-righteousness. True and saving knowledge of God looks only to God in Christ (*theologia crucis*). Only the theology of the cross leads to true knowledge of God, to his heart, his will to save, and to justification and salvation.[143]

On the one hand, this means that we can never mount an adequate defense of the Christian faith based on natural theology. It is true that Luther never completely dismissed the value of rational arguments in defending the Christian faith, provided that they are in agreement with Scripture. Siegbert Becker, in his studies on Luther's views on reason and apologetics, demonstrates how Luther both advocated and engaged in a kind of negative rational apologetics against opponents of the Christian faith. That is, in Socratic style he turned their use of reason against them, to show the unreasonableness of their objections to the Christian faith.[144] Becker also demonstrates how Luther regarded the natural knowledge of God and his Law as both genuine revelation and a point of contact for Christian proclamation.[145] Luther writes,

> Were it not naturally written in the heart, one would have to teach and preach the law for a long time before it became the concern of conscience. The heart must also find and feel the law in itself. Otherwise it would become a matter of conscience for no one. However, the devil so blinds and possesses hearts, that they do not always feel this law. Therefore one must preach the law and impress it on the minds of people till God assists and enlightens them, so that they feel in their hearts what the Word says.[146]

Yet although Luther saw some value in natural revelation in this limited way, he was opposed to all attempts to build faith on this foundation.[147] This is partly because of the weakness and instability of natural reason, as we will see in the next chapter. Even more, it is because of the inability of natural reason to know the Gospel. Since natural reason only knows the God of the Law and not the God of grace, it will always provide a distorted picture of God. The danger then in relying too heavily on natural theology without always

---

143 Öberg, *Luther and World Mission*, 63.

144 Becker, *The Foolishness of God*, 176–84; Siegbert W. Becker, "Luther's Apologetics," *Concordia Theological Quarterly* 10 (Oct. 1958), 754–59.

145 Becker, *The Foolishness of God*, 25–60.

146 *Against the Heavenly Prophets*, LW 40:97 = WA 18:80.35–81.3. Cf. WA 16:447.27–39.

147 Becker, *The Foolishness of God*, 154–75; Becker, "Luther's Apologetics," 750–54.

subsuming it under the higher revealed Word is that we end up presenting to people a false god of the Law. In our attempts to bring people to God we then might achieve the opposite, by appealing to the self-righteous and making them secure in their idolatry, while crushing broken sinners without binding them up through Christ. Natural theology might succeed in a limited sense in that it can raise the right questions, but it fails in that it does not supply the right answers, which only come via God's special revelation in his Word. By nature we know the accusing voice of the Law, but not how to silence this accusation through the Gospel. By nature we can know there is a God, but not his true identity in Christ. By nature we can see our need for divine help in times of trouble, but not where to find it. By nature we reason that a wise ruler rewards the innocent and punishes the guilty, but we are totally unprepared for the surprise that in Christ God punishes the innocent One and lets the guilty go free.[148] If we try to supply these answers for ourselves, we will end up constructing a false god based on some form of legalistic thinking.[149] The only way to avoid this is to allow the true God to speak, as he reveals himself to us by the Spirit through the Word.

An example of a god of natural reason is the god of moralistic therapeutic deism we encountered in previous chapters. The authors of the National Study of Youth and Religion note that adherents of this creed show little interest in absorbing or adhering to any authoritative doctrine, apart from "what seems right to me."[150] This is more than simple neglect. It often involves an aversion to the very idea of religious authority, as if to be persuaded by a higher authority is an affront to the sovereign right of the individual to choose his or her own beliefs.[151] The authors then go on to describe the resultant god in the following terms:

> Moralistic Therapeutic Deism is about belief in a particular God: one who exists, created the world, and defines our general moral order, but not one who is particularly personally involved in one's affairs—especially affairs in which one would prefer not to have God involved. . . . God sometimes does get involved in people's

[148] Luther, *Church Postils*, 8.12; LW 17:221, 228 = WA 31/2:432, 438; Becker, "Luther's Apologetics," 744.

[149] Note Luther's insight, discussed in chapter 6, that both legalism and antinomianism are two sides of the same coin. They are both expressions of thinking that is shaped by the Law and not the Gospel.

[150] Christian Smith and Melinda Lundquist Denton, *Soul Searching: The Religious and Spiritual Lives of American Teenagers* (New York: Oxford University Press, 2005), 131–37, 165, 262; Christian Smith and Patricia Snell, *Souls in Transition: The Religious and Spiritual Lives of Emerging Adults* (New York: Oxford University Press, 2009), 156–57.

[151] Smith and Denton, *Soul Searching*, 143–45; Smith and Snell, *Souls in Transition*, 156–57.

> lives, but usually only when they call on him, mostly when they have some trouble or problem or bad feeling that they want resolved. In this sense, the Deism here is revised from its classical eighteenth-century version by the therapeutic qualifier, making the distant God selectively available for taking care of needs. . . . Like the deistic God of the eighteenth-century philosophers, the God of contemporary teenage Moralistic Therapeutic Deism is primarily a divine Creator and Lawgiver. He designed the universe and establishes moral law and order. But this God is not trinitarian, he did not speak through the Torah or the prophets of Israel, was never resurrected from the dead, and does not fill and transform people through his Spirit. This God is not demanding. He actually can't be, because his job is to solve our problems and make people feel good. In short, God is something like a combination Divine Butler and Cosmic Therapist: he is always on call, takes care of any problems that arise, professionally helps his people to feel better about themselves, and does not become too personally involved in the process.[152]

From Luther's perspective nothing in this creed is surprising. When the sinful nature rears its ugly head, people rebel at the thought of being instructed by authority from above, and choose to be their own teachers instead. When they do this, they may retain aspects of true belief that can be known by natural reason, such as belief in a divine Creator and Lawgiver. Yet they will lose those things that can only be known through special revelation, such as knowledge of the Trinity and the Gospel of Jesus Christ. Therefore they will adopt a legalistic opinion concerning whatever god they worship. Then, even this remnant of knowledge will become twisted in self-serving ways. In the case of moralistic therapeutic deism, the moral law gets watered down to make it non-threatening, and God gets turned into a tame god who is at our beck and call. Thus the moralistic and therapeutic aspects of moralistic therapeutic deism flow quite naturally out of its deism, that is, its attempt to approach God from below, using human thoughts as its guide.

A CHRISTIAN RESPONSE: REFOCUSING PEOPLE ON THE WORD

Luther's goal in denouncing the idol of autonomous human reason was to redirect people to God's Word, so that they could be taught by God. So how do we proclaim the same message to people today?

---

[152] Smith and Denton, *Soul Searching*, 164–65. By permission of Oxford University Press, USA.

First, like Luther we can seek to expose the futility of dealing with God in any other way. This futility should be obvious to all. How could we possibly claim to have secure knowledge about a God who is hidden from our sight unless he chooses to reveal himself to us? Nevertheless, this point seems to be lost on many people, particularly in our modern world that has such confidence in autonomous human thought. I have lost count how many times I have heard someone say, "this is what I think about God," without bothering to ground this in any word from God, as if mere human opinion counts for anything in this regard. Therefore we may have to work at uncovering the futility of such an approach to divine things. One way to do this is to point out how consistently people try to remake God in their own image by adjusting their picture of God in self-serving ways, and pointing out how unlikely it is that God would change to suit human opinion in this way.

Second, like Luther we can regard the natural knowledge of God not as a secure basis on which to construct our picture of God but as a point of contact for Christian proclamation. Richard Keyes argues along these lines. He notes how Jesus and the apostles in the New Testament vary their proclamation considerably depending on to whom they are speaking. He then suggests that the way they adapt their message to their audience suggests that they have first asked two questions: (1) "What do these people already know of God?" and (2) "What have they done with what they know of God? What sort of idol have they created with what they know of God?" He then proposes that this is a good pattern for us to follow in dealing with non-Christians.[153] Although any knowledge they have of God has been twisted into idolatry, we should still consider how this knowledge provides us with starting points for dialogue. For instance, we do not need to convince moralistic therapeutic deists that there is a God; we merely need to introduce them to the true God. Likewise, we do not need to start from scratch in convincing moral relativists that God's Law is binding on them. Deep down they already know this. We merely need to break through the layers of denial and draw this knowledge out.

Third, like Luther, we can point people to God's Word as the font of true wisdom. We can clear the ground by deconstructing the authorities people use to critique and discredit Scripture, and then invite then to taste and see that the Lord is good.

One of the challenges we face here is that in our world of relativism and postmodern literary theory people have lost confidence that any text can speak clearly. Furthermore, they are frequently exposed to umpteen conflicting interpretations of the Bible in place of the Word itself. In dealing with this problem we can take a leaf out of Luther's book, who argues that a major rea-

[153] Richard Keyes, "Giving a Word Back," www.bethinking.org/what-is-apologetics/giving-a-word-back.htm (accessed Nov. 17, 2006).

son why Scripture appears obscure to people is that they are too lazy to study it properly. Just because Scripture seems unclear to us does not mean it is unclear in itself. To give an analogy, one of my parishioners is a mechanic. After I visited him one day he walked with me out to my car. As soon as he heard me start my engine he said, "You've got a problem with your resonator box." Sure enough, when I had it checked out he was right. This was clear to him, but it was not clear to me, because I had not spent sufficient time familiarizing myself with car mechanics. Likewise, the more we study Scripture the clearer it becomes. The first time I read books like Isaiah and Jeremiah I found large sections to be dry and obscure, but every time I have read them since I have gotten more out of them, so that now I find them wonderfully rich and enlightening. Luther, who read Scripture from cover to cover twice every year,[154] could speak with authority about the kind of insight that diligent study of Scripture can bring. Rather than trying to argue with people about the clarity of Scripture, a more effective method is to invite them to engage with it, so they can experience firsthand the kind of enlightenment this can yield.

Finally, we can imitate Luther in giving people the key to unlocking the Scriptures, the Gospel of Jesus Christ. In doing so we provide them with the central thesis of Scripture that enables them to makes sense of the whole. Furthermore, only this can release them from an evil conscience, so that instead of finding the Scriptures oppressive, and twisting their words to justify themselves, they can begin to delight in what the Bible has to say.

---

[154] *Table Talk* No. 1877 (Oct. 1532), LW 54:165 = WA TR 2:244.

Chapter Nine

The Idol of the Self and Repentance

For those who are engaged in the ministry of the Gospel, no question is more important than how we can lead people to repentance. How can we not only fill church pews, but also change people's hearts so that faith in Jesus Christ and love for God and neighbor flow out? To put it differently, how do we root out idolatry and establish true faith in the living God?[1] So far in this book we have looked at how Luther's theology of idolatry can help us to diagnose different kinds of idolatry. So now that the diagnosis is done, what is the cure?

For Luther, God is the only one who can produce this change in us. He does this through his Holy Spirit, who dethrones the idols in our hearts and creates in us true faith in the true God. As a result, he is also the one who is responsible for producing the fruits of faith in our lives. This reveals another subtle form of idolatry to us. If we think we can purify our own hearts from idolatry by means of our own efforts and willpower, and in this way produce faith and its fruits in ourselves and others, we have again set ourselves in the place of God.

Luther's Teaching

Luther's best-known articulation of the Holy Spirit's role in bringing us to faith is in his Small Catechism, where he writes,

> I believe that I cannot by my own reason or strength believe in Jesus Christ, my Lord, or come to Him. But the Holy Spirit has called me by the Gospel, enlightened me with His gifts, sanctified and kept me in the true faith. In the same way He calls, gathers, enlightens, and

---

[1] The topic under consideration here is not merely the initial conversion from unbelief to faith in a person's life, but also the ongoing repentance that Luther regarded as a daily struggle for every Christian (LW 31:25; SC IV 12 = WA 30/1:382.6–383.2). Each day we must turn from our sin and the idolatry that stands at the heart of it, and turn again in faith to the true God.

> sanctifies the whole Christian Church on earth and keeps it with Jesus Christ in the one true faith.[2]

What is less well known is how Luther develops this thought with explicit reference to idolatry. One place he does this is in his lectures on Zechariah. Here he writes that although human hands can smash statues and destroy sacred groves, they cannot cleanse the heart. Only the Holy Spirit can remove the idols from our hearts.[3] When he does, the external idols also fall, for "once the truth is known, once the Holy Spirit has been sent, the idols topple by themselves. The Spirit—not mortal hands—breaks them."[4]

Another place he connects the work of the Holy Spirit with the destruction of idolatry is in his commentary on Psalm 117:1, "Praise the Lord, all you heathen,"[5] where he writes:

> Now if all heathen are to praise God, this assumes that He has become their God. If He is to be their God, then they must know Him, believe in Him, and give up all idolatry. One cannot praise God with an idolatrous mouth or an unbelieving heart. And if they are to believe, they must first hear His Word and thereby receive the Holy Spirit, who through faith purifies and enlightens their hearts.[6]

Elsewhere, Luther argues that if we think that by our own free will we can create true faith in our hearts, and thereby keep the First Table of the Law, then we have made our natural human will into an idol. In this way we worship ourselves instead of God by trusting in ourselves instead of God's Holy Spirit.[7] Instead, a person must recognize that "this blessing of deliverance from idolatry has its source, not in his own merits or powers but solely in a God who pities and calls."[8] It is God's work to create us as new creatures who are holy to the Lord.[9] The Spirit must purify and regenerate us

---

[2] SC II = WA 30/1:367.4–368.3.

[3] LW 20:145; cf. Martin Luther, *Martin Luther's Complete Commentary on the First Twenty-Two Psalms*, trans. Henry Cole (2 vols.; London: W. Simpkin and R. Marshall, 1826), 2:153–54.

[4] *Lectures on Zechariah: The Latin Text* (1526), LW 20:145 = WA 13:663.37–38; cf. LW 13:378 = WA 31/1:418; LW 20:145 = WA 13:663; LW 26:224–25 = WA 40/1:357–58; LW 35:351 = WA DB 12:315–16.

[5] *Commentary on Psalm 117* (1530), LW 14:3 = WA 31/1.223.2.

[6] *Commentary on Psalm 117* (1530), LW 14:9 = WA 31/1:228.33–229.4; cf. LW 14:11 = WA 31/1:231.4–7.

[7] *The Misuse of the Mass* (1521), LW 36:216–17 = WA 8:552–53; LW 33:75; 54:110.

[8] *Lectures on Genesis* (1535–38), LW 2:246 = WA 42:437.2–3.

[9] *Sermon on St. Thomas' Day, Ps 19:1* (1516), LW 51:18–22 = WA 1:111–15.

through his Word so that we trust in God our Father, praise his name with a cheerful heart, and delight in his Word.[10] To think that we can do something to work saving faith and its fruits in ourselves is presumption. It is to trust in ourselves when we must trust wholly in God.[11] Such presumption cannot be purged by human effort, but God must teach us to despair of ourselves and to rely on him completely.[12]

Luther insists that the life of faith is purely passive. By this he does not mean that faith is inactive, since he also insists that faith is "a living, busy, active, mighty thing."[13] What he means is that it is receptive. On the one hand, it receives from God a righteousness that is not its own but comes through the merits of Christ.[14] On the other hand, the very faith by which it receives this righteousness is also a gift. A person must receive it through the working of God's Spirit. We can only lie like clay in the potter's hand as he purges away our trust in ourselves and other creatures, and renews our minds and wills so that we trust in God alone. He must move us, carry us along, form us, cleanse us, and impregnate us with his Word if our faith, hope and love are to be anchored in him. Only as he puts us in motion are we able to cooperate with him in any spiritual good such as praying or working.[15] Then, even when this work is begun in us, we cannot advance it by ourselves. Instead, we must pray that God would increase our faith, and we must turn to the Word of the Gospel so that through it he may do his work in us.[16]

This means that God is the one who must build his church and tear down the idols that oppose it. Christ alone can defend his church against idolatry and lies, and destroy them by attacking the devil's kingdom.[17] He is the one who must defeat the Antichrist by the word of his mouth,[18] and he is the one who must turn the enemies of the church into its friends by changing their hearts.[19] We can only cooperate in this struggle when we use the spiritual tools he gives us. We must put all our confidence in him through prayer and

---

[10] LW 20:9 = WA 13:550–51; LW 22:144–45 = WA 46:661–63; LW 24:110–12 = WA 45:560–62.

[11] *The Bondage of the Will* (1525), LW 33:61–62 = WA 18:632–33.

[12] *Lectures on Isaiah* (1527–30), LW 17:49–50 = WA 31/2:298–300.

[13] *Preface to Romans* (1522), LW 35:370 = WA DB 7:11; cf. LW 26:11–12 = WA 40/1:50–51.

[14] Luther, *Commentary on the First Twenty-Two Psalms*, 1:247–48; LW 3:102; 26:4–11, 25, 259, 392.

[15] Luther, *Commentary on the First Twenty-Two Psalms*, 1:258–62 = *Operationes in Psalmos* (1519–21), WA 5:175–77; cf. LW 1:84–85; 2:246; 5:258; 13:137; 26:392; 33:157–58; 54:260.

[16] *A Meditation on Christ's Passion* (1519), LW 42:11–14 = WA 2:138–42; LC I 101–2.

[17] LW 12:222 = WA 40/2:494–501; LW 34:213–15 = WA 50:270–73.

[18] LW 36:263 = WA 10/2:37–38; cf. Dan 8:25; 2 Thess 2:8.

[19] Luther, *Commentary on the First Twenty-Two Psalms*, 1:411, 459–63 = *Operationes in Psalmos* (1519–21), WA 5:261–62, 289–91.

perseverance, and then use the sword of the Spirit.[20] God's Word is the only sword by which we can attack the Antichrist and actually achieve something.[21] To believe otherwise is to have an idolatrous trust in human beings.[22] Luther uses the example of his struggle against the papacy, with its idols such as indulgences. In this struggle he knew he could achieve nothing apart from God's power contained in the Gospel.[23]

THE SPIRIT TEARS DOWN IDOLS AND PLANTS TRUE FAITH

In order to create faith in us and build the church God must carry out a twofold work. He must put to death the idolatrous sinful self, and plant in its place a new believing self. Luther refers to this as God's alien and proper work, and attributes both to the Holy Spirit. He writes,

> The Holy Spirit speaks to us in this manner: "I am a God who kills and brings to life, brings down to Sheol and raises up, makes poor and makes rich (cf. 1 Sam. 2:6–7). Not separately or disjunctively. Killing is not the only thing I do. No, this would be devilish. But I am a God who kills and brings to life. I bring down to Sheol, but in such a way that I bring back."[24]

God's alien work is the work of his Law, by which he puts to death our idolatrous sinful nature. This involves both the proclamation of the Law and our experience of the Law as we deal with its consequences in our lives. God's proper work is the work of the Gospel, by which he raises us up as new creatures who live by faith in him. This involves the proclamation of the Gospel, and also our experience of the Gospel as we receive a foretaste of God's promised blessings. In his antinomian disputations, Luther talks about four ways in which God instructs us toward salvation: he terrifies by threats, comforts by promises, admonishes by afflictions, and attracts by benefits.[25] This is an elaboration of the alien and proper work of God. By talking about four ways Luther is indicating that both the alien and proper work of God

---

[20] Luther, *Commentary on the First Twenty-Two Psalms,* 1:349–50, 363, 508–9; 2:312–13, 321; LW 8:245; 12:176–77; 14:54–56, 333–35; 16:99; 36:263; 46:32.

[21] *Preface to the First Book of Maccabees* (1533), LW 35:351 = WA DB 12:315–16; cf. Luther, *Commentary on the First Twenty-Two Psalms,* 1:39, 68–69, 360–61, 363; 2:192–93, 312–13, 321.

[22] *Commentary on Psalm 118* (1530), LW 14:67 = WA 31/1:105–14.

[23] LW 7:134–35 = WA 44:397–99; LW 34:16 = WA 30/2:281–83; LW 14:67; 36:263.

[24] *Lectures on Genesis* (1543–45), LW 8:10 = WA 44:586.25–29.

[25] Martin Luther, *Solus Decalogus Est Aeternus: Martin Luther's Complete Antinomian Theses and Disputations,* ed. and trans. Holger Sonntag (Minneapolis, MN: Lutheran Press, 2008), 247 = WA 39/1:357.7–12.

take place in our experience as well as in our hearing.[26] God carries out his alien work as we hear his threats and experience his afflictions; he carries out his proper work as we hear his promises and experience his benefits.

God's alien work: The Spirit dethroning our idols. God's alien work is focused on putting to death our sinful nature. Luther frequently refers to it as the mortification of the flesh. This also means the destruction of our idolatry. As we noted in chapter 5, the flesh for Luther is not one part of the self but the whole self as it is curved in on itself through original sin. It is the idolatrous self that is wrapped in its self-idolatry and strives to use everything around it including God as idols to serve itself. Therefore mortification of the flesh means destroying our idolatrous self-love and self-confidence and the idols we use to support this chief idol.

The first way the Spirit carries out this alien work is by publishing God's Law. This exposes our sin and the idolatry that lies at the root of it, and calls us to put it to death.[27] Aided by the Spirit we can do this,[28] yet left to ourselves we do not heed this call.[29] Our flesh despises God's Word and does not want to die.[30] It is smug, and does not believe God when he threatens judgment.[31] It does not want to give up its sin,[32] submit to God's will,[33] denounce its own

---

[26] On the one hand, Luther emphasizes that the Holy Spirit works faith in us through the Word, and we are to trust this Word even when it is contrary to our experience (e.g., LW 4:94; 8:199; 15:207–8; 17:328; 26:387; 52:68). Yet on the other hand, he frequently speaks about the importance of experience in training us in faith and the knowledge of God (e.g., LW 2:283; 4:321, 358, 376; 7:138, 326; 8:309; 9:93; 12:406; 14:60–61; 17:410; 21:306–7; 22:209, 378; 24:51, 87, 151–52; 26:323–24; 27:27, 234; 28:107, 304; 34:287; 35:61; 36:340; 38:224; 40:66, 276; 50:21; 54:7, 371; Luther, *Commentary on the First Twenty-Two Psalms*, 1:117–18). At first glance these two themes seem to contradict each other. Is experience contrary to faith, or does experience strengthen and confirm faith? Yet the contradiction is only apparent. As Oswald Bayer points out, when Luther says that "experience alone makes the theologian" (LW 54:7) he does not mean experience per se, but experience with the Word of God (Oswald Bayer, *Martin Luther's Theology: A Contemporary Interpretation,* trans. Thomas H. Trapp [Grand Rapids, MI: Eerdmans, 2008], 37). He means experience that can only be gained when we live by faith in God's Word. Only when we cling to God's promises in the face of troubles that seems to contradict them do we truly discover how powerful and sweet God's Word is, and experience that his promises are ultimately vindicated in the lives of those who live by faith. This experience then confirms our faith and strengthens it to face future trials.

[27] Luther, *Antinomian Theses and Disputations*, 245; LW 24:336 = WA 39/1:356.19–24.

[28] *Preface to Romans (*1522), LW 35:377 = WA DB 7:21–23.

[29] *Lectures on Isaiah* (1527–30), LW 16:232–33 = WA 31/2:166–67.

[30] LW 11:230 = WA 4:81–82; LW 14:335, 337–39 = WA 5:63–65.

[31] *Lectures on Genesis* (1543–45), LW 8:202–4 = WA 44:726–28.

[32] Luther, *Commentary on the First Twenty-Two Psalms*, 2:39 = *Operationes in Psalmos* (1519–21), WA 5:389.

[33] *An Exposition of the Lord's Prayer for Simple Laymen* (1519), LW 42:48–49 = WA 2:104–5.

righteousness,[34] or live by faith in God's promises.[35] Nor will it give up its fixation with its own wellbeing. Those who live by the flesh will only follow the Lord when he is serving their true god, themselves, not when he calls them to suffer or die to self.[36] The flesh howls miserably when it experiences misfortune. Unwilling to wait for God's deliverance, it demands immediate and visible consolation and help.[37] So the ungodly resist the discipline of the Lord. The godly on the other hand recognize that the flesh must be mortified. Yet weakened by the flesh they cannot carry out this work by their own strength but must allow God to do it in them.[38]

Since we are poor at heeding God's Law, the Spirit must cause it to penetrate our hearts so that we feel it.[39] He does this not only by infusing his proclamation with his power,[40] but also by allowing us to experience the Law at work in our lives as we come under its judgment. That is, he allows us to taste some of the shameful and destructive consequences of our sin and the futility of the idols we serve.[41] This means bringing suffering and the cross upon us.

By the cross of the Christian Luther means the trials and sufferings that God brings upon his people. Luther acknowledged that God does not work evil directly, but we experience evil because the devil, the world, and our sinful selves stand in opposition to God. Yet Luther did not think this gets God "off the hook," as if anything can happen without his knowledge and permission. Since God allows this evil to persist for a time and allows us to experience it, it is true to say that he brings it upon us. Yet even when he does this he is gracious and merciful. He is turning around what his fallen creatures intend for evil and using it for his saving purposes.[42] One of Luther's favorite texts for talking about the cross of the Christian is Romans 8:28: "We know that for those who love God all things work together for good."[43]

---

[34] *Sermon on St Thomas' Day, Ps 19:1* (1516), LW 51:18–22 = WA 1:111–15.

[35] *Lectures on Genesis* (1538–42), LW 5:206–7 = WA 43:570–71.

[36] Luther, *Commentary on the First Twenty-Two Psalms*, 1:164–69; 2:158; LW 23:393.

[37] Luther, *Commentary on the First Twenty-Two Psalms*, 1:485–486; LW 5:203–4; 7:131–32; 14:49, 58, 89.

[38] LW 5:319–20; 7:132–34; 8:8–11; 16:229–30; 20:330; 44:77–78; 51:21–23.

[39] LW 12:372; Luther, *Commentary on the First Twenty-Two Psalms*, 2:204, 420 (sic).

[40] *Lectures on Deuteronomy* (1525), LW 9:64 = WA 14:604–5.

[41] LW 12:372–73; 17:5; 19:99–102; 20:12–13; 26:117, 341; Luther, *Commentary on the First Twenty-Two Psalms*, 1:146.

[42] LW 12:372–74; 13:135; 24:197, 201; 29:134–37; Luther, *Commentary on the First Twenty-Two Psalms*, 1:46, 54, 304, 501–2, 513.

[43] LW 2:378–79; 3:333–36; 5:304; 6:59, 73, 181, 236; 7:222, 273; 8:37, 328; 17:184–85; 19:16, 21, 27; 31:354–55; 32:66; 42:158; David Jonathan Terry, *Martin Luther on the Suffering of the Christian* (Ann Arbor, MI: UMI Dissertation Service, 1991), 20–21.

Luther identifies two saving purposes that God advances through Christian suffering. The first is his alien work of purifying our faith by purging us from sin. The second is to use us as agents of righteousness, who suffer for the sake of righteousness in a world that hates Christ and the righteousness he brings.[44] In a letter to Frederick the Wise to comfort him when he was ill, Luther says that Christians suffer either because of their sins or because of their righteousness, and both kinds of suffering have been sanctified by Christ.[45]

Luther regarded both as necessary if we are to be conformed to Christ's image. We must suffer to mortify all our ungodliness, and we must join with Christ in suffering for the sake of righteousness.[46] Luther had much to say about the suffering Christians experience because of righteousness, as we struggle to be faithful to our callings against the opposition of the devil, the world, and our sinful selves. He regarded such suffering as a mark of the church, and a necessary part of living a Christ-like life in this fallen world that opposes our Lord.[47] Yet to deal with this theme in detail would take us away from the topic of idolatry. Therefore we will merely note it and focus on the second saving purpose God advances through suffering: his alien work of destroying our idolatry.

When Luther describes God's work of putting to death our sin as his "alien work," he is borrowing an expression Isaiah used to describe God's wrath against sin (Isa 28:21). Luther latched on to this as an apt expression, since he recognized that God's true nature is to show mercy, not to vent his wrath. His proper work is to heal and give life, not to work death.[48] Yet in order to carry out his proper work in a sinful world he must first carry out his alien work. When as Christians we experience God's judgment against sin, we should know that he does not judge us out of hatred but out of love, since his

---

[44] Thus Luther's view of the cross of the Christian differs significantly from that of John Howard Yoder. Yoder insists that Christians are only bearing the cross in a New Testament sense when their suffering is innocent, and they suffer because they are imitating their Lord's servanthood and his forgiving love toward their enemies (John Howard Yoder, *The Politics of Jesus* [2nd ed.; Grand Rapids, MI: Eerdmans, 1994], 127–33). Luther acknowledged this as one part of the cross the New Testament calls Christians to bear. Yet he also acknowledged another aspect to the cross, whereby our flesh with its worldly passions is crucified (cf. 2 Cor 4:7–12, and Luther's interpretation of Gal 5:24 and 6:14 at LW 27:96–104, 133–37).

[45] LW 42:140–42; cf. LW 43:27; 51:207–8; Luther, *Commentary on the First Twenty-Two Psalms*, 2:383.

[46] LW 13:347; 16:229–30; 17:233; 20:41; 29:136; 30:23, 117–18, 127; 31:89, 225; 35:375; 43:165, 184–85; 51:19–20, 198–99, 206–8.

[47] LW 4:22; 12:222; 13:259–63, 333–34; 14:56–58, 85–86, 89, 96; 16:310–11; 19:183; 20:41; 26:418–22, 428, 450–57; 27:3, 6, 19, 24, 43–45, 133–37, 143–44; 30:84, 117–18; 34:215; 41:164–65; 42:13–14; 43:184; 46:29–31, 36; 51:199–201, 206; 54:275–76; Luther, *Commentary on the First Twenty-Two Psalms*, 1:51, 178, 360–61, 412–13, 436, 540, 558; 2:424.

[48] LW 2:134; 29:134–37; 51:18–19.

goal is to produce good in us. As Luther writes, "He kills our will that His may be established in us . . . [and] subdues the flesh and its lusts that the spirit and its desires may come to life."[49] Thus he is acting as a loving Father, who disciplines the children he loves.[50]

Above all, subduing the flesh means destroying the idolatry that is the chief work of the flesh and the root of all its evils.[51] It is not enough for God to purge us of lesser sins. He must also cure us of the idolatry that is the cause of all sins,[52] and teach us to trust in him alone.[53] Therefore God may cause us to hunger for a time so that we learn that he is our God and not our bellies, and that his Word is more important than bread (Deut 8:3). Likewise, he may take away our wealth or other earthly blessings for a time, so that we learn that he is all we really need. Through such experiences, he trains us to live by faith in his promises and not by sight.[54] Luther writes that many people claim that the Lord is their God, until he begins to show them that he alone is their good, by taking everything else away—their wealth, good name, life, righteousness, and all they possess. It then becomes evident whether he was their God or not. This will lead those whose faith is merely skin deep to fall away.[55] Yet those whose faith is genuine will be driven to prayer and the Word. Then their faith will be strengthened and refined as they learn through experience that God is good, and his Word is comforting, and he really does keep his promises.[56]

Luther stresses that God must put to death one idol in particular, the self.[57] This means destroying our self-righteous presumption by teaching us

---

[49] *Operationes in Psalmos* (1519–21), LW 14:335 = WA 5:64.2–4; cf. Gal 5:16–24.

[50] LW 7:131–33, 226; 22:144–45; 21:301; 24:193–94; 42:125–26; 44:77; Heb 12:5–11. Luther also draws on many other biblical images to speak about this. God diagnoses our disease and forces us to recognize it so that we see our need for the cure (LW 19:57–59; 22:143–45; 51:19–23; Luther, *Commentary on the First Twenty-Two Psalms*, 2:42). He purges the rotten and unclean disease of sin from us so that he can make us clean and holy (LW 8:5–13; 24:211–13; 29:130; 35:375, 377–78; Luther, *Commentary on the First Twenty-Two Psalms*, 1:184, 586–87; 2:26, 424 (sic); Ps 51:7; 103:3; Ezek 36:25–27; Hos 6:1–3; Mal 3:1–4; Luke 5:31–32). He prunes away the unfruitful branches so that we may bear more fruit (LW 24:193–201, 209–10; John 15:1–2). He plows us and uproots the weeds so that he can plant good seed in us and make his flowers grow (LW 16:234–37; Isa 28:24–29).

[51] LW 11:522; 17:12; 21:303–6; 25:350–54; 27:87–91; 30:119; 33:288; Gal 5:19–20.

[52] Luther, *Commentary on the First Twenty-Two Psalms*, 2:309 = *Operationes in Psalmos* (1519–21), WA 5:567.

[53] LW 30:119; 44:30–31.

[54] *Operationes in Psalmos* (1519–21), LW 14:343 = WA 5:69–70; LW 5:202–3; 8:200–201; 9:93–96; 27:405.

[55] Luther, *Commentary on the First Twenty-Two Psalms*, 2:116, 156–57; cf. LW 19:21; Luke 8:13.

[56] LW 13:333–34; 14:49–50, 59–61; 20:151; 30:17, 126–27; 34:286–87; 35:12, 19; 42:185–86.

[57] Luther, *Commentary on the First Twenty-Two Psalms*, 1:184 = *Operationes in Psalmos* (1519–21), WA 5:128–29.

that we are sinners. It also means destroying our confidence in our own wisdom and strength.[58] If we are to have a pure hope in God, we must be stripped of all the other things in which we trust or boast, from our works, honor, and wisdom to our property and health.[59] That is, we need to experience the cross,[60] which God gives us to destroy our empty pride.[61]

When God comes to kill this idol it appears that he is our enemy, except to the eyes of faith.[62] Since we are our own worst enemies, when God slays our great enemy he seems to be fighting against us, when in reality he is acting as our truest friend. Luther writes that by instructing us to pray "your will be done," God "teaches us that we have no greater enemy than ourself."[63] Since we want our will to be done, God is asking us to pray against ourselves. This means asking him to put our self-will to death through the cross.[64]

Luther summarizes many of these thoughts in his Isaiah commentary, where he writes,

> The cross and the chastening of God casts this idol down that we may abide in God's First Commandment, that we may fear and dread and love God. . . . those who in their presumption trust in their own power, wisdom, and wealth, these choose their own things as divine worship and spurn God, as we see in tyrants, heretics, and hypocrites. These rely on their own power, wisdom, and wealth contrary to God's First Commandment. This is what it means to commit idolatry. The saints and godly, however, are kept by the cross and chastening in the fear of God and are estranged from trust in themselves. This is the fruit of the chastisement of God, that it teaches us not to flee but to approach God and, what is greatest, that it kills that supreme idolatry, trust in oneself. This killing is much greater than the outward mortification of the flesh, of lust, and of other outward things that cannot be compared with this killing. But the cross casts out this idol so that we do not rely on ourselves. Even so all hypocrites on the basis of a little good (as it

---

[58] LW 3:333–35; 4:44; 8:5–11; 9:68, 70, 104; 16:216, 233–36, 346–47; 17:49–50; 19:21, 114–15; 24:210–11; 27:404–5; 33:61–62; Luther, *Commentary on the First Twenty-Two Psalms*, 1:184, 391, 395; 2:53, 213–14, 220, 422.

[59] Luther, *Commentary on the First Twenty-Two Psalms*, 1:239–40, 248–54, 291; LW 14:94–95; 35:236; 44:108.

[60] LW 43:184; 52:246; Luther, *Commentary on the First Twenty-Two Psalms*, 1:72, 331.

[61] *Lectures on Galatians* (1535), LW 27:101–4 = WA 40/2:129–33.

[62] Luther, *Commentary on the First Twenty-Two Psalms*, 1:148–49 = *Operationes in Psalmos* (1519–21), WA 5:108–9.

[63] *An Exposition of the Lord's Prayer for Simple Laymen* (1519), LW 42:48 = WA 2:105.

[64] *An Exposition of the Lord's Prayer for Simple Laymen* (1519), LW 42:42–49 = WA 2:99–105.

> seems) have such confidence in themselves that it knows no bounds, as happened to me once upon a time. How much pride came over me when I correctly celebrated one Mass! Shame on you! So it happens also to all other hypocrites with their glittering works. They defend their idolatry with their works. This idolatry God's unique chastisement casts out. . . . Thus with the chief presumption of the heart removed, we will not easily fall into another kind of idolatry. All the prophets who were active against this idolatry were slain because of it, since the flesh cannot bear to have its own opinion cast aside. Therefore the Lord's chastening is necessary.[65]

Since our fallen human hearts are naturally bent in the direction of idolatry, God must chasten us all. He does this by showing us through experience that our idols are not God. When we invest idolatrous trust in ourselves and created things, God exposes the futility of this faith by allowing these things to fail. When our love and joy are bound in earthly things and earthly well-being, God allows these things to disappoint us or to be taken away. This is not because he is cruel. Rather, it is because he does not want these things to blind us to where true joy is found and our confidence must reside. Indeed, Luther insists that God gives us the cross out of kindness, and it leads to a joy the world cannot know.[66] This is not because Luther downplayed in any way the genuine pain that comes with the cross,[67] but because he recognized that the cross drives us to cling to the one who alone is God and the true source of every joy. Luther writes,

> Anyone who has come to the point that he can see and feel in the Scriptures the Father's love toward us will easily be able to bear all the misfortune that there may be on earth. On the other hand, anyone who does not feel it cannot be genuinely happy, even though he is bathed in pleasure and joy throughout the world.[68]

Furthermore,

> It is impossible that he should not be filled with sorrow, who does not hope in the Lord, when any tribulation shall come upon him. . . . On the other hand, it is impossible that he should not rejoice, who hopes in God: and even if the whole world should burst upon

---

[65] *Lectures on Isaiah* (1527–30), LW 16:215–16 = WA 31/2:153.21–154.11.

[66] LW 8:47; 12:296; 17:407; 30:23; Luther, *Commentary on the First Twenty-Two Psalms*, 1:263–71.

[67] Cf. *Sermon at Coburg on Cross and Suffering* (1530), LW 51:198–99 = WA 32:28–30.

[68] *Preface to The Four Psalms of Comfort* (1526), LW 14:210 = WA 19:553.14–18.

> the head of such a one, he would stand unmoved amid the falling ruins.[69]

Thus God trains us through adversity to know through experience that he can give us joy even in adversity, so that we would learn to look to him and not the fleeting things of this world as the ultimate source of joy.

God's proper work: The Spirit raising up true faith. God carries out his alien work simply to clear the ground for his proper work. His proper work is to work life and salvation by creating in us the kind of faith that grasps hold of God's mercy.[70]

This faith is a new work of creation,[71] and therefore must be produced not by us but by God alone.[72] The Holy Spirit must enlighten our hearts and give us faith in Christ, and he must preserve us in this faith. He accomplishes this by working through the Gospel to awaken and nourish true faith in us.[73] First and foremost we receive this faith simply by hearing the Word. Yet for those who cling to this Word, even in the face of experience that seems to contradict it, it is ultimately confirmed by experience as God's promises come true.[74]

The reason why God's Word has the power to create faith is that it is not merely information, but a vehicle by which the Spirit comes to us and does his work in us.[75] As Luther writes, "Holy Scripture's inseparable companion is the Holy Spirit,"[76] and "It has thus pleased God to impart the Spirit, not without the Word, but through the Word."[77] Indeed, Luther insists that the Holy Spirit works nothing without the Word and the Sacraments.[78] He therefore urges us to seek the Spirit in these external means and nowhere else.[79] At the Marburg Colloquy he asserted that,

> Faith [in Christ] is a gift of God which we cannot earn with any works or merit that precede, nor can we achieve it by our own strength, but the Holy Spirit gives and creates this faith in our

---

[69] Luther, *Commentary on the First Twenty-Two Psalms*, 1:270 = *Operationes in Psalmos* (1519–21), WA 5:182.3–4, 9–11.

[70] LW 13:135; 14:335; 16:233; 26:314; 29:135; 44:77; 51:19–20.

[71] *Lectures on Genesis* (1535–38), LW 1:17 = WA 42:14.

[72] LW 15:277; 23:181; 30:6, 14, 39; 31:56; 43:233.

[73] LW 24:171, 212, 297–98; 26:64, 208; 36:301–2; 38:86–87; LC I 101; II 38–45, 58–64.

[74] See footnote 26 on page 213.

[75] LW 24:212; 26:64, 208; 38:86–88; 40:147; WA 47:184; Eugene Klug, *From Luther to Chemnitz: On Scripture and the Word* (Grand Rapids, MI: Eerdmans, 1971), 76–80.

[76] *Exposition of Psalm 90* (1534), LW 13:111 = WA 40/3:543.

[77] *The Bondage of the Will* (1525), LW 33:155 = WA 18:695.28–29.

[78] *Lectures on Genesis* (1538–42), LW 3:275 = WA 43:71.

[79] LW 24:141; 29:83.

> hearts as it pleases him, when we hear the gospel or the word of Christ.[80]

It is this sacramental view of God's Word that enables Luther to avoid quietism while at the same time directing all confidence away from ourselves to God. Luther acknowledges that we can cooperate with God in furthering his work of creating faith in human hearts. We can preach the Word. We can administer the Sacraments. We can turn to the Word ourselves and allow it to do its work in us.[81] Yet this does not mean trusting in our own strength or contributing something of our own to this work. Rather, it means receiving the gifts God has given us and trusting that they will be powerful and effective in the way that he has promised. Luther's view is epitomized in a sermon from 1522:

> I simply taught, preached, and wrote God's Word; otherwise I did nothing. And while I slept [cf. Mark 4:26–29], or drank Wittenberg beer with my friends Philip and Amsdorf,[82] the Word so greatly weakened the papacy that no prince or emperor ever inflicted such losses upon it. I did nothing; the Word did everything.[83]

Not only does the Holy Spirit use the Word and its promises as his tool for creating faith, but the faith God calls for is always faith in these promises. Luther identifies confidence in God's promises as a mark for distinguishing true faith from idolatry. He writes,

> [1 Peter 5:7]: "Casting every care upon Him, because He Himself takes care of you"; and Ps. 34:10: "Those seeking God shall lack no good thing." To understand these and similar wonderful and faithful promises of God is truly to understand the promise of the First Commandment, in which He says: "I am the Lord your God." "Yours, yours," He says, "who will show and display Myself to you as God and will not forsake you, if only you believe this." All such promises depend on and flow from the First Commandment. On the other hand, not to believe them is indeed not to understand the Commandment but to have other gods.[84]

---

[80] *The Marburg Articles* (1529), LW 38:86 = WA 30/3:163.7–14; cf. LW 36:217.

[81] *Lectures on Genesis* (1538–42), LW 3:274–75 = WA 43:71; *The Bondage of the Will* (1525), LW 33:155 = WA 18:695.

[82] Philip Melanchthon and Nicholas von Amsdorf.

[83] *Eight Sermons at Wittenberg* (1522), LW 51:77 = WA 10/3:18.14–16, 19.1–3.

[84] *Lectures on Deuteronomy* (1525), LW 9:94 = WA 14:631–32.

> For what more sinful idolatry can there be than to abuse God's promises with perverse opinions and to neglect or extinguish faith in them? For God does not deal, nor has he ever dealt, with man otherwise than through a word of promise, as I have said. We in turn cannot deal with God otherwise than through faith in the Word of his promise.[85]

> This was the cause of all the idolatry among the people of Israel . . . For they wanted to be led and governed in such a way that they did not live from faith in the promise but from what was actually present.[86]

Idolatrous faith judges spiritual matters by what its eyes can see. It looks to what is temporally and visibly present and is characterized by impatience. It concludes that God is favorable when temporal things go well, and that his favor has turned away when trouble comes.[87] This means that it misjudges, since God loves the afflicted.[88] When his promises are in the process of coming to fulfillment our experience frequently contradicts them, so that we are forced to cry out "how long O Lord!"[89] This is not a sign that he has abandoned us, but that he is giving us opportunity to put our faith into practice. Through such testing our faith is shown to be genuine. It is also strengthened and purified as we learn through experience that God is for us and is our only refuge in every trouble.[90] Idolaters fail this test. When God appears slow in carrying out his threats and fulfilling his promises, they despise his Word, and seek after a god who will bless them immediately. Yet when we cling to God's promises instead, we are assured that he loves us whether temporal things are going well or badly, and are taught to trust him whether the temporal things we need are at hand or absent.[91] When we do this we discover two things: first, that he is able to sustain us inwardly and give us joy even when outwardly we are afflicted;[92] and second, that in his good timing he fulfills all his

---

[85] *The Babylonian Captivity of the Church* (1520), LW 36:42 = WA 6:516.

[86] *Lectures on Genesis* (1543–45), LW 8:200 = WA 44:725.

[87] LW 4:28–30; 19:176–77.

[88] LW 5:319–20; 12:406; 21:299–302.

[89] *Lectures on Genesis* (1543–45), LW 8:199–200 = WA 44:724–25.

[90] Luther, *Commentary on the First Twenty-Two Psalms*, 1:81, 116–20, 123–24, 239, 141–42, 145–46, 151, 156–57, 169–70, 173, 246, 260–61, 281–82, 313, 325–26, 330, 455, 458, 564; 2:116; Rom 5:3–5.

[91] LW 4:30; 44:77–78; Luther, *Commentary on the First Twenty-Two Psalms*, 1:36; 2:344.

[92] Luther, *Commentary on the First Twenty-Two Psalms*, 1:32, 169–71, 234; 2:314; LW 7:326; 16:300–301; 20:32; 26:133; 27:22.

promises so abundantly that they outweigh everything we may suffer while we wait.[93]

THE FRUIT OF FAITH VS. THE FRUIT OF IDOLATRY

The result of this killing and raising work of God is that the believer is sanctified from the inside out. The faith that God creates in the heart makes a person inwardly righteous, and this inner righteousness then produces outward manifestations in the believer's life. Idolatry on the other hand stems from a covetous and self-centered heart, and can at best lead to an external righteousness but not a righteousness of the heart.

Luther writes that when the chief work is absent, which is true faith in the true God, then all other works "are nothing but mere sham, show, and pretense with nothing behind them."[94] He acknowledges that the Law by itself can restrain outward behavior to a certain extent. He even says things like, "Externally there is not much difference between the Christian and another socially upright human being."[95] Yet for Luther this is faint praise, since he constantly stresses that a righteousness that does not penetrate the heart is seriously defective. Thus the righteousness of idolaters is a hollow shell. They may at times keep the letter of the Law outwardly, yet even when they do, the spirit is wrong.[96] They may not kill, but they are angry; they may not steal, but they are greedy; they may not commit adultery, but they are filled with lust. And since they are bent on justifying themselves, they will judge and condemn others.[97] Inwardly they will hate God's Law and will only keep it when it is convenient or suits their purposes in some way, not when it is difficult or calls them to bear the cross with no expectation of personal reward.[98] Ultimately this lack of inner righteousness will find outward expression. So Luther writes,

> Did not the Romans enact the most excellent and salutary laws? Did they not curb and restrain proud nations by justice? Why then did they so bitterly persecute Christ and his Christians? Why, but

---

[93] LW 5:202–7; 7:131–38, 313–16; 8:4–13, 200–204; 9:92–96; 13:347–48; 14:58, 62, 68, 86–88, 342–43; 16:237; 29:129–30; 30:23; 42:157–52; 43:185–86; 51:199–205; Luther, *Commentary on the First Twenty-Two Psalms*, 1:100–102, 106–12; 2:15–16, 42–43.

[94] *Treatise on Good Works* (1520), LW 44:31 = WA 6:210.16–17; cf. LW 27:131–32.

[95] *Lectures on Galatians* (1535), LW 26:376 = WA 40/1:573.

[96] *Treatise on Good Works* (1520), LW 44:30–33 = WA 6:209–12.

[97] LW 21:217; 51:22.

[98] LW 14:295; 22:141–44; 35:366–67, 375–76; Luther, *Commentary on the First Twenty-Two Psalms*, 2:22, 228–29, 391 (sic), 407–10 (sic), 418 (sic).

> because their righteousness was only an external appearance in the sight of men, and was nothing in the sight of God?[99]

Faith in the true God, on the other hand, brings with it hope and love. It moves people to love God and their neighbor from the heart and, ultimately, to keep all God's commandments.[100] Its fruits are peace and joy, and in the midst of trouble it produces confidence, assurance, boldness, courage, and hope.[101] It also leads those who have experienced mercy to show mercy to others.[102] Those who possess this faith will genuinely love God's Law and regard it as holy and good, rather than merely keeping it out of fear of punishment or hope of reward. Therefore, those who live by faith are steadfast in doing good and do not flinch when God calls them to suffer for the sake of righteousness.[103] Luther talks about such faith in the following terms:

> Faith is a living, daring confidence in God's grace, so sure and certain that the believer would stake his life on it a thousand times. This knowledge of and confidence in God's grace makes men glad and bold and happy in dealing with God and with all creatures. And this is the work which the Holy Spirit performs in faith. Because of it, without compulsion, a person is ready and glad to do good to everyone, to serve everyone, to suffer everything, out of love and praise to God who has shown him this grace. Thus it is impossible to separate works from faith, quite as impossible as to separate heat and light from fire. . . . Pray God that he may work faith in you. Otherwise you will surely remain forever without faith, regardless of what you may think or do.
>
> Righteousness, then, is such a faith. It is called "the righteousness of God" because God gives it, and counts it as righteousness for the sake of Christ our Mediator, and makes a man to fulfil his obligation to everybody. For through faith a man becomes free from sin and comes to take pleasure in God's commandments, thereby he gives God the honor due him, and pays him what he owes him. Likewise he serves his fellow-men willingly, by whatever means he

---

[99] Luther, *Commentary on the First Twenty-Two Psalms*, 1:466 = *Operationes in Psalmos* (1519–21), WA 5:293:26–29.

[100] LW 35:36:374; 42; 44:30–31; 51:23.

[101] *Preface to Romans* (1522), LW 35:374 = WA DB 7:17.

[102] LW 16:215; 51:18; Luther, *Commentary on the First Twenty-Two Psalms*, 1:134–35, 137, 161–63.

[103] LW 14:59–61, 295, 297, 300; 22:144–46; 35:375–76; Luther, *Commentary on the First Twenty-Two Psalms*, 2:416–19 (sic).

> can, and thus pays his debt to everyone. Nature, free will, and our own powers cannot bring this righteousness into being. For as no one can give himself faith, neither can he take away his own unbelief. How, then, will he take away a single sin, even the very smallest?[104]

One of Luther's favorite ways to talk about good works in the Christian life was to use Jesus' teaching that "every healthy tree bears good fruit, but the diseased tree bears bad fruit" (Matt 7:17). This means that the way to change the fruit is to change the tree, not the other way round (Matt 12:33–35).[105] When we are justified through faith in Christ we become good trees who produce good fruit. While we are still wrapped in the idolatry of our sinful nature we are bad trees who produce bad fruit. No amount of human effort can change this, since we cannot produce good fruit by idolatrous means, or root out things like covetousness and selfishness from our hearts. At best we can turn ourselves into hypocrites: that is, people who make an effort to do the right thing outwardly, but without genuine love of God and neighbor in our hearts. What we need is for God to make us into good trees through his Spirit: first, by doing his alien work of rooting out the disease of our idolatry; then, by doing his proper work of planting in us the good seed of his Word, from which the good tree of faith grows. Then the fruits will naturally follow.

Contemporary Application

Luther insists that only God can liberate us from our idols. What is more, he also identifies God's method of carrying out this work: his alien work of mortification and his proper work of the Gospel. This knowledge of how God works should inform the church as it joins in his work of producing true faith and its fruits in people's hearts. In particular, it can enable us to avoid both quietism and self-reliance. The call is not for us to do nothing; nor is it for us to build the church by our own reason and strength. Instead it is to take up our cross (as Christ has called us) and faithfully carry out the task of proclaiming the Gospel (which he has given us), all the while trusting that in this way he will be at work in and through us.

This reveals two ways in which the contemporary church can hinder the Spirit's work of building the church, instead of acting as his faithful instrument. First, we can flee the cross that he gives us. Second, we can neglect the proclamation of the Gospel and substitute for it our own efforts to influence and persuade.

---

[104] *Preface to Romans* (1522), LW 35:370–71 = WA DB 7:10–13.

[105] LW 1:328; 5:9; 12:385; 18:401; 19:23; 20:38; 21:259–68; 22:280–81; 23:151–52; 26:154–55, 257; 30:242, 264; 31:270, 361–62; 32:84; 33:275; 34:111; 43:280–81; 45:89; 52:151.

MORTIFICATION OF THE IDOLATROUS SELF AND THE CONTEMPORARY FLIGHT FROM SUFFERING

In chapter 5, we noted that both contemporary society and the contemporary church frequently display an obsession with personal happiness and subjective wellbeing. The consequence of this is an aversion to suffering. For moralistic therapeutic deists and prosperity Gospel preachers it is God's job to shield us from suffering and make us happy. Therefore suffering should not play a big part in the Christian life. This view is promoted in no uncertain terms by the prosperity preacher Kenneth Copeland:

> One of the major deceptions Satan is sowing in the Church today is that our problems, our trials and our temptations are sent to teach and develop us spiritually, physically and in other ways. The very extreme of this says that God is the author of our troubles, or that God is the One Who makes us sick in order to teach us something. This is absolutely against the Word of God. The basic principle of the Christian life is to know that Jesus bore our sin, sickness, disease, sorrow, grief and poverty at Calvary. For Him to put any of this on us now would be a miscarriage of justice. . . . A loving God doesn't send or even permit death and destruction in His children's lives to instruct them.[106]

For Luther, the first problem with this sense of entitlement to a suffering-free life is that it builds false expectations. He writes,

> God has allotted us much tribulation in this world, and, at the same time, offered us no other consolation than his holy Word. Thus Christ has promised us, "In the world you will have tribulation, but in me you will have peace" [John 16:33]. Therefore, if you are willing to have God's kingdom come to you and have God's will be done, do not resort to evasive measures. It cannot be otherwise: God's will is done only if yours is not done. That is to say, the more adversity you experience, the better is God's will done; this is especially true in the hour of death. It has been ordained—and no one can alter this—that in this world we find unrest, and in Christ we find peace.[107]

---

[106] Kenneth Copeland Ministries Australia, "Understanding Chastisement," www.kcm.org.au/content/understanding-chastisement (accessed Feb. 2, 2016). Reproduced with permission of Kenneth Copeland Ministries, Locked Bag 2600, Mansfield Delivery Centre, QLD 4122, Australia.

[107] *An Exposition of the Lord's Prayer for Simple Laymen* (1519), LW 42:50 = WA 2:106.

Since God neither promises nor delivers a trouble-free life in this world, this leads to a second problem. When we are led to believe that this is something we should want and expect, we end up trying to manufacture it for ourselves. This means attempting to be our own saviors. Luther writes that those who think they can rid themselves of the trouble God allots them, instead of standing their ground faithfully and waiting for God's deliverance, show thereby that "they want to be their own saviors and redeemers and are unwilling to wait for God to relieve them of their cross."[108]

This does not mean that Luther thought we should seek out suffering. He rejected self-chosen crosses,[109] and was convinced that any cross we choose for ourselves will only nourish our sinful nature by feeding our pride. He taught that only God's Law and the trials he tailors to our individual needs can successfully mortify our flesh.[110] However, Luther also taught that we must not flee suffering if God brings it upon us. We must always be willing to suffer for the sake of righteousness, and must not flee suffering if doing so would mean disobeying God's commandments or abandoning the callings he has given us.[111] To flee this suffering would be to flee the saving work that God wants to do in and through us in a futile attempt to save ourselves.

A theology that refuses to face up to the alien work of God hinders the work of God's Spirit in at least two ways. First, it builds in people an expectation that they can and should avoid the cross, instead of teaching them to endure patiently the Lord's discipline and to rejoice in the privilege of suffering with Christ. Thus it breeds unfaithfulness to the hard work of Christian vocation, since many of the crosses God calls us to bear come from being faithful to what God has called us to do. Second, it comforts the self-secure while heaping more affliction on the afflicted. It reverses the beatitudes, and says, "Blessed are you who are rich and full now; blessed are you who laugh now; blessed are you when all people speak well of you, for this is a sign that God loves you; but woe to you who are poor, hungry, weeping, or persecuted, for not only does this world hate you, but obviously your life is not right with God, since he does not seem to care for you either" (cf. Luke 6:20–26). Thus it fails to humble those who are rich in this world and to teach them to hope in God alone. Instead, it sets them up for a fall by teaching them carnal security. At the same time, it fails to comfort the poor and afflicted with the knowledge that God loves them, and that he will use even their sufferings for their benefit. It robs them of the joy they should derive from their suffering, that

---

[108] *An Exposition of the Lord's Prayer for Simple Laymen* (1519), LW 42:50–51 = WA 2:106–7.

[109] LW 4:22; 7:113–14; 17:294; 20:261–62, 329–30; 22:55; 30:109–10; 40:81; 43:183–84; 51:198–99.

[110] LW 17:49–50; 20:330; 27:31; 43:165.

[111] Luther, *Commentary on the First Twenty-Two Psalms*, 1:151, 283, 285; LW 1.214–15; 20:330; 43:120–22.

through it God is developing in them endurance, character, and hope (Rom 5:3–5).

THE PROPER WORK OF THE GOSPEL AND HUMAN PERSUASION

As we have seen, Luther teaches that the Gospel alone can produce in us true faith in the true God. This has enormous practical significance for the church's mission. Other means of persuasion may be successful in leading a congregation to grow, by getting those who are already Christians to move from one congregation to another. Other methods of persuasion may perhaps be effective in preparing the way for the Gospel by gaining a hearing for it. Yet only the Gospel can convert the heart from idolatry to faith in the living God. The Lutheran theologian C. F. W. Walther echoes Luther's position accurately when he writes, "The Word of God is not rightly divided when one makes an appeal to believe in a manner as if a person could make himself believe or at least help toward that end, instead of preaching faith into a person's heart by laying the Gospel promises before him."[112] This provides a clear focus for all the church's efforts in mission: to preach faith into people's hearts by proclaiming the Good News.

The church growth movement. From Luther's perspective, many contemporary church growth strategies are misdirected because they have lost this singular focus. By giving as much if not more attention to human methods of persuasion than to the power of the Gospel, they have enthroned human strength and ability as an idol alongside the Spirit-filled Word.

One example of this is provided by Rick Warren, who talks about God's power and human effort as if they are virtually equal partners in God's mission. Warren rightly warns against the dangers of both "practical humanism" and "pious irresponsibility" when it comes to ministry. On the one hand, he identifies the error of thinking that all it takes to grow the church is organization, management, and marketing. On the other hand, he notes the error of quietism, which says that our only role in mission is to sit back and watch God do his thing.[113] He then seeks to avoid both these errors by placing God's power and human effort side by side. He teaches that prayer and dedication to God's Word are important, but not sufficient to lead a church to grow. Instead, human skill must be added to the Word.[114] With this thought in mind he writes,

---

[112] C. F. W. Walther, *The Proper Distinction between Law and Gospel*, trans. W. H. T. Dau (St. Louis: Concordia, 1928), 260.

[113] Rick Warren, *The Purpose Driven Church: Growth Without Compromising Your Message and Mission* (Grand Rapids, MI: Zondervan, 1995), 58–59.

[114] Ibid., 56–60.

> Church growth is a partnership between God and man. Churches grow by the power of God through the skilled effort of people. Both elements, God's power and man's skilled effort, must be present. We cannot do it without God but he has decided not to do it without us![115]

Warren bases his thoughts here on Paul's words in 1 Cor 3:9, "We are God's fellow workers."[116] In some regards he is right. He is right to say that God works through us. He is right to reject the attitude that it is enough for us to be hearers of the Word, without also being doers of it, who faithfully work in God's kingdom. Yet from a Lutheran perspective he is also wrong. He is wrong to suggest that prayer and dedication to God's Word are not enough, and he is wrong to put human skill on the same level as God's power. He latches on to one verse but fails to pay sufficient attention to what Paul says only two verses earlier, "So neither he who plants nor he who waters is anything, but only God who gives the growth" (1 Cor 3:7).

What Warren lacks to help him hold these two verses together is a strong theology of the means of grace as the instruments by which the Holy Spirit does his work both in us and through us. He can see the dangers of both human activism and pious inactivity, yet the only way he can see to avoid both is to prescribe a little bit of each. What he fails to consider adequately is that the competency required for ministry is itself a product of the Word.[117] For Luther, the Word shapes us into what we need to be if we are to be effective workers in God's kingdom, and the same Word is what we need to proclaim to others if they, too, are to be transformed. Therefore the Word is always enough! It will do its work where and when it pleases God, and we cannot add anything to make it more effective other than using all the means at our disposal to get it out, as it impels us to do. The result of Luther's theology is not pious inactivity but receptive activity that is driven by the Word, so that when our activity has ceased we can say, "I did nothing; I let the Word do its work."[118]

A second example is the work of Christian A. Schwarz on natural church development. In contrast to Luther, the premise behind Schwarz's work is that the Holy Spirit is not the inseparable companion of Scripture, and that

---

[115] Ibid., 60.

[116] Ibid., 60.

[117] "Not that we are sufficient in ourselves to claim anything as coming from us, but our sufficiency is from God, who makes us competent to be ministers of a new covenant" (2 Cor 3:5–6). "All Scripture is breathed out by God and profitable for teaching, for reproof, for correction, and for training in righteousness, that the man of God may be competent, equipped for every good work" (2 Tim 3:16–17).

[118] *Eight Sermons at Wittenberg* (1522), LW 51:77–78 = WA 10/3:17–19.

Scripture by itself is dead and lifeless.[119] Schwarz makes a distinction between the static/institutional pole of the church's existence and the dynamic/organic pole, and assigns things like doctrine, the biblical canon, the Sacraments, and the proclamation of the Gospel to the static pole.[120] Only when the Spirit is added, so that a word-event takes place, do these things become God's living Word that is able to produce dynamic things like faith, love, spiritual gifts, and evangelism (something that Schwarz distinguishes from the proclamation of the Gospel).[121] For Schwarz, the dynamic pole is where the real action takes place in leading a church to grow. He does not advocate dispensing with the static pole, since he recognizes that it is frequently useful in producing the dynamic pole. Yet he says that we should feel free to modify it based on our perception of its functionality in producing the dynamic pole.[122]

Schwarz then proposes eight quality characteristics of healthy churches, and contends that if they are all present in a sufficiently high degree the church is guaranteed to grow.[123] These characteristics are empowering leadership, gift-oriented ministry, passionate spirituality, functional structures, inspiring worship services, holistic small groups, need-oriented evangelism, and loving relationships.[124] Whereas the New Testament always equates spiritual health with sound doctrine,[125] Schwarz equates adherence to fixed doctrine with unhealthy legalism,[126] and excludes it from his list of quality characteristics. This is a serious omission. Nevertheless, the main problem with these characteristics from a Lutheran perspective is not with the categories themselves, which can all be given a Lutheran slant. The problem instead is with the premise that lies behind Schwarz's categories, and his suggestions for how to measure and instill these qualities. The premise is this: that the Word is not enough, and something else must always be added to give that Word life. Therefore many of Schwarz's proposals amount to techniques for finding that

---

[119] Christian A. Schwarz, *Paradigm Shift in the Church: How Natural Church Development Can Transform Theological Thinking* (Carol Stream, IL: ChurchSmart Resources, 1999), 70–71.

[120] Ibid., 99; Christian A. Schwarz, *Natural Church Development: A Guide to Eight Essential Qualities of Healthy Churches* (St. Charles, IL: ChurchSmart Resources, 2000), 95.

[121] Schwarz, *Paradigm Shift*, 112, 116–19, 199.

[122] Ibid., 18, 65–74, 108–11, 121–23.

[123] Schwarz, *Natural Church Development*, 40.

[124] Ibid., 22–37; Schwarz, *Paradigm Shift*, 21.

[125] Apart from Jesus' ironical statement in Luke 5:31, every time the New Testament talks about health (ὑγιαίνω [*hugiainō*] and its derivatives) in a spiritual rather than physical sense it explicitly connects this health to sound doctrine (1 Tim 1:10; 6:3; 2 Tim 1:13; 4:3; Tit 1:9; 1:13; 2:1–2; 2:8; 3 John 2).

[126] Schwarz, *Paradigm Shift*, 26; Schwarz, *Natural Church Development*, 26.

something extra,[127] and confidence in the Word itself fades into the background.

This assumption that the Word is not enough has been the working premise of the church growth movement since its inception. Like Schwarz, Donald McGavran, who is widely regarded as the founder of the movement, made a distinction between the proclamation of the Gospel and evangelism, between sharing the good news and persuading people to believe it.[128]

For those who are steeped in a church growth mentality it would therefore be surprising to discover that the Word itself stands unrivalled as a means for converting people to the Christian faith. This was the finding of a recent study entitled *Surprising Insights from the Unchurched* by Thom Rainer, dean of the Billy Graham School of Missions, Evangelism and Church Growth. Many other church growth researchers have assumed that the way to optimize the church's evangelism efforts is to interview unchurched people, ask them what they would want in a church, and then give them what they want, as if the church can grow by supplying people who are still bound in the idolatry of the flesh with what they want. Rainer instead decided to interview recent converts and ask them what made the difference.[129] The most "surprising" result from a church growth perspective was that biblical preaching and teaching was by far the top response, and was listed as a factor by nearly all of the participants.[130]

From a church growth perspective these results may be surprising, but from Luther's perspective there is no surprise at all. Rather, it confirms Luther's emphasis on the importance of the Word in changing the hearts of those who are outside God's kingdom. Furthermore, the next most common group of responses clustered around personal relationships and contacts.[131]

---

[127] Christian A. Schwarz and Christoph Schalk, *Implementation Guide to Natural Church Development* (St. Charles, IL: ChurchSmart Resources, 1998), 47–122.

[128] Donald A. McGavran, *Understanding Church Growth* (Grand Rapids, MI: Eerdmans, 1978), 34, 44; Donald A. McGavran and Winfield C. Arn, *Ten Steps for Church Growth* (San Francisco: Harper & Row, 1977), 51–54.

[129] Thom S. Rainer, *Surprising Insights from the Unchurched: and Proven Ways to Reach Them* (Grand Rapids, MI: Zondervan, 2001), 22–23.

[130] When Rainer asked the open ended question of "What factors led you to this church?" 90 percent of the participants listed the pastor and his preaching, and 88 percent listed the church's doctrine. Each of these had nearly double the response rate of the next highest response (Rainer, *Surprising Insights from the Unchurched*, 21). When the participants were asked more directly if these two things were factors, the responses were even higher (97 percent and 91 percent respectively) (ibid., 46, 55). When Rainer asked a follow up question to determine what in particular about the pastor and his preaching influenced people, the top response was preaching that taught the Bible and Christian doctrine (ibid., 57–59).

[131] Rainer, *Surprising Insights from the Unchurched*, 74–79.

This, too, is an expected result for Luther, when we remember that he lists the "mutual conversation and consolation of brethren" as a means of the Gospel.[132] In other words, he would expect personal relationships to be a means of converting people, provided that they are used as a vehicle for sharing the Good News.

Apologetics. Just as evangelists can be tempted to replace the power of the Gospel with human efforts to influence and persuade, so can those who work in the closely related field of apologetics.

Luther's consistent position is that God's Word is its own best defense.[133] In his comments on 1 Pet 3:15, the foundational text for apologetics, Luther affirms that every Christian should be prepared to give an account of the reason for their faith. From this he concludes that every Christian must be a student of Scripture, so they can defend their faith on the basis of Scripture. In particular, he emphasizes that we should know those parts of Scripture that tell us most clearly about Christ and salvation through him.[134] He insists that Christians must take their stand on God's Word alone, and not substitute a human word in its place: neither the statements of the pope, nor the church fathers, nor Aristotle, nor the light of natural reason.[135]

As we saw in the last chapter, it would be wrong to conclude from this that Luther granted no validity to arguments based on natural reason, at least when they concur with Scripture. It would also be wrong to conclude that he assigned no place to the natural knowledge of God when it comes to Christian proclamation, at least when it comes to finding points of contact for the proclamation of the Law. Furthermore, it would be wrong to conclude that Luther was against using human reason to point out logical weaknesses in the attacks people make against the truth as taught by Scripture.[136] What he

---

[132] SA III 4.

[133] Siegbert W. Becker, *The Foolishness of God: The Place of Reason in the Theology of Martin Luther* (Milwaukee, WI: Northwestern, 1999), 161–68.

[134] As we noted in the previous chapter, it would be wrong to conclude from Luther's emphasis on the doctrine of Christ and the Gospel that he considered the other doctrines of Scripture to be unimportant or expendable. Since Scripture provides a comprehensive worldview it speaks to all of life in one way or another, and gives immense scope for addressing alternative truth claims. Luther's emphasis on the biblical word as the best defense of the Christian faith should not be misconstrued to mean that once we've preached a few select themes like justification by faith we've done our job, and no further defense or engagement with the culture is necessary. Luther's views are not inconsistent with the emphasis of the L'Abri Fellowship, which is that defending the Christian faith means using the Word of God to engage with every area of life (L'Abri Fellowship, "History of L'Abri," www.labri.org/history.html [accessed Aug. 4, 2011]).

[135] *Sermons on First Peter* (1522), LW 30:105–8 = WA 12:360–62.

[136] Becker, *The Foolishness of God*, 168–76.

refused to do was to take the next step and attempt to establish the Christian faith on the basis of human reason.

In the previous chapter we noted Luther's primary objection to natural reason, that it does not know the Gospel. However, he also supplies two further objections. The first is that reason is too uncertain and fragile a basis on which to build faith. Luther writes,

> No reason is so firm that it can not again be overthrown by reason. There is no counsel, no matter how wise, no thing, no edifice, no matter how magnificent or strong, which cannot again be destroyed by human counsel, wisdom, and strength. And this can be seen in all things. Only the Word of God remains to all eternity.[137]

Furthermore,

> the attempt to guard or to base God's order upon reason, unless previously it has been grounded in and illumined by faith, is the same as if I wanted to illumine the sun with a dark lantern or use a reed as the foundation for a rock.[138]

Luther's final objection to our confidence in natural reason is that it does not have the power to break the human heart out of its rebellion against God. Only God's Word bears the Spirit's power to change the human heart and give it the gift of faith in Christ.

Much ink has been spilled in recent times regarding apologetic method. Should apologetics focus on logical proofs, and logical criteria for evaluating the validity of competing worldviews? Should it focus on grounding the Christian faith in empirically verifiable facts? Should it focus on critiquing the fundamental presuppositions of non-Christians? Or should it focus on reasons of the heart, and the value of the Christian faith in meeting existential needs? Luther would see a certain validity in all these approaches. They can all help to respond to objections to the Christian faith, to point out the inadequacy of competing worldviews, and perhaps to find a point of contact for Christian proclamation. However, he would absolutely object to any attempt to modify God's Word to make it "reasonable" according to a human standard of reason.[139] Furthermore, his focus and confidence would always be

---

[137] WA TR 1:530.14–18. Translated by Becker, *The Foolishness of God*, 37–38.

[138] *On the Papacy in Rome, Against the Most Celebrated Romanist in Leipzig* (1520), LW 39:63 = WA 6:291.8–11.

[139] "Now this is the will of the Father, that we be intent on hearing what the Man Christ has to say, that we listen to His Word. You must not cavil at His Word, find fault with it, and dispute it. Just hear it. Then the Holy Spirit will come and prepare your heart, that you may sincerely believe the preaching of the divine Word, even give up your life for it, and say: 'This is God's

elsewhere, on God's Spirit-filled Word, and its power to both defend itself and change the human heart.

The words of Charles Spurgeon, the great London preacher from the 19th century, echo the spirit of Luther on this point:

> Extenuations, explanations and apologies may be produced from the best of motives. But too often they suggest to opposers that it is admitted that God's most Holy Word contains something in it which is doubtful, or weak, or antiquated. It looks as though it needed to be defended by human wisdom. Brethren, the Word of the Lord can stand alone, without the propping which many are giving it. These props come down and then our adversaries think that the Book is down, too. The Word of God can take care of itself and will do so if we preach it and cease defending it. See that lion? They have caged him for his preservation—shut him up behind iron bars to secure him from his foes!
>
> See how a band of armed men have gathered together to protect the lion. What a clatter they make with their swords and spears! These mighty men are intent upon defending a lion. O fools and slow of heart! Open that door! Let the lord of the forest come forth free. Who will dare to encounter him? What does he want with your guardian care? Let the pure Gospel go forth in all its lion-like majesty and it will soon clear its own way and ease itself of its adversaries.[140]

Like Spurgeon, Luther encourages us to let the Gospel go forth in its lion-like majesty, rather than thinking we can build or preserve God's kingdom with our own might. Yes, we need to think about how best to get the Word out and ensure that it is heard. Yes, we can point out weaknesses in the

---

Word and the pure truth.' But if you insist that you be heard, that your reason interpret Christ's Word; if you presume to play the master of the Word, to propound other doctrines; if you probe it, measure it, and twist the words to read as you want them to, brood over them, hesitate, doubt, and then judge them according to your reason—that is not hearing the Word or being its pupil. Then you are setting yourself up as its schoolmaster. In that way you will never discover the meaning of Christ's Word or of His heavenly Father's will" (*Sermons on John* [1530–32], LW 23:229 = WA 33:362–63). Cf. LW 23:51, 80; 23:229–30; 28:69–70; 40:197; Becker, *The Foolishness of God*, 93–114, 153–61.

140 Spurgeon, "Sermon No. 2004: The Lover of God's Law Filled With Peace," in *Spurgeon's Sermons Volume 34: 1888* (Grand Rapids, MI: Christian Classics Ethereal Library, n.d.), www.ccel.org/ccel/spurgeon/sermons34.pdf (accessed 24 Jan. 2016), 31; cf. Spurgeon, "Sermon No. 2467: Christ and his Co-Workers," in *Spurgeon's Sermons Volume 42: 1896*, 265–77 (Grand Rapids, MI: Christian Classics Ethereal Library, n.d.), www.ccel.org/ccel/spurgeon/sermons42.pdf (accessed Jan. 24, 2016), 267–68.

objections people raise to the Christian faith. Yet we cannot build faith on any other foundation than the Spirit-breathed Word that points us to Christ; nor do we have any other means for changing hearts. Whenever we replace God's Word with human efforts to influence and persuade, we will find that we have put a feeble idol in the place of the Spirit's mighty sword.

THE FRUIT OF IDOLATRY: HYPOCRISY

The final theme in this chapter has been the contrast between the fruit of idolatry and the fruit of faith in Christ, and how only the Gospel can produce the fruits of the Christian faith in us. This provides us with a useful tool for diagnosing a person's spiritual state. When professing Christians fail to practice what they preach, or put on an outward show of sanctity with little sincerity behind it, this should tell us they have a problem with idolatry.

Christians are often accused of being hypocrites who fail to live up to the standards they seek to impose on others. The sociologist Os Guinness compiled a list of academics who have made this charge,[141] including the following:

> Friedrich Nietszche: "In truth, there was only one Christian, and he died on the cross."[142]
>
> Ralph Waldo Emerson: "Every Stoic was a Stoic; but in Christendom where is the Christian?"[143]
>
> Bertrand Russell: " 'If thou wilt be perfect, go and sell that which thou hast, and give to the poor.' That is a very excellent maxim, but, as I say, it is not much practised."[144]
>
> The philosopher C. M. Joad, before he converted to Christianity: "For God's sake don't touch the Church of England. It is the only thing that stands between us and Christianity."[145]
>
> Finally, a quip that is widely attributed to George Bernard Shaw: "Christianity might be a good thing if anyone ever tried it."[146]

---

[141] Os Guinness, "The One Unanswerable Objection to the Christian Faith: Christians," March 13, 2006, Veritas Forum, www.veritas.org/Media.aspx#!/v/216 (accessed Aug. 6, 2011).

[142] Friedrich Nietszche, "The Anti-Christ," in *The Portable Nietszche*, trans. and ed. Walter Kaufmann (New York: Penguin Books, 1977), 612.

[143] Ralph Waldo Emerson, "Self-Reliance," in *Self-Reliance and Other Essays* (Mineola, NY: Courier Dover Publications, 1993), 36.

[144] Bertrand Russell, "Why I Am Not a Christian," in *Bertrand Russell: Why I Am Not a Christian and Other Essays on Religion and Related Topics*, ed. Paul Edwards (New York: Touchstone, 1967), 15. Quoted with permission of the Bertrand Russell Peace Foundation.

[145] C. E. M. Joad, *The Present and Future of Religion* (London: Ernest Benn, 1930), 27.

The opinion that Christians are poor representatives of the faith they profess is not restricted to such academics from the past. For instance, a research study published in 2007 by the Barna Group looked at the attitudes that sixteen- to twenty-nine-year-old non-Christian Americans have toward Christians and found that the attitudes were predominantly negative.[147] The most common complaints were that Christians are:

- Hypocrites, who act as if they are morally superior when they are not.
- More focused on winning converts than genuinely caring for people.
- Unloving toward homosexuals.
- Sheltered, and unwilling to get involved in the grit and grime of people's lives.
- Too political and focused on legislating a right wing agenda.
- Judgmental toward others rather than loving.[148]

Many things could be said in response to such accusations. Many attacks against Christians are deeply unfair and factually untrue, and say more about the people making the attacks and their antipathy toward Christ than they do about Christians. Jesus told his followers to expect unfair treatment, and said, "Blessed are you when others revile you and persecute you and utter all kinds of evil against you falsely on my account" (Matt 5:11). Many attacks also show little understanding of the central Christian claim, that we are forgiven sinners who can boast of no moral perfection but instead "proclaim not ourselves, but Jesus Christ as Lord" (2 Cor 4:5). Yet such responses only go so far. Jesus expected that despite our ongoing struggle with sin our faith would still make a significant enough difference in our behavior that we would be like a city on a hill, with our love and good deeds being evident to all (Matt 5:13–16; John 13:35; 1 Pet 3:16). Furthermore, it is not just the enemies of the church who have observed the failure of its people to live up to the teachings of Christ; countless Christians down through the centuries have lamented the failure of church members to live lives worthy of the Gospel.

---

[146] I hesitate to repeat this quotation, since although it is frequently attributed to Shaw (e.g., in Os Guinness, *The Call: Finding and Fulfilling the Central Purpose of Your Life* [Nashville, TN: Thomas Nelson, 2003], 103), I have been unable to track down the original source of the quote. However, even if the quote has been falsely attributed to Shaw, it captures both his gift for memorable one-liners and his attitude toward Christianity.

[147] David Kinnaman and Gabe Lyons, *Unchristian: What a New Generation Really Thinks about Christianity . . . and Why it Matters* (Grand Rapids, MI: Baker Books, 2009), 24–29.

[148] Ibid., 28–30.

One who has bemoaned this sad reality is Tim Keller. He calls it the great scandal of our church that so many who confess faith in Christ fail to exhibit changed lives. He then suggests a reason for this: we as a church have failed to discern and expose people's idols. Instead, we have allowed people to worship the Lord and their idols too. As a result, their most fundamental commitment in many areas of their lives is not to the life-changing Gospel of Jesus Christ, but to some idol instead.[149] Furthermore, he suggests that in many cases the Christian faith itself has become idolatrous. It has become centered in a moral performance narrative instead of the Gospel and therefore breeds self-righteous contempt for others instead of graciousness and love. What needs to happen if the lives of professing Christians are to display genuine love for others is that they need to be truly centered in the One who gave his life for sinners.[150]

Christian Smith and his colleagues back up Keller's contention that the true Gospel has often morphed into a moral performance narrative. If they are correct, and moralistic therapeutic deism is really the dominant religion in America even among professing Christians, then hypocrisy is what we should expect. Such a faith cannot produce the kind of gracious love that Christ calls for in his followers. Moralistic therapeutic deism is idolatrous in relation to all three Articles of the Creed: it is centered on love of self rather than love of God; it places confidence in human righteousness rather than the righteousness of Christ; and it is informed more by the natural light of human reason than by God's Word. It is what Luther identifies as the natural religion of the Law rather than a genuine expression of the Christian faith. When people claim the name of Christ but live out a creed like this instead, they will inevitably bring dishonor to his name.

A CHRISTIAN RESPONSE: RECEPTIVE SPIRITUALITY

When I first applied to go to seminary as a twenty-year-old, I had an interview with Dr. Andrew Pfeiffer, the head of the pastoral ministry program at Luther Seminary in Adelaide, South Australia.[151] I told him that my interest in studying at the seminary was prompted by my interest in theology and that I was not sure if I was cut out to be a pastor. He then encouraged me to see that I had one of the best qualifications for ministry—a desire to get deeply

[149] Timothy Keller, "The Grand Demythologizer: The Gospel and Idolatry," April 20, 2005, The Gospel Coalition, thegospelcoalition.org/resources/video/The-Grand-Demythologizer-The-Gospel-and-Idolatry (accessed March 3, 2010).

[150] Timothy Keller, "A Conversation with Tim Keller: Belief in an Age of Skepticism?" March 4, 2008, Veritas Forum, www.veritas.org/Media.aspx#!/v/47 (accessed Aug. 5, 2011).

[151] This institution has now changed its name to Australian Lutheran College.

into God's Word, since everything in ministry flows out of this. He then encouraged me to simply come and dedicate myself to prayer and God's Word and let God worry about the rest. God might prepare me through this Word to be a better-equipped lay person; or, if he wanted me to be a pastor, he would make this clear to me over time, and he would get me into shape.

Several months later, I sat as a newly enrolled student and listened to Dr. Pfeiffer present the inaugural lecture at Luther Seminary for the new academic year. The topic of the lecture was Luther's view of *tentatio,* or God's alien work of testing us through the cross. As a class we laughed about this afterwards, "What an encouraging introduction to seminary—now that you are here you are going to suffer!" Yet it was an encouraging message. As I have experienced my share of struggles in subsequent years, it has fortified me to know that nothing unusual is happening to me. Instead, this is God's program for his people: prayer, listening to God's Word, and then learning through experience the truth of his Word as we cling to it in the trials of life. It is both heartening and liberating to know that in this way God does his work in us, to cleanse us from our idolatry and to plant faith and its fruits in us.

Our efforts as Christians to denounce the idolatry of our culture will always be hindered if we fail to provide an alternative by modeling repentance from it. Before we take the speck out of anyone else's eye we need to take the plank out of our own. So how do we do that? Not by our own strength, or we will be attempting to root out one idol with another. Instead, we need to learn a receptive spirituality centered on prayer, God's Word, and faithful perseverance. Through prayer, we put our trust in what God's Spirit can do, not what we can do. Through God's Word, we listen to his voice instead of human wisdom, and learn to have both our faith and our resultant actions directed by him. Then, by faithfully persevering with prayer and the Word in the midst of trouble, we learn through experience the power of God.

Unfortunately, this kind of receptive spirituality is sadly lacking in many churches in the Western world. Instead, prayerlessness and biblical illiteracy have become commonplace. In a recent sermon, I asked the gathered congregation to put up their hands if they had read the Bible from cover to cover at least once in their life. Apart from my wife and me, only one person could honestly say yes. When we pause to consider that virtually everyone in the Western world can read and has access to a Bible, it is staggering to consider that the vast majority of people who call themselves Christians have never bothered to read the only book that is authored by God.

In this situation, we need to learn how to preach and teach the Third Article of the Creed, and not merely the Second Article. Too often I have heard people say, "I have my faith [presumably in Jesus?], and that is all I need, and so I do not need to go to church or read and study the Bible." We need to say to such people, “You believe now, and that is great. But will you still have faith when you die? And what about your children? How will they learn to believe?” Then we can talk to them about the wonderful way God has made himself available to us through prayer and the Word to give us the gift of faith and to preserve us in it.

This neglect of God’s Word means that God has put a wide-open door in front of us for improving the spiritual state of our church. At a recent synodical convention, one of the pastors of my church told the assembly that he was the pastor of a large congregation that had been involved in several different activities and outreach programs over many years. Yet now most of the people in his congregation were getting old and tired and did not have the energy to keep all those programs going. So they decided that for a time, they would simply focus on prayer and God’s Word. And lo and behold, before long this recharged them, and they regained their enthusiasm for mission.

Until we learn to be people of prayer and God’s Word, more programs and strategic planning will not help us in our mission to the world. Yet if we are people of the Word, then the Word will become like a fire within us, and we will find ways of getting it out, so that the plans and strategies will fall into place. Furthermore, our programs will find their right focus, which needs to be on getting the Word out, since this alone can change the human heart.

If idolatry really does make people blind to God and deaf to his Word, as the Scriptures teach (Ps 115:4–8; 135:15–18; Isa 6:9–10), then we really are impotent to battle against it with our own strength. For how can we preach to the deaf and open the eyes of those who are blind to the things of God? So instead of trying harder to build God’s kingdom by the strength of our arms, we need to confess our impotence and learn to rely fully on God.

CONCLUSION

LUTHER'S APPROACH TO IDOLATRY

Luther deals with idolatry in much the same way that a bank teller detects a counterfeit bill or an art critic detects a forgery: not by developing some abstract theory, but by being well enough acquainted with the genuine article to know the difference between it and a fake. Luther first asks the question "Who is God?"[1] He then answers that he is the One who reveals and gives himself to us in a highly specific economy of salvation, as the Father who created us and provides for us, as the Son who has redeemed us and reveals to us the Father, and as the Spirit who speaks to us through the Word to enlighten and empower us. Furthermore, he is a God who gives us everything by grace, and calls us to fear, love, and trust him with all our hearts, in every area of our lives. When we know who this God is it is easy to identify idols. They are all the things we fear, love and trust more than him.

THE VALUE OF STUDYING LUTHER ON IDOLATRY

The main goal of this study has been to systematize Luther's thoughts on idolatry so they can be used as a tool for spiritual diagnosis. This can help us to focus our application of Law and Gospel in our preaching, teaching, evangelism, and pastoral care. This is still the main value of this book.

However, as I studied Luther's theology of idolatry I received a pleasant surprise, and that is the extent to which it yielded insights into his theology as a whole. In hindsight, this should not be surprising. To borrow an image from Halbertal and Margalit, studying idolatry is like mapping out the wall that surrounds the city of God and separates the community of the faithful within from the strange gods without.[2] This wall defines both what is outside the boundary and what is within. Since true faith and idolatry are binary opposites, a precise understanding of one necessarily entails a precise understanding of the other. Only when we clearly distinguish God from everything that is not God does our picture of God come into sharp focus.

It is in this regard that this book can contribute to Luther studies as a whole. As we noted in the introduction, the topic of idolatry has been largely neglected in Luther studies. Yet if all we ever examine is Luther's thoughts

[1] Cf. LC I 1 = WA 30/1:132.34–133.1.

[2] Moshe Halbertal and Avishai Margalit, *Idolatry*, translated by Naomi Goldblum (Cambridge, MA: Harvard University Press, 1992), 236.

regarding true faith and the true God, not false faith in false gods, then our understanding of his picture of God will always be fuzzy around the edges. Only when we consider the enormous amount of thought Luther gave to the binary opposite of saving faith will we be able to see both sides of his theology clearly. The following are some examples:

1. Most scholars contrast Luther's theology of the cross with the theology of glory, without realizing that "theology of glory" is just an expression Luther used at one brief stage of his career and then never used again. For the rest of his career he talked about idolatry instead.[3] If we fail to see that the most significant contrast for Luther is between the theology of the cross and idolatry, then we will fail to understand fully this important aspect of Luther's thought.
2. Unless we see that the opposite of justification by faith for Luther is not simply works righteousness, but any form of self-justification, we will fail to see why Luther lumps legalists and antinomians together as enemies of Christ and his salvation.
3. If we fail to see Luther's concern with how easily human reason gets turned into an idol, we will fail to understand why Luther can praise reason with one breath and curse it with the next.
4. The Reformation was essentially a battle against idolatry, which the reformers believed had corrupted the church. Unless we understand how Luther's theology of idolatry differed from that of other reformers like Calvin and Zwingli, we will never fully understand why his reform took a different turn from theirs.

SUMMARY OF LUTHER'S THOUGHT

Luther talks about idolatry in relation to every domain of life, including all three Articles of the Creed. In relation to the First Article, he talks about idols we use to provide for ourselves and to orient our existence. In relation to the Second Article, he talks about idols we use to justify ourselves and climb up to God to secure his favor and blessing. In relation to the Third Article, he talks about idols we use to enlighten and empower our hearts and minds.

In all these domains, the self is the greatest idol. Although we cling to many idols apart from ourselves, we recruit these with the intention of making them serve ourselves. The problem is as follows: in relation to the First Article, we want divine self-sufficiency, and we want the universe to revolve around us and our desires; in relation to the Second Article, we want to claim that we are righteous in and of ourselves, and if we acknowledge a God above

---

[3] See chapter 2, footnote 18.

us, we want to relate to him on our terms; and in relation to the Third Article, we want to claim that we are enlightened and wise, instead of acknowledging that our minds are dark unless they receive light from above.

A summary of the different types of idolatry that Luther discusses is provided in the table below. The consequences of each form of idolatry are particularly important for Christian proclamation, since these reveal the futility of the idolatry. It is at these points, when people's idols start to fail them, that we have the best opportunities to disenchant people from their idols and to proclaim the benefits of faith in the true God.

First Article	
Providence	**Love**
Key Issues • Trust in God's providence vs. trust in human strength to provide • Using the masks of God (while trusting in God) vs. trusting in the masks themselves Key Texts Ps 127:1; Deut 8:17–18 Consequences of idolatry in this area of life • Insecurity • Fear • Exhaustion	Key Issues • Love of God vs. self-interest • Love of God's will vs. self-will Key Texts Mark 12:30; 1 Cor 13:5; Matt 16:25 Consequences of idolatry in this area of life • Lack of joy and contentment • Frustrated desire

Second Article	
Justification	**The Worship of God Incarnate**
Key Issues • Justification through Christ and his righteousness vs. self-justification through our own righteousness • The true Gospel vs. legalism, antinomianism, and all attempts to deny our sin or tailor the Law to justify ourselves Key Texts Luke 5:31–32; Rom 1–4.	Key Issues • God ordained worship through Christ-and-the-Gospel vs. self-chosen worship • Trying to devise our own path to God in heaven vs. knowing him and having him as he has come down to earth in Christ-and-the-Gospel Key Texts Exod 33:18–23; John 1:17–18; 14:6–10; Col 2:16–23.

Consequences of idolatry in this area of life • An unstable conscience, that can easily swing between pride and despair • The justification of sin, which leads to an increase in wickedness beneath a hypocritical pretense of righteousness • A sense of entitlement, which leads us to condemn God instead of thanking him • Judgmentalism over against others • Condemnation by God on the last day	Consequences of idolatry in this area of life • Vain worship in which God and his grace and blessing are absent • A legal knowledge of God rather than an evangelical knowledge of him

THIRD ARTICLE	
God's Word	**Repentance**
Key Issues • Enlightenment through the Spirit-given Word vs. self-enlightenment through human wisdom (i.e., human reason, tradition and experience, when these are not informed and governed by God's Word) Key Texts 1 Cor 1:18–2:16; 2 Pet 1:16–21 Consequences of idolatry in this area of life • Foolishness • Making a god in our own image (who allows us to justify ourselves and pursue our own desires) instead of knowing the true God	Key Issues • Confidence in the Spirit to work repentance, faith, and the fruits of faith in us vs. confidence in our own willpower and ability to produce spiritual good in ourselves • Faithfulness in vocation and patient endurance vs. avoidance of the cross • Receptive spirituality and ministry centered in the means of grace vs. efforts to produce faith and its fruits by our own powers Key Texts Isa 28:21; Matt 12:33–35; Rom 10:17; 1 Cor 12:3; Gal 5:16–24. Consequences of idolatry in this area of life • Hypocrisy • Failure to produce true faith or its fruits in ourselves or others

LUTHER AND CONTEMPORARY IDOLATRY

The original goal of this study was to aid in the spiritual diagnosis of contemporary Western society, and to sharpen our proclamation of Law and Gospel within it. Luther's theology of idolatry is particularly useful for this task because of its vast scope and ready applicability. Other scholars have dealt with idolatry in one or two areas of life, but Luther has looked at every major area of life, and provides us with a comprehensive framework and methodology for dealing with idolatry of any kind. Furthermore, his thought is readily applicable to a secular context, where many of the idols people worship are not obviously religious in nature. When Luther describes idolatry as primarily a matter of faith, and defines idols in terms of the function we expect them to play in our lives, he exposes the idolatrous nature of all kinds of things that at first glance appear to be secular. This combination of vast scope and ready applicability makes Luther's theology of idolatry a powerful tool for analyzing human rebellion, so that we can challenge idolatry in every area of life, and provide an alternative through the Gospel.

Here we can take our cue from Jesus in the Gospels. The Gospels devote much attention to Jesus' clash with the Pharisees. The Pharisees were not idolaters in an obvious sense, since they did not bow down to gods of wood or stone. Yet Jesus challenged their idolatry on at least three levels. He challenged their greed (First Article idolatry), and exposed its idolatrous nature by telling them they could not serve both God and money (Luke 16:13–15). He challenged their self-righteousness (Second Article idolatry), and showed how out-of-step this made them with the will of the Father and the Savior he had sent (Luke 5:27–32; 7:36–50; 15:1–32; 18:9–14). He challenged their devotion to human traditions (Third Article idolatry), and told them that by setting aside God's Word for the sake of their traditions they showed that their hearts were far from him (Mark 7:1–13). Evidently Jesus was not content to allow idolatry to reign in any part of their hearts and minds. Likewise, he is not satisfied until all our self-confidence is destroyed and we have learnt to trust in God's gracious provision in every area of our lives.

Just as Jesus uncovered multiple idols in the lives of the Pharisees, so Luther can help us to uncover multiple idols in the lives of people today. This can help us to proclaim Law and Gospel in such a way that it addresses the real issues in every dimension of people's lives.

Whenever the Law uncovers our sin, the answer is always found in Christ and the Gospel. However, it is easy to fall into the trap of proclaiming the Gospel in a one-dimensional way so that people fail to see how it answers their need.[4] One way this frequently happens in the Lutheran Church is that we proclaim the central message of the Gospel—that God justifies sinners through faith in Jesus Christ—but fail to proclaim how the Gospel then spills over and affects all of life. Christ's atoning death on the cross for our salvation

---

[4] One helpful resource on how to proclaim the biblical message of the Gospel in all its richness is Jacob A. O. Preus, *Just Words: Understanding the Fullness of the Gospel* (St. Louis: Concordia, 2000).

must remain central in any faithful proclamation of the Gospel. Nevertheless, we fail to proclaim the Gospel in all its fullness if we fail to proclaim its implications for the rest of our lives, as it flows into God's undeserved gifts and gracious promises in every area of life. The God who saved and redeemed us from the condemnation of our sin is the same God who gives us his good gifts in creation, "Without any merit or worthiness in me."[5] The God who sent his Son to die is the same God who overcomes our spiritual blindness and causes us to believe in Jesus Christ when we could not do this by our own reason or strength.[6] The God who forgives sins is the same God who now hears our prayers because we are forgiven.[7] And so on. For "He who did not spare his own Son but gave him up for us all, how will he not also with him graciously give us all things?" (Rom 8:32).

Until we have led people to trust in God's gracious gifts and faithful promises not only as their ticket to heaven but in every area of their lives we have not completed the work of Law and Gospel proclamation. Often in our pastoral dealings with people, their need for the Gospel emerges more obviously in other areas of their lives than it does in any discussion of justification before God on the last day. The Gospel is obviously relevant to someone who does not know what it is to be justified through faith in Jesus Christ. Yet what about the pastor who preaches salvation by faith, but when it comes to growing the church trusts more in human programs and methods of persuasion than he does in God? What about the woman who believes in Jesus, but still thinks that it is her ability to charm a man or build a happy family that is the key to a happy life? What about the man who says that Jesus is his Lord and Savior, but whose sense of self-worth is bound more with the pride he takes in his business acumen, and who trusts more in his own shrewdness than in God's Word when it comes to making decisions for his everyday life? All of these need to grapple more deeply with what it means to live by faith in the unmerited kindness of God.

LIBERATION

While I was doing this research on Luther, someone asked me what I was writing about. When I told him that I was writing on idolatry, he responded, "That must be a depressing topic to spend so much time on." Yet I have not found it depressing at all. Instead, it reinforces who the true God is, a God who wants to give us everything by grace, in every area of life. Furthermore, since idols enslave us and choke the life out of us, every time we uncover a

---

[5] SC II = WA 30/1:365.2–3.

[6] SC II 6.

[7] SC III 16.

new idol we discover a new avenue for life and freedom. If we have hitched our wagon to the wrong star, it is liberating to realize this, and to see that we have a brighter star who will not disappoint us.

Luther's insights into the idolatry of the self—and how the deepest idols we struggle with amount to an idolization of ourselves and our own human power—reinforce this point. What could be more oppressive than attempting to shoulder a burden we cannot possibly bear, the responsibility of being gods? What a joy to relinquish this burden and to come to the One whose yoke is easy and whose burden is light! As Luther writes:

> No one who believes in Christ is strong by his own power, but is weak and suffers all things. Nor does he avenge or liberate himself, even if he is able, but he gives glory to God, and waits for his liberating and avenging power. . . . No one [who believes in Christ] is wise in his own wisdom, but becomes a fool in his own eyes and before all people, and gives the glory of wisdom to God alone, who, when he has been tested, will give him the glory of wisdom in heaven. In the same way no Christian is righteous in his own righteousness, but gives the glory of righteousness to God.[8]

What Luther teaches about idolatry can be summarized in this way: What a burden it is to have to secure my earthly wellbeing by the strength of my own arm! How liberating to know that God the Father will provide for me, and to trust in his power. What a burden to be bound by my own self-love! How liberating to be caught up in love for the Lord instead. What a burden to have to justify myself with my own paltry righteousness! How liberating to be justified by the righteousness of Christ. What a burden to grope vainly for an unknown god, and to have to invent ways to climb to him or please him! How liberating to know and worship the God who comes down to me and is pleased with me through Christ. What a burden to have to make myself wise with my puny brain and limited vision! How liberating to receive heavenly wisdom through the Word. And what a burden to engage in ministry by my own strength, to strive by my own power to instill faith and its fruits in myself and others! How liberating to know that God feeds our faith and makes it fruitful by his Holy Spirit through the Word.

Soli Deo Gloria

---

[8] *Operationes in Psalmos* (1519–21), WA 5:250.26–33.

Bibliography

Abraham, William J. "Inclusivism, Idolatry and the Survival of the (Fittest) Faithful." In *The Community of the Word: Towards an Evangelical Ecclesiology*, edited by Mark Husbands and Daniel J. Treier, 131–45. Downers Grove, IL: InterVarsity, 2005.

Achtemeier, Paul J. "Gods Made with Hands: The New Testament and the Problem of Idolatry." *Ex Auditu* 15 (1999): 43–61.

Althaus, Paul. *The Theology of Martin Luther*. Translated by Robert C. Schultz. Philadelphia: Fortress, 1966.

Arand, Charles P. "Luther on the God Behind the First Commandment." *Lutheran Quarterly* 8 (Winter 1994): 397–423.

Aronson, Elliot. "The Rationalizing Animal." In *Psychology is Social: Readings and Conversations in Social Psychology*, edited by Edward Krupat. 2nd ed. Dallas:b Scott, Foresman, 1982.

Assmann, Jan. *The Search for God in Ancient Egypt*. Translated by David Lorton. Ithaca, NY: Cornell University Press, 2001.

Augustine of Hippo. *Confessions and Enchiridion*. Translated and edited by Albert C. Outler. Library of Christian Classics, Vol. 7. Philadelphia: Westminster, 1955.

_____. *Eighty-Three Different Questions*. Translated by David L. Mosher. Fathers of the Church Series 70. Washington D.C.: CUA Press, 2002.

_____. *On the Holy Trinity; Doctrinal Treatises; Moral Treatises*. Edited by Philip Schaff. Nicene and Post-Nicene Fathers, First Series, Vol. 3. Edinburgh: T & T Clark, 1988.

_____. "On the Morals of the Catholic Church." *In St Augustin: The Writings Against the Manichaeans and Against the Donatists*. Edited by Philip Schaff. Nicene and Post-Nicene Fathers, First Series, Vol. 4. Grand Rapids, MI: Christian Classics Ethereal Library, n.d. www.ccel.org/ccel/schaff/npnf104.html (accessed 18 Nov. 2010).

_____. *St. Augustin's: City of God and Christian Doctrine*. Edited by Philip Schaff. Nicene and Post-Nicene Fathers, First Series, Vol. 2. Edinburgh: T & T Clark, 1988.

_____. *St Augustin: Lectures or Tractates on the Gospel According to St. John*. Translated by John Gibb and James Innes. Edited by Philip Schaff. Nicene and Post-Nicene Fathers, First Series, Vol. 7. New York: The Christian Literature Company, 1888.

Australian Bureau of Statistics. *Australian Social Trends 1994.* ABS Catalogue No. 4102.0. Canberra: Australian Bureau of Statistics, 1994. www.ausstats.abs.gov.au/ausstats/free.nsf/0/1CC597199AA4BD14CA25722500049553/$File/41020_1994.pdf (accessed May 21, 2010).

Barna Group, "Americans Are Most Likely to Base Truth on Feelings." Feb 12, 2002. www.barna.org/barna-update/article/5-barna-update/67-americans-are-most-likely-to-base-truth-on-feelings (accessed Jan 28, 2010).

_____. "Surveys Show Pastors Claim Congregants Are Deeply Committed to God But Congregants Deny It!" Jan. 10, 2006. www.barna.org/barna-update/article/5-barna-update/165-surveys-show-pastors-claim-congregants-are-deeply-committed-to-god-but-congregants-deny-it (accessed Jan. 28, 2010).

Barr, James. *Holy Scripture: Canon, Authority, Criticism.* Philadelphia: Westminster, 1983.

Bauer, Walter. *A Greek-English Lexicon of the New Testament and Other Early Christian Literature.* Translated and edited by William F. Arndt, F. Wilbur Gingrich, and Frederick W. Danker. Chicago: University of Chicago Press, 1979.

Bayer, Oswald. "Law and Freedom: A Metacritique of Kant." In *Freedom in Response: Lutheran Ethics: Sources and Controversies*, translated by Jeffrey F. Cayzer, 138–55. New York: Oxford University Press, 2007.

_____. *Living by Faith: Justification and Sanctification.* Translated by Geoffrey W. Bromiley. Grand Rapids, MI: Eerdmans, 2003.

_____. *Martin Luther's Theology: A Contemporary Interpretation.* Translated by Thomas H. Trapp. Grand Rapids, MI: Eerdmans, 2008.

_____. *Theology the Lutheran Way.* Edited and Translated by Jeffrey G. Silcock and Mark C. Mattes. Grand Rapids, MI: Eerdmans, 2007.

Beale, G. K. *We Become What We Worship: A Biblical Theology of Idolatry.* Downers Grove, IL: IVP Academic, 2008.

Becker, Siegbert W. *The Foolishness of God: The Place of Reason in the Theology of Martin Luther.* Milwaukee, WI: Northwestern, 1999.

_____. "Luther's Apologetics." *Concordia Theological Quarterly* 10 (Oct. 1958): 742–49.

Berger, Peter L. *Pyramids of Sacrifice: Political Ethics and Social Change.* New York: Basic Books, 1974.

Bernard of Clairvaux. *On Loving God.* Grand Rapids, MI: Christian Classic Ethereal Library, n.d. www.ccel.org/ccel/bernard/loving_god.html (accessed 25 July 2014).

Biden, Joseph. "Opening Statement, Senator Joseph R. Biden, Chairman of the Judiciary Committee Hearing on the Confirmation of Clarence Thomas to be an Associate Justice to the U.S. Supreme Court." Sept 10, 1991.

www.gpoaccess.gov/congress/senate/judiciary/sh102-1084pt1/6-21.pdf (accessed May 12 2009).

Biel, Gabriel. "The Circumcision of the Lord." In *Forerunners of the Reformation: The Shape of Late Medieval Thought Illustrated by Key Documents*, edited by Heiko Oberman, 165–74. Philadelphia: Fortress, 1981.

Bornkamm, Heinrich. *Luther and the Old Testament*. Translated by Eric W. Gritsch and Ruth C. Gritsch. Edited by Victor I. Gruhn. Philadelphia: Fortress, 1969.

Breen, Quirinius. *John Calvin: A Study in French Humanism*. Grand Rapids, MI: Eerdmans, 1931.

Budziszewski, J. *The Revenge of the Conscience: Politics and the Fall of Man*. Dallas: Spence Publishing, 1999.

_____. *What We Can't Not Know: A Guide*. Dallas: Spence Publishing, 2003.

Calvin, John. *Calvin: Institutes of the Christian Religion* [1559]. Edited by John T. McNeill, translated by Ford Lewis Battles. Louisville, KY: Westminster John Knox, 2006.

_____. *Calvin's Commentaries: The Gospel According to St. John and the First Epistle of John*. Translated by T. H. L. Parker. Edited by David W. Torrance and Thomas F. Torrance. Grand Rapids, MI: Eerdmans, 1961.

_____. *Commentaries on the Book of the Prophet Jeremiah and the Lamentations*. Translated and edited by John Owen. Grand Rapids, MI: Eerdmans, 1950.

_____. "Confession of Faith concerning the Eucharist." In *Calvin: Theological Treatises*, edited by J. K. S. Reid, 167–77. Louisville, KY: Westminster John Knox, 2006.

_____. *John Calvin's Sermons on the Ten Commandments*. Edited and translated by Benjamin W. Farley. Grand Rapids, MI: Baker Book House, 1980.

_____. *Letters of John Calvin*. Vol. 2. Edited by Jules Bonnet. Philadelphia: Presbyterian Board of Publication, 1858.

_____. "Short Treatise on the Holy Supper of our Lord and Only Saviour Jesus Christ." In *Calvin: Theological Treatises*, edited by J. K. S. Reid, 140–66. Louisville, KY: Westminster John Knox, 2006.

_____. "The clear explanation of sound doctrine concerning the true partaking of the flesh and blood of Christ in the Holy Supper: to dissipate the mists of Tileman Heshusius." In *Calvin: Theological Treatises*, edited by J. K. S. Reid, 257–324. Louisville, KY: Westminster John Knox, 2006.

_____. *Writings on Pastoral Piety*. Translated and edited by Elsie Anne McKee. Mahwah, NJ: Paulist Press, 2001.

Cary, Phillip. *Good News for Anxious Christians: 10 Practical Things You Don't Have to Do*. Grand Rapids, MI: Brazos, 2010.

_____. *Outward Signs: The Powerlessness of External Things in Augustine's Thought.* Oxford: Oxford University Press, 2008.

_____. "Why Luther is not quite Protestant: The Logic of Faith in a Sacramental Promise." *Pro Ecclesia* 14 (Fall 2005): 447–86.

Christensen, Jens. *Mission to Islam and Beyond: A Practical Theology of Mission.* Blackwood, South Australia: New Creation Publications, 2001.

Colman, Paul. "Selfish Song." In *New Map of the World*, track 8. Franklin, TN: Essential Records, 2002.

Concordia: The Lutheran Confessions. 2nd ed. Edited by Paul McCain et al. St. Louis: Concordia, 2006.

Cooper, Terry D. *Sin, Pride, & Self-Acceptance: The Problem of Identity in Theology & Psychology.* Downers Grove, IL: InterVarsity, 2003.

Cyril of Alexandria. *On the Unity of Christ.* Translated by John Anthony McGuckin. Crestwood, NY: St. Vladimir's Seminary Press, 1995.

_____. "The Third Letter of Cyril to Nestorius." In *Christology of the Later Fathers*, edited by Edward R. Harvey, 349–54. Louisville, KY: Westminster John Knox, 2006.

Davis, John Jefferson. *Worship and the Reality of God: An Evangelical Theology of the Real Presence.* Downer's Grove, IL: IVP Academic, 2010.

Dawkins, Richard. *The God Delusion.* Boston: Houghton Mifflin, 2006.

Dollard, Maureen F., Anthony Harold Winefield, and Helen R. Winefield. *Occupational Stress in the Service Professions.* London: Taylor & Francis, 2003.

Eire, Carlos M. N., *War against the Idols: The Reformation of Worship from Erasmus to Calvin.* Cambridge: Cambridge University Press, 1986.

Ellul, Jacques. *The Ethics of Freedom.* Translated and edited by Geoffrey W. Bromiley. Grand Rapids, MI: Eerdmans, 1976.

_____. *The Humiliation of the Word.* Translated by Joyce Main Hanks. Grand Rapids, MI: Eerdmans, 1985.

Emerson, Ralph Waldo. "Self-Reliance." In *Self-Reliance and Other Essays*, 19–38. Mineola, NY: Courier Dover Publications, 1993.

Epley, N., et al. "Believers' estimates of God's beliefs are more egocentric than estimates of other people's beliefs." *Proceedings of the National Academy of Sciences,* 106 (2009), 21533–38. www.pnas.org/content/106/51/21533.full.pdf+html (accessed 28 Nov. 2011).

Forde, Gerhard O. "When the Old Gods Fail: Martin Luther's Critique of Mysticism." In *The Preached God*, edited by Mark C. Mattes and Steven D. Paulson, 56–68. Grand Rapids, MI: Eerdmans, 2007.

Frankl, Viktor. *Man's Search for Meaning.* New York: Washington Square Press, 1985.

Fred Hollows Foundation. "About Fred." www.hollows.org/AboutFred/ (accessed May 18, 2010).

Gallup, George H. Jr. "American Spiritual Searches Turn Inward." 2003. www.gallup.com/poll/7759/Americans-Spiritual-Searches-Turn-Inward.aspx (accessed July 27, 2010).

Gay, Craig M. *The Way of the (Modern) World, or, Why It's Tempting to Live as if God Doesn't Exist*. Grand Rapids, MI: Eerdmans, 1998.

Geisler, Norman. *Chosen But Free: A Balanced View of Divine Election*. Minneapolis, MN: Bethany House Publishers, 2001.

_____, and William C. Roach. *Defending Inerrancy: Affirming the Accuracy of Scripture for a New Generation*. Grand Rapids, MI: Baker Books, 2011.

Gerrish, B. A. *Grace and Reason: A Study in the Theology of Luther*. Oxford: Oxford University Press, 1962.

Gilkey, Langdon. *Shantung Compound: The Story of Men and Women Under Pressure*. New York: Harper and Row, 1966.

Götze, Alfred. *Frühneuhochdeutsches Glossar*. 5th ed. Berlin: Walter de Gruyter, 1956.

Guinness, Os. *The Call: Finding and Fulfilling the Central Purpose of Your Life*. Nashville, TN: Thomas Nelson, 2003.

_____. "The One Unanswerable Objection to the Christian Faith: Christians." March 13, 2006. Veritas Forum. www.veritas.org/Media.aspx#!/v/216 (accessed Aug. 6, 2011).

Halbertal, Moshe, and Avishai Margalit. *Idolatry*. Translated by Naomi Goldblum. Cambridge, MA: Harvard University Press, 1992.

Halik, Tomas. "The Soul of Europe: An Altar to the Unknown God." *International Review of Mission* 95 (Jul–Oct 2006), 265–70.

Hamm, Berndt. "Volition and Inadequacy as a Topic in Late Medieval Pastoral Care of Penitents." In *The Reformation in the Context of Late Medieval Theology and Piety: Essays by Berndt Hamm*, edited by Robert J. Bast, 88–127. Boston, MA: Brill, 2004.

Hildebrand, Joe. "Fred Hollows Remembered at Ceremony in Bourke." *The Daily Telegraph*, Feb. 11, 2008. www.dailytelegraph.com.au/news/nsw-act/a-vision-well-remembered/story-e6freuzi-1111115519873 (accessed May 18, 2010).

Hoffman, Bengt. "Introduction." In *The Theologia Germanica of Martin Luther*, translated by Bengt Hoffman, 1–50. New York: Paulist Press, 1980.

Holifield, E. Brooks. *A History of Pastoral Care in America: From Salvation to Self-Realization*. Eugene, OR: Wipf and Stock, 1983.

Horney, Karen. *Neurosis and Human Growth: The Struggle Toward Self-Realization*. New York: W. W. Norton, 1950.

Hunter, Cornelius G. *Darwin's God: Evolution and the Problem of Evil.* Grand Rapids, MI: Brazos, 2001.

Jenson, Matt. *The Gravity of Sin: Augustine, Luther and Barth on Homo Incurvatus In Se.* London: T & T Clark, 2006.

Joad, C. E. M. *The Present and Future of Religion.* London: Ernest Benn, 1930.

Johnson, Phillip E. "Nihilism and the End of Law." *First Things* (March 1993). www.firstthings.com/article.php3?id_article=5101&var_recherche=natural+law (accessed May 14, 2009).

Jonas, Eva, and Peter Fischer. "Terror Management and Religion: Evidence That Intrinsic Religiousness Mitigates Worldview Defense Following Mortality Salience." *Journal of Personality and Social Psychology* 91 (2006): 553–67.

Jones, Ernest. *The Life and Work of Sigmund Freud.* Edited and abridged by Lionel Trilling and Steven Marcus. New York: Basic Books, 1961.

Jones, Gregory L. "The Psychological Captivity of the Church in the United States." In *Either/Or: The Gospel or Neopaganism*, edited by Carl E. Braaten and Robert W. Jenson, 97–112. Grand Rapids, MI: Eerdmans, 1995.

Kaldor, Peter, et al. *Build My Church: Trends and Possibilities for Australian Churches.* NCLS Research. Adelaide, South Australia: Openbook Publishers, 1999.

Keel, Othmar, and Christoph Uelinger. *Gods, Goddesses, and Images of God in Ancient Israel.* Translated by Thomas H. Trapp. Minneapolis: Fortress, 1998.

Keller, Timothy. "A Conversation with Tim Keller: Belief in an Age of Skepticism?" March 4, 2008. Veritas Forum. www.veritas.org/Media.aspx#!/v/47 (accessed Aug. 5, 2011).

_____. *Counterfeit Gods: The Empty Promise of Money, Sex, and Power, and the Only Hope that Matters.* New York: Dutton Adult, 2009.

_____. "How the Cross Changes Us." 2007. Christian Life Conference (Second Presbyterian of Memphis, TN). www.2pcmedia.org/get.php?web=2007-01-19_How_the_Cross_Changes_Us.mp3 (accessed Sept. 15 2009).

_____. "How the Cross Converts Us." 2007. Christian Life Conference (Second Presbyterian of Memphis, TN). www.2pcmedia.org/get.php?web=2007-01-19_How_the_Cross_Converts_Us.mp3 (accessed Sept. 15, 2009).

_____. "Reaching the 21st Century World For Christ." 2005. The Gathering. thegathering.com/gws/media/_mp3/2005/2005-Tim%20Keller-Reaching%20The%2021st%20Century%20World%20For%20Christ.mp3 (accessed Sept. 15, 2009).

_____. "Smashing False Idols: Gospel Communication." 2007. The Evangelists Conference. www.evangelists-conference.org.uk/2F014-02GospelCommunication.mp3 (accessed Sept. 15, 2009).

_____. "Smashing False Idols: Gospel Realisation." 2007. The Evangelists Conference. www.evangelists-conference.org.uk/1F014-01GospelRealisation.mp3 (accessed Sept. 15, 2009).

_____. "Talking About Idolatry in a Postmodern Age." April 2007. www.stevekmccoy.com/keller-idoaltry.pdf (accessed March 4, 2010).

_____. "The Grand Demythologizer: The Gospel and Idolatry." April 20, 2005. The Gospel Coalition. thegospelcoalition.org/resources/video/The-Grand-Demythologizer-The-Gospel-and-Idolatry (accessed March 3, 2010).

Kenneth Copeland Ministries Australia. "Understanding Chastisement." www.kcm.org.au/content/understanding-chastisement (accessed Feb. 2, 2016).

Kenny, Anthony. *An Illustrated Brief History of Western Philosophy*. Malden, MA: Blackwell Publishing, 2006.

Keyes, Richard. "Giving a Word Back." www.bethinking.org/what-is-apologetics/giving-a-word-back.htm (accessed Nov. 17, 2006).

_____. "The Dynamics of Idolatry." www.bethinking.org/spirituality/the-dynamics-of-idolatory.htm (accessed Nov. 17, 2006).

_____. "The Idol Factory." In *No God but God: Breaking with the Idols of our Age*, edited by Os Guinness and John Seel, 29–48. Chicago: Moody, 1992.

Kinnaman, David, and Gabe Lyons. *Unchristian: What a New Generation Really Thinks about Christianity . . . and Why it Matters*. Grand Rapids, MI: Baker Books, 2009.

Kittel, Gerhard, Gerhard Friedrich, and Geoffrey W. Bromiley, eds. *Theological Dictionary of the New Testament*. 10 Volumes. Translated by Geoffrey W. Bromiley. Grand Rapids, MI: Eerdmans, 1964.

Kleinig, John. *Grace upon Grace: Spirituality for Today*. St. Louis: Concordia, 2008.

_____. "Where is your God? Luther on God's Self-Localisation." In *All Theology Is Christology. Essays in Honor of David P Scaer*, edited by Dean O. Wenthe et al., 117–31. Fort Wayne, IN: Concordia Theological Seminary Press, 2000.

Klug, Eugene F. *From Luther to Chemnitz: On Scripture and the Word*. Grand Rapids, MI: Eerdmans, 1971.

_____. "Word and Scripture in Luther Studies Since World War II." In *Biblical Authority and Conservative Perspectives: Viewpoints from Trinity Journal*, edited by Douglas Moo, 117–54. Grand Rapids, MI: Kregel Publications, 1997.

Kolden, Marc. "Luther on Vocation." *Word and World* 3 (Fall 1983): 382–90.

Kutsko, John F. *Between Heaven and Earth: Divine Presence and Absence in the Book of Ezekiel*. Winona Lake, IN: Eisenbrauns, 2000.

L'Abri Fellowship. "History of L'Abri." www.labri.org/history.html (accessed Aug. 4, 2011).

Lasch, Christopher. *The Culture of Narcissism: American Life in an Age of Diminishing Expectations*. New York: W. W. Norton, 1978.

Lasch-Quinn, Elisabeth. "Introduction 2006." In *The Triumph of the Therapeutic: Uses of Faith After Freud*, by Philip Rieff. Wilmington, DE: ISI Books, 2006.

Lash, Nicholas. *Easter in Ordinary: Reflections on Human Experience and the Knowledge of God*. Charlottesville: University Press of Virginia, 1988.

_____. *The Beginning and the End of "Religion"*. Cambridge, UK: Cambridge University Press, 1996.

Lewis, C. S. *God in the Dock: Essays on Theology and Ethics*. Edited by Walter Hooper. Grand Rapids, MI: Eerdmans, 1970.

Little, Joyce. *The Church and the Culture War: Secular Anarchy or Sacred Order*. San Francisco: Ignatius Press, 1995.

Locher, Gottfried W. *Zwingli's Thought: New Perspectives*. Leiden, The Netherlands: E. J. Brill, 1981.

Lohse, Bernhard. *Martin Luther: An Introduction to His Life and Work*. Translated by Robert C. Schultz. Philadelphia: Fortress, 1986.

Lotz, David W. "Sola Scriptura: Luther on Biblical Authority." *Interpretation* 35 (July 1981): 258–73.

Luther, Martin. *Luthers Werke im WWW: Weimarer Ausgabe*. 127 Volumes. Proquest, 2000–2010. An electronic reproduction of *Luthers Werke: Kritische Gesamtausgabe*. Weimar: Hermann Böhlau, 1883–1993.

_____. *Luther's Works*. American Ed. 56 Volumes. St. Louis: Concordia; Philadelphia: Fortress, 1955–86.

_____. *Martin Luther's Complete Commentary on the First Twenty-Two Psalms*. 2 Volumes. Translated by Henry Cole. London: W. Simpkin and R. Marshall, 1826.

_____. *Sermons of Martin Luther: The Church Postils*. 8 Volumes. Edited by J. N. Lenker. Translated by J. N. Lenker et al. Grand Rapids, MI: Baker Books, 1995.

_____. *Sermons of Martin Luther: The House Postils*. 3 Volumes. Edited by Eugene F. A. Klug. Translated by Eugene F. A. Klug et al. Grand Rapids, MI: Baker Books, 1996.

_____. *Solus Decalogus Est Aeternus: Martin Luther's Complete Antinomian Theses and Disputations*. Edited and translated by Holger Sonntag. Minneapolis, MN: Lutheran Press, 2008.

_____. *The Bondage of the Will*. Translated by J. I. Packer and O. R. Johnston. London: James Clarke & Co., 1957.

_____. *What Luther Says: A Practical In-Home Anthology for the Active Christian*. Compiled by Ewald M. Plass. St. Louis: Concordia, 1959.

Maxfield, John A. "Martin Luther and Idolatry." In *The Reformation as Christianization: Essays on Scott Hendrix's Christianization Thesis*, edited by Anna Marie Johnson and John A. Maxfield, 141–68. Tübingen: Mohr Siebeck, 2012.

McGavran, Donald A. *Understanding Church Growth*. Grand Rapids, MI: Eerdmans, 1978.

_____, and Winfield C. Arn. *Ten Steps for Church Growth*. San Francisco: Harper & Row, 1977.

McGrath, Alister E. *Luther's Theology of the Cross: Martin Luther's Theological Breakthrough*. Oxford: Basil Blackwell, 1985.

Melanchthon, Philip. "Loci Communes Theologici." In *Melanchthon and Bucer*, Library of Christian Classics, edited by Wilhelm Pauck, 1–152. Louisville, KY: Westminster John Knox, 2006.

Menninger, Karl. *Whatever Became of Sin?* New York: Hawthorn Books, 1973.

Mettinger, Tryggve. *No Graven Image?: Israelite Aniconism in Its Ancient Near Eastern Context*. Stockholm: Almqvist and Wiksell International, 1995.

_____. "The Veto on Images and the Aniconic God in Ancient Israel." In *Religious Symbols and Their Functions*, edited by Haralds Biezais, 15–29. Uppsala, Sweden: Almqvist and Wiksell International, 1979.

Murdoch, Iris. *Existentialists and Mystics: Writings on Philosophy and Literature*. Edited by Peter Conradi. New York: Penguin, 1999.

Myers, David. *The Inflated Self: Human Illusions and the Biblical Call to Hope*. New York: Seabury Press, 1981.

Najovits, Simson. *Egypt, Trunk of the Tree: A Modern Survey of an Ancient Land*. 2 Volumes. New York: Algora, 2003–4.

Niebuhr, H. Richard. *Radical Monotheism and Western Culture, With Supplementary Essays*. New York: Harper & Brothers, 1960.

Nietszche, Friedrich. "The Anti-Christ." In *The Portable Nietszche*, translated and edited by Walter Kaufmann, 565–656. New York: Penguin Books, 1977.

Nygren, Anders. *Agape and Eros*. Translated by Philip S. Watson. New York: Harper Torchbooks, 1969.

Öberg, Ingemar. *Luther and World Mission: A Historical and Systematic Study*. Translated by Dean Apel. St. Louis: Concordia, 2007.

Oberman, Heiko A. "Simul Gemitus et Raptus: Luther and Mysticism." In *The Dawn of the Reformation: Essays in Late Medieval and Early Reformation Thought*, 126–54. Edinburgh: T & T Clark, 1986.

_____. *The Harvest of Medieval Theology: Gabriel Biel and Medieval Nominalism*. Durham, NC: Labyrinth, 1983.

Osteen, Joel. *Become a Better You: 7 Keys to Improving Your Life Every Day*. Large print ed. Detroit: Thomson Gale, 2007.

_____. *Your Best Life Now: 7 Steps to Living at Your Full Potential.* New York: Time Warner Book Group, 2004.

Parsons, Michael. "Luther on Isaiah 40: the Gospel and Mission." In *Text and Task*, edited by Michael Parsons, 64–78. Waynesboro, GA: Paternoster, 2005.

Partee, Charles. *Calvin and Classical Philosophy*. Leiden, Netherlands: E. J. Brill, 1977.

_____. "The Soul in Plato, Platonism, and Calvin," *Scottish Journal of Theology* 22 (Sept. 1969): 278–95.

Pelikan, Jaroslav. "Luther's Works on the New Testament." In *The Sermon on the Mount (Sermons) and the Magnificat*, Vol. 21 of *Luther's Works*, edited by Jaroslav Pelikan. St. Louis: Concordia, 1956.

Peters, Albrecht. *Commentary on Luther's Catechisms: Ten Commandments*. Edited by Charles P. Schaum. Translated by Holger K. Sonntag. St Louis: Concordia, 2009.

Peterson, Kurt W. " 'The Spirit Gives Life, but the Letter Kills': Bible-olatry in American Protestantism." *Ex Auditu* 15(1999), 119–36.

Pew Forum on Religion and Public Life. "Many Americans Say Other Faiths Can Lead to Eternal Life." pewforum.org/docs/?DocID=380 (accessed Jan. 29, 2010).

_____. "U.S. Religious Landscape Survey: Religious Affiliation: Diverse and Dynamic." June 2008. religions.pewforum.org/pdf/report-religious-landscape-study-full.pdf (accessed Jan. 28, 2010).

_____. "U.S. Religious Landscape Survey: Religious Beliefs and Practices: Diverse and Politically Relevant." June 2008. religions.pewforum.org/pdf/report2-religious-landscape-study-full.pdf (accessed Jan. 28, 2010).

Posset, Franz. "Bernard of Clairvaux as Luther Source: Reading Bernard with Luther's 'Spectacles.'" *Concordia Theological Quarterly* 54 (Oct. 1990): 282–84.

Powlison, David. "Idols of the Heart and 'Vanity Fair.'" *The Journal of Biblical Counseling* 13 (Winter 1995): 35–50.

Powlison, David. *Seeing With New Eyes: Counseling and the Human Condition Through the Lens of Scripture*. Phillipsburg, NJ: P & R Publishing, 2003.

Prenter, Regin. *Spiritus Creator*. Translated by John M. Jenson. Eugene, OR: Wipf and Stock, 2001.

Preus, Jacob A. O. *Just Words: Understanding the Fullness of the Gospel*. St. Louis: Concordia, 2000.

Preus, Robert. *The Inspiration of Scripture: A Study of the Theology of the 17th-Century Lutheran Dogmaticians*. St. Louis: Concordia, 1957.

Prothero, Stephen. *American Jesus: How the Son of God Became a National Icon*. New York: Farrar, Straus and Giroux, 2003.

Pyszczynski, Tom, Sheldon Solomon, and Jeff Greenberg. *In the Wake of 9/11: The Psychology of Terror*. Washington DC: American Psychological Association, 2003.

Rabinowitz, Louis Isaac. "Idolatry." Pages 1227–37 in vol. 8 of *Encyclopaedia Judaica*. New York: Macmillan, 1971.

Rahner, Karl. *Karl Rahner in Dialogue: Conversations and Interviews 1965–82*. Edited by Paul Imhof and Hubert Biallowons. Translation edited by Harvey D. Egan. New York: Crossroad, 1986.

Rainer, Thom S. *Surprising Insights from the Unchurched: and Proven Ways to Reach Them*. Grand Rapids, MI: Zondervan, 2001.

Rieff, Philip. *The Triumph of the Therapeutic: Uses of Faith After Freud*. Wilmington, DE: ISI Books, 2006.

Russell, Bertrand. "Why I Am Not a Christian." In *Bertrand Russell: Why I Am Not a Christian and Other Essays on Religion and Related Topics*, edited by Paul Edwards, 3–23. New York: Touchstone, 1967.

Sasse, Hermann. *This Is My Body: Luther's Contention for the Real Presence in the Sacrament of the Altar*. Adelaide, South Australia: Lutheran Publishing House, 1977.

Schaff, Philip, and Henry Wace, eds. *The Seven Ecumenical Councils*. Nicene and Post-Nicene Fathers, Second Series, Vol. 14. Grand Rapids, MI: Eerdmans, 1982.

Schwarz, Christian A. *Natural Church Development: A Guide to Eight Essential Qualities of Healthy Churches*. St. Charles, IL: ChurchSmart Resources, 2000.

_____. *Paradigm Shift in the Church: How Natural Church Development Can Transform Theological Thinking*. Carol Stream, IL: ChurchSmart Resources, 1999.

_____, and Christoph Schalk. *Implementation Guide to Natural Church Development*. St. Charles, IL: ChurchSmart Resources, 1998.

Schweitzer, Albert. *The Quest of the Historical Jesus: A Critical Study of its Progress from Reimarus to Wrede*. Translated by W. Montgomery. London: Adam and Charles Black, 1910.

Schwiebert, E. G. *Luther and His Times: The Reformation from a New Perspective*. St. Louis: Concordia, 1950.

Second Council of Constantinople. "The Anathemas of the Second Council of Constantinople (Fifth Ecumenical)." In *Christology of the Later Fathers*, edited by Edward R. Harvey, 378–81. Louisville, KY: Westminster John Knox, 2006.

Second Vatican Council. "Lumen Gentium." Nov. 21, 1964. In *Vatican Council II: Constitutions, Decrees, Declarations—The Basic Sixteen Documents*, edited by Austin Flannery, 1–95. Northport, NY: Costello, 1995.

Singer, Irving. *The Nature of Love: Plato to Luther*. New York: Random House, 1966.

Sipe, Dera. "Struggling with Flesh: Soul/Body Dualism in Porphyry and Augustine." *Concept* (2006): 2–39. www.publications.villanova.edu/Concept/2006/Sipe.pdf (accessed April 29, 2010).

Smith, Christian. *Moral, Believing Animals: Human Personhood and Culture*. New York: Oxford University Press, 2003.

_____, and Melinda Lundquist Denton. *Soul Searching: The Religious and Spiritual Lives of American Teenagers*. New York: Oxford University Press, 2005.

_____, and Patricia Snell. *Souls in Transition: The Religious and Spiritual Lives of Emerging Adults*. New York: Oxford University Press, 2009.

Solomon, Sheldon, Jeff Greenberg, and Tom Pyszczynski. "The Cultural Animal: Twenty Years of Terror Management Theory and Research." In *Handbook of Experimental Existential Psychology*, edited by Jeff Greenberg, Sander L. Koole, and Tom Pyszczynski, 13–33. New York: Guilford Press, 2004.

Sonntag, Holger. "Translator's Preface." In *Solus Decalogus Est Aeternus: Martin Luther's Complete Antinomian Theses and Disputations*, edited and translated by Holger Sonntag, 11–21. Minneapolis, MN: Lutheran Press, 2008.

Spitzer, Robert J., Robin A. Bernhoft, and Camille E. De Blasi. *Healing the Culture: A Commonsense Philosophy of Happiness, Freedom, and the Life Issues*. San Francisco: Ignatius, 2000.

_____. "Toward a Philosophy of the Pro-Life Movement: Personhood, Rights, and 'Purpose in Life.'" Jan. 27, 2006. The Maclaurin Institute. www.maclaurin.org/mp3_group.php?type=MacLaurin+Campus+Lectures (accessed Jan. 17, 2008).

Sproul, R. C. "Explaining Inerrancy: A Commentary." 1980. International Council on Biblical Inerrancy Foundation Series 2. 65.175.91.69/ICCP_org/Documents_ICCP/English/White_Papers/01_Biblical_Inerrancy_Paper.pdf (accessed Oct. 25, 2012).

Spurgeon, Charles. "Sermon No. 2004: The Lover of God's Law Filled with Peace." In *Spurgeon's Sermons Volume 34: 1888*, 26–38. Grand Rapids, MI: Christian Classics Ethereal Library, n.d. www.ccel.org/ccel/spurgeon/sermons34.pdf (accessed 24 Jan. 2016).

_____. "Sermon No. 2467: Christ and his Co-Workers." In *Spurgeon's Sermons Volume 42: 1896*, 265–77. Grand Rapids, MI: Christian Classics Ethereal Library, n.d. www.ccel.org/ccel/spurgeon/sermons42.pdf (accessed 24 Jan. 2016).

Suk, Tae Jun. *The Theology of Martin Luther between Judaism and Roman Catholicism: A Critical-Historical Evaluation of Luther's Concept of Idolatry*. Ann Arbor, MI: UMI Dissertation Services, 2001.

Swanson, Robert Norman. *Religion and Devotion in Europe, c. 1215 – c. 1515*. Cambridge, UK: Cambridge University Press, 1995.

Taber, Charles R. "God vs. Idols: A Model of Conversion." *Journal of the Academy for Evangelism in Theological Education* 3 (1987–88): 20–32.

Taylor, Charles. *Sources of the Self: The Making of the Modern Identity.* Cambridge, MA: Harvard University Press, 1989.

Teigen, Erling T. "The Clarity of Scripture and Hermeneutical Principles in the Lutheran Confessions." *Concordia Theological Quarterly* 46 (April–July 1982): 147–66.

Terry, David Jonathan. *Martin Luther on the Suffering of the Christian.* Ann Arbor, MI: UMI Dissertation Service, 1991.

The Theologia Germanica of Martin Luther. Translated by Bengt Hoffman. New York: Paulist Press, 1980.

Third Council of Constantinople. "The Statement of Faith of the Third Council of Constantinople (Sixth Ecumenical)." In *Christology of the Later Fathers,* edited by Edward R. Harvey, 382–85. Louisville, KY: Westminster John Knox, 2006.

Thomas Aquinas. *On Charity.* Translated by Lettie H. Kendzierski. Milwaukee: Marquette University Press, 1960.

_____. *Summa Theologica.* Translated by Fathers of the English Dominican Province. Benzinger Brothers, 1947. www.ccel.org/ccel/aquinas/summa.i.html (accessed June 2, 2010).

Thompson, Mark D. *A Sure Ground on Which to Stand: The Relation of Authority and Interpretive Method in Luther's Approach to Scripture.* Carlisle, Cumbria, UK: Paternoster, 2004.

Turner, Philip. "An Unworkable Theology." *First Things* 154 (June/July 2005): 10–12.

Twenge, Jean M. *Generation Me: Why Today's Young Americans Are More Confident, Assertive, Entitled—and More Miserable Than Ever Before.* New York: Free Press, 2006.

_____, and W. Keith Campbell. *The Narcissism Epidemic: Living in the Age of Entitlement.* New York: Free Press, 2009.

Tyrell, George Tyrell. *Christianity at the Cross-Roads.* London: Longmans, Green, and Co., 1910.

United States Supreme Court. *Planned Parenthood of Southeastern Pennsylvania et al. v. Casey, Governor of Pennsylvania, et al.* 505 U. S. 833 (1992). supremecourtus.gov/opinions/boundvolumes/505bv.pdf (accessed Jan. 29, 2010).

Vajta, Vilmos. *Luther on Worship.* Philadelphia: Muhlenberg Press, 1954.

Wallach, Michael A., and Lise Wallach. *Psychology's Sanction for Selfishness: The Error of Egoism in Theory and Therapy.* San Francisco: W. H. Freeman, 1983.

Walther, C. F. W. *The Proper Distinction between Law and Gospel.* Translated by W. H. T. Dau. St. Louis: Concordia, 1928.

Warren, Rick. *The Purpose Driven Church: Growth Without Compromising Your Message and Mission*. Grand Rapids, MI: Zondervan, 1995.

_____. *The Purpose Driven Life: What on Earth Am I Here For?* Grand Rapids, MI: Zondervan, 2002.

Watson, Philip S. *Let God Be God!: An Interpretation of the Theology of Luther*. London: Epworth, 1947.

Wright, Christopher J. H. *The Mission of God: Unlocking the Bible's Grand Narrative*. Downers Grove, IL: IVP Academic, 2006.

Yeago, David S. "Gnosticism, Antinomianism, and Reformation Theology: Reflections on the Cost of a Construal." *Pro Ecclesia* 2 (Winter 1993): 37–49.

_____. "Lutherans and the Historic Episcopate: Theological Impasse and Ecclesial Future." *Lutheran Forum* 26 (Nov. 1992): 36–45.

_____. "The Catholic Luther." In *The Catholicity of the Reformation*, edited by Carl E. Braaten and Robert W. Jenson, 13–34. Grand Rapids, MI: Eerdmans, 1996.

Yoder, John Howard. *The Politics of Jesus*. 2nd ed. Grand Rapids, MI: Eerdmans, 1994.

Zachman, Randall C. *Image and Word in the Theology of John Calvin*. Notre Dame, IN: University of Notre Dame Press, 2007.

_____. "The Idolatrous Religion of Conscience." In *The Assurance of Faith: Conscience in the Theology of Martin Luther and John Calvin*, 19–39. Minneapolis, MN: Fortress, 1993.

Zwingli, Huldrych. "Friendly Exegesis, that is, Exposition of the Matter of the Eucharist to Martin Luther, February 1527." In *Huldrych Zwingli Writings*, Vol. 2, translated by H. Wayne Pipkin, 233–385. Allison Park, PA: Pickwick Publications, 1984.

_____. *Huldreich Zwinglis Sämtliche Werke*. 14 Volumes. Edited by Emil Egli et al. Corpus Reformatorum Vol. 88–101. Zürich: Theologischer Verlag, 1982–91.

_____. *Huldreich Zwingli's Werke*. 7 Volumes. Edited by Melchior Schulero and Johannes Schultess. Zürich: Friedrich Schulthess, 1830–41.